Oxford EAP

A course in English for Academic Purposes

ADVANCED / C1

Edward de Chazal & Julie Moore

OXFORD
UNIVERSITY PRESS

MW01009123

Contents

LISTENING	SPEAKING	VOCABULARY
Lectures (1) Using the introduction and navigational language to understand a lecture Note-taking (1): evaluating different note-taking techniques Signposting (1): Guiding the audience	**Student discussions** Preparing for a discussion individually and collaboratively Active listening: checking, clarifying, and confirming Interaction (1): Checking and confirming	**Flexibility** Recognizing word forms and how they are used Using different word forms to express perspective
Lectures (2) Topic signposting in a lecture Listening critically and evaluating an argument Signposting (2): Focusing on the main theme	**Seminars (1)** Contributing to a discussion: developing, presenting, and supporting an argument Introducing, interrupting, and turn-taking Interaction (2): Interrupting and linking	**Accuracy** Choosing prepositions in noun phrases Identifying adjective / verb + preposition combinations
Lectures (3) Establishing key words and themes from the introduction Note-taking (2): using different techniques	**Seminars (2)** Reading in preparation for a seminar discussion Summarizing ideas from written sources Citations (2): Referring to sources in a discussion	**Identifying senses** Identifying general and specialized senses Understanding grammatical differences in usage
Presentations (1) Identifying and explaining key components in a poster Listening to the question and answer stage of a poster presentation Evaluating a poster and presentation	**Presentations (2)** Planning, researching, and giving a poster presentation Viewing posters and preparing critical questions Asking questions about a poster: Spatial expressions, and question forms	**Variety** Understanding how synonyms alter meaning Using antonyms to avoid negatives
Lectures (4) Making notes on a chronological sequence Recognizing citations and references in lectures Citations (6): References to people, works, and ideas	**Teamwork** Planning and conducting team research Preparing and giving a group presentation Hedging (2): Reaching agreement	**Lexical patterns** Recognizing verb + verb patterns Identifying and using clause patterns Identifying repeated patterns to decode long sentences
Lectures (5) Understanding the main points of a lecture Summarizing a key concept from a lecture Combining and comparing information from two lectures	**Seminars (3)** Reading and preparing a logical argument for a seminar Asking questions about a contribution Conducting a seminar discussion and summarizing main points Asking critical questions: Questioning the logic of a contribution	**Collocation** Recognizing collocations in a text Identifying academic & discipline-specific collocations

Introduction

Welcome to *Oxford English for Academic Purposes* – a complete course for anyone preparing to study in English at university level.

What is in the course?

Oxford EAP is designed specifically to improve your ability to study effectively in English, whether you are planning to embark on an undergraduate or postgraduate programme. Whatever your academic background and chosen subject, *Oxford EAP* will help you develop your knowledge and skills in all of the following areas:

- reading and understanding a range of authentic academic texts
- listening to lectures and presentations
- writing a variety of essays and other assignments
- participating in seminars and group discussions
- preparing and giving presentations
- improving study skills such as planning, note-taking and research techniques
- critical thinking
- recognizing and using academic grammar
- learning and using academic vocabulary.

What is in a unit?

Oxford EAP has twelve units. Each unit starts with a preview page showing the learning objectives for that unit, plus a short discussion task to get you thinking about the unit theme.

The **academic focus** of each unit covers an important aspect of academic study relevant to all subject areas – for example: presenting an argument; comparing, contrasting, and evaluating; cause, effect, and association; problems, solutions, and evaluation. This focus is maintained throughout the unit.

The units are divided into four main modules – Reading, Writing, Listening, Speaking – plus a one-page Vocabulary module, combined with a Research project in Units 7–12. Each module starts with a rationale (a short explanatory text), and develops the main skill in relation to the academic focus of the unit through a sequence of tasks.

Reading uses extracts from authentic academic texts (see page 239 for a list of sources). It usually starts with a short task to get you thinking about the subject matter, or to predict the content of the text. Subsequent tasks help with comprehension strategies and an analysis of textual features or academic language, and often end with an evaluation task where you respond critically to what you have read.

Writing focuses on key aspects of academic writing in the first part of the book, such as planning and organization in relation to written assignments. You will typically analyse a written model, followed by a series of tasks that help you build up to your own piece of writing. Later in the course, you move on to different types of essay and looking at key aspects of organization, style and use of language, as well as citation and criticality.

Listening focuses mainly on listening to lectures. It uses short, video-based extracts from authentic lectures to help you understand key information and language, as well as aspects of style and structure. Effective note-taking is a key part of most modules, and the module usually ends with a critical thinking task evaluating the content of the lecture.

Speaking includes participating in seminars and informal discussions, and giving presentations. It covers key communication strategies for these contexts, and reviews and practises useful language. An initial listening or reading task to introduce the context and present examples of the target language and strategies is included. At the end of the module there is an opportunity to reflect on and evaluate your own performance in the previous discussion or presentation task.

Vocabulary looks at key aspects of academic vocabulary using language from the unit, and focuses on the most useful vocabulary-learning strategies. In Units 7–12 this module is combined with work on the different stages of a **Research project** from planning to submission.

What else is included?

Each unit also includes:

- **Academic language** (grammar and useful phrases) related to the academic focus of the unit, with examples taken from the texts or video / audio transcripts. Where relevant, there is a cross-reference to the language reference at the back of the book for supporting or related information.
- **Critical thinking** tasks encouraging you to evaluate and reflect on the content of each module, and on your own performance in writing and speaking tasks.

At the back of the book there are the following:

- **Glossary** of common academic terms used in this book
- **Academic language reference** with additional information on key aspects of academic grammar
- **Checklists** for evaluating aspects of your learning and assessing your performance in a range of tasks
- **Additional material** relating to the content of individual units
- **Video and audio transcripts**.

UNIT 1 Behaviour

LEARNING OBJECTIVES

This unit covers:

Reading
- Identifying genre, audience, purpose, and perspective in texts
- Navigating texts

Writing
- Personalizing the writing process: planning, preparation, and working with ideas
- Analysing, planning, and writing a coherent essay introduction

Listening
- Using the introduction and navigational language to understand a lecture
- Note-taking (1): evaluating different note-taking techniques

Speaking
- Preparing for a discussion individually and collaboratively
- Active listening: checking, clarifying, and confirming

Vocabulary
- Flexibility

Discussion

1 **Work in groups. Take turns to present yourself. Include:**
   - brief biodata (name, origin, educational background)
   - your main skills, areas of interest, key achievements
   - the subject or discipline you are studying / plan to study
   - specific skills you want to learn and improve on
   - your preferred learning styles.

2 **Do you agree with the following statement? Think about your own discipline or subject area. Explain why (not).**

   'Anthropology is the study of humans and their behaviour, but all disciplines are concerned with how humans behave.'

   Example: *I mainly agree with this idea. In my subject, economics, an important area is 'consumer behaviour', that is, what people buy and why.*

3 **Decide which factors affect your behaviour.**
   - social background and parenting
   - education
   - financial gain
   - positive feedback from a colleague, friend, teacher ...
   - habit
   - fear of punishment
   - other ...

   Agree on the three most significant factors.

4 **Present your main ideas from 2 and 3 to the class.**

There are many types of academic text: a textbook chapter, a scientific article, a lecture, an essay, and longer texts like dissertations. We often refer to text type as **genre**, and texts from the same genre share a similar structure, style, and content. Closely related to genre is **audience** – the intended readers (e.g. students of a particular discipline). A further characteristic of academic texts is their **purpose** – the main reason for writing the text (e.g. to explain a concept, or persuade the audience through argument). The author may consider a number of **perspectives** (e.g. economic, historical). You need to be able to **navigate** a text effectively, work out the genre, audience, and purpose, and identify its perspectives.

This module covers:
- Identifying genre, audience, purpose, and perspective in texts
- Navigating texts

TASK 1 Understanding genre, audience, and purpose in texts

1 **Work in pairs. Describe the characteristics of genres 1–10 in the table. Identify the** *audience* **and** *purpose* **of each.**

Example: *A subject-specific dictionary lists short definitions in alphabetical order for key concepts in a discipline (e.g. medicine). It is written for students and …*

	Genre (What?)	Audience (For whom?)	Purpose (Why?)
1	subject-specific dictionary	students / staff of the subject	to define technical terms / explain key concepts
2	university textbook		
3	abstract of a journal article		
4	journal article		
5	newspaper article		
6	encyclopaedia entry		
7	essay		
8	review / critique		
9	scientific report		
10	Master's dissertation		

2 **Discuss the questions.**

1 Which genres in 1 have you read in your first language / in English? How often?

2 Which genres do you consider to be academic? Give reasons and examples.

3 Which genres do you think are important for you to be able to read for your academic study?

TASK 2 Understanding reading lists and references

1 **Look at the reading list. Identify the genres for references a–d.**

> a Black, J., Hashimzade, N., & Myles, G.D. (2009). *Oxford Dictionary of Economics* (3rd ed.). Oxford: Oxford University Press. _subject-specific dictionary_
> b Herlihy, J., Gleeson, K., & Turner, S. (2010). What assumptions about human behaviour underlie asylum judgments? *International Journal of Refugee Law*, 22: 351–366. _journal article_
> c Hothersall, S. J. (2008). Review of human behaviour and the social environment micro-level: individuals and families, Katherine van Wormer, Oxford University Press, USA, in *British Journal of Social Work*, 38: 1447–1449. _journal article_
> d Jones, K. & Creedy, D. (2008). *Health and Human Behaviour* (2nd ed.). Oxford: Oxford University Press. _university textbook_

2 **Find one or two examples of each feature below in the references in 1.**

author surname(s)   author initial(s)   edition   page numbers
place of publication   publisher   title of article   title of book
title of journal   volume number   year of publication

3 **Compare answers and explain why you made these choices.**

TASK 3 Identifying and comparing features of a genre

1 Read Texts 1–4 quickly. Ignore any unknown language at this stage. Match the texts to references a–d in Task 2.1 and complete rows 1 and 2 in the summary table.

2 Discuss what information in the texts helped you complete 1.

3 Choose one or two key words or phrases for each text. Complete row 3 in the summary table. Decide which one word or phrase links all four texts. *human behavior*

	SUMMARY	Text 1	Text 2	Text 3	Text 4
✓ 1	Reference (a, b, c, or d)	d	b	a	c
✓ 2	Genre	university textbook	journal article	subject-specific dic	review / journal article
3	Key words	behavior / basic needs motivation / next level of needs	behavior / assumption asylum / judg	behavior / economic decision	behavior / individual society
✓ 4	Purpose	b	c	a	d

Motivation *based on a content* **TEXT 1**

Most people think about **motivation** in terms of needs that must be met to achieve a state of comfort. When behaviour occurs, we assume that it has done so to achieve some goal. If the behaviour succeeds, the result is satisfaction; if not, frustration. The study of motivation is, therefore, concerned with those factors that arouse, sustain, and direct behaviour.

One useful analysis of human motivation (Maslow, 1970) suggests that we have a hierarchy of needs that we will be concerned with satisfying. Our most basic needs come first, then we are able to direct energy at higher level needs. The most basic needs are the fundamental physiological ones - hunger, thirst, and avoidance of pain. Only when these are satisfied are we able to worry about the next level - which Maslow described as the safety needs - to feel secure and out of danger: shelter, defence, etc. The next level of needs is seen to be social - the need to belong to a group, to be loved and wanted. Esteem comes next - the need to feel competent, to achieve something, to gain the approval of our fellows. Maslow completes his pyramid of needs with the need for self-actualisation, to be the best that we can possibly be, to fulfil our own unique potential.

What assumptions about human behaviour underlie asylum judgments? **TEXT 2**

In order to claim recognition as a refugee, individuals must give a 'plausible' account of persecution. Decision-makers must then decide on the truthfulness of the account, and whether the person fits the legal definition of a refugee. Decision-makers often have little corroborating evidence, and must make an assessment of credibility, largely a subjective response, involving a reliance on assumptions about human behaviour, judgments, attitudes, and how a truthful account is presented. This article describes a study of the assumptions in judgments made by UK immigration judges. Assumptions were defined and a coding structure used to systematically extract a list of assumptions from a series of written determinations. These assumptions were then submitted to an inductive thematic analysis. The resulting themes are compared briefly to the psychological and psychiatric literature, raising the question of whether assumptions used in asylum decision-making are in line with current empirical evidence about human behaviour. The article recommends cross-disciplinary research to build an evidence base in order to help inform the decision-making process in this crucial area of law.

TEXT 3

behavioural economics An approach to economic analysis that incorporates psychological insights into individual behaviour to explain economic decisions. Behavioural economics is motivated by the observation of anomalies that cannot be explained by standard models of choice. It provides an explanation for the anomalies by introducing human and social cognitive and emotional biases into the decision-making process.

TEXT 4

Volume 2 (the *macro* level) has as its focus the interrelationships across, between and within the wider social milieu and the influences these have at the individual level. The focus is from the *macro* to the *micro*, looking at social structures and structural forces and offering theoretical frameworks to guide the reader's thinking on these matters. There are subsequent chapters on the social psychology of group behaviour, the family within society, the relevance of culture in relation to societal structures and functions, the notion and role of community and community development, the organizational context, the natural environment and the faith community. [...] This two-volume set offers the reader a good overview of a number of important perspectives relating to the individual and society (Volume 1) and society and the individual (Volume 2) and there are many signposts to a range of other materials. The writing is generally insightful and, a clear strength here, pragmatically oriented to the realities of social life in the twenty-first century and the social work task within that. There is a sense of balance to the volumes, although, if pushed to choose between the two, Volume 2 has more to offer, and is, as mentioned above, better constructed, in my view.

TASK 4 Identifying purpose in texts

√ 1 **Look at the list of verbs which can be used to express the main purpose of a text.**

claim   define   describe   evaluate   exemplify   explain   outline   state

Example: *This text **defines** the concept of 'motivation.'*

Match the verbs with definitions 1–8.

define 1   to give the exact meaning of a word, phrase, or concept

exemplify 2   to give an example in order to make something clearer

evaluate 3   to form a judgement about something after thinking about it carefully

explain 4   to give reasons for something

outline 5   to give only the main facts or points involved in something

describe 6   to give an account of something, saying what it is like

claim 7   to put forward an idea which has not been proved / which others may not agree with

state 8   to formally write or say something, especially in a careful and clear way

√ 2 **Read Texts 1–4 on page 009 again. Decide which phrase best expresses the main purpose of each text. Complete row 4 in the summary table.**

a   to define a technical term

b   to outline and explain a topic and theory

c   to give background information on a topic and state the aims, method, and conclusion

d   to describe and evaluate another text (i.e. to review)

3   **Compare answers and decide how effectively each text achieves its purpose.**

TASK 5 Identifying perspective in texts

how you look at sth

√ 1 **Read ideas 1–4 from Text 1. Check unknown words in a dictionary. Decide which perspectives are being expressed. Choose one or more from the list for each extract.**

academic   philosophical   physiological   social   theoretical

1   The study of motivation is, therefore, concerned with those factors that arouse, sustain, and direct behaviour. *Social / Academic / theoretical*

2   The basic needs are the fundamental ones – hunger, thirst, avoidance of pain. *Physiological theoretical*

3   The next level of needs is social – the need to belong to a group, to be loved. *Social / philosophical*

4   Maslow completes his pyramid of needs with the need for self-actualization, to be the best that we can possibly be, to fulfil our own unique potential. *theoretical / philosophical*

2   **Which of the perspectives in 1 are** *explicit*, **i.e. clearly stated, and which are** *implicit*, **i.e. suggested without being directly expressed?**

ACADEMIC LANGUAGE ▸ Language reference page 204 5.2

Perspective Words and phrases expressing perspective

Academic texts typically contextualize and analyse an issue from a number of perspectives: academic, economic, philosophical, political, psychological, social, theoretical, etc.

Notice how perspectives can be expressed explicitly using nouns, adjectives, or adverbials.

- the perspectives of 'the individual' and 'society' are shown using nouns:
  *This two-volume set offers the reader a good overview of a number of important perspectives relating to **the individual** and **society**.* (Text 4)

- the 'human', 'social cognitive', and 'emotional' perspectives are shown using adjectives:
  *It provides an explanation for the anomalies by introducing **human** and **social cognitive** and **emotional** biases into the decision-making process.* (Text 3)

Alternatively, a perspective may be stated more implicitly, using related words.

- the content, and nouns *refugee* and *persecution*, suggest a 'political' perspective:
  *In order to claim recognition as a **refugee**, individuals must give a 'plausible' account of **persecution**.* (Text 2)

TASK 6 Understanding the language of perspective

1 Find more examples of perspective in Texts 1–4 on page 009. Note words / phrases that signal these perspectives.

   Examples: an individual perspective – *our own unique potential (Text 1)*;
              a legal perspective – *the legal definition (Text 2)*

2 Use the correct form to complete expressions 1–4.

   politics *(n)*   political *(adj)*   politically *(adv)*

   1 from a _____ perspective
   2 as far as _____ is concerned
   3 _____ speaking
   4 in terms of _____

3 Work in pairs. Write down at least three observations on human behaviour from different perspectives. Use the expressions in 2.

   Example: *From a linguistic perspective, all humans are naturally motivated to learn the language of their immediate environment.*

TASK 7 Using cover and Contents to navigate a textbook

1 Look at the textbook cover. Note down:
   • the audience of the book, i.e. the profile of the expected readers
   • specific topics and perspectives that you think might be covered
   • any limitations, i.e. what might not be covered.

2 Turn to page 214. Look at the Contents of the textbook and check your answers to 1.
   1 What else can you say about the audience profile?
   2 How do the headings for Parts 1–4 relate to the chapters in those parts?

3 Using the Contents, decide where you would find:
   1 definitions of technical terms used in the book
   2 details of sources cited in the book
   3 discussion of different influences on health and behaviour
   4 an explanation of the aims of the book
   5 a detailed overview of the meaning of 'health' and related issues.

TASK 8 Navigating and analysing a textbook extract

1 Read Text 5 on page 12. Which text (1–4) does it follow directly on from?

2 Decide which statement a–d best expresses the purpose of Text 5.
   a to define and describe a theory of motivation
   b to outline and evaluate different theories of motivation
   c to argue for, explain, and exemplify contrasting perspectives relating to motivation
   d to give an overview of a contrasting theory

Motivation

[1]While Maslow's theory makes good intuitive sense, a number of objections have been made to it. All of us can think of times when we ignored a basic need to look after a higher one, and examples of people who have sacrificed their own security for the benefit of others are too common to ignore. [2]Clearly, circumstances can lead to a reordering of the hierarchy. Maslow's theory also does not really give a detailed picture of the workings of needs - where they originate, how they push or pull behaviour, and why humans do things that are quite clearly not in their own interests. [3]To begin to understand them, we need to examine genetic, biological, and higher mental (cognitive) factors that influence motivation.

Genetic factors

Much of animal behaviour seems to be based on [4]instincts - patterns that are hard-wired or programmed to occur in response to internal or external events, including events such as the migration of birds, aggression between species, and so on. [5]What holds for animals might hold for humans as well. Early psychologists such as James (1890) believed that social behaviour showed patterns that looked like instinct, and the psychoanalyst Freud (see, for example, Hall, 1979) believed that instincts relating to sex and aggression were basic to much of human behaviour. [...]

Biological factors

[6]Some drives do quite clearly ensure the survival of the individual and are so based in bodily states that they must have a key biological focus. Physiological needs, in Maslow's terms, give rise to internal states focused on satisfying those needs, states that are commonly referred to as [7]primary drives (Hull, 1943). In a primary drive, either deprivation (of food or water, for example) or stimulation (pain or sexual arousal, for example) produce a need state in the organism, which in turn gives rise to a drive to satisfy that need. This drive is not just a general state; it also has a direction. This direction in the case of hunger is to find food, in the case of pain to move away from the source. [8]Thus, a drive does not just produce behaviour, but also produces certain specific behaviours related to the desired goal. [...]

Cognitive factors

The fact that motivated behaviour has direction - we tend to hold off eating until we can eat preferred foods, for example - clearly indicates the role of cognition (our thought processes) in motivation. As already mentioned, motivation can be modified by learning, which means that higher mental processes can play a significant role in our understanding of motivation and our responses to it. [9]Much, if not most, of the time, our behaviour appears to be mindful, that is, rational and sensible. We do not usually grab and eat other people's lunches just because we are hungry, or sexually assault everyone who appeals to us.

In some cases, [10]cognitive appraisals - judgements that people make about the situations they are in - lead individuals to make regulatory decisions that look pretty irrational in terms of their biological needs. [...] Another way we regulate behaviour is by the postponement of gratification, at which we are far better than most other organisms. Graduation, for example, is hard to predict on the basis of biological needs, yet you will work hard over a number of years to become university graduates. In summary, motivation is an interaction of influences that come from the genetic, biological, cognitive, and social levels.

[1] *Argues against Maslow's theory*

[2] *Makes a claim*

[3] *States the purpose of the text*

[4]

[5]

[6]

[7]

[8]

[9]

[10]

3 Look at the ten sections a student has annotated in Text 5. Decide whether each section 4–10:

  1 makes a claim and/or offers explanation

  2 introduces and defines a technical term.

4 Using the student notes, identify the key terms introduced and defined in Text 5. Explain how these terms relate to the three sub-headings in the text.

TASK 9 Independent research - text navigation

1 Review your work in this module using Checklist A on page 209.

2 Search for further texts on the topic of human behaviour and motivation, including one or more related to your discipline. Record the reference information for each text, identify the genre, audience, and purpose, and use features of the text to navigate for further information.

3 Compare with the class. How many different disciplines did you find texts from?

As a first step, planning and writing an effective introduction will help you organize your academic writing and focus on your aims. You need to state your writing purpose, typically in a **thesis statement**, describe your **rationale**, and explain your concepts, including **definition** of key terms. Your writing throughout should focus on relevance, logic, and conciseness (avoid anecdote and digression). When you make a claim, support it with **evidence** and follow this by **analysis** and **evaluation**. Include your own evidence, plus **citation** (material brought in from another source through quotation, paraphrase, or summary) to support your **argument**.

This module covers:
- Personalizing the writing process: planning, preparation, and working with ideas
- Analysing, planning, and writing a coherent essay introduction

TASK 1 Critical thinking – evaluating academic writing ability

1 Read statements 1–8 and tick the appropriate column.

		Always	Usually	Sometimes	Never
1	I can understand a writing task and decide what is relevant to include.				
2	I can develop an argument and express this in my writing.				
3	I can identify what further material I need, and I know how to search for it.				
4	I can critically respond to what I read, and select from it.				
5	I can write an effective introduction and conclusion for my text.				
6	I can accurately reference the material I have cited.				
7	I can use appropriate and accurate language to express my ideas.				
8	Other people can read my text and fully understand it.				

2 Compare answers. Give examples from writing tasks you have done.

Example: *I can usually understand a writing task, but I don't always find it easy to work out my main argument and find material to support it, for example …*

TASK 2 Understanding the purpose of writing

1 Read writing tasks 1–4. Describe the genre specified. Complete the table.

Task 1: website guidelines

> You are invited to write a summary of your presentation (max. 800 words) to be considered for the university publication *Conference Proceedings*, which is read by over 3,000 readers worldwide.

Task 3: formal printed task handout

> **Research essay** Write an essay of 2,000 words based on a topic within your subject area. Titles must be discussed and agreed with your tutor.

Task 2: a question on an examination paper

> **Time allowed: 2 hours. Candidates must answer both questions.**
> 1   To what extent have recent changes in equality legislation in the UK contributed to higher wages?
> 2   …

Task 4: formal printed task handout

> Write up your research project following the scientific report format given in the 'Writing Guidelines' section of the department website. Remember that your report may be read by tutors outside the department, including external examiners.

	Genre	Audience	Purpose	No. of words	Comments
1	summary	academics within the discipline	to give the main points of a presentation	800	Most of the audience did not see the presentation.
2					
3					
4					

2 Analyse writing tasks you have done using the headings in the table in 1.

TASK 3 Reflecting on your own writing process

1 **Read the possible stages in the writing process. Decide whether each stage is part of the *pre-writing, while-writing,* or *post-writing* process.**
- write the body of the text
- generate ideas
- read good examples of similar texts written by other students / academics
- logically organize your ideas
- write the introduction to the text
- narrow down the topic to a clear focus
- decide on which perspectives to include
- critically read what you have written to check the logic, and rewrite as necessary
- work with other students and discuss your ideas
- delete any points that are not relevant
- search for sources – research the topic to find supporting evidence and examples
- critically evaluate the chosen sources

2 **Add more *pre-, while-,* or *post-writing* stages that you might follow.**

Example: *work out your main argument (pre-writing)*

3 **Which stages in 1 do you think are the most important for writing a short, researched essay? Put these in order. Which stages are you most likely to repeat?**

4 **Work in pairs. Compare ideas.**
1 What are the differences between your writing processes? How significant are these?
2 Choose one stage and explain your approach in more detail.

Example: *When working out my ideas, I like to arrange my material visually, so I make a mind-map. I also annotate the texts I'm using …*

TASK 4 Identifying features in an introduction

1 **Think about the introduction to an academic text such as an essay or article. Decide whether a–i are essential (E) or optional (O).**
a gain the reader's interest by offering an opening statement, or 'hook'
b give background and context by moving from the general to the particular
c provide a rationale for researching and writing the text
d define any core terms necessary to the understanding of the text
e present evidence and citations to support your argument
f state limitations, e.g. to previous research, to the current text
g state the overall purpose and aims of the text
h state how the whole text is organized
i indicate the conclusion of the text

2 **The *thesis statement* is a key feature of many introductions. Read thesis statements 1–4 and decide which items a–i in 1 are most likely to form the basis of a thesis statement.**
1 In this essay, I investigate the causes of inner-city social discontent using cases from UK cities, and assess the impact of anti-social behaviour arising from this discontent.
2 The aim of this report is to compare the outcomes of cognitive behaviour therapy using both quantitative and qualitative methods.
3 This paper sets out the main arguments for the adoption of the private funding model, first by examining the arguments and then assessing cases in Sweden and Singapore.
4 By tracing the development of education initiatives in three young offenders' institutes, we show that early intervention is the most effective means of reducing reoffending.

TASK 5 Analysing an introduction

1 Read the essay title and Introduction A. Identify the thesis statement.

> **TITLE:** *Many people apparently behave in an altruistic or 'selfless' way, for example, by offering help or money to someone they do not know. What are the main motivating factors for such selfless human behaviour?*

Introduction A

[1] It has long been recognized that human behaviour does not always have to be focused towards the gain of the individual and their circle of family and friends. [2] Many people behave in altruistic ways that seem to help unknown people for no obvious reason, for example, by giving money to distant charities. [3] Altruism may be defined as 'helping behavior that is motivated by a selfless concern for the welfare of another person' (Psychology and Society, n.d.). [4] This phenomenon has been studied from a number of perspectives. [5] The work of Reuter, Frenzel, Walter, Markett, and Montag (2011, pp.662-668) approaches the issue from a genetic perspective, identifying the neurotransmitter dopamine as a key factor affecting human altruism. [6] Other research adopts an evolutionary perspective, investigating group selection as an explanation for altruism (e.g. Cooper & Wallace, 2004). [7] A key reason for the importance of understanding altruistic behaviour is the increasing influence of the charity and non-profit sectors in many economies. [8] This essay aims to examine altruistic behaviour from an evolutionary perspective, leading to three possible motivating factors, which are then evaluated.

2 Match sentences 1–8 in Introduction A with some of the features a–i in Task 4.1. Which items in 4.1 are *not* included?

3 As a class, decide the most appropriate ending to the following sentence.

Example: *By the end of the introduction, the audience of the text should ...*

ACADEMIC LANGUAGE   ▸ Language reference page 206 8.1

Noun phrases (1) Expressing information concisely using noun phrases

Academic writers frequently discuss abstract concepts, events, and actions, and often use noun phrases to express such ideas clearly and concisely. The following clause (subject - verb - ...) can be expressed more concisely as a noun phrase:

> *Many people behave in altruistic ways* (clause) → *people's altruistic behaviour* (noun phrase)

Noun phrases enable you to express a lot of information in part of a sentence instead of a whole sentence, or to use one sentence instead of two. Compare how the information in 1 below is presented as a **noun phrase** in 2:

1 *It is very important for people to be able to understand altruistic behaviour. This is because the non-profit sectors in many economies are becoming increasingly influential.*

2 ***A key reason for the importance of understanding altruistic behaviour** is the increasing influence of the non-profit sectors in many economies.*

To do this, you have to make a number of grammatical changes. You need to make a **head noun,** i.e. the main noun around which other information is added (e.g. by changing the adjective *important* into the noun *importance*). You may start the noun phrase with a determiner (e.g. *the, any, our*), and then add further detail to modify the head noun, using adjective(s) or noun(s):

> *many* **people**   *human* **behaviour**   *three possible motivating* **factors**

You can also add a structure following the head noun, usually a prepositional phrase and/or a relative clause:

> *an* **explanation** *for altruism* (prepositional phrase)
> *helping* **behavior** *that is motivated by selfless concern for others* (finite relative clause)
> *a key* **factor** *affecting human altruism* (non-finite relative clause)

TASK 6 Using noun phrases

1 Rewrite sentences 1–6 as noun phrases. Use the bold word to make the head noun.

Example: People often **assess** human behaviour in different ways. → *people's different assessments of human behaviour*

1 In a variety of global contexts, individuals **behave** in predictable ways.

2 Psychologists have recently been **researching** into altruistic behaviour.

3 Individuals can **benefit** in both psychological and financial terms.

4 Further **studies** have been carried out into how people behave when they are stressed.

5 People are sometimes motivated to **act** in certain ways for self-gain.

6 Tensions in the workplace often relate to **changes** in the way employees behave.

2 Use your noun phrases as grammatical subjects or objects. Write new sentences.

Example: *People's different assessments of human behaviour can lead to misunderstandings between individuals.*

3 Write three sentences containing noun phrases to define key concepts in your discipline. Underline the noun phrases in your sentences.

Example: *Artificial intelligence is the branch of computer science which aims to create 'intelligent' machines.*

TASK 7 Evaluating essay introductions

1 Read the essay title and plan below. Then read Introduction A (in Task 5), and Introductions B and C on page 017. Use Checklist B to decide which is the most effective.

CHECKLIST B Evaluation criteria for an essay introduction

1 Is the introduction closely relevant to the essay question?
2 Does it contain the essential features of an introduction (see Task 4)?
3 Is it logically organized?
4 Are the aims and rationale of the essay clearly given?
5 Does it contain appropriate academic language for an essay introduction?
6 Is it the right length (e.g. a 750-word essay may have an introduction of up to 150 words)?

Checklists:
page 209

TITLE: *Many people apparently behave in an altruistic or 'selfless' way, for example, by offering help or money to someone they do not know. What are the main motivating factors for such selfless human behaviour? Write about 750 words.*

Introduction

Body paragraph 1: Evolutionary background and developments related to altruistic behaviour

Body paragraph 2: Three possible motivating factors

Body paragraph 3: Evaluation of these factors

Conclusion

References

Cooper, B. & Wallace, C. (2004). Group selection and the evolution of altruism. *Oxford Economic Papers*, 56: 307-330.
Psychology and Society (n.d.). retrieved January 20, 2012, from http://www.psychologyandsociety.com/altruismdefinition.html.
Reuter, M., Frenzel, C., Walter, N.T., Markett, S., & Montag, C. (2011). Investigating the genetic basis of altruism: the role of the COMT Val158Met polymorphism. *Social Cognitive and Affective Neuroscience*, 6: 662- 668.

Introduction B

What is altruism? Why is it important? These are clearly important questions. Altruism has been talked about in academic settings and within a lot of disciplines, from psychology to sociology. It is a defining feature of humans and human behaviour. Many people have carried out useful research into the area. For example, the researchers Reuter, Frenzel, Walter, Markett, and Montag (2011, pp.662-668) conducted research into altruistic behaviour from a genetic perspective. There are other researchers too, such as Cooper and Wallace (2004), who have searched to reach a deeper understanding of altruistic behaviour. This essay investigates how factors relating to altruistic or 'selfless' behaviour can motivate people, for example, offering money to an unknown person.

Introduction C

Human behaviour encompasses many variations, many of which are culturally constructed. In many cultures, altruism is an important aspect of human behaviour. Research into human behaviour includes important work by Reuter, Frenzel, Walter, Markett, and Montag (2011, pp.662-668). These researchers look into genetic factors, which may to some extent affect aspects of human behaviour, such as altruistic behaviour. In certain cultures, such as Asian cultures, altruistic behaviour can be highly valued, for example, a rich person giving money to poor people from another area. Arguably, different cultures approach the notion of altruistic behaviour in different ways; these differences have so far not been well-researched. Cooper and Wallace (2004) examined the much-researched notion of 'group selection'. The aim of this essay is to offer three motivating factors which may affect altruism and altruistic behaviour, with a particular emphasis on evolutionary theories relating to it.

2 Compare answers. Give reasons why the introduction you chose is the most effective.

3 Choose another introduction and discuss ways in which it could be improved.

TASK 8 Planning, writing, and evaluating an introduction

1 Read the essay title below and plan your introduction following the guidelines.

> **TITLE:** *To what extent should people visiting or temporarily living in a foreign country adapt their behaviour in response to local conditions and customs? Write about 750 words.*

Guidelines for planning an introduction

1 Narrow the topic and focus, e.g. by limiting the discussion to one or two geographical areas.
2 Decide on relevant perspectives, e.g. cultural, educational, linguistic ...
3 Work out your main argument (i.e. how important you think it is for people to adapt their behaviour). Summarize this in one sentence.

2 Write your introduction. (Do not write the body paragraphs.)

3 When you have finished, check your writing using Checklist B (Task 7).

4 Work in groups. Exchange your introductions and offer critical feedback based on the criteria in Checklist B. Suggest possible improvements.

Example: *The introduction doesn't give a clear rationale for writing the essay. How about ...?*

TASK 9 Independent research – introduction techniques

1 Search for three published introductions within your subject area. Analyse them following a similar process to that in Tasks 4 and 5. Note similarities and differences.

2 Draw up your own list of preferred features to use when writing introductions.

3 Look again at the stages in the writing process in Task 3.1. Formulate an action plan for your next piece of writing, based on these stages.

It is often a challenge to understand a lecture effectively, as you will be dealing with the language, content, and **delivery** of the lecture. You may have to process information from a wide variety of different media, such as visuals, audio-recordings, **handouts**, and textbook / article extracts, as well as lecturer and audience input.

This module covers:

- Using the introduction and navigational language to understand a lecture
- Note-taking (1): evaluating different note-taking techniques

TASK 1 Predicting the content of a lecture

1 **Work in groups. Discuss the questions.**

  1 Think about a recent course. How much content was delivered through lectures?

  2 What difficulties have you encountered in listening to lectures in your first language and/or English?

  3 How useful and accessible are lectures as an information source?
  as much as possible *make benefits of sth* *best of sth*

2 **You are going to watch extracts from a lecture called *Making the most of higher education in English-speaking countries*. Predict which two aspects will be included.**

  a an overview of the history of education and thought

  b advice for the lecture audience on ways of studying and learning

  c a comparison between higher education in English-speaking and other countries

  d discussion of theories relating to education and learning

TASK 2 Navigating a lecture: understanding the introduction

Rational (adj) logical
Rationale (n) Reason
what gonna hap

1 **Decide whether the features below are best communicated orally (O), visually (V), or both.**

  - lecture title and topic *both*
  - lecturer biodata (the lecturer's name and educational background) *both*
  - limitations, i.e. a list of things the lecturer is *not* going to cover *orally*
  - *reason* rationale and aims of the lecture, including the main questions to be addressed *both*
  - interaction with the audience (e.g. stating what the lecturer wants them to do) *both* *exp*

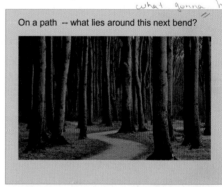

On a path -- what lies around this next bend?

Slide 1

2 ▷1.1 **Watch Extract 1 and note down information on the lecture features in 1. Does the lecturer present each item orally, visually, or both?**

3 **Turn to Checklist C on page 209. Use part A to make notes about general information on the lecture.**

TASK 3 Using navigational language to aid listening

Learning as...

trunk

OR

A) Quantitative increase *= how much*

B) A qualitative change/transformation *= how*

Slide 2

1 **Work in pairs. Discuss the questions.**

  1 Say how the lecturer used Slide 1, and how it contributed to your understanding.

  2 Try to work out the meaning of Slide 2. Speculate how the lecturer might use it.

2 **Match terms 1–2 with definitions a–b.**

  1 qualitative *a*   a concerned with how good something is

  2 quantitative *b*   b connected with the amount or number of something

Signposting (1) Guiding the audience
GPS for presentation → whats coming next

Lecturers use a wide range of expressions to help the audience focus attention on a particular point, and noticing these should enable you to follow the lecture more effectively.

The following examples from the lecture are used to

- refer to what will happen later in the lecture:

  So our talk addresses three main questions today ...

  So I'll highlight some key ideas from the field of ...

- interact with the audience:

  To get the most from the lecture, I'd like you to ... *take notes, answer the questions*

  I'm assuming that most of you are ... *say examples*

The lecturer may also review or refer back to what has already been said:

  So those are the two main ways of looking at this.

  So if we go back to my example from ...

recap = review = sum up = summarize

TASK 4 Navigating a lecture

1 Read sentences 1–7 from Extract 2 of the lecture. Identify the signposting language.

  1 First we need to clarify the meaning of 'university learning' and we need to clarify the meaning of 'learning'. We need to understand what it means from a variety of ...

  2 So your first reflection question is very briefly to think about, 'What does it mean to learn something?'

  3 Now let's take a look at some research that outlines a variety of different conceptions of learning that are commonly held, and how those relate to what is expected ...

  4 On the right hand side, you'll see a little face that looks like a monkey.

  5 ... he came up with five major conceptions of learning, which can be broken into these two rough categories ...

  6 So I could give you an example from my own experience of viewing learning as ...

  7 Another way of looking at things is a more qualitative change, which is not really what I did with my own vocabulary tests when I was 12 years old ...

2 Match functions a–g to sentences 1–7.

  2 a asking the audience a direct question

  4 b referring to a visual

  7 c discussing and evaluating

  3 d presenting several theories based on research

  6 e introducing an example

  5 f presenting the results of one researcher

  1 g intr...
  the...

3 ▶ 1.2 Watch Extract 2. Then turn to Checklist C on p...
  about the delivery of the lecture.

4 Watch again, and identify the main point following e...
  Check your answers in the transcript on page 224.

5 ▶ 1.3 Watch Extract 3, the concluding part of the le...
  how the lecturer sums up and rounds off her lecture.

TASK 5 Note-taking (1) – evaluating dif...

1 Compare the notes you made for the three lecture ex...
  Checklist C to overview the lecture (for Extracts 1 an...
  (for Extract 3)? Explain why (not).

2 Compare your notes with other students. Discuss dif...

  - quantity - clarity - language - use of sym...

3 Discuss what note-taking techniques you have found

meaning of university learning and learning.

what does it mean to learn sth. How do you know you have learned

Variety of different conception of learning

changing our way of looking (visual)

five major conception of learning →(result)

example of my own experience → quantitative (exp)

more qualitative change (evaluate)

Discussions in academic contexts often revolve around lectures or reading given by your tutor. You need to prepare by **responding** to this material. Responding means checking your understanding of language and meaning, asking **critical questions** such as 'How reliable is this information?', and considering points arising from the material. Depending on your preferred **learning style**, you can do this preparation individually (on your own), or **collaboratively** (with other students).

This module covers:

- Preparing for a discussion individually and collaboratively
- Active listening: checking, clarifying, and confirming

TASK 1 Evaluating your discussion and seminar skills

1 **Read statements 1–7 and decide the extent to which you agree or disagree.**

strongly agree   mostly agree   partly disagree   strongly disagree

1 I prefer to prepare carefully for a discussion and find it hard to speak spontaneously. *without preparation mostly agree*

2 I prepare more effectively working collaboratively than working individually. *strongly agree*

3 I am a good listener and I try to understand what everyone is saying in a discussion. *strongly disagree*

4 I find it easy to think of interesting points to contribute to the discussion. *mostly agree*

5 I feel more comfortable speaking in small groups than large groups. *srongly agree*

6 I like to build on what other people say by adding my own ideas and examples. *partly disagree*

7 I check understanding and ask for clarification whenever I do not understand something. *mostly agree*

2 **Work in pairs. Compare responses.**

ACADEMIC LANGUAGE

Interaction (1) Checking and confirming

To ensure that you have understood something correctly, you can use functional expressions:
  That seems mostly clear, but there's just one thing that I'd like to check …
  So, by (x) do you mean (y), or …?
  In other words, you're defining (x) as …
  If I understand you correctly, you're saying that …
You can often use the key word of the function in your expression:
  to **clarify** → Could you just **clarify** that for me, please?
  to **define** → Could you **define** what you mean by …?
  to **exemplify** → It would be useful if you could give us an **example**.
Using these expressions in discussions allows the speaker to correct your understanding if necessary, so that you can participate more effectively.

TASK 2 Individually preparing and discussing

1 **Work alone. Look at the four 'Reflection' points from Dr Quinlan's lecture (1C). Prepare personal responses for each point, including reasons and examples.**

Reflection 1	Reflection 2	Reflection 3	Reflection 4
What does it mean to 'learn' something? How do you know if you have 'learned' something?	Can you think of an example of when you experienced learning as a quantitative increase? Can you think of an example of when you experienced learning as a qualitative change?	Think of a situation in which you learned something deeply. What did you do? What helped you the most?	Why do you want a higher education? How will you be different because of the experience? What do you want to be able to do?

2 Conduct a group discussion around the Reflection points in 1, based on the responses you have prepared. Follow the guidelines below. Choose one student observer to check how effectively the group performs.

> ### Guidelines for conducting a group discussion
>
> 1 Keep focused on the content of the discussion, i.e. the material in the slides and arising from it. Avoid irrelevant comments and digressions.
>
> 2 Listen and recognize when other students express the ideas / comments that you have prepared. Ensure all the points you prepared are covered by you or others.
>
> 3 Listen closely to and build on other students' contributions, adding your own ideas where relevant.
>
> 4 Check your understanding and ask for clarification as necessary, using expressions from the Academic Language box.
>
> 5 Reach an agreement and draw a conclusion if possible.

TASK 3 Collaboratively preparing and discussing

1 Work in threes. Read Slides 3–5 from the lecture. Discuss the questions.

1 Check that you understand all the concepts expressed on the slides. Help each other by explaining any difficult points.

2 From the slides, note down
   a advice for students generally
   b the most useful advice for you personally.

3 Should the advice be any different for students whose first language is not English? Give reasons and examples.

2 Form new groups to discuss the questions. Follow the guidelines in Task 2.2. Choose one student observer to check how effectively the group performs.

1 What types of advice does the lecturer give to students, based on Slides 3–5?

2 To what extent do you agree with her advice?

TASK 4 Critical thinking – evaluating discussion skills

1 Review your own contribution to each discussion.

1 Did you manage successfully to put forward the ideas you had prepared?

2 What did you learn from other students?

3 Is there anything you would do differently next time?

2 Compare and evaluate the individual and collaborative processes of preparing for a discussion in Tasks 2 and 3, using the '3Es' below.

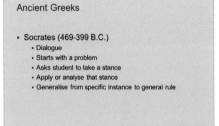

Ancient Greeks

- Socrates (469-399 B.C.)
  - Dialogue
  - Starts with a problem
  - Asks student to take a stance
  - Apply or analyse that stance
  - Generalise from specific instance to general rule

Slide 3

The *process* of university learning in English-speaking universities

- Reading
- Listening (actively)
- Writing
- Laboratories or practical experiences
- Discussion
- Debate
- Critique
- Questioning
- Developing and supporting an argument (YOUR argument)
- Finding your voice and your place in a re-made world

Slide 4

7 Principles for making the most of your Higher Education

1. Interact with your teachers
2. Learn with other students – learning is a social process
3. Active learning
4. Notice and act on feedback given to you
5. Spend time on your studies
6. Believe in yourself – set high goals and work out strategies for getting there
7. Respect diverse talents and ways of learning

Based on Chickering, A.W. & Z.F. Gamson (1987). *Seven principles of good practice in undergraduate education.* AAHE Bulletin, March 1987.

Slide 5

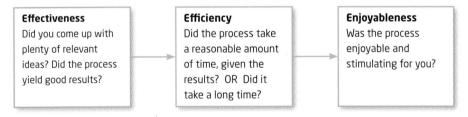

Effectiveness	Efficiency	Enjoyableness
Did you come up with plenty of relevant ideas? Did the process yield good results?	Did the process take a reasonable amount of time, given the results? OR Did it take a long time?	Was the process enjoyable and stimulating for you?

3 Which preparation process suits you best: working individually or collaboratively?

Vocabulary F

In order to express what you want to say in an
core academic vocabulary flexibly. To use key
language in this unit, you need to know the di
adverb) and be able to switch between them t
Switching between word forms is also a key sk

Handwritten notes (top right box):

① the origins of this conflict are rooted in history.

②
• The first society for a young child is the
family and home.

• Socially speaking, the first years of a child's
life are affected by where they grow up

③ economically
• The value of the long-term benefits is greater than
the short-term costs.

• To weight up the long term and short term profits
of the changes, the first one seems more reasonable economically.

④ According to the law, condition of the vehicle is the driver's responsibility.

TASK 1 Recognizing word forms

✓ 1 Choose the best form of the words in italics

1 Decision-makers often have to make an
a subjective response, involving a *rely* /
human behaviour.

2 Examples of people who have sacrificed
of others are too *commonly* / *common* to
(adv) (adj)

3 Behavioural economics is an approach t
incorporates psychological insights into
economic decisions.

2 In pairs, compare your answers and identify the word class (noun, verb, adjective
or adverb) of the words in *italics* in 1. Use a dictionary if necessary.

3 Create new phrases or sentences using the alternative word forms in 1. Use the same
context where possible.

Example: *Decision-makers have to assess how **credible** asylum seekers are.*

TASK 2 Using different word forms to express perspective

✓ 1 Complete the table with the correct forms of these perspective words.

Noun	Adjective	Adverb
1 finance	financial	financially
2 the economy / economics	economic	economicly
3 history	historical	historically
4 geography	geographical	geographically
5 science	scienctific	scienctifically
6 society	social	socially
7 psychology	psychological	psychologically
8 medicen	medical	medically
9 the law	ligol	ligolly
10 technology	technological	technologically
11 language	linguestic	linguestically
12 culture	cultural	culturally
13 behaviour	behavioural	behaviourally
14 theory	theoretical	theoretically

Handwritten notes (right):
about country
{ economic reasons
  economical reasons
about personal finance

✓ 2 Complete sentences 2–4 using an appropriate perspective word from the table in 1.

1 _____Historically_____ speaking, the roots of this conflict go back many centuries.

2 In their early years, a child's immediate environment is the ___social / cultural___
context of family and home.

3 From an ___economic___ perspective, the long-term profits of such changes far
outweigh the short-term costs.

4 As far as ___the law___ is concerned, it is the driver who is responsible for the
condition of the vehicle.

✓ 3 Rewrite the sentences in 2 using an alternative phrase to express the perspective.

Example: *In a historical context, the roots of ...*

UNIT 2 Sustainability

ACADEMIC FOCUS: DISCURSIVE TEXTS – PRESENTING AN ARGUMENT

LEARNING OBJECTIVES

This unit covers:

Reading
- Understanding an argument and recognizing a writer's stance
- Identifying arguments and supporting evidence

Writing
- Presenting an argument and incorporating citation
- Planning and writing a body paragraph of a discursive essay

Listening
- Topic signposting in a lecture
- Listening critically and evaluating an argument

Speaking
- Contributing to a discussion: developing, presenting, and supporting an argument
- Introducing, interrupting, and turn-taking

Vocabulary
- Accuracy

Discussion

1 **Work in groups. Think about the adjectives** *sustainable* **and** *unsustainable*. **Note down two or three characteristics relating to these words.**

2 *Sustainability* **has become a buzzword in many different contexts. Agree a clear definition of 'sustainability'. Then discuss how it relates to the following topics. Give examples.**

energy   food   population   tourism
transport   waste   water

3 **Choose one of the topics you discussed in 2. Set out two contrasting points of view.**

Example: *In many parts of the world, mass tourism is damaging areas of outstanding natural beauty. As far as some developing countries are concerned though, tourism is important for the economy, and income from tourism can be also used to support conservation projects.*

An argumentative text puts forward an academic viewpoint – an argument – which develops a topic or issue. The writer sets out their argument in a number of main points, supported by examples and evidence, to convince the reader about their **stance**, i.e. how they stand in relation to the issue. They may also present opposing arguments in order to show that these are weaker than their own argument. In an argumentative text, the writer structures points in a logical order to help the reader follow their argument. It is important to recognize the main points and stages in an argument, and to be able to identify the writer's stance.

This module covers:
- Understanding an argument and recognizing a writer's stance
- Identifying arguments and supporting evidence

TASK 1 Establishing a purpose for reading

1 **Before you read a text it is important to decide why you are reading it. Look at the flow chart of a reading process. Answer the questions.**

1 Where can you usually find the main topic of a text?

2 Why do you think these stages are important as part of an academic course?

Give reasons.

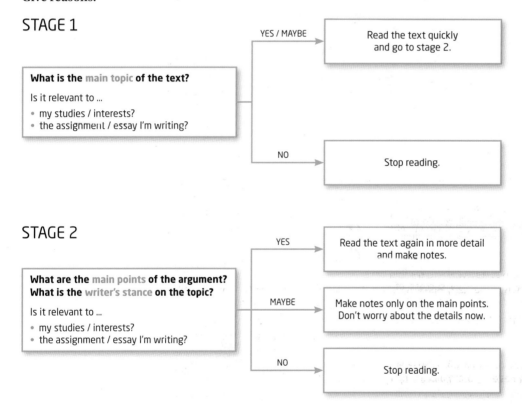

STAGE 1

What is the **main topic** of the text?

Is it relevant to …
- my studies / interests?
- the assignment / essay I'm writing?

YES / MAYBE → Read the text quickly and go to stage 2.

NO → Stop reading.

STAGE 2

What are the **main points** of the argument?
What is the **writer's stance** on the topic?

Is it relevant to …
- my studies / interests?
- the assignment / essay I'm writing?

YES → Read the text again in more detail and make notes.

MAYBE → Make notes only on the main points. Don't worry about the details now.

NO → Stop reading.

2 **You are going to read an extract from one chapter of a textbook. Look at the cover and information. What do you expect to be the main topic of the chapter?**

Book: *Winds of Change: The Environmental Movement and the Global Development of the Wind Energy Industry*, by Ion Bogdan Vasi

Chapter: *The Puzzling Development of the Wind Energy Industry*

3 **Work in groups. Discuss how these perspectives might be relevant to the topic.**

economic environmental political technological

Example: *Oil will become much more expensive in the future because it is running out. So **from an economic perspective**, alternative energy sources, like wind power, will become more important.*

TASK 2 Understanding the topic of a text

1 Read Text 1 paragraph 1. Answer the questions.

1 Which pair of adjectives best describes the development of the wind energy industry?

   (a) fast but uneven   b splashy and successful   c strong and dependable

   possibly   *actually*

2 Explain the difference between *energy potential* and *installed capacity*.

   what there is   *what they can use*

2 Match each style 1–3 in Text 1 to the purpose of the text a–c.

b 1 **bold** text   a gives examples and evidence

c 2 normal text   b expresses the main point of the paragraph

a 3 grey text   c explains the arguments

3 Which parts of the text (bold, normal, grey) do you need to focus on to understand:

a the overall topic?   b the main points?   c the details?

   Bold   *Bold and normal*   *grey*

The puzzling development of the wind energy industry   TEXT 1

1 **What drives the relatively fast but uneven growth of the wind energy industry worldwide? In other words, why is it that wind power stands out as one of the splashiest success stories in renewable energy, but has failed to reach its potential and developed irregularly in different parts of the world? This uneven global development is puzzling.** *not equally balanced* Many countries and regions with some of the best wind energy potential do not have the highest installed capacity, as is the case with the United Kingdom, which has by far the best wind energy potential of all the European Union countries. Recent studies show the United Kingdom has the strongest, most dependable, and most convenient onshore winds, as well as the highest offshore wind potential (CNN, 2001). However, the United Kingdom ranked sixth in Europe in installed wind power capacity at the beginning of 2008 and was generating almost 10 per cent less wind energy than Germany. Conversely, some leading US regions and states in installed wind power capacity did not have the best wind power resources. For example, California was the leading US wind energy producer in 2005, although it was ranked just seventeenth in wind generation potential. North Dakota has frequently been called the 'Saudi Arabia of wind' – the state's persistent winds are capable of generating enough power for more than a quarter of the nation. Yet in 2006 it ranked fifteenth in installed capacity (AWEA, n.d.).

2 **Two perspectives dominate accounts of the growth of the wind energy industry - and research on new industries generally. The technological perspective argues that the development of new industries is influenced primarily by technological innovations and traditions.** In this view, the global growth of the wind energy industry results from decreasing costs in wind power generation due to continuous improvements in blade, gearbox, and generator technology, while cross-national variation results from differences in technological approaches. Numerous academic studies have used this framework to show that differences in technological approaches account for the early success of wind turbine manufacturers in some countries and not others (Heymann, 1998; Est, 1999; Karnøe, Kristensen, & Anderson, 1999; Johnson & Jacobsson, 2000; Garud & Karnøe, 2003; Boon, 2008). Wind power advocates frequently employ this framework and argue that the industry's global development is inevitable, given that it is driven by continuous technological advances. Paul Gipe – a well-known wind energy pioneer – wrote in the mid-1990s, 'From the deserts of California to the shores of the North Sea, wind energy has come of age as a commercial generating technology. Wind turbines now provide commercial bulk power in California, Hawaii, Minnesota, Alberta, Denmark, Germany, Great Britain, Spain, Italy, Greece, the Netherlands, China and India, and the list continues to grow' (Gipe, 1995).

3 **The market perspective, on the other hand, argues that the emergence of new industries is shaped by various economic forces.** Academic research taking this perspective examines how the interaction between factors such as the adoption of specific energy policies, the supply of wind turbine components, or the deregulation of electric utilities determines wind energy price and market penetration. Several studies have compared public policies such as purchase power agreements, investment and production incentives, and renewable set-asides to assess whether they create efficient markets for renewable energy (Redlinger, Anderson, & Morthorst, 2002; Lauber, 2005). Energy professionals often debate the growth of the renewable energy sector in terms of the costs associated with specific policies. A 2008 report of the International Energy Agency exemplifies this approach:

GLOSSARY

splashy *(splashiest) (adj)* very easy to notice; widely covered in the media

> The group of countries with the highest effectiveness ... used feed-in tariffs (FITs) to encourage wind power deployment. Their success in deploying onshore wind stems from high investment stability guaranteed by the long term FITs, an appropriate framework with low administrative and regulatory barriers, and relatively favorable grid access conditions. In 2005, the average remuneration levels in these countries (USD 0.09-0.11/kWh [kilowatt-hours]) were lower than those in countries applying for quota obligation systems with tradable green certificates (TGCs) (USD 0.13 -0.17/kWh). (IEA, 2008)

4   **These two dominant perspectives cannot fully explain the puzzling development of the wind energy industry.** The first perspective can explain why Denmark, which adopted a specific approach to technology, was successful in wind turbine innovation; it cannot explain why the wind energy industry also developed in countries and regions that did not use the Danish technological approach. The second perspective can explain why the wind energy industry developed faster in countries and regions that adopted policies such as feed-in tariffs, but cannot explain why only certain countries and regions adopted these policies.

5   **An uncommon approach to understanding burgeoning industries considers the influence of social movements. This perspective acknowledges the importance of technological or economic factors, but centers primarily on the role played by social movements in the growth of new industries.** In the case of the wind energy industry, this perspective analyzes how the environmental movement has influenced the industry's growth in various national and subnational contexts. (This book argues that the global development of the wind energy industry cannot be understood without examining the interactions of environmental activists and organizations with governments, energy sector actors, various institutions, and the general public over the last four decades.)

SOURCE: Vasi, I (2011). pp.4-7. *Winds of Change: The Environmental Movement and the Global Development of the Wind Energy Industry.* Oxford: Oxford University Press.

GLOSSARY

burgeoning *(adj)* growing very rapidly

TASK 3 Identifying the main points and stages in a text

1 Read the whole of Text 1. Focus mainly on the **bold text**, using the normal text if you need to. Ignore the grey text at this stage. Complete the main points in the table.

Paragraph	Stage in the argument	Main point
1	Describes the background and identifies an issue / question.	The development of the wind energy industry worldwide is uneven. Why?
2	Puts forward one perspective on the situation.	*technological* .... mainly influence the growth of the wind energy industry.
3	Puts forward *another perspective* on the situation.	*Economic issues mainly influence the growth ... energy industry*
4	Critiques these two perspectives.	These views *cannot explain* why the development of wind energy is so uneven in different parts of the world.
5	Puts forward *a different perspective on ...*	*main the ... of the wind industry has been social splash in environmental*

2 It is often possible to ignore the exact meaning of unknown words and phrases when you are trying to understand the main points of a text. Complete the headings for each of these groups of words in the text.

Paragraph 2: Words to do with ....
blade
gearbox
generator technology
wind turbine

Paragraph 3: Words to do with ....
deregulation
market penetration
purchase power agreements
production incentives

(handwritten top right: Perspective stance)

TASK 4 Recognizing the writer's stance

1 Which statement a–c best describes the writer's stance on this topic?

  a Technological, economic, and political factors can all explain the uneven development of the global wind energy industry.

  ✓ b The development of the wind energy industry in different countries has been heavily influenced by the efforts of environmental groups.

  c The uneven growth of the wind energy industry in different parts of the world cannot easily be explained.

2 Find the paragraph in Text 1 that shows the writer's stance. Identify one sentence which best shows what the writer's position is. What sentence opening does the writer use to signal stance? *(handwritten: last sentence)*

3 Why do you think the writer expresses his own stance in this paragraph and not earlier? *(handwritten: a counter argument)*

TASK 5 Recognizing citations in a text

1 Look at some of the people mentioned in Text 1. Decide whether each refers to a specific published text (S) or to a general group of people (G).

  G CNN, 2001
  S Johnson & Jacobsson, 2000
  S Paul Gipe
  S Redlinger, Anderson, & Morthorst, 2002
  G the International Energy Agency

  S Heymann, 1998
  G wind power advocates
  S Lauber, 2005
  G energy professionals

2 Which of the people or groups above are mentioned in connection with:

  1 the uneven development of the wind energy industry? *(handwritten: CNN)*

  2 the technological perspective? *(handwritten: Heymann, Johnson and Jacobsson, Paul Gipe, wind power advocates)*

  3 the market perspective? *(handwritten: Redlinger, Anderson, and Morthorst / energy professionals / international energy agency / Lauber)*

3 How do the references at the end of sentences a and b add to the information in grey? *(handwritten: they give approval to show what you said is true. cite your source (who says so?))*

  a Numerous academic studies have used this framework to show that differences in technological approaches account for the early success of wind turbine manufacturers in some countries and not others (Heymann, 1998; Est 1999; Karnøe, Kristensen, & Anderson, 1999; Johnson & Jacobsson, 2000; Garud & Karnøe, 2003; Boon, 2008).

  b Several studies have compared public policies such as purchase power agreements, investment and production incentives, and renewable set-asides to assess whether they create efficient markets for renewable energy (Redlinger, Anderson, & Morthorst, 2002; Lauber, 2005).

ACADEMIC LANGUAGE   ▸Language reference page 206

Noun phrases (2) Using nouns to present alternative arguments

In discursive writing, noticing the ways different points of view can be expressed will help you identify and compare sections of the argument in a text.

- A general noun introduces a widely held point of view:
  The technological / market **perspective** argues that …
  This **approach** focuses on …
  Two **views** have emerged …

- Writers also use noun phrases to refer to research that supports a particular perspective:
  Numerous academic studies have used this framework to show …
  Academic research taking this perspective examines …

- Plural nouns are frequently used to refer to people who support or oppose a particular view:
  Wind power advocates frequently employ this framework …
  Critics have claimed that …
  Social psychologists have proposed …

TASK 6 Presenting alternative arguments

1 **Put the nouns in list a into five pairs with a similar meaning.**

[handwritten: Supporter –] a advocate *[handwritten: (v) advocate (n) advocate]*   b air travel
[handwritten: Opponent –] critic   alternative energy
[handwritten: Professional –] expert   climate change
[handwritten: trend] movement   environmental
               opponent   population
               professional   public transport
[handwritten: Studies –] research   recycling
               studies   waste
               supporter
               trend

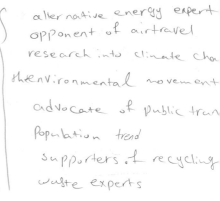

[handwritten margin notes: alternative energy expert / opponent of air travel / research into climate cha / the environmental movement / advocate of public tran / Population trend / supporters of recycling / waste experts]

2 **Combine nouns in list a with nouns in list b to form at least six different noun phrases using different patterns. Add a preposition (e.g. *of*) where necessary.**

[handwritten margin notes: climate change trend / opponents wasting / environ al research / public sport advoca]

   Example: *supporters of alternative energy / alternative energy supporters ...*

3 **Rewrite sentences 1–5 to show whose argument is being expressed. Use noun phrases from 2.**

   Example: Wind power could produce 20% of our energy by 2050. – *Supporters of alternative energy predict that wind power could produce 20% of our energy by 2050.*

   1 Recycling campaigns are only effective if there is a real market for recycled materials.
   2 Areas with restrictions on car use see a surge in demand for public transport.
   3 Many consumer goods are now so cheap, they are seen as disposable.
   4 Global weather patterns are becoming less predictable.
   5 Greenhouse gas emissions from aviation are increasing at an unsustainable rate.

TASK 7 Identifying supporting evidence in a text

1 **Look again at Text 1 on page 025. The grey sections of text mainly give supporting evidence, examples, and reasons. Find one piece of support for:**
   a the uneven growth of the wind energy industry
   b the technological perspective
   c the market perspective.

2 **Which of these different types of support are used in the text? Underline examples.**
   a specific examples or statistics from research by others
   b specific examples or statistics from the author's own research
   c general arguments put forward by other writers
   d the author's own reasons and logical conclusions

3 **Work in groups. Discuss the questions.**
   1 How does the support (evidence, examples, etc.) contribute to the text?
   2 Which type of support is most convincing?
   3 How important is it to understand the details of the evidence to understand the main points of the text?
   4 If this was your specialist area, which references do you think would be the most important to look up? Why?

Discursive writing is common across most disciplines, in essays that discuss different arguments on a particular issue, or in the discussion section of a longer piece of writing. You will be expected to develop arguments that include a claim – your main point or **thesis** – and reasons why it is convincing, followed by examples or evidence to support your claim. You need to include citation, with a **reference** to the source, e.g. *(Jones, 2011, p.34)*. Evidence can include research, theories, and wider ideas within your discipline. An argument can be a single main point expressed in one paragraph, or it can be an overall **position** argued across a whole text; in this case, a thesis statement in the introduction will be supported by a number of points in following paragraphs. The structure of your argument should be clear and logical so that your reader can easily follow your line of thought.

This module covers:
- Presenting an argument and incorporating citation
- Planning and writing a body paragraph of a discursive essay

TASK 1 Presenting an argument at paragraph level

1 Read the two paragraphs, Texts 1 and 2. Write brief notes for each paragraph.

	Text 1	Text 2
the main point		
supporting points		
evidence		

2 Work in groups. Discuss what the two paragraphs have in common and in what ways they are different. Consider:
- the general topic
- the perspectives mentioned and the stance of the writers
- the source – genre, audience, and purpose
- the use of citation.

Congestion charges

`TEXT 1`

The primary objective of a congestion charge is to reduce traffic congestion. The congestion tax system introduced in London, for example, led to a reduction in city-center traffic of 12 percent, of which 50-60 percent shifted to public transport (Transport for London, 2004). It is estimated that daily inbound traffic would be reduced by 5 percent in New York if a toll (set at the level of current tolls on the two parallel Metropolitan Transportation Authority (MTA) tunnels) or a variable charge (with MTA tolls modified to match it) were introduced on the East River Bridge. A London-type congestion charge would reduce daily traffic volume in the city by 9 percent; if full variable pricing were introduced, the reduction could reach 13 percent (Zupan & Perrotta, 2003).

SOURCE: Timilsina, G. & Dulal, H. (2011). p.169. Urban road transportation externalities: costs and choice of policy instruments. *World Bank Research Observer*, 26 (1): 162-191.

GLOSSARY

congestion charge *(n)* a fee that drivers have to pay each time they drive into the centre of a city

toll *(n)* a charge paid for using a particular road, bridge, tunnel, etc.

The motivated consumer

Two strategies dominate discussions about curbing greenhouse gas emissions and oil use: vehicle efficiency and low carbon fuels. But there's a third strategy that's also very important: motivating better behavior. People, acting as consumers, travelers, voters, and investors, are central to all strategies to reduce oil use and carbon footprints; with the rest of the world following America's lead in mobility matters, it's especially important for Americans to adjust their behavior. The primary challenge is to awaken an American public largely ignorant of the energy and climate implications of their decisions, and to motivate American consumers to align their choices with the greater public good – what US Senator John McCain has repeatedly called 'a cause greater than self-interest'.

SOURCE: Sperling, D. & Gordon, D. (2009). pp.151-152. *Two Billion Cars: Driving Toward Sustainability.* Oxford: Oxford University Press.

TASK 2 Critical thinking – generating and organizing ideas

1   Read the essay title. How are the ideas in Texts 1 and 2 relevant to this essay?

> TITLE: *'Today there are over a billion vehicles in the world, and within twenty years, the number will double, largely a consequence of China and India's explosive growth. Given that greenhouse gases are already creating havoc with our climate and that violent conflict in unstable oil-rich nations is on the rise, will matters only get worse? Or are there hopeful signs that effective, realistic solutions can be found?' (Sperling & Gordon, 2009)*
> *Discuss the effectiveness of solutions to this issue currently being tried around the world.*

2   Complete the arguments below which could be used as part of the essay.

   From Text 1: One strategy for reducing ... (Timilsina & Dulal, 2011)

   From Text 2: Strategies to reduce our dependence on fossil fuels for transport will only be effective if ... (Sperling & Gordon, 2009)

3   Work in groups. Use the prompts to make a list of other points and arguments that might be relevant to the essay. Add others, drawing on your own experience.

   alternative fuels   education   energy efficiency
   incentives / disincentives   regulation   urban planning

4   Organize your ideas according to the perspective from which they approach the issue (*technological, political, economic*, etc.).

5   Discuss and write down possible stances you could take on this topic.

   Example: *There are plenty of examples of effective and realistic solutions to this problem, but they require political will to implement them globally.*

6   Work alone. Using the ideas generated in your group, make notes on these questions.

   ● Which stance will you adopt in your essay?

   ● How many of the points discussed could you include in a 1,000-word essay?

   ● How could you group your points into paragraphs?

TASK 3 Analysing and evaluating a main body paragraph

1 Which features a–j would you expect to find in a main body paragraph of a discursive essay? Write essential (E), optional (O), or not relevant (N).

a the main point of the paragraph expressed clearly

b a thesis statement

c additional supporting points

d explanation of a concept

e definition of key terms

f examples or other supporting evidence

g citations

h comment on or evaluation of the main points

i a concluding sentence recapping or summarizing the main idea

j a link to the next paragraph

2 Read a main body paragraph from a student essay.

- Which perspective does the paragraph present?
- Which of the features in 1 can you identify?
- What is the stance of the writer on this point?
- What do you think will follow in the next paragraph?

In recent decades, there has been a focus on the development of cleaner, more fuel-efficient vehicles, and huge progress has undoubtedly been made in vehicle technology. Increasing awareness of the damage done by greenhouse gas emissions, along with rising oil prices, has prompted manufacturers to develop and market cars with smaller, more efficient engines as an 'eco' alternative. As Sperling and Gordon (2009, p.151) point out, even in the United States, the market for large, 'gas-guzzling' SUVs has been shrinking, and demand for hybrids has increased. Perhaps the most prominent development has been electric cars, which run on batteries recharged by plugging the vehicle into a charging point, and which produce almost zero emissions. Hybrids use similar technology, but have the capacity to switch to using more conventional fuel, such as petrol or diesel, when batteries are running low. This overcomes the problems currently associated with short battery life and limited access to charging points. Studies have shown that the adoption of electric and hybrid cars can significantly reduce atmospheric emissions and, after the initial investment, they could be comparable in cost terms in the future (Cruickshank & Kendall, 2012). However, whilst progress in vehicle technology seems promising, there are still a number of issues and problems to consider around so-called 'green' vehicles.

3 Evaluate the body paragraph in 2 using Checklist D.

CHECKLIST D Evaluation criteria for a body paragraph

1 Does the writer state their main argument clearly?

2 Do supporting points flow logically? Give evidence.

3 Are key concepts / terms clearly defined and/or explained? Give evidence.

4 Does the evidence chosen support the main argument? Explain why (not).

5 Does the writer include comment and/or evaluation to make their own stance clear? Give evidence.

Checklists:
page 209

Citations (1) Incorporating references

In academic writing, there are several ways of incorporating citations, i.e. evidence from
sources. In each case, it is important to include a reference to show clearly the source of
the idea or information. Academic references have two parts: an in-text reference, and full
reference details in a reference list or bibliography at the end of the text.

In-text references

Many academic texts use an **author-date system**, where the name of the author(s) (*only* the
family name, *not* the first name or initial) and the date of publication appear in the in-text
reference. You also include a page number where you use a direct quotation or paraphrase a
specific point. The reference can appear

- before the citation with the name(s) as the subject of a reporting verb and the date (and
  page number) in brackets:
  Timilsina and Dulal (2001, p.169) *cite the example of London's congestion charge scheme ...*
- after the citation with the name(s) and date in brackets:
  Several studies have compared ... ***(Lauber, 2005; Redlinger, Anderson, & Morthorst, 2002)***.

Texts in some disciplines, especially law, science, and engineering, use **numerical systems**,
where a number appears in the text instead of the author and date, and links to the full
reference details in a footnote or a numbered reference list at the end of the text.

Bibliography

The full reference details of all sources appear at the end of your text in a reference list or
bibliography. The details will typically include the name(s) and initials of the author(s), the date
of publication, the title of the book or article, and other details of the publication to help your
reader find the source for themselves.

- Reference for a **book**:
  Vasi, I. (2011). *Winds of Change: The Environmental Movement and the Global Development
  of the Wind Energy Industry.* Oxford: Oxford University Press.
- Reference for a **journal article**:
  Timilsina, G. & Dulal, H. (2011) Urban road transportation externalities: costs and choice of
  policy instruments. *World Bank Research Observer,* 26(1): 162-191.

Whichever system and format you choose, it must be clear to your reader which ideas in a text
are your own and which come from sources. If references to ideas from sources are not clearly
shown using appropriate referencing conventions, this may constitute plagiarism.

TASK 4 Incorporating citation in an essay

1 **Look again at the body paragraph in Task 3 on page 031. For each sentence, decide:**
   a Does it express the student's own ideas?
   b Is it a citation from a source text? If so, how is the in-text reference given?

2 **Is it clear throughout which ideas are the student's own and which come from sources?**

3 **Read Text 3, another extract from the book by Sperling & Gordon.**

TEXT 3

The modest reduction in driving by Americans in the face of high fuel prices is largely a result of their
increasing dependence on cars, and the lack of alternatives. Increased suburbanization and sprawled
development have led to longer distances to work, shopping, and other destinations, and have
reduced the viability of walking, transit, and biking. Children used to go to school by foot, bicycle, or
bus. Now many are driven, or drive themselves as soon as they get a license. Greater car dependence
and greater sprawl has reduced Americans' flexibility in responding to high fuel prices.

SOURCE: Sperling, D. & Gordon, D. (2009). p.161. *Two Billion Cars: Driving Toward Sustainability.* Oxford: Oxford
University Press.

4 Look at ideas a–e from Text 3. Answer the questions.

  1 Do the ideas:
  - paraphrase an idea from a single sentence in the original text? OR
  - summarize ideas expressed in more than one sentence?

  a Despite rising fuel prices, Americans remain heavily dependent on their cars.

  b Most Americans drive to work, to the shops, or to school because there are few viable alternatives.

  c In the US, increased suburbanization and urban sprawl mean that many are forced to travel long distances to work or school.

  d Poor urban planning often means that people are no longer able to walk or cycle to work or school.

  e Americans have struggled to reduce car usage in response to rising fuel prices because the American lifestyle has become so dependent on driving.

  2 To what extent do sentences a–e:
  - use the language of the original text? OR
  - paraphrase the ideas using different language?

5 Edit ideas a–e in 4 to write citations that could appear in an essay. Use the formats in the Academic Language box on page 032.

  Example: *Sperling and Gordon (2009, p.161) maintain that despite rising fuel prices, Americans remain heavily dependent on their cars.*

TASK 5 Writing a body paragraph of a discursive essay

> **TITLE:** *'Today there are over a billion vehicles in the world, and within twenty years, the number will double, largely a consequence of China and India's explosive growth. Given that greenhouse gases are already creating havoc with our climate and that violent conflict in unstable oil-rich nations is on the rise, will matters only get worse? Or are there hopeful signs that effective, realistic solutions can be found?' (Sperling & Gordon, 2009)*
> *Discuss the effectiveness of solutions to this issue currently being tried around the world.*

1 Read the essay title again, and review the issues and arguments in this module.

  1 Look back through the module and make a list of the issues and arguments discussed.

  2 Note down relevant perspectives that the essay could include.

  3 Work out two opposing stances that it would be possible to take.

2 Choose one perspective on the topic and one main argument that could be included in the essay. Draft a single main body paragraph of 200–250 words. Follow the guidelines below.

> **Guidelines for drafting a body paragraph**
>
> 1 State your main argument clearly.
> 2 Include supporting points in a logical order.
> 3 Explain or define any key terms or concepts where necessary.
> 4 Use relevant evidence to support your points - from this module or your own research.
> 5 Ensure that citations are appropriately presented and referenced.
> 6 Include comment and/or evaluation to make your own stance clear.

3 Exchange your paragraph with another student.
  - Evaluate each other's writing using Checklist D (Task 3.3).
  - Check the citations are correct.
  - Give each other feedback on both positive points and possible weaknesses.
  - Redraft your paragraph in the light of the feedback.

The purpose of academic lectures is often to give an overview of main points, perspectives and arguments on a topic, and to help students see how different positions fit together. The important thing is to follow the main points rather than the details, which you can go away and read about later. As you are listening, you need to think critically about the arguments being presented in order to be able to evaluate and discuss them in a **seminar** or essay.

This module covers:
- Topic signposting in a lecture
- Listening critically and evaluating an argument

TASK 1 Critical thinking – evaluating an argument

1 **Work in groups. Discuss to what extent you agree with this statement from the introduction to a lecture. Put forward specific support or criticisms.**

'The world's residents are in general young and poor, and living in cities, and are part of an unequal and unsustainable network of global production and consumption.'

Example: *I know it says 'in general', but surely there are as many people in the world living in rural areas as there are in cities.*

2 **Work alone. Note down key words and phrases that you think might come up.**

3 **Now compare words and phrases. Explain how they are connected to the topic.**

TASK 2 Establishing the topic of a lecture from the introduction

1 ▶2.1 **Watch Extract 1 of a lecture by Dr David Howard. Tick the topic that Dr Howard talks about most in this part of the introduction.**

.... sustainable cities .... urbanization .... population growth .... poverty

2 ▶2.2 **Watch Extract 2, the second part of the introduction. Which topic in 1 will be the main focus of the rest of the lecture? Explain how you know.**

3 **Did Dr Howard use any of the words and phrases you noted in Task 1.2? Check transcripts 2.1 and 2.2 on page 225.**

4 **What is the purpose of the introduction? Does it capture your attention?**

ACADEMIC LANGUAGE

Signposting (2) Focusing on the main theme

In a discursive lecture, a lecturer will often repeat the focus on the main theme of the lecture. Noticing this will help you see how each point is connected to the theme:

Particularly I'm looking at …
But really what we're concerned with today is …
So today we are going to focus this lecture on …
For (the) purposes of this lecture, I'm going to be concentrating on …
I'm not going to look at … as a whole …, I'm going to focus narrowly on …

TASK 3 Recognizing signposting language

1 ▶2.3 **Watch Extracts a–d from four different lectures and note down the main focus of each lecture.**

2 **Watch again and note down which signposting expressions the lecturers use.**

3 **Check transcripts 2.1 and 2.2 on page 225 again. Find other signposting expressions.**

TASK 4 Listening critically

1 In Extract 3, Dr Howard describes a school of thought known as *New Urbanism*, an approach to designing cities. Work in groups. Look at some of the key terms that he uses. Discuss how they might relate to urban planning.

   sense of community   liveable   social mix   high quality design   walkable   public spaces

   Example: *I think that 'walkable' means that people can walk to work or to school and they don't have to drive. So schools and offices have to be near where people live.*

Seaside

2 ▷ 2.4 Watch Extract 3. Using the key terms in 1 as your headings, make notes about the main features of New Urbanism.

3 Discuss the questions.

   1 Do you think a New Urbanist city would be a good place to live?
   2 In what ways would it be sustainable?
   3 What possible criticisms could you put forward?

4 You are going to watch a longer extract which describes two examples of New Urbanist design and then critiques them. Dr Howard starts by saying that 'the New Urbanists have been critiqued for being too Utopian'.

Celebration

   1 What do you understand by the phrase 'too Utopian'?
   2 Does this match any of the criticisms you discussed in 3?

5 Look at groups of words / phrases a–c from the lecture. Briefly explain the terms.

   a mixed neighbourhoods   b ideal   c Utopian
      conformity   1930s townships   market economy
      quaint   clean   gentrified
      social code   small scale   community
                                    walkability   problematic
                                                             affordable
                                                             social mixing

6 Look at the photos of New Urbanist towns. Match the groups of words in 5 to the headings in the table below.

Features of New Urbanist developments		Critiques of New Urbanism
Seaside	Celebration	

7 ▷ 2.5 Now watch Extract 4. Make notes under the headings in 6.

8 Work in A or B groups. A groups prepare an oral summary of how the principles of New Urbanism have been put into practice in Seaside and Celebration. B groups prepare a summary of the criticisms of the two developments.

TASK 5 Critical thinking – evaluating an argument

1 Work in groups. Dr Howard sums up Extract 4 as follows:

   'Sustainable development isn't purely looking at urban design. It's not focusing on the economic or environmental aspects alone; it's the social aspect which many would argue is the most important form of creating a liveable city.'

   Evaluate his argument. Consider:

   • the examples you have seen of New Urbanist developments
   • some of the economic and environmental aspects of sustainable development
   • what you understand by the 'social aspect' of sustainable cities
   • other projects and schemes you know about to make cities more sustainable
   • what you think is most important in creating sustainable cities for the future.

2 Present a summary of your discussion to the class.

In a seminar discussion, you may be asked to put forward your own arguments on a topic or issue. An academic argument is different from a personal opinion because it is based on your academic knowledge of the topic and is supported by evidence drawn from reading and lectures, as well as your own experience. A good discussion, however, isn't just a series of monologues in which individuals present their own arguments. Participants in a discussion need to link their ideas together in order to come to a better overall understanding of the topic. Listening and responding is sometimes as important as getting your prepared point across.

This module covers:
- Contributing to a discussion: developing, presenting, and supporting an argument
- Introducing, interrupting, and turn-taking

TASK 1 Developing an argument

1 **You are going to discuss the question below. Work alone, and quickly write down your first response.**

> **DISCUSSION:** *What makes a city liveable? Argue for the most important factor in determining people's quality of life in the area where they live.*

Example: *I think it's important to live in an area that's clean and safe.*

2 **Work in pairs. A read Text 1 on page 215. B read Text 2 on page 217. Decide:**
- Does the text mention the factor you chose in 1?
- Does the text persuade you to adapt your ideas?

Summarize the information in your text to your partner.

3 **Use the language in the texts to develop your response in 1 into an academic argument.**

Example: *A clean, pleasant environment and a low crime rate help to create a sense of well-being in a community.*

4 **Present your argument. Work in pairs to improve your main points.**

5 **Present to the class. How many different factors did you come up with?**

TASK 2 Supporting an argument with evidence

1 ◀)) 2.6 **Listen to a seminar discussion about what makes a liveable city. Note the main argument and support each person (A–C) contributes.**

	Main argument	Support	Type of evidence
A	*Transport is a key factor.*		
B		*The cities at the top of the list in Text 1 can afford to spend money on urban planning because they don't have to deal with so much poverty and crime.*	
C			

2 **Classify the type of evidence each student uses. Give examples.**
1 ideas from the texts in Task 1
2 evidence from other sources in this unit
3 examples from their own general knowledge
4 examples from their own experience

3 **Work in groups. Discuss which type of support was most effective and why.**

Interaction (2) Interrupting and linking

Try to use techniques to help a discussion move forward effectively. Listen carefully to other speakers; linking what you say to a previous speaker's point helps a discussion to flow.

- You can politely interrupt a speaker in order to add your own point, or to ask a question:
  Sorry, can I just interrupt you there?   *I just wanted to say something about …*
  If I could interrupt you for a second …   *Can I ask something?*
- You can acknowledge the previous speaker's point, and add to the point:
  Yes, and like you said …   *Exactly, I think that's a really important point …*
- You can also acknowledge the previous speaker's point, but add a different point:
  Well, I completely agree about …, but …   *Yes, of course we need to consider …, but …*

TASK 3 Introducing your argument and linking to others' ideas

1 **Look at the pairs of comments. Add suitable expressions to link them together.**

a Culture is really important in enriching people's quality of life. I came to study in Europe because there's so much diversity in terms of art, theatre, music, and so on.

b Culture isn't only art and music; it includes social activities and a sense of community - you know, the way people interact with each other generally.

c I'm not sure if I trust the survey. It seems to be looking at quality of life from a privileged, Western perspective. I'd like to know exactly what factors they looked at and how they calculated the scores.

d Surely what's important in one culture, or in one context, may not be as important to someone living in a very different culture or context.

e If we're going to create more sustainable cities, then we really have to address the issues of consumption and waste. We can't just keep dumping more stuff, because we'll end up with mountains of waste.

f Perhaps the issue we really need to address is population growth. All these other problems around sustainability come about because the world's population is growing out of control.

2 **Work in pairs. Which ideas a–f do you agree or disagree with? Take turns to read out one of the comments, then introduce your own point using a linking expression.**

TASK 4 Participating in a seminar discussion

1 **Work in groups. You are going to take part in a discussion about 'what makes a place liveable'. Select one person to take notes on the discussion. Follow the guidelines below.**

Guidelines for conducting a seminar discussion (1)

1 Try to include different perspectives in your arguments.
2 Include evidence and examples to support your arguments.
3 Listen carefully to others and link your ideas to what has been said before.
4 Interrupt appropriately if you want to ask a question or add a relevant point.
5 Include all participants equally. Try to avoid anyone dominating the discussion.

2 **Summarize the main points of your discussion and present these to the class.**

TASK 5 Reflecting on performance in a seminar

1 **Evaluate your discussion based on the guidelines in Task 4.1. Think about how you can contribute more effectively in your next discussion.**

2E Vocabulary Accuracy

In academic writing, an apparently minor error, for example, a wrong choice of preposition, can subtly alter the meaning of information or lead to ambiguity. Repeated minor errors can undermine the strength of an academic argument or text, by calling into question the reliability of the writer. Checking grammatical words, such as prepositions that link together noun phrases, can significantly improve the accuracy and impact of your writing.

TASK 1 Choosing prepositions in noun phrases

1 The most common preposition to follow nouns in academic texts is *of* (*the role of, consumption of*, etc.), but different prepositions are typical after particular nouns (e.g. *approach to*). Decide which prepositions typically follow these nouns.

debate   interaction   investment   participation   research

2 Complete these sentences using a suitable preposition in each gap.

  1 The emergence .... new industries is shaped by various economic forces.

  2 Two perspectives dominate accounts .... the growth .... the wind energy industry and research .... new industries generally.

  3 Political scientists might suggest that individual well-being is dependent on the quality .... political institutions and the level .... participation .... the democratic process.

  4 This research examines how the interaction .... factors such as the adoption .... specific energy policies, the supply .... wind turbine components, or the deregulation .... electric utilities determines wind energy price.

3 Some nouns can be followed by more than one preposition in the same context, with little change in meaning (e.g. *a debate on/about wind energy, research on/into alternatives*). Some nouns are used with different prepositions depending on the information that follows (*investment in infrastructure, an investment of $5 million*). Explain what typically follows the noun + preposition pairs 1–3.

Example: the **attitudes** of consumers: *attitude + of + the person/people with this belief*

  1 positive **attitudes to** technology

  2 strong **evidence for** a link

  3 little **evidence of** reform

4 Write noun phrases using these noun + preposition pairs and explain the difference in meaning in each case.

  1 relevance + of, relevance + to   2 role + of, role + in

TASK 2 Identifying adjective / verb + preposition combinations

1 Look at the prepositions highlighted in sentences 1–8, then complete each sentence with the adjective or verb that best fits the meaning and grammar of that sentence.

appropriate   benefitted   capable   ignorant
incorporate   oriented   participated   responding

  1 Consumers have been slow in .... **to** higher fuel prices.

  2 Only a small proportion of the workforce .... **in** the survey.

  3 The treatment is not .... **for** children under five years old.

  4 The course is very interactive and specifically .... **towards** young adolescents.

  5 This allows users to .... stricter security checks **into** their online systems.

  6 The public are largely .... **of** the environmental implications of their decisions.

  7 Families from the surrounding villages .... greatly **from** the new health clinic.

  8 The wind turbines are .... **of** generating power 98% of the time.

2 Choose four of the adjective/verb + preposition pairs in 1 and write your own example sentence for each.

UNIT 3 Creativity

ACADEMIC FOCUS: SUMMARIZING TEXTS

LEARNING OBJECTIVES

This unit covers:

Reading
- Identifying the features and structure of abstracts
- Navigating journal articles and using abstracts for research

Writing
- Ensuring coherence and cohesion throughout an essay
- Analysing, writing, and evaluating a conclusion

Listening
- Establishing key words and themes from the introduction
- Note-taking (2): using different techniques

Speaking
- Reading in preparation for a seminar discussion
- Summarizing ideas from written sources

Vocabulary
- Identifying senses

Discussion

1 **Work in groups. Study the quotation and discuss the questions.**

'The lives of artists and inventors suggest that creativity is often not recognized or distinguished from eccentricity, that society is generally opposed to innovation, and fickle when it does reward creative works. Yet modern society is committed to progress and is rapidly changing its attitude toward scientists, if not toward all creative individuals.' (Weibe, 1962)

- According to the writer, do creative people always have a positive image in society?
- Think of examples of when creative people are portrayed by society as eccentric (for example, in the media and popular culture, such as films).
- To what extent have attitudes changed since this was written? Think of at least two examples.

2 **Discuss how creativity and innovation are relevant in your own subject areas. Use the ideas below. Give reasons and examples.**

developing new techniques / theories / methods
changing ideas / attitudes
finding new applications for technology
finding solutions to new problems

Example: *Historians have to innovate, for example, using new technologies such as carbon dating to date archaeological finds more accurately.*

Academic **journal articles** are an important genre for anyone undertaking academic study. They are an essential part of academic research, publishing up-to-date ideas and **research findings** in specific areas. Journal articles are typically **primary sources**; they report directly on research undertaken by the authors. **Secondary sources**, such as textbooks, report on research carried out by others. In your own research and writing, it is better to find and read a primary source where possible. Understanding how to use journal articles is a key skill that will make your research more efficient. Learning to use **abstracts** will maximize your reading time by helping you to select articles more quickly that are relevant to your research question. Within an article, using section headings will enable you to go to the most important sections first.

This module covers:
- Identifying the features and structure of abstracts
- Navigating journal articles and using abstracts for research

TASK 1 Understanding academic journal articles

1 **What is your experience of journal articles? Answer the questions.**

  1 Have you read journal articles in your subject area (in English / your own language)?

  2 If so, did you search for the articles yourself, or were they suggested to you, for example, by a tutor, or on a reading list?

  3 Did you read the journal online or did you read it in print in a library?

2 **Work in pairs. Decide how far you agree with statements a–j. Give reasons.**

Articles in academic journals …

  a are about more specific areas of study / research than academic textbooks

  b are more formal in style than other academic genres

  c report on primary research

  d are peer-reviewed

  e can be written by one person or a team of people

  f are often more up-to-date than information in books

  g are available online

  h are between 4,000 and 7,000 words in length

  i start with an abstract

  j follow a fixed format.

TASK 2 Navigating journal articles

1 Look at the section headings of two journal articles. For each article, decide which section(s) you would look in for a–i.

		Article 1	Article 2
a	a summary of the contents of the article		
b	a thesis statement / statement of aims		
c	background information on the topic		
d	a literature review (a summary of what has already been written about the topic)		
e	a description of the research		
f	details of the results of the research		
g	a discussion of the results		
h	the wider implications of this research		
i	full details of references		

1

Making humour work: creativity on the job

1. Abstract
2. Introduction
3. Humour and workplace relationships
4. Humour and creativity
5. Database and methodology
6. Conclusion
7. Acknowledgements
8. Footnotes
9. References

2

The territorial dynamics of innovation in China and India

1. Abstract
2. Introduction
3. Geographies of innovation in China and India
4. Model and data
5. Results of the empirical analysis
6. Conclusion: the territorial innovation processes of India and China
7. Funding
8. Acknowledgements
9. Appendix
10. Footnotes
11. References

2 Which section(s) of the articles would you read if you wanted to:

1 decide quickly whether the article is relevant to an essay you are researching?

2 find out what the research discovered?

3 use the article as a starting point to learn more about this topic?

3 Match extracts A–D with article sections 1–4:

1 Funding   2 Acknowledgements   3 Appendix   4 Footnotes

A   The authors would like to thank ChinChih Chen and Max Nathan for their excellent research assistance. They would also like to thank the editors and the anonymous referees for their suggestions to previous versions of the paper.

B   [5] For India data are available for 18 States and 3 Union Territories. Bihar and Rajasthan are included in descriptive statistics but not in the regression analysis due to the limited number of observations available over time.

C   **Table A1** Definitions of variables for China

Variable	Definition	Source
PCT applications per capita (per 1000 persons)	Number of provincial PCT applications (count) / total regional population	OECD.Stat

D   Financial support by ESPON 2013-KIT (European Observation Network of Territorial Development and Cohesion - Knowledge, Innovation, Territory) Project and the LSE-SERC, as well as by the European Research Council under the European Union's Seventh Framework Programme (FP/2007-2013)/ERC grant agreement no. 269869 and of a Leverhulme Trust Major Research Fellowship, is gratefully acknowledged.

1 **Look quickly at the two abstracts, Text 1 and Text 2. Make notes on:**
  - the journals they come from
  - the disciplines they are from
  - the authorship, i.e. a single author or a team
  - the estimated number of words in each abstract (count the words in one line and multiply by the number of lines).

2 **Work in pairs. Write a short definition of an *abstract*. Include what it is and how you can use it.**

Making humour work: creativity on the job

TEXT 1

Abstract

There is a long research tradition associating humour with creativity, although relatively little research which focuses on the use of humour among professionals in particular workplaces. **Addressing this gap, this paper analyses** ordinary everyday workplace interaction in a range of New Zealand white collar organizations in order to examine claims about the beneficial effects of workplace humour, including claims that humour is associated with creativity at work. **The analysis provides evidence that** humour not only contributes to the construction of effective workplace relationships (the *creative use of relational humour*), but may also stimulate intellectual activity of direct relevance to the achievement of workplace objectives (the *use of humour to foster workplace creativity*). **The analysis suggests that** the first category is pervasive and examples abound throughout our data set, whilst humour associated with workplace creativity is less frequent and tends to characterize some communities of practice more than others. Interestingly, the effective use of workplace humour to generate new ideas and stimulate intellectual progress is strongly associated with what has been labelled 'transformational' leadership.

SOURCE: Holmes, J. (2007). Making humour work: creativity on the job. *Applied Linguistics*, 28 (4): 518-537.

The territorial dynamics of innovation in China and India

TEXT 2

Abstract

This article analyses the geography of innovation in China and India. **Using a tailor-made panel database for regions in these two countries, we show that** both countries exhibit increasingly strong polarization of innovative capacity in a limited number of urban areas. But the factors behind this polarization and the strong contrasts in innovative capacity between the provinces and states within both countries are quite different. In China, the concentration of innovation is fundamentally driven by agglomeration forces, linked to population, industrial specialization and infrastructure endowment. Innovative areas in China, rather than generate knowledge spillovers, seem to produce strong backwash effects. In India, by contrast, innovation is much more dependent on a combination of good local socioeconomic structures and investment in science and technology. Indian innovation hubs also generate positive knowledge spillovers to other regions.

SOURCE: Crescenzi, R., Rodríguez-Pose, A., & Storper, M. (2012). The territorial dynamics of innovation in China and India. *Journal of Economic Geography*, 12 (5): 1055-1085.

GLOSSARY

agglomeration *(n)* a collection of things together in one place

backwash effect *(n)* when economic growth in one area has an effect on surrounding areas

community of practice *(n)* a group of people who work in the same field

dynamics *(n)* the way in which people or things react to each other in a situation

pervasive *(adj)* existing in all parts of something

polarization *(n)* the process of dividing into completely opposite groups

spillover *(n)* when something spreads to another area

ACADEMIC LANGUAGE

Style (1) Describing and summarizing aims

The aims, results, and conclusions of a journal article are typically summarized in the abstract and introduction.

- Writers may refer to themselves and their co-authors using personal pronouns:
  In this paper / article, **I** *explore* …
  In this essay, **I** *will argue that* …
  We (*will*) *focus on* …

- It is also common to focus on the text or the research itself rather than the writer, using impersonal structures:
  This paper / article *analyses* …
  The aim / purpose of **this essay** *is to* …
  The analysis *suggests that* …
  The findings *indicate* …
  It is suggested *that* …

Common verbs describing research aims:
*address   analyse   argue   consider   describe   discuss   examine
explore   focus on   report   investigate   look at   show   study*

TASK 4 Describing aims

1 Look again at Texts 1 and 2. Which style is used in each text?

a direct reference to the writer (*I, we*)

b reference to the text (*this paper / article*, etc.).

2 Complete these statements of aims from journal abstracts using six different constructions from the Academic Language box, and the verb in brackets.

1 .... (examine) the role of universities in industrial innovation systems.

2 .... (investigate) possible spillover effects of the UK minimum wage.

3 .... (discuss) the findings of a case study of a European health promotion project.

4 .... (study) how internal and external factors affect biological systems.

5 This article is not intended to be an exhaustive review; .... (focus on) some new developments and techniques.

6 .... (suggest) that the decision-making processes change across the lifespan.

TASK 5 Identifying the features and structure of abstracts

1 Read Texts 1 and 2 again carefully. Find phrases / sentences that refer to:

a background to the topic

b aims of the text

c research and methodology

d findings / results of the research

e implications and conclusions from the findings.

2 Work in pairs. Compare answers and discuss how the two abstracts are similar in structure and how they differ.

3 Based on the abstracts, discuss which article you would find most interesting to read. Give reasons.

Example: *I'm studying economics, so I think I'd find the article about China and India more interesting. I'd like to understand why the two countries are so different in terms of business innovation.*

TASK 6 Using abstracts for writing and research

1 You often have limited time to research an essay, so you have to prioritize your reading. Abstracts help you decide what to read. Based on the abstracts in Task 3, decide which articles you would read as research for essay topics a–d. Would each article be:

✓✓ high priority – directly relevant to the topic?
✓ medium priority – useful background reading?
? low priority but worth noting – possibly relevant to the topic?
✗ ignore – not relevant?

	Essay topic	Article 1	Article 2
a	Factors affecting innovation and creativity in business		
b	Innovation, development, and economic policy		
c	Encouraging innovation in the workplace		
d	The role of humour in building effective teams		

2 Choose an essay topic in 1 that relates closely to one of the articles. Use the Contents pages in Task 2.1. Decide how you would use the article to research the essay.

- Which section(s) in the Contents would you focus on? Give reasons.
- How could you use the article to find other useful sources?

3 It is important always to note down the details of any sources that you might use in your writing. Work in groups. Which techniques 1–6 do you think are most useful for keeping track of journal references? Give reasons.

1 Write down the author and title of each journal article in a notebook.
2 Write down all the reference details of each article in a notebook.
3 Print out a hard copy of the article.
4 Cut and paste the details of references into a document.
5 Cut and paste the link to a journal article into a document.
6 Use reference management software to organize your references, e.g. *Mendeley*.

TASK 7 Independent research – exploring journal abstracts

1 Choose a key phrase associated with a topic in your subject area that interests you.

Example: *marketing innovation*

Use an academic search engine (such as Google Scholar) or a university library portal to search for journal articles on this topic. Look at just the abstracts and note down:

1 the length of the abstract
2 whether it is a research article or a discussion article
3 which of the features from Task 2 it includes
4 what language is used to describe the aims (*I* / *we, this paper* / *article*, 'research aims' verbs).

2 What patterns and features do you notice in journal abstracts in your subject area? Were most of the abstracts you found similar in style, or was there a lot of variation?

3 In many journals, key words accompany the abstract. Keep a record of the key words of the abstracts you read. Compile a list of important key words which occur across several articles. Use these key words to help improve and refine your online searches.

Key words

• innovation • R&D • socio-economic conditions • geography • regions • China • India

4 Note down three important academic journals in your subject area. Look at the Contents pages for three or more issues, to gain an overview of the topics included.

The **conclusion** of an essay often summarizes the main points, but it should not just repeat them. It shows how the arguments relate to each other and back to the thesis statement. It also draws wider conclusions such as **implications** of the ideas discussed, practical **applications**, **predictions** for the future, and suggestions for further research. The conclusion may also acknowledge any **limitations** of the essay, for example, points that were not discussed. Throughout, your essay must be **coherent**, i.e. containing logically connected ideas, and **cohesive**, i.e. with points connected through carefully-chosen language.

This module covers:
- Ensuring coherence and cohesion throughout an essay
- Analysing, writing, and evaluating a conclusion

TASK 1 Identifying features of a conclusion

1 Read the title and conclusion of a student essay. Decide what the writer thinks. Write one sentence summarizing the writer's stance.

> **TITLE:** *It has been suggested that there is a link between learning disabilities, such as dyslexia, and increased creativity. Discuss the extent to which this may be true.*

[1]It seems clear from the studies examined here that individuals with dyslexia are more likely than average to exhibit creative talents, and indeed, many successful innovators in different fields are dyslexic. [2]What is less conclusive is the evidence showing whether these talents result from an ability to visualize the world in a different way, or are simply a result of individuals' attempts to compensate for deficits in other areas. [3]More research is needed to understand the exact nature of this association, and this essay has not considered whether similar tendencies exist in individuals with other learning disabilities. [4]However, an understanding of the creative abilities of those with dyslexia could clearly be applied to improving education for this group of students.

2 Tick any features a–g that apply to sentences 1–4 in the essay conclusion in 1.

Sentence	1	2	3	4
a recap the topic / thesis statement				
b summarize main points of the essay				
c refer to findings of research				
d acknowledge limitations of the essay				
e identify areas for further research				
f comment on the implications / application of the findings				
g offer predictions for future developments				

ACADEMIC LANGUAGE   ▸Language reference page 205

Hedging (1) Modal verbs, tentative verbs, and adverbs

Minimizing language, sometimes known as 'hedging' language, is used to 'soften' what you write, so that your ideas are not presented as absolute facts. It is used particularly in conclusions, where you are presenting possible implications or offering predictions.
- Modal verbs:
  *Such insights **could** be applied to improving education for this group.*
  *Future research **may** uncover clearer associations.*
- Tentative verbs:
  ***It seems clear** from the studies examined here that …*
  ***It remains to be seen** how this role may change over time.*
- Adverbs:
  *The introduction of this technology could **potentially** reduce costs at each stage.*

TASK 2 Using minimizing language

1 Look back at the abstracts on page 042. Identify examples of minimizing language.

2 Choose three sentences from the abstracts or the Academic Language box on page 045 and remove the minimizing language. What difference does this change make? What criticism could be levelled at the writers?

3 Edit sentences 1–6 to add a variety of minimizing language.

Example: The storage of health information online has significant implications in terms of security and privacy.
*The storage of health information online **may** have **potentially** significant implications in terms of security and privacy.*

1 The application of stricter visa controls will have knock-on effects in both the business and education sectors.

2 With general acceptance that recorded cases are only the 'tip of the iceberg', more thorough risk assessment is needed.

3 The recent research on dyslexic students shows that they are more creative than the rest of the population.

4 Less developed countries place the blame for their slow growth rates on outside factors such as colonial legacies and free trade.

5 Children from wealthier, well-connected backgrounds are at an advantage in the careers market.

6 Economic, social, and technological developments have resulted in greater inequalities between different income groups in the world.

TASK 3 Ensuring coherence throughout an essay

1 For an essay to be *coherent*, the introduction (including the thesis statement), main points, and conclusion should follow logically from each other, using connected ideas. Read the essay title and outline below. Note down the meaning of the following terms used in the Introduction.

traditional manufacturing   the knowledge economy
emerging economies   falling / lagging behind

> **TITLE:** *'In an age of innovation, ideas are currency.' Discuss the role of creativity and innovation in the modern global economy.*

Introduction:
In a rapidly changing modern world, innovation and creativity are more highly valued than ever. Many developed economies are now based more on ideas and information than on traditional manufacturing – the so-called 'knowledge economy'. Some, however, argue that countries such as the United States, traditional leaders in the field of innovation, are now falling behind the emerging economies of countries like China and India (Kao, 2007). The World Bank's 'knowledge index' (2009), which measures a country's ability to 'generate, adopt, and diffuse knowledge', is based on three key areas; education, innovation, and ICT (information and communications technology).

Thesis statement: This essay focuses on the first two areas, education and innovation, and explores how creativity can be encouraged both in education and in the workplace, looking at why Western countries are now lagging behind in the global, innovation-based economy.

Paragraph 1: Discussion and examples of encouraging creativity in education and training → esp. in emerging economies

Paragraph 2: Encouraging innovation in the workplace → esp. in emerging economies

2   **Work in pairs. Read the two possible conclusions, A and B, and discuss which one best fits the essay outline in 1.**

Does the conclusion:

1   match the thesis given in the introduction?

2   summarize the main points in the body paragraphs?

3   express a stance consistent with the arguments in the introduction and main body?

Conclusion A

Traditionally, the strength of an economy was judged by its heavy industry and manufacturing capacity. However, in today's rapidly changing, globally-oriented, knowledge-based economies, traditional industries are becoming less important. The potential of creative industries can be illustrated by powerful global drivers of growth such as the Apple corporation. In a modern global economy, where goods can be made anywhere and transported easily to markets worldwide, it is those with the capacity to manage such multi-national operations and come up with innovative new products and solutions who will be successful. The knowledge economy is here to stay; therefore the importance of encouraging creativity and innovation in corporations around the world cannot be underestimated. In short, 'knowledge is power'.

Conclusion B

As we have seen, many of the emerging economies of the BRIC nations have moved on in recent years from acting as cheap manufacturing bases for Western businesses to generating their own new ideas and innovations. We are now seeing a significantly increased knowledge flow within emerging nations – ideas and information which completely bypass more traditional knowledge bases such as the United States (Brahmbhatt & Hu, 2010). It seems that these shifts are due largely to changing ideas about education, especially in East Asia, and new business organizations which have learnt from and improved upon best practices in terms of encouraging innovation in the workplace. It remains to be seen how the traditional economies of the West will react to these changes.

GLOSSARY

BRIC *(abbr)* an acronym that refers to Brazil, Russia, India, and China, countries at a newly advanced stage of economic development

3   **Check your choice of conclusion. Identify which of the features of conclusions in Task 1.2 (a–g) it includes.**

4   **Identify examples of minimizing language in Conclusion B. What effect do they have on the text?**

TASK 4 Understanding coherence and cohesion

1   **Look back at Task 3.1. Then place the concepts of *coherence* and *cohesion* on the line.**

         ideas   meaning   language

2   **For writing to be *cohesive*, ideas are connected through the choice of language. Find these words / phrases in the student introduction in Task 3.1.**

knowledge economy   emerging economies   education   innovation

Now read Conclusion B again. Find examples of repeated words or synonyms of these terms.

TASK 5 Writing a coherent conclusion

1 **Work in groups. Read the essay title and outline below.**

- Discuss what you understand by *creative and critical thinking skills*.
- Check any other unknown vocabulary.
- Identify the aims stated in the Introduction.
- Discuss what points you might expect to find in the main body paragraphs, based on the outline.

TITLE: *'In a rapidly changing modern world, where anyone can check information online easily and quickly, education is no longer about simply learning lists of facts by heart. Creative and critical thinking skills are receiving increased emphasis in education systems around the world.'* Discuss the implications of this trend for teachers and students.

Essay outline

Introduction:

The 'empty vessels' view of education, whereby students' minds are simply to be filled with facts by their teachers, has long been criticized (see Friere, 1970; Vella, 2004). However, education systems around the world still place a great emphasis on students learning lists of facts to be reproduced in exams. In an internet age though, where simple information of all kinds is readily available online, this memorization of facts seems increasingly less relevant. Education is becoming more about teaching creative and critical thinking skills to enable young people to effectively process the information they encounter, and ultimately, to channel these skills into 'the production of novel, socially valued products' (Mumford, Gustafson, & Sigrid, 1988, p.27). This essay will first examine what we mean by creative and critical thinking skills, and will then focus on two implications of this shift in education: how it might affect the nature of classroom activities, and the relationship between teachers and students.

Paragraph 1: Explanation of what is meant by creative and critical thinking skills

Paragraph 2: Discussion and examples of the teaching of critical thinking skills: asking questions, challenging assumptions, identifying bias and questioning reliability of information, thinking 'outside the box'

Paragraph 3: The relationship between teachers and students: more dialogue, more student participation, students need to feel confident to challenge the traditional sources of authority (e.g. teachers and texts)

2 **Work alone. Write a conclusion for this essay. Write 100–150 words.**

TASK 6 Critical thinking – evaluating a conclusion

1 **Evaluate your conclusion from Task 5.2 using Checklist E.**

CHECKLIST E Evaluation criteria for an essay conclusion

1 Does the conclusion match the thesis statement and the points in the main body?
2 Does the conclusion summarize the main points logically?
3 Does it refer back to findings of research?
4 Is the focus / stance consistent throughout?
5 Does it state any limitations?
6 Does it comment on implications, or offer predictions for future developments?
7 Is there appropriate use of minimizing language?
8 Is the writing cohesive, repeating words or synonyms from the Introduction?

Checklists:
page 209

2 **Read at least two other students' conclusions. As a group, discuss any differences between your writing, and explain the reasons for your approach. Offer each other critical feedback.**

3C Listening Lectures (3)

Academic lectures can present a wide variety of different types of information, including: general theories and models, different perspectives for analysis, detailed technical information and examples, issues and problems. As a student, it is important to link the information from a lecture to what you already know - from your previous studies, reading, or general knowledge and experience - and think about how you might use that information in the future in essays, seminar discussions, etc.

This module covers:

- Establishing key words and themes from the introduction
- Note-taking (2): using different techniques

TASK 1 Preparing for a lecture

1 **You are going to watch extracts from a lecture. Look at the information from the lecture schedule and make notes on the questions.**

> **Faster, Higher, Stronger: Hero Materials in Sport**
>
> **by Jennifer Tilley**
> Biomaterials DPhil Student,
> University of Oxford

1 What is the lecturer's subject area?
2 What application of her subject will she be talking about?
3 Do you recognize the quotation in the lecture title?
4 What ideas do you think the lecture will cover?
5 What do you already know about this topic? Give examples from your general knowledge.

2 **Work in groups. Compare answers to 1, then discuss how the following words might relate to the lecture. Add three more words or phrases that might appear.**

composition   controversial   fibre   Paralympics   properties   (world) record   strength   structure

TASK 2 Establishing key themes in an introduction

1 ▷3.1 **Work in pairs. Watch Extract 1, the first part of the introduction to the lecture. Each note down key words mentioned in connection with *one* of the topics below.**

People and disciplines involved in materials science	Words / phrases related to materials
biomaterials scientist	*structure*

2 **Compare your lists of words. Then look back at your predictions in Task 1.2 about how the key words might be used. Which words have not been mentioned yet?**

3 **Complete the definition.**

Materials science is an interdisciplinary subject that is concerned with ...

4 ▷3.2 **Watch Extract 2, the last part of the introduction. Note down the three reasons given for improved sporting performance over the past century.**

5 **Discuss which of the reasons in 4 you think is the most significant, and why.**

TASK 3 Inferring the meaning of unknown vocabulary

1 There are several ways of inferring the meaning of unknown vocabulary in a lecture. Look at examples a–e and match them with techniques 1–5 that Jennifer Tilley uses.

   a the Romans added some tiny, tiny little particles, **nano-particles**, of gold

   b **biomaterials**

   c Now **ceramic** is probably a material that you think of as the plates that you use every day.

   d **Elasticity** is the ability of a material to deform linearly, like a spring when I apply a force and then return to its original shape when I remove that force.

   e Physical demonstration (see photo).

   1 parts of the word (prefixes / suffixes)   4 definitions

   2 visual cues   5 examples

   3 synonyms

2 Work in pairs. Discuss the meaning of terms 1–6 from Extracts 1 and 2 of the lecture. Which do you find easier to understand, and why? Check your ideas in transcripts 3.1 and 3.2 on page 227. What technique(s) from 1 did you use to understand the words?

   1 massive structure   4 nano-wires

   2 biochemist   5 double amputee

   3 atomic structure   6 biomechanical engineering

TASK 4 Note-taking (2) – using different techniques

1 You are going to watch another extract from Jennifer Tilley's lecture about one use of a synthetic material called polyurethane. Work in A, B, C groups. Turn to page 219.

2 ▷3.3 Watch Extract 3 and make notes to help you answer the questions.

   1 What are the properties of polyurethane swimsuits?

   2 Why was the use of polyurethane swimsuits in competitions controversial?

3 Compare notes. Discuss the questions.

   1 Are Student C's notes more similar to A's or B's?

   2 Which style of notes do you think is most effective for this type of information? Why?

4 Work collaboratively. Combine your notes into one final version (this might use a mix of styles). Then write a description of the use of polyurethane in the sport of swimming.

TASK 5 Critical thinking – developing your stance

1 Work in groups. Discuss the questions.

   1 Do you think that the use of high-tech materials in sport is fair? Why (not)?

   2 Use your notes to respond to one of the points raised by the lecturer related to high-tech materials. Comment on the implications.

   3 What other materials could be controversial? Do you know of any examples?

2 Look at the sequence below. Can you think of other examples, perhaps from your discipline, where innovations have been controversial?

research / innovation → application → implications

Many seminar discussions are based on reading you have been asked to prepare in advance. The purpose of such a discussion is to help you understand the ideas in the **literature** better through the process of explaining them in your own words, and working together with other students to build up a clear picture of the key arguments and what lies behind them. Discussion should also help you to develop your own stance on the topic. Making notes on a text beforehand will help you to summarize the key ideas and arguments in your own words. As in academic writing, it is important to show in a seminar discussion where ideas you express come from, i.e. whether they are your own ideas or from your reading.

This module covers:
- Reading in preparation for a seminar discussion
- Summarizing ideas from written sources

TASK 1 Reading in preparation for a seminar discussion

1 **Do you think all drugs should be banned in sport? Write your stance in one sentence.**

2 **Read Text 1 quickly. Does the writer believe that all drugs should be banned in sport?**

TEXT 1

Why wage a war on drugs in sport?

Barry Houlihan has summarised the historical arguments used to ban drugs in sport.[13] Firstly, doping harms athletes; secondly, doping is unfair to the athlete's competitors; thirdly, doping undermines sport in society. Contrast this with the arguments against recreational drugs. Firstly, drugs harm an individual; secondly, drugs harm those with whom an individual interacts; thirdly, drugs harm the moral structure of society. There are clear parallels in the first and third arguments. Even the second has resonance. For where a heroin user steals money directly from other people, a steroid doper steals gold medals and fame from other athletes.

Does sport have a unique nature that makes it easy to legislate without controversy? Sometimes the waters can seem just as muddy. [...] Athletes consciously and continuously put their health at risk without risking the ire of the sporting authorities. In some sports, such as boxing, the risks may be self-evident. However they hold for any contact sport. In fact, it is a rare sport, contact or otherwise, that is not harmful to health at the elite level. Exercise may be good for you; elite sport demonstrably isn't. Waddington and Smith illustrate this point with numerous relevant examples.[14] In the US, for example, the average length of career for an American football player is under four years, with injury being one of the main reasons for this lack of longevity. Between 1997 and 2007 on average, five fatalities per year were directly attributable to American football, the majority of these being high school students.[15] In the round ball version, professional footballers in the UK run a 1,000 times higher risk of injury than other so-called high-risk jobs such as construction and mining,[16] although it has been said that in football, incidents are only rarely life-threatening. [...] A UK House of Commons report in 2007 noted that, while it was difficult to ascertain the precise number of deaths caused by anabolic steroids worldwide, for it to be anywhere near the deaths caused by contact sports it would need to be in the hundreds or even thousands a year; it was suggested this was very unlikely to be the case.[17] [...]

Basing a ban merely on drugs being harmful to athletes would of necessity result in elite sport itself being banned. So what about the second argument? Do drugs create an unfair playing field and so harm other non-drug-taking athletes? Previous chapters in this book suggest that, with the right genes and training regimes, drugs may not be necessary for top performance, at least in males. But this is clearly a debatable argument and certainly not true of female athletes. A sense of fairness is a powerful argument for fans who like to know that they are observing an event that is the true test of the athletes themselves. However, emotionally attractive as it is, basing a decision to ban drugs solely to level the playing field does not really stand up to close scrutiny. There are lots of cases where sport is not 'fair'. Athletes are always after 'the edge' - knowledge that will make the difference between success and failure. There is no desire to share this information with others. In most sports, key information is a well-kept secret. Witness the British team that dominated the track cycling medals at the Beijing Olympics in 2008, claiming seven of the ten gold medals on offer. As well as a well-funded and well-oiled support infrastructure, this success was made more likely due to superior, though completely legal, equipment - termed 'technological doping' by its critics.

There is no doubt that being born in the UK in the 1980s meant that you were more likely to win a cycling gold medal in the Beijing Olympics than if you had the same genes, but were born in Morocco. Is it fair that rich athletes and countries can afford the best equipment?

SOURCE: Cooper, C. (2012). pp.228–230. *Run, Swim, Throw, Cheat: The science behind drugs in sport.* Oxford: Oxford University Press.

Note: Numbers 13–17 (13, etc.) refer to footnotes in the original text.

3 Read Text 1 on page 051 again, in preparation for a seminar discussion. As you read, make notes on the following points. Annotate the text (using numbering, underlining, highlighting), make separate notes, or use a combination of techniques.

Textual information

- the main arguments in the text
- background information and citation, including supporting evidence and examples
- the different stances presented (Who said what?)

Personalized information

- any points that you find difficult to understand (What questions do you have?)
- your reactions (Do you agree or disagree? What problems / questions are raised?)
- key language in the text that you can use when discussing the topic

4 Compare your notes with the example on page 216. Find examples of notes relating to the points in 3 above. Develop your own personalized annotation style.

5 Add any extra notes to your own text that you think might be useful.

ACADEMIC LANGUAGE ▸ Language reference page 200 1.3

Citations (2) Referring to sources in a discussion

Although we do not use the same academic conventions to refer to sources in speech as we do in writing, it is still important to make it clear in discussion which ideas are your own and which are from your reading.

> Cooper **argues** that …
> **According to** Jones, …
> Walsh **outlines** …
> He **goes on** to say that … → Continue

Make it clear when you are giving your interpretation of what you have read:

> Overall, I think what Perez is saying is … overall view
> What Perez is suggesting is …
> Perez seems to be arguing for …

Common verbs for referring to sources:

argue believe compare consider defend demonstrate describe differentiate between emphasize examine explain explore focus on illustrate look at outline point out propose report say suggest

---

TASK 2 Summarizing ideas from written sources

1 Work in fours. Choose one observer, who should look at the guidelines on page 053. Students A, B, and C, prepare to summarize *one* idea from the text *in your own words*.

Student A: summarize the traditional arguments against drugs in sport

Student B: summarize the writer's argument against 'doping harms athletes'

Student C: summarize the writer's argument against 'doping is unfair'

Follow the guidelines below.

Guidelines for preparing a spoken summary

1 Focus on the notes you made in Task 1 rather than on the detail of the original text.

2 You don't have to present ideas in the same order as in the text.

3 You may want to use some key words or phrases from the text, but don't 'memorize' long stretches of the text; it will sound awkward and unnatural.

4 A summary doesn't usually include specific examples or evidence.

5 Acknowledge the source of any ideas using reporting language.

---

2 Students A, B, and C: present your oral summary to your group, without looking at the text or your notes. Observer: follow the guidelines below. Using your notes, feed back on the students' reporting language.

3 Discuss the questions as a group, using feedback from the observer.

   1 Did everyone make it clear where / who the information they were reporting came from? If not, how could they have made it clearer?

   2 How did different group members refer to the source: using the name of the writer (*Cooper argued …*) or referring to the text itself (*According to the text …*)?

   3 In what circumstances are each of these methods (author's name or 'the text') most effective?

Guidelines for observer

- Reread Text 1 on page 051 while the other students are preparing.
- During the discussion, listen carefully to the other group members as they each summarize an idea from the text. Note down the *reporting language* they use. For example:

    According to Cooper …
    The writer argues that …
    The text outlines …

  There is no need to try and write down everything they say, just the reporting phrases, and if possible, the main point they then make.

TASK 3 Participating in a seminar discussion

1 Conduct a group discussion around the question, 'Should all drugs in sport be banned?'. Cover:

- main issues / arguments
- different stances
- any personal reactions or questions.

Refer to material in the source text to support specific points.

TASK 4 Critical thinking – evaluating performance

1 Look back at the notes you prepared in Task 1, before the discussion.

   1 Did your preparation help you to participate in the discussion?

   2 Did you manage to refer to the text in the discussion?

   3 Which notes were most useful?

2 Do you have a better understanding of the ideas in the text as a result of the discussion? What helped you most to improve your understanding?

   1 explaining the ideas in your own words

   2 listening to other students' ideas

   3 comments from your teacher

3 Has your stance on the topic changed as a result of your reading or the discussion?

Each academic discipline has its own set of specialized terminology which you will learn as part of your studies (e.g. *hydrophobic*, *isotope*, *iambic*). There are, however, many words in English which have specialized as well as general, everyday senses. Commonly, these senses are linked in meaning, but the specialized sense usually has a more narrow usage. For example, *quarter* means 25% in general usage, but in Economics it refers specifically to the four three-month periods which a year is divided into for financial purposes. You need to look out for and identify the narrower, more specific usage of these words within your own discipline.

TASK 1 Identifying general and specialized senses

1 In pairs, identify the general meaning of these words. Give an example for each.

concentration   corridor   corruption   majority   metre   stress

Example: *A corridor is a narrow passage between rooms in a building.*
       For example, 'Students wait in the corridor before they go into class.'

2 Match sentences 1–6 with the disciplines they are from.

Chemistry   Computer Science   Ecology   Engineering   Law   Literature

1   There is a scale of parental rights from birth to the age of **majority**.
2   Some species of plant are confined to the river **corridor**.
3   There are a number of methods for protecting data from accidental **corruption**.
4   It breaks with the lyric convention of not altering a poem's **metre**.
5   The joint is liable to crack under high tensile **stress**.
6   The samples contain high **concentrations** of organic and inorganic salts.

3 In your pairs, speculate on the possible specialized meanings of the bold words above.

Example: *If a corridor is a narrow passage, then in Ecology, I guess it refers to a narrow*
       piece of land, maybe along a river.

TASK 2 Understanding grammatical differences in usage

1 In the dictionary entry for *concentration*, identify how the general and specialized senses differ grammatically.

concentration *noun* **1** [uncountable] the ability to direct all your effort and attention on one thing, without thinking of other things: *This book requires a great deal of concentration.*
4 [countable, uncountable] the amount of a substance in a liquid or in another substance: *glucose concentrations in the blood*

Source: Oxford Advanced Learner's Dictionary

2 For each of the pairs of phrases 1–6, identify the meaning of the words in bold.

1   a   the **generation** of electricity using solar power
    b   three **generations** of the same family
2   a   one of the **exhibits** at the Museum of Modern Art
    b   both countries **exhibit** similar trends
3   a   insights into human **behaviour**
    b   specific **behaviours** related to the desired goal
4   a   this is not always possible in **practice**
    b   environmentally friendly work **practices**
5   a   the 'international community' is a theoretical **construct**
    b   it took only eighteen months to **construct**
6   a   a new **means** of mass communication
    b   the arithmetic **mean** of all the samples

3 For each pair in 2, identify how the words in bold differ grammatically, in terms of:
   •   different parts of speech (e.g. noun, verb, adjective)
   •   countable, uncountable, or plural uses of a noun.

UNIT 4 Information

ACADEMIC FOCUS: COMPARING, CONTRASTING, AND EVALUATING

LEARNING OBJECTIVES

This unit covers:

Reading
- Evaluating objectivity in texts
- Identifying the main points in texts for a summary
- Identifying cohesive words to confirm themes
- Comparing and evaluating information in different texts

Writing
- Analysing an essay question and writing a basic essay plan
- Using source texts: selecting, comparing, and evaluating points across multiple texts
- Planning and writing a comparison essay

Listening
- Identifying and explaining key components in a poster
- Listening to the question and answer stage of a poster presentation
- Evaluating a poster and presentation

Speaking
- Planning, researching, and giving a poster presentation
- Viewing posters and preparing critical questions

Vocabulary
- Variety

Discussion

1   Work in groups. Explain the following concepts related to *information*. Give examples.

Example: *Information technology refers to the use of computers and other electronic devices for processing and storing information ...*

2   Note down and explain further words and concepts related to information.

Examples: *misinformation, bioinformatics*

3   Discuss the questions.
- How do you organize the information you need for your administrative and educational life?
- How do you learn new information most effectively?
- How can you find the information you need in an increasingly complex and information-rich world?

4   What kind of information is most important in your discipline?

Example: *In linguistics, there is a focus on information which derives from any of the languages of the world.*

When you read extracts from textbooks in your subject area, you need to notice how different authors select and present information. Textbooks may appear **objective**, for example, in the way that they compare and contrast information. However, in many ways textbooks are **subjective**, because comparing and contrasting first involves selecting and evaluating information, and different textbook authors do this in different ways to support their academic purpose, chosen perspectives, and stance.

This module covers:

- Evaluating objectivity in texts
- Identifying the main points in texts for a summary
- Identifying cohesive words to confirm themes
- Comparing and evaluating information in different texts

TASK 1 Critical thinking – evaluating objectivity in texts

1 **Decide whether each word below is associated more with *objectivity* or *subjectivity*.**

critique   fact   guesswork   interpretation   investigation   news story   observation
opinion   prediction   proof   reporting   speculation   viewpoint

2 **Compare answers and explain your choices in 1.**

Example: *Observation – You conduct an experiment and write up your observations in a factual report. But an artist can observe an object and interpret it (subjectively) in a painting.*

3 **Give examples of how the following can be both subjective and objective.**

a newspaper article / editorial   the discussion section of a research article
a university prospectus   a university textbook on media studies

Example: *A newspaper article reports factual news and events, which is mostly objective. It also offers comment and interpretation on the news, which is subjective.*

TASK 2 Engaging with a text

1 **Work in pairs. Identify at least four key characteristics of a *journalist*. Use these to write a definition of the job.**

2 **Rate the following statements from 1 (strongly disagree) to 4 (strongly agree).**
   1 The language of journalism is the language of facts.
   2 Objectivity requires facts to be checked against two or more sources.
   3 Newspaper reporters are expected to interpret the news.

3 **Read the first section of Text 1, *Proof*. Choose the best answer. Give reasons.**
   1 Who is the likely audience for the text?
      a the general public   b students of journalism   c newspaper reporters
   2 What is the main point made in this section of the text?
      a Facts are not always straightforward or easy to check.
      b Newspaper reporters must check their facts with two reliable sources.
      c Woodward and Bernstein checked their facts using two sources.
   3 What does paragraph 3 suggest may happen if reporters do not check their facts?
      a A reporter who does not check their facts will mainly lose their credibility.
      b People will stop reading the articles of a reporter who does not check their facts.
      c Other people may be seriously affected if a reporter does not check their facts.

4 Read all of Text 1 and identify the authors' stance in relation to statements 1–3 in 2.

Facts

TEXT 1

PROOF

1 Not all facts are as straightforward as a name, an address or an age. Where people's reputations are at stake, information requires corroboration as well as attribution, no matter how carefully it's reported.

2 Charges against people, unless they are made during trials or other official proceedings, are not just double-checked to make sure they have been transcribed properly. They must be, in some sense, proven.

3 During their celebrated Watergate investigation, Bob Woodward and Carl Bernstein of *The Washington Post* refused to report on any charge until it had been confirmed by two sources – two reliable sources. That should be taken as a minimum standard for any reporter who has been handed some ready-to-fling mud. When records are available, such documented proof is even better. One source saying that the state attorney general is a hidden partner in a race track invites further investigation, not a story. A trustworthy form of confirmation, and an interview with the accused person, will be needed before the charge can appear in print – carefully attributed, of course. Much more than the reporter's credibility rests on the confirmation of such a 'fact'.

INTERPRETATION

4 Newspaper readers will not always be satisfied with different accounts of who said what to whom when. They often have seen the newsmakers themselves talking on television the previous evening. When their newspaper comes out the next morning, they may want to know a little more: Why did they say that? What did it mean? Newspaper reporters increasingly are asked to *interpret* the news.

5 There are dangers here. Interpretation too often leads to guesswork and subjectivity. For an example, we turn to an event some years ago: a presidential visit to Britain by Ronald Reagan. In writing of that visit, one *New York Times* reporter said that 'In style, Mr Reagan pleased and almost charmed Britain' with his 'genial and relaxed manner'. Three days later, another *New York Times* reporter wrote that British newspapers, in assessing the same visit, 'commented on the lack of spontaneity or common touch to his [Reagan's] appearances'.

6 Where are the facts there? Where are the facts when the *Los Angeles Times* concludes that a speech by Reagan before the British Parliament was 'generally well-received', while *The New York Times* reports a day later that the same speech 'stunned many Britons, including a number of leading conservatives'.

7 Too frequently, reporters take their orders to explain causes and effects as license to take leave of the facts. They certainly do their readers no service with unsupported and possibly unfounded speculation that a speech was 'generally well-received'.

8 As usual in journalism, the solution is to include more facts. Facts do not just fill all the little holes in a story; they anchor it and keep it from wandering too far from observable reality. Instead of indulging in guesswork, R.W. Apple of *The New York Times* managed to say something about reaction to that speech Reagan gave by noting the generally overlooked fact that 'only about 30 of the 225 members of the Labour Party' chose to show up to hear the US president address Parliament.

9 It is more difficult to find a fact illustrating reaction to a speech than simply to take a stab at summing up that reaction yourself. But good reporters always are ready to make the extra effort. The order to interpret, to analyse, to explain the news should be seen as an order to find more, not fewer, facts – to conduct that extra interview in search of a quote that might explain why, to read that extra document in search of a crucial explanation, to observe the scene more closely in search of a telling detail.

10 Reporters are people who watch, read, ask and listen, with notebook out and pen in hand. They should also be interested in nuances, concepts and ideas, but they should be looking to translate these subtler thoughts into what is essentially the language of journalism – the language of facts.

SOURCE: Lanson, J. & Stephens, M. (2008). pp.192–4. *Writing and Reporting the News* (3rd ed.). New York: Oxford University Press.

GLOSSARY

Watergate a US political scandal that forced President Nixon to leave office in 1974

TASK 3 Identifying main points in a text for a summary

1 Read Text 1 on page 057 again, and follow this procedure for each paragraph 1–10.

1 Identify the main point in the paragraph. This may be expressed in one sentence, or may be based on information throughout the paragraph.

2 As you work, use a dictionary to check the meanings of important words and phrases in the text, e.g. *corroboration, attribution*. Keep a record of these words.

3 Write a sentence summarizing the main point. Do not include details and examples. You can use some of the original language of the text, making grammatical changes and changes in word form.

Example: (paragraph 1) *Reporters need to corroborate and attribute facts in order to protect people's reputations.*

2 Work in groups.

1 Compare your sentences from 1. Choose the most effective one for each paragraph.

2 Select the most important points to include in a summary of the whole text. Some paragraphs have similar or related main points, and these can be combined.

TASK 4 Summarizing a text

1 Read the student summary of *Proof* (Text 1). Match parts 1–4 with descriptions a–d.

[¹The section on 'proof'] [²(Lanson and Stephens, 2008, p. 192-3)] [³states that] [⁴newspaper reporters must check their facts with two reliable sources before printing a story.]

a the main point of the source text

b a reference to the source text

c the introduction to the summary

d the reporting verb structure

2 Write a 50-word summary of *Interpretation* (Text 1 on page 057). Follow the guidelines below.

Guidelines for summarizing a section of a text
1 Decide how to introduce your summary.
2 Include all the parts, a–d, in Task 4.1.
3 Base your summary on the material you selected in Task 3.2.
4 Try to use your own language, including synonyms and related words where possible.

3 Read at least two other students' summaries and:

1 compare the points which are included in each summary

2 compare the style of each summary

3 evaluate the summaries to decide which one is the clearest and most complete.

ACADEMIC LANGUAGE	▸Language reference page 201 2.2

Cohesion (1) Using related words and synonyms in a text

Lexical cohesion, the use of related words running through a text, helps you identify key ideas and see how they are connected. In Text 1, cohesion is achieved in many ways, including:

- **repeating key contextual terms** to emphasize what is being discussed. Here the context of journalism and reporting is expressed through the words highlighted in green:
  report – reporter; news – newspaper – newsmakers; journalism

- **using synonyms and related words** with similar meanings. Here the key idea of information-checking is expressed through the related words highlighted in yellow:
  proof → corroboration → double-checked → proven → confirmed → confirmation

TASK 5 Identifying cohesive words to confirm themes

1 Decide which *one* word in each set has a slightly different meaning from the others.

  1 attribute, confirm, corroborate, double-check

  2 better, credible, reliable, trustworthy

  3 information, interview, records, sources

2 Rank each set of words from Text 1 on page 057 from *most objective* to *most subjective*.

  1 attributed, documented, unfounded, unsupported

  2 guesswork, interpretation, reality, speculation

  3 comment, interpret, report, transcribe

3 Find the following words in Text 1 and put them into two categories.

~~facts~~ information corroboration attribution
double-checked transcribed investigation ~~report~~
sources records confirmation interview attributed

  1 Words related to facts: *facts* ...

  2 Words related to activities around facts: *report* ...

4 What function do the following words have in Text 1? Find more examples.

carefully properly proven confirmed reliable

TASK 6 Extracting and noting down key information in texts

1 Use your analysis of Text 1 to complete the 'Text 1' column of the table.

		Text 1	Text 2
1	Date of publication		
2	Place of publication	*USA: New York*	
3	Genre	*textbook, professional handbook*	*textbook*
4	Audience		
5	Purpose	*to present an argument*	
6	Main topic & themes	*reporting, journalism, establishing facts*	
7	Main point		
8	Authors' stance		

2 Read the title and source information of Text 2 and complete rows 1–4 of the table.

3 Read Text 2, focusing on the two highlighted word groups to identify the main topic.

4 Work in pairs. Identify two aspects of the topic 'Media' from the words highlighted in a) yellow, and b) green.

'The infotainment monster that ate the news industry' `TEXT 2`

1 Infotainment, it has been argued, is not only now fulfilling the role of the Fourth Estate, but it is also engaging, informing and entertaining the public far more effectively than the traditional news outlets. Australian media academic Stephen Stockwell (2004) says that television infotainment (including subgenres like lifestyle shows, reality television, and talk shows), when considered as a totality, actually offer greater diversity of viewpoints, acuity of representation and depth of critique than traditional news and current affairs programs in Australia presently provide (Stockwell, 2004:14).

2 Stockwell (2004:14) argues that reality television 'provides a more intense account of experience than either news or entertainment can supply, and a deeper reading of what it is to be a human'. He points to amateur footage of natural disasters, which places the viewer with the citizen at the dramatic moment of challenge; for example, the amateur footage of the devastating 2004 Boxing Day tsunami, which provided an immediate and shocking understanding of the horror and devastation of that disaster in a way that no journalist reporting in the aftermath could hope to accomplish.

GLOSSARY

Fourth Estate *(n)* newspapers and journalists in general and the political influence that they have

3   By 2011 traditional news outlets had learnt their lesson, and had the resources in place - along with a well-established online presence - to reverse this deficiency in disaster coverage. The news coverage of the 2010-11 Queensland floods saw mainstream news journalists filing reports and footage from the epicentre of the unfolding floods. It was this ability of journalists across the vast flood regions to file timely stories and footage of the unfolding disaster - both on traditional formats (particularly television and radio) and online - that brought audiences back to mainstream news coverage.

4   Nonetheless, audiences today still often emerge with news and current affairs through outlets other than news bulletins. In general, it is evident from the ratings that the public are turning to infotainment shows, tabloid current affairs, YouTube and Facebook for their information. [...]

5   There is no doubt that the tabloid entertainment style of journalism captures our attention. In her work on media effects, Grabe (2000, cited in Stockwell, 2004:7-8) found that the flamboyant tabloid - or infotainment style of packaging news and current affairs - increased arousal and attention. [...]

6   While audiences voraciously consume celebrity stories they still expect their news media to provide reliable information from trustworthy sources in a timely manner, and to expose corruption and wrongdoing. [...]

7   Carl Bernstein, veteran journalist of Watergate fame (cited in Stockwell, 2004) maintains that the problem with news and news journalism today is epistemological: journalism has become 'illusionary and delusionary - disfigured, unreal and disconnected from the real context of our lives... distorted by gossip; by sensationalism.' By giving way to the audience's base desires, one commentator claimed that it was 'the infotainment monster that ate the news industry' (Rapping, cited in Stockwell, 2004).

SOURCE: Bainbridge, J., Goc, N., & Tynan, L. (2011). pp.43-44. *Media and Journalism* (2nd ed.). Melbourne: Oxford University Press.

GLOSSARY

epistemological *(adj)* relating to the way we think about knowledge

tabloid *(n)* a newspaper with small pages, short articles and lots of pictures and stories about famous people, often thought of as less serious than other newspapers

5   Read Text 2 again carefully and complete rows 5–8 of the table in 1.

6   Write a summary of Text 2 using the techniques in Tasks 3 and 4. Write about 60 words.

TASK 7 Comparing and evaluating information in two texts

1   Compare and contrast Texts 1 and 2. Use the information in the table in Task 6.1, and your summaries of the texts. Find similarities and differences in:

- **content:** points about fact, interpretation, reliability, journalism, and reporting
- **commonalities:** specific people, events, or types of media mentioned in both texts
- the authors' **stance**.

2   Work in groups. Evaluate the information in Texts 1 and 2 using Checklist F.

> **CHECKLIST F** Evaluation criteria for information in a source text
>
> Consider:
> 1   the context and currency of the texts, i.e. where and when they were published
> 2   the examples given in the texts: where and what type
> 3   the interest, relevance, and usefulness for you of the information in the texts
> 4   how clearly the information in each text is presented
> 5   the difficulty of the texts, in terms of language, concept, and cultural understanding
> 6   the application of the texts: how generally / specifically the information and arguments apply.

Checklists:
page 209

TASK 8 Independent research - comparing sources

1   Carry out an exploratory research project.

1   Search for academic texts in your discipline. Work with at least four different texts, including textbooks and journal articles.

2   Go through the References sections at the end of each text to find out how many different types of sources are used in each text. Are many media sources used?

3   Compare the types of sources between the genres and identify any differences.

Comparison and contrast are very frequent in academic texts, and may form part of a text or the whole text, e.g. an essay. A comparison essay typically moves from comparison and contrast through to evaluation. You start by selecting the information to compare and contrast, which you can present in the form of facts, ideas, and research. To limit the **scope**, you can focus on different perspectives, such as technological, psychological, sociological. You can then evaluate the material in different ways, for example, by assessing its significance, effectiveness, or feasibility. Evaluation may be integrated throughout an essay or presented near the end of the body of the essay.

This module covers:
- Analysing an essay question and writing a basic essay plan
- Using source texts: selecting, comparing, and evaluating points across multiple texts
- Planning and writing a comparison essay

TASK 1 Analysing an essay question

1 **Read the essay title, and match each part of the question with its description.**

instruction   limitation   main topic

> **TITLE:** *Compare and contrast the presentation of information in two different types of media today, focusing on how effectively the information is communicated.*

2 **Add two or more relevant points for each part of the essay question.**

Media types to compare	*radio & television …*
Main topic: How is information presented?	*radio & TV – information presented is chosen by the broadcaster …*
Limitation / focus: How effectively is information communicated?	*radio & TV – audiences don't have control over the information …*

3 **Read these initial notes on the essay question. Select the most relevant items.**

- Historical overview of changing media – growth of internet and social media
- Global emergence of individuals contributing to media, e.g. through blogs
- Definition and discussion of what we mean by 'effective communication'
- Analysis of how information is presented
- Selection of media: TV broadcasting, and individually-accessible media (blogs, social media)
- Speculation on future of media – movement to regional hubs?
- Major types of information presented: news / current affairs; public service info.; personal info.
- Survey of media ownership – major global media corporations

4 **Look at the essay question again. Think of different ways you could interpret the idea of *effective communication*. Choose from the points (right) and expand them to describe themes you could focus on.**

Example: **currency** = *how up-to-date the information is, e.g. radio / TV news is constantly updated, newspapers are always slightly out-of-date by the time you read them*

TASK 2 Writing a basic essay plan

1 Write a basic essay plan following the stages below.

- Select a number of relevant themes and points to focus on from Task 1.
- Decide on the paragraph topics – one topic per paragraph.
- Add in some detail for each paragraph – main point, examples.
- Finalize the order for your material.

2 Compare essay plans using Checklist G. Make notes on the main points of your discussion.

CHECKLIST G Evaluation criteria for a basic essay plan

1 Does the sequence of body paragraphs follow a coherent (logical) structure?
2 Does each paragraph have a clear topic, expressed in a topic sentence? Is this relevant to the essay question?
3 Are the items in each paragraph relevant to the paragraph topic?
4 Which order of body paragraphs is the most effective? Why?
5 Is there any material in the plan which is not relevant to the essay question?

Checklists:
page 209

3 Redraft your plans based on your notes.

TASK 3 Researching: selecting relevant material in a source text

1 Read Text 1 and complete the notes on the text.

Date and place of publication:

Context and relevance to essay task:

Main point(s):

TEXT 1

YouTube and Facebook

The digital and electronic revolution of the past twenty years has had a significant impact on the way we access news and information. While the most dramatic impact of the internet on the traditional news media has been on the decline of newspaper circulation figures, the more recent phenomenon of sites such as YouTube and Facebook have started to have a significant impact on television viewing. According to Sorensen (2007), 'Every day millions of people choose to watch dubious quality amateur videos on the screens of their personal computers'. She said that no one anticipated the trend, and 'no one foresaw that, within a couple of years, media watchers would be talking about an end to the TV era.' [...] Australian academic Axel Bruns (cited in Sorensen, 2007) claims that what we are seeing with YouTube and Wikipedia is the 'user-led future of communications'. He says that YouTube and Wikipedia are changing the power relations between producers and users, and that we are seeing a 'fundamental shift in the model of consumption that grew out of the industrial revolution'.

SOURCE: Bainbridge, J., Goc, N., & Tynan, L. (2011). pp.45-46. *Media and Journalism* (2nd ed.). Melbourne: Oxford University Press.

---

2 Identify two or three relevant pieces of information in Text 1 to cite in the Task 1 essay. Using your essay plan from Task 2, decide where the material fits in the essay, and how it can provide appropriate evidence for a specific point.

3 Write three sentences incorporating the material you have selected, using different types of citation (quotation, paraphrase, or summary). Use the following ways of presenting the citations.

Bainbridge, Goc, and Tynan (2011, p.45) claim / report that ...

It has been argued that ... (Bainbridge, Goc, and Tynan, 2011)

The impact of ... on ... suggests ...

YouTube and Facebook have ... / Television has ...

Comparing and evaluating Using adjectives, adverbs, nouns, and verbs

Comparison typically involves an element of evaluation. Your choice of language reflects how you judge the things you are comparing; which is greater, more significant, etc.

Look at sentence 1 (from Text 1), comparing traditional and new media. Notice how slightly different language changes the meaning of sentence 2.

1 *While **the most dramatic impact** of the internet on the traditional news media has been on the decline of newspaper circulation figures, the **more recent phenomenon** of sites such as YouTube and Facebook have started to have a **significant impact** on television.*

2 ***Clearly the most obvious impact** of the internet on the traditional news media has been on the decline of newspaper circulation figures, while the **more peripheral influence** of sites such as YouTube and Facebook have so far had **a limited impact** on television.*

'Comparison + evaluation' can be expressed using a variety of adjective and adverb constructions:

*Their struggle becomes **that much more urgent** in an era when anyone can grab a megaphone.* (comparative adjective)

*Not all facts are **as straightforward as** a name, an address or an age.* (as + adjective + as)

*Infotainment, it has been argued, is **not only** now fulfilling the role of the Fourth Estate, **but** it is **also** engaging, informing and entertaining the public **far more effectively than** the traditional news outlets.* (not only ... but also; comparative adverb)

When comparing, you also typically evaluate different elements of the two ideas. This can be expressed using a variety of structures, with different degrees of evaluation, from strong to more tentative:

*It **fails to** capture the reality of Britain's hybrid media system.* (strong)

***In general, it is evident** from the ratings that the public are turning to infotainment shows, tabloid current affairs, YouTube and Facebook for their information.* (neutral, evidence-based)

*This article **suggests that** while this label is **accurate in many respects**, it is also **partial** and therefore **misleading**.* (tentative)

TASK 4 Comparing and evaluating ideas

1 **Work in pairs. Compare the media below, using appropriate comparative and evaluative language. You could compare their effectiveness, popularity, reliability, or speed.**

news websites   newspapers   radio   television   Twitter   YouTube

Example: *Although radio doesn't have **as much visual impact as** media like television or the internet, it is **more flexible**; you can listen anywhere. And in developing countries especially, **it clearly manages to** reach a **much wider audience**.*

2 **Work in groups. Critically evaluate the ideas in Text 1 on page 062, using the questions.**

1 How effective is the argument?

2 How convincing is the use of citation in the text?

3 How broad is the range of sources?

4 Is the cited material appropriately explained and evaluated?

5 Can you think of any relevant points which are missing?

Example: *The text states that newspaper circulation figures have been declining, but it does not mention that these newspapers' online content is expanding.*

3 **When incorporating a citation, in some disciplines it is important to evaluate it. Evaluate the citations you selected in Task 3.3. Either continue the same sentence or add a separate sentence.**

Example: *Bainbridge, Goc, and Tynan (2011) report that newspaper circulation figures have declined as a result of the internet, but **they fail to mention** that these newspapers' online content is expanding.*

TASK 5 Comparing specific points across multiple texts

1 Read Text 2 and write a sentence expressing the main point of the text.

Facts

TEXT 2

Reporters should be suspicious of any story that can't be tied to solid fact. They should be uncomfortable with predictions, speculations and attempts at mind reading. The best reporters continually struggle to cut through the evasions and the distortions of newsmakers, but they do so by piecing together patterns of fact, not by voicing an opinion. Their struggle becomes that much more urgent in an era when anyone can grab a megaphone by starting a blog and discourse about news has become that much louder (but not that much clearer) on all-talk TV. Ultimately, facts do matter. They are the basis of news.

SOURCE: Lanson, J. & Stephens, M. (2008). p.191. *Writing and Reporting the News* (3rd ed.). New York: Oxford University Press.

2 Complete the table for Texts 1 and 2.

		Text 1	Text 2
1	Date of publication		
2	Place of publication		
3	Genre		
4	Audience		
5	Purpose		
6	Main topic & themes		
7	Main point		
8	Specific media mentioned		

3 Identify examples of evaluative language in each text. Explain how they demonstrate the authors' stance in relation to each type of media.

4 Compare and evaluate the main points and arguments of Texts 1 and 2. Use the questions in Task 4.2.

TASK 6 Focusing back on the essay question

1 Read the essay title again (from Task 1). Decide which statements 1–4 you agree with.

> **TITLE:** *Compare and contrast the presentation of information in two different types of media today, focusing on how effectively the information is communicated.*

1 You should select exactly two media types for the main focus of the essay.
2 You can limit the scope of the essay by focusing on one part of the world.
3 You should offer appropriate support in the form of citations from a range of sources.
4 Your 'voice' should emerge, particularly through your evaluation of the argument and citations.

2 Compare and discuss answers, explaining how relevant each statement is to the title.

TASK 7 Structuring an essay

1 Study three possible essay structures, and decide which one(s):

   1 a present evaluation at the end of the essay
      b integrate evaluation throughout the essay.

   2 a have a 'theme-driven' focus (see Task 1.4, e.g. reliability, global reach, etc.)
      b have a 'media types-driven' focus.

STRUCTURE 1
- **Introduction**
- **Paragraph 1:** description of media type 1
- **Paragraph 2:** description of media type 2
- **Paragraph 3:** overview of theme 1
- **Paragraph 4:** overview of theme 2
- **Paragraph 5:** comparison and contrast of the material in paragraphs 1–4
- **Evaluation and Conclusion**

STRUCTURE 2
- **Introduction**
- **Paragraphs 1 and 2:** comparison, contrast, and evaluation of the two media types in the context of theme 1
- **Paragraphs 3 and 4:** comparison, contrast, and evaluation of the two media types in the context of theme 2
- **Conclusion**

STRUCTURE 3
- **Introduction**
- **Paragraphs 1 and 2:** comparison, contrast, and evaluation of the two themes in media type 1
- **Paragraphs 3 and 4:** comparison, contrast, and evaluation of the two themes in media type 2
- **Conclusion**

2 Compare these structures to your basic essay plans from Task 2. Decide which structure is the most effective for the essay question in this module.

TASK 8 Planning and writing a comparison essay

1 You are going to write a 1,000-word essay in response to the essay question (see Task 6.1). Plan your essay. Follow the guidelines below.

> **Guidelines for planning an essay**
>
> 1 Decide on the two types of media, the two themes, and the structure you will use for your essay.
> 2 Work out the main points you want to make in each paragraph. Note down the topics for each paragraph, and sketch out topic sentences.
> 3 Read the texts in 4A Reading and 4B Writing modules, and select relevant material to use in your essay. Use two or three different sources.
> 4 Search for further sources using library services you have access to and online resources.
> 5 Critically evaluate what you read, and include this evaluation in your essay.
> 6 Write a draft thesis statement to clarify the focus of the essay and how it will develop.
> 7 Keep content directly relevant to the essay title. Delete any irrelevant material.
> 8 Focus on structure and organization. Refine and adapt your plan as necessary.

2 Write your essay, paying attention to the guidelines in 1. Actively expand your language to include language of cohesion, comparison, and evaluation.

3 Carefully check your introduction, main body, and conclusion using Checklist H on page 210.

TASK 9 Critical thinking – peer review and feedback

1 Exchange essays with another student. Read their essay to establish:

- the two types of media they have chosen to compare
- their main themes and perspectives
- their stance.

   Ask questions about any of these that are not immediately clear.

2 Evaluate their essay using Checklist H.

3 Compare your approaches to the essay question. Give each other feedback on positive points and areas that could be improved.

Poster presentations are playing an increasingly important role in academic settings including assessment. They are a shorter, more informal way for students and researchers to present their work. They are displayed at events like conferences and university open days, for a wider audience. People can read the information on the poster, then presenters give a short presentation. Audience members have the opportunity to ask for clarification and to ask critical questions directly to the presenters. Posters are a useful way to learn about new topics or to keep up-to-date with the work in your department.

This module covers:
- Identifying and explaining key components in a poster
- Listening to the question and answer stage of a poster presentation
- Evaluating a poster and presentation

TASK 1 Identifying and explaining key components in a poster

1 **Work in the same pairs throughout this module. Look at the poster on page 067 and match sections 1–5 with items a–e.**

   a problems associated with the main topic

   b definition and explanation of key terms

   c an illustration of a process

   d citations and references speculating on the future of publishing

   e citations and references relating to business and universities

2 **Choose two each from sections 1–4 on the poster. Carefully read your sections, checking the meaning of key terms and language. Prepare to explain the material.**

3 **Take turns to explain your sections. Make notes while listening.**

TASK 2 Comparing a poster and a poster presentation

1 ▷4.1 **Watch Extract 1 and make notes about the three sections discussed.**

2 **Compare with your notes from Task 1.3. What extra information is included?**

3 ▷4.2 **Turn to transcript 4.2 on page 228. Watch and read four clips from Extract 1. Identify the comparative and evaluative language used by the presenters.**

TASK 3 Listening to a question and answer stage

1 **Read section 5 of the poster. Work out the meaning of the two quotations.**

2 ▷4.3 **Watch Extract 3 and note down the presenters' answers to the questions.**

3 **Read the following audience question. Discuss possible answers.**

'How do you see the future of knowledge transfer and in particular, publishing in, say, five years?'

4 ▷4.4 **Watch Extract 4 and note down the presenter's answer to this question. How does this compare with your answer?**

TASK 4 Critical thinking – evaluating a poster presentation

1 **Turn to Checklist I on page 211 and evaluate the success of the poster and presentation.**

2 **For the points you are critical of, suggest specific ways of improvement.**

   Example: *The presentation would benefit from a clearer structure and signposting in some parts.*

TRANSFERRING KNOWLEDGE IN HIGHER EDUCATION: FROM THE UK TO THE WORLD?

1 WHAT IS **KNOWLEDGE TRANSFER?**

- Knowledge transfer is the exchange and dissemination of knowledge and information, particularly research.
- Knowledge transfer is closely related to information transfer & technology transfer.

2 A KNOWLEDGE TRANSFER STRATEGY

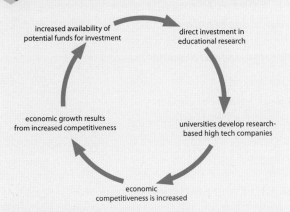

increased availability of potential funds for investment

direct investment in educational research

universities develop research-based high tech companies

economic competitiveness is increased

economic growth results from increased competitiveness

4 KEY **ISSUES** AND **CHALLENGES**

- Investment costs – including money and time.
- Working in the current economic and political environments.
- Increasing competition from other universities globally.

3 **PUBLISHING** RESEARCH: OPPORTUNITIES AND CHALLENGES OF **OPEN ACCESS**

'"Open access" publishing in science … allows readers to access papers free of charge … The aim is to broaden opportunities for high-quality research findings to be widely disseminated and freely available, to advance biomedical research worldwide.'
The UK Medical Research Council

'The peer-review process is still viewed as the best method of ensuring quality control in the publication process.'

'Plagiarism continues to be a problem in the academic community – but publications stored electronically can be easily identified through anti-plagiarism software.'
Policy Briefing, *Publishing research results: the challenges of open access*. (2007). p.6. Universities UK.

5 **ANALYSIS** AND **EVALUATION**

'Harnessing innovation in Britain is key to improving the country's future wealth creation prospects… [Britain] must invest more strongly than in the past in its knowledge base, and translate this knowledge more effectively into business and public service innovation.'
The Science and Innovation Investment Framework (2004–2014, para.1.1.)

'University research has a **distinctive contribution** to make in **creating value** through supporting company innovation processes, and thus has a role in contributing to **economic impact**. But there are **dangers** in positioning university research too close to market and thereby crowding out company innovation and undermining its value.'
Ternouth, P., Herrman, K., & Docherty, D. (2010). p.3. *Absorbing research: the role of university research in business and market innovation*. The Council for Industry and Higher Education.

Poster researched and presented by Carolina Burquart and Ben Foster

Poster presentations typically involve an initial time when people can read the posters, a short presentation stage, and then a more interactive question and answer or discussion stage. As with other types of presentation, key skills include presenting clearly and concisely within a limited timeframe, and providing accurate and accessible answers to often unpredictable questions. It is also important to be able to ask questions about other people's posters.

This module covers:

- Planning, researching, and giving a poster presentation
- Viewing posters and preparing critical questions

TASK 1 Critical thinking – selecting a topic

1 **Work in pairs. Choose three of the following topics. Quickly decide how you could present them effectively on a poster. Make rough notes and sketches.**

a description of a process   a plan for a redesigned city square
a sequence of exercise routines   an argument for a specific approach
a debate for and against a motion   a chemical experiment   a case study
a detailed analysis of works of literature   a textile design   a prototype engine

Example: *A description of a process lends itself to a poster presentation because the process can be represented graphically on the poster using something like a flow chart. The presenters can then add extra information and respond to questions.*

2 **Which topics seem more difficult to present on a poster? Give reasons.**

Example: *A detailed analysis of works of literature wouldn't work visually because it involves a lot of text. You could summarize the key themes under headings …*

TASK 2 Planning and researching a poster presentation

1 **Work in groups of two or more. Use one of the topics in Task 1.1, or your own ideas. Plan the poster design, using the flow chart to guide you.**

Stage 1: Developing a topic
- Choose one of the following topics related to the theme of information:
  information technology   managing information   searching for information   transferring information
- Decide on up to five specific aspects of the topic that you would like to cover. These will form the sections of your poster.
- Summarize your main points for each aspect.

Stage 2: Research
- Find three pieces of information related to your topic from the resources available, such as online resources and libraries / library search facilities.
- Choose key statements from each source to use as citations.
- Note down the reference for each statement.

Stage 3: Developing your material
- Write the title and main message for your poster.
- Divide the poster space into sections to present the different aspects effectively.
- Write and present your text, including your citations and key statements.
- Search for visuals and/or prepare your own. Visuals should be relevant and informative, not just decorative.

Stage 4: Making your poster
- Use appropriate software, such as a Word file, to design your poster.
- Refine your material to fit the space, adding / cutting where necessary.
- Pilot your poster by showing it to a person outside your group. Get critical feedback.
- Check language, spelling, and accuracy of your citations and references.
- Critically view the poster, making sure that it stands alone.

---

2 Plan the spoken presentation stage. Follow the guidelines below.

Guidelines for planning a spoken presentation

1 Check the time available, including the question phase.

2 Negotiate who will present different stages in the presentation.

3 Plan what needs to be presented:
   - the main message of the poster
   - the main points in each section, plus which sections to focus on
   - how you will add in the additional spoken information.

4 Note down and prioritize the points: what is necessary to say, and what is optional.

5 Predict possible audience questions. Prepare brief answers.

6 Assemble any necessary aids, such as a pointer, objects, or handouts.

ACADEMIC LANGUAGE

Asking questions about a poster Spatial expressions and question forms

Using and recognizing spatial language is helpful when presenting or viewing posters.

Start by using spatial expressions to focus attention on a point you are interested in:

In the top right-hand corner of the poster *it says '...' - could you explain what that means?*

Can you tell me more about the section **at the bottom of your poster***?*

You can ask more critical questions to get further detail from the presenter:

The quotation *in the central column seems to assume that information is presented neutrally,* **but what about the question of** *who originally selects the information?*

I'm not quite sure why you bring in the topic of *motivation -* **why is this relevant***?*

The citation in section 3 is not very current *- hasn't the field of information technology moved on since then?*

I'm not sure what you mean by *'enabling information in a different space' -* **could you explain it, and tell me how it fits in with** *the message at the top of your poster?*

TASK 3 Viewing posters and preparing critical questions

1 Display all the posters. Read the other posters, noting down points for possible questions.

2 Write at least three critical questions for different posters, using the language above.

TASK 4 Giving a poster presentation

1 Take turns to give your presentations, allowing sufficient time for audience questions.

2 During the question phase, ask and answer the questions you prepared in Task 3.2.

TASK 5 Evaluating a poster presentation event

1 In your groups, review the main stages in the poster presentation event: preparation, delivery, and questions. Consider:
   - how you worked in the research and preparation stage (Task 2)
   - the overall results (using Checklist I on page 211)
   - how well you worked collaboratively throughout.

   Discuss and make brief notes on what worked well and less well.

2 Prepare two points of critical feedback on your own group's performance.

3 Critically review another group's presentation.

In a long academic text, it is important to link new points to the main themes and arguments. There are a number of ways to avoid repeating the same words and phrases while maintaining cohesion. You can use a **synonym** (a word / phrase with a similar meaning), e.g. *electronic media - online communications*, but bear in mind that you may not always be able to substitute one word directly for another. Sometimes you can use an **antonym** (a word / phrase with an opposite meaning) instead of a negative, e.g. *not reliable - unreliable*. Looking out for these alternatives in your reading and using them in your own writing will help you to achieve a more varied and readable style.

TASK 1 Understanding how synonyms alter meaning

1 **Read part of an entry from a learner's thesaurus and decide which of the synonyms can be used in sentences 1–3.**

> **traditional ◆ conventional ◆ mainstream ◆ classical ◆ orthodox**
> These words all describe things or ideas that are based on what has happened or been accepted in the past.
>
> **traditional** (*sometimes disapproving*) following older methods and ideas rather than modern or different ones: Traditional attitudes to divorce were changing. **OPP modern**
>
> **conventional** [usually before noun] (of an idea or method) following what is usually done and is not particularly new: *It's not a hotel in the conventional sense, rather a whole village turned into a hotel.* **OPP alternative**
>
> ● TRADITIONAL OR CONVENTIONAL? **Traditional** emphasizes how old a method or idea is; **conventional** emphasizes how usual it is now.
>
> **mainstream** [usually before noun] following the ideas that are thought to be normal because they are shared by most people: *Many sports are not adequately covered in the mainstream media.*
>
> Source: Oxford Learner's Thesaurus

1 The youth market is more receptive to marketing on websites such as YouTube and Facebook than they are to *traditional / conventional / mainstream* media such as television.

2 An increasing number of patients are seeking alternatives to *traditional / conventional / mainstream* medicine, such as herbal remedies.

3 In the *traditional / conventional / mainstream* practice of arranged marriages, the families, not the prospective bride and groom, are the primary actors.

2 **In pairs, discuss how these sets of near synonyms are similar and how they differ in meaning and usage.**

a range, choice, diversity
b disclose, uncover, leak
c analyst, critic, commentator
d information, data, statistics

3 **Choose one of the sets a–d and write one sentence using each word.**

TASK 2 Using antonyms to avoid negatives

1 **Identify possible antonyms for the bolded words in sentences 1–6.**

Example: The evidence in the case was **not straightforward.** *complex*

1 Much of the so-called evidence put forward in the news media is **not at all precise.**

2 In the past, there was **not** the **diverse** range of news media we have available today.

3 Media scare stories play on people's fears that are **not rational**.

4 News organizations who do not have an **innovative** approach to new technologies will not survive.

5 In the interview, he was clearly **not relaxed** and **not eager** to answer many of the questions.

6 Many academics are wary of crowd-sourced information which they condemn as **not reliable.**

2 **Rewrite the sentences using the antonyms. Make any other necessary changes.**

UNIT 5 Patterns

ACADEMIC FOCUS: CITATION AND REFERENCING

LEARNING OBJECTIVES

This unit covers:

Reading
- Identifying arguments and supporting evidence from sources
- Recognizing different types of citation and comment
- Understanding focus in citations

Writing
- Understanding the use of citations and avoiding plagiarism
- Varying reporting structures and citing accurately from sources
- Identifying, using, and recording references in writing

Listening
- Making notes on a chronological sequence
- Recognizing citations and references in lectures

Speaking
- Planning and conducting team research
- Preparing and giving a group presentation

Vocabulary
- Lexical patterns

Discussion

1 **Much academic research is about identifying patterns, for example, patterns in population. Work in groups. Discuss the differences between these words to describe patterns. Give examples.**

cycle   distribution   structure   tendency   trend

Example: *A trend refers to a pattern of general change in something over time. Sociologists are interested in demographic trends – changes in birth rates and family size during a specific period.*

2 **Choose an aspect of each topic which could demonstrate a *trend*.**

culture   family relationships   health
natural world   technology   wealth

Example: health – *trends in life expectancy*

3 **Choose one of the aspects in 2. Describe a trend across:**
- time (e.g. 1950 v. 2010 / a 16-year-old v. a 50-year-old)
- place (e.g. West Africa v. Northern Europe).

Example: **Topic:** *health*   **Aspect:** *trends in life expectancy*
Time trend: *Over the past century, average life expectancy has risen hugely with better diet and healthcare.*
Place trend: *Life expectancy still varies considerably; it is much lower in poorer countries than in more developed countries.*

An essential element in most journal articles is a **literature review**. This forms part of the background, and appears towards the start of the article, in or following the introduction. It summarizes and evaluates published writing or research relevant to the topic, and helps you understand how the ideas of one author fit in with other research in the field. The style and length of a literature review will vary: an article discussing a theory or an issue might focus on well-known names or experts in the field and their individual arguments; an article reporting research is more likely to focus on the findings of previous studies in the same area. A literature review typically includes a lot of citations. These may be **quotation**, **paraphrase**, or **summary**, and are always identified using an **in-text reference**, using either an author-date or a numerical system linked to the full reference at the end of the article. In many online journals, this appears as a hyperlink, allowing you to click directly to the reference.

This module covers:

- Identifying arguments and supporting evidence from sources
- Recognizing different types of citation and comment
- Understanding focus in citations

TASK 1 Critical thinking – analysing and evaluating a definition

1 **Work in groups. Read the definition of *people in poverty* and check the meaning of any unknown words.**

> **people in poverty**
> people with a household income below 60 per cent of the national median income

2 **Discuss the extent to which a person who falls into this category in the UK might be viewed as *poor* from the perspectives of people a–d.**

   a   a British person with an average income

   b   a person living in the same neighbourhood

   c   someone from another European country

   d   someone living in a developing country

3 **Do you agree with the definition of *people in poverty* in 1? Give reasons why (not).**

4 **Identify what problems there might be in defining *poverty* across:**

   - an individual country
   - a wider region (such as the European Union)
   - internationally.

TASK 2 Identifying arguments from sources

1 **You are going to read Text 1, an extract from the introduction to an article entitled *Comparing poverty indicators in an enlarged European Union*. Use the source information at the end. Make notes.**

Genre	Journal
Audience	Sociologists / Europe
Purpose of the text	Comparison of poverty indicators
Date of publication	2010

2 **Work in pairs. Read Text 1 and discuss:**
   - what you understand by *an EU-wide 'at risk of poverty' indicator* who can afford minimally way of living / meets minimum standards
   - what possible issues and problems have been raised with this measure The dividing line between poor and rich
   - which ideas in the text overlap with what you discussed in Task 1. become more and more

Poverty in the EU is normally defined in terms of income thresholds established at the level of each member state. The 'at risk of poverty' (ARP) indicator identifies those individuals falling below 60 per cent of the national median disposable equivalent income appropriately adjusted for household composition. The conceptual foundations of this approach can be found in **Townsend's (1979) definition of poverty** as 'exclusion from ordinary living patterns and activities due to lack of *b* resources'. Those falling more than a certain 'distance' below a nationally defined income level are understood to be excluded from a minimally acceptable way of life.

The current set of common EU-indicators of poverty relies heavily on such measures. The emphasis on a purely relative perspective **has been justified by the European Commission in the following terms**:

> An absolute notion is considered less relevant for the EU for two basic reasons. First the challenge for Europe is to make the whole population share the benefits of high average prosperity and not to reach basic standards of living as in less developed parts of the world. Secondly, what is regarded as minimal acceptable living standards depends largely on the general level of social and economic development, which tends to vary considerably across countries **(European Commission, 2004)**.

However, as **Guio (2005) observes**, enlargement of the EU and the consequent widening of the gap in living standards between the richest and the poorest member states have provoked concern about the ability of the current portfolio of indicators to satisfactorily reflect the situation of the New Member States and facilitate meaningful comparison between them and the 'old' Member States. **Förster (2005, p.32) notes that** the labelling of the relative income measure as 'at risk of poverty' reflects the tendency of governments to interpret it as an indicator of inequality in income distribution rather than as a measure of poverty as such.

These paradoxical findings have produced a number of interrelated responses. The first focuses on the limitations imposed by the entirely national frame of reference. **Fahey (2007) argues for** the development of an EU-wide measure alongside a nationally relative measure and **recent exercises of this sort include Brandolini (2007), and Kangas and Ritakallio (2007)**. An alternative critique focuses on the fact that low income fails to identify those experiencing the forms of deprivation that one would expect to characterize those excluded from customary living patterns.[1] *e*

[1] **For a recent review of this evidence, see Nolan and Whelan (2007).**

SOURCE: Whelan, C. & Maître, B. (2010). pp.713-714. Comparing poverty indicators in an enlarged European Union. *European Sociological Review*, 26 (6): 713-730.

GLOSSARY

New Member States the countries which joined the European Union in 2004, many of which were former Eastern bloc countries, such as Poland and Lithuania

3 Read Text 1 again and match sources 1–6 with statements a–f.

e 1 Townsend (1979)   *d* 4 The European Commission (2004)
b 2 Förster (2005)   *c* 5 Fahey (2007), Brandolini (2007), Kangas & Ritakallio (2007)
a 3 Guio (2005)   *f* 6 Nolan & Whelan (2007)

a Current poverty measures do not take into account the large gap between the richer and poorer EU countries.

b Current poverty indicators really measure income inequalities, not poverty.

c A separate EU measure of poverty is needed as well as individual national measures.

d Within the EU, poverty should be defined in relative terms, not as absolute poverty (where someone does not have the basics to live).

e Poverty can be defined as 'exclusion from ordinary living patterns and activities due to lack of resources'.

f Simply looking at low income may not be a fair way to measure poverty.

4 Which of the sources cited in the text would you read to find out more about the following? Give reasons.

1 the background to currently used definitions and indicators of poverty *1*

2 possible alternative measures of poverty across the EU *6*

3 limitations and criticisms of the current ARP indicators *2*

Citations (3) Quotation, paraphrase, and summary

Information and ideas from sources, or citations, can take a number of forms.

- **Quotation** Quotations give the exact words of another author, shown inside quotation marks '...'. Quotations are used where the wording of the original author is especially important or unusual. Quotations can be just a few words, a single sentence, or a longer section of a text.

  Townsend's (1979) definition of poverty as 'exclusion from ordinary living patterns and activities due to lack of resources'.

Most citations, however, are summarized to fit in with the flow of the text and the writer's own 'voice'.

- **Paraphrase** An idea described in one or two sentences in the original source may be paraphrased, i.e. expressed using the writer's own language. In this case, the page number is typically given:

  Förster (2005, p.32) notes that the labelling of the relative income measure as 'at risk of poverty' reflects the tendency of governments to interpret it as an indicator of inequality in income distribution rather than as a measure of poverty as such.

- **Summary** An idea that is described through a whole article or a chapter of a book can be summarized when cited:

  Fahey (2007) argues for the development of an EU-wide measure alongside a nationally relative measure.

In-text reference In each case, an in-text reference is given to show the source of the citation. There are a number of different systems for referencing citations (see page 032). Even similar systems, such as author-date systems (e.g. APA, MLA, and Harvard) have many minor variations between them.

TASK 3 Recognizing different types of citation

1 Identify the citations in Text 1 on page 073. For each, decide the type of citation, a–f.

a a short quotation   d a summary

b a long quotation   e a footnote

c a paraphrase   f more than one reference to support the same point

2 Suggest reasons why the writers chose types of citation a–f in Text 1.

Example: *In a definition, the exact wording is important, so the writers use a short quotation to cite Townsend's definition.*

3 Identify the types of citation a–e.

a It is important to remember, however, that the data used to create the dollar-a-day poverty line have their own reliability issues (Deaton & Zaidi, 1999).

-b Wealth indices are widely used for measuring health inequalities (Sastry, 2004; Machado & Hill, 2005; Sastry & Burgard, 2005; Subramanian et al., 2006; Cuong et al., 2007; Dieu et al., 2007).

c Former US Federal Reserve Chairman Alan Greenspan has warned that ageing in the United States 'makes our social security and Medicare programmes unsustainable in the long run' (Greenspan, 2003).

d The World Economic Forum (2004) is concerned, but similarly cautious, suggesting that with large numbers of non-working elderly, 'we face the prospect that the historical rates of improvement in standards of living might slow or even decline'. Appropriately, the Forum's report goes on to stress the value of raising the retirement age and points out that both governments and businesses can play a role in encouraging workers to continue working.

e ² **For a detailed analysis of several measures of population ageing, see Lutz et al. (2008).**

4 Work in pairs. Note down conventions that are associated with each type of citation, such as punctuation, abbreviations, or position of in-text references.

Example: *Short quotations are always shown within quotation marks, i.e. '...'.*

TASK 4 Differentiating between cited material and comment

1 **The way a writer presents a citation can show their stance in relation to the source. Look at the example below from Text 1 and identify:**

  a the material from the source

  b the in-text reference

  c specific language showing the writers' evaluation / stance.

> The current set of common EU-indicators of poverty relies heavily on such measures. The emphasis on a purely relative perspective has been justified by the European Commission in the following terms:
>
> > An absolute notion is considered less relevant... (European Commission, 2004).

2 **Compare an alternative version of the citation below with the original in 1. Does it contain evaluative language? Does it express the writer's stance?**

> The current set of common EU-indicators of poverty is based on such measures. The reasons for this relative perspective are explained by the European Commission as follows: ...

3 **Look again at citations a–e in Task 3.3.**

  1 Which citations include evaluative comment by the writer?

  2 Identify the evaluative language.

  3 Explain the stance of the writer in relation to the idea cited.

TASK 5 Identifying supporting evidence from sources

1 **Text 2 is part of the introduction to an article about patterns of employment over the course of people's lives. Read the text and tick the points below which are mentioned.**

  1 The number of women in the workforce has grown significantly since the 1970s. ✓

  2 On average, people now work shorter hours. ✓

  3 People spend less time on household chores because of new technology. ✓

  4 Women often have to make difficult choices between family and career. ✗

  5 Women spend more time in paid work than they did in the past. ✓

  6 Most housework is still done by women. ✓

  7 Men do a greater share of housework than in the past. ✓

  8 Women's incomes are still significantly lower than men's. ✗

TEXT 2

Several common trends in employment and household transitions over the life course have emerged in advanced economies since the 1970s. Women account for a growing proportion of the labour force, producing a shift away from the single-earner 'male breadwinner' to 'dual-earner' working arrangements in couples. Working life has been compressed into a narrower age range through the extension of education and retirement systems. There has also been a substantial increase in the amount of 'free time' in societies over many decades. Reductions in average annual working hours have also been achieved (Bosch et al., 1994). Time devoted to housework has also fallen as many elements of domestic production have been outsourced to market services and the public sector (aspects of food preparation, cleaning, repairs, childcare, etc.), and technological innovation in 'labour-saving' consumer goods has also played a role (washing machine, dishwasher, microwave, etc.).

However, pronounced gender inequalities in time-use persist. Women's time allocation to employment during the 'working years' has increased since the 1960s (Blossfeld & Hakim, 1997; Rubery et al., 1999; Blossfeld & Drobnič, 2001), partly offsetting the reduction among men. Yet the bulk of unpaid housework and care activities are still predominantly performed by women, even though men's relative contribution has increased in most countries (Gershuny, 2000; Anxo et al., 2002). The resilience of this traditional gender division of labour has dynamic implications across the life course in terms of gender inequalities in career prospects, lifetime earnings and the accumulation of pension and other welfare entitlements.

SOURCE: Anxo, D., Fagan, C., Cebrian, I., & Moreno, G. (2007). pp.235–236. Patterns of labour market integration in Europe – a life course perspective on time policies. *Socioeconomic Review*, 5 (2): 233–260.

2 For each of the points in 1 mentioned in Text 2, identify what evidence, if any, the writer provides in the form of citations.

   Example: 2 On average, people now work shorter hours. – *'Reductions in average annual working hours have also been achieved' (Bosch et al., 1994)*

3 **Why do some of the points not have a supporting citation? Choose the best answer.**

   a There are many possible citations and it is difficult to choose one.

   b Common knowledge does not need a citation.

   c The writers should have added a citation.

ACADEMIC LANGUAGE   ▸Language reference page 200 1.1-1.2

Citations (4) Focus on author or content

A writer's choice of citation style depends on what they want to emphasize.

Author-content Where the author or source of a citation is considered significant, the author's name is given first, followed by the content. This style is used to present arguments, theories, or definitions that were put forward by particular authors.

• author + reporting verb (e.g. *argue, claim, mention, note, observe, point out, report, say, state*):
  Fahey (2007) argues *for the development of an EU-wide measure ...*

• author + noun (*argument, definition, model, observation, theory*):
  Townsend's (1979) definition *of poverty as ...*

Content-author Where the content is more important than the individual author(s), then the reference can be shown in brackets at the end. In this case, the citations provide support (from other authors or research) for an idea being put forward by the writer:

  Reductions in average annual working hours have also been achieved **(Bosch et al., 1994)**.

This style is particularly used when citing evidence for the same idea from several different sources:

  Women's time allocation to employment during the 'working years' has increased since the 1960s **(Blossfeld & Hakim, 1997; Rubery et al., 1999; Blossfeld & Drobnič, 2001)**.

In some cases, one style or another is more appropriate. Sometimes, either style could be used. An in-text reference is always given to identify the source of the citation.

TASK 6 Understanding focus in citations

1 **Which statements a–d best describe Text 1 and which best describe Text 2?**

   a The text presents different perspectives and issues already raised around the topic.

   b The text gives a brief overview of the historical background to the topic.

   c The citations provide evidence for facts and trends which have been observed or researched.

   d The citations show some of the arguments already put forward.

2 **Work in pairs. Compare the use of citations in Texts 1 and 2 in terms of:**

   • the number / density of citations

   • the type of citation (quotation, paraphrase, summary)

   • the focus of citations (author–content, content–author).

TASK 7 Independent research – citation in your discipline

1 **Search for two or three journal articles in your subject area. Focus on the introduction section and identify examples of citation. Note down:**

   1 the type of citations you find:

      a quotation or paraphrase / summary

      b author–content or content–author focus.

   2 the style of in-text references used (author-date, a numerical system, footnotes).

2 **Report back to the class, giving an overview of your findings.**

An academic writer does not write in a vacuum, expressing only their own ideas on a topic. An academic text needs to be situated within the context of what others have written on the same topic. How do your ideas fit in with other ideas, theories, or research? As an academic writer, you need to refer to sources (journal articles, books, research findings) to outline the general thinking about your topic, typically in an introduction or literature review, and to provide specific evidence to support your main points. Understanding how to select and refer to sources, use correct referencing conventions, and avoid misrepresentation and **plagiarism**, are key skills in writing an academic text. The full reference for each citation needs to be included in your **references section** (sometimes known as a **bibliography**).

This module covers:
- Understanding the use of citations and avoiding plagiarism
- Varying reporting structures and citing accurately from sources
- Identifying, using, and recording references in writing

TASK 1 Critical thinking – why do we reference sources?

1 **Work in groups. Read comments 1–9 about reasons for including sources in academic writing. Discuss to what extent each comment is true for you, and generally valid.**

1 'I can't write 1,000 words of my own ideas – I need sources to pad out my essay.'

2 'My argument sounds stronger if a professional academic has written the same thing.'

3 'My tutor said we have to include references to at least three sources.'

4 'If I put forward an idea, I need to back it up with evidence from real research.'

5 'To write a balanced essay, I need to show a range of ideas from different sources, including opposing arguments sometimes, not just my personal point of view.'

6 'It shows my readers (e.g. my tutor) that I've read about the subject.'

7 'I have to include references so that my audience can find the sources.'

8 'Reading information from different sources helps me to formulate my own ideas.'

9 'Through referencing, I can "pay back" the cited authors for the "loan" of their ideas.'

2 **Look at three different versions 1–3 of part of the introduction to a student biology essay. Which do you think is clearest and most persuasive? Why?**

1 In nature, animals need to use different strategies for finding different types of food, depending on the typical distribution patterns of the food source. Nectar from flowers usually comes in patches as one plant often has several flowers and the food source is generally renewable, whereas dead insects are usually randomly distributed and depletive.

2 In natural conditions, animals need to use different strategies for finding different types of food. For example, food from plants is often found in patches, as one plant has several flowers or fruits and the source is renewable (Schultheiss & Cheng, 2013), thus allowing the animal to return to the same source time and again. Whereas foraging for dead insects, for example, is less predictable, as they are randomly distributed, laying wherever the insects happened to die (*ibid.*) and so clearly demands a different search strategy.

GLOSSARY
ibid. *(abbr)* from the same source as the one which was last mentioned

3 In natural conditions, animals need to use different strategies for finding different types of food. According to Schultheiss and Cheng (2013) 'Certain types of food [...] have typical distribution patterns'. They explain that nectar from flowers usually comes in patches as one plant often has several flowers and this is a renewable source. On the other hand, dead insects are usually randomly distributed as they remain where the insect happened to die, and they are depletive.

3 **Identify the citation types used in extracts 1–3.**
- Are they a quotation, paraphrase, or summary?
- Do they have an author–content or content–author focus?

TASK 2 Attributing citations

1 **Work in groups. Discuss how far each of these situations constitutes plagiarism.**

   a submitting an essay written by someone else as your own work

   b cutting and pasting a paragraph from an article into your essay

   c using a phrase (four or five words) from something you have read

   d using ideas that are not your own in an assessed piece of work

2 **Read Text 1 and check your answers to 1, according to the text.**

TEXT 1

Cheating (plagiarism)

The computer age has brought easier access to sources of information through electronic searching and the 'cut-and-paste' facility. It has also tempted some undergraduates to cheat, either by downloading whole reports or essays, or by cutting and pasting paragraphs from articles. Assessments are supposed to be your own work, which means that they should be your own ideas and your own words. If the ideas or words are not your own, you should indicate the source by referencing them. Failure to do this is called plagiarism. Not only will you not learn anything by cheating, but you will also be subject to your institution's penalties. Scientists make their living by the facts they discover and the communication of these facts. This is why you must always acknowledge the sources of your information and this is why there are severe penalties if you do not. If you are still tempted, please bear in mind that if you can find these articles, so can others, and it is surprisingly easy to spot the use of essay bank work and content that has been cut and pasted from another source.

SOURCE: Holmes, D., Moody, P., & Dine, D. (2011). p.369. *Research Methods for the Biosciences* (2nd ed.). Oxford University Press: Oxford.

---

3 **Compare answers. Specify in what circumstances statements a–d in 1 would or would not be plagiarism.**

4 **Discuss what you know about:**

   • possible reasons for plagiarism by students

   • the difference between intentional and accidental plagiarism

   • how teachers and examiners can spot plagiarism

   • the possible penalties for plagiarism.

TASK 3 Avoiding plagiarism

1 **Work in pairs. Compare extracts 1–3 in Task 1 with the original source text, Text 2. Are any phrases / sentences taken directly from the original with no attribution?**

TEXT 2

In nature, food sources can occur at very different densities (sparse or dense) and distributions (patchy or randomly distributed), and food sources can be renewable or depletive (Stephens & Krebs, 1986; Bell, 1991). Certain types of food, however, have typical distribution patterns. Nectar from flowers, for example, usually comes in patches, as one plant often has several flowers, and the food source is generally renewable as the nectar is replenished; the same is true for honeydew excretions from aphids. Dead insects on the other hand are usually randomly distributed as they remain where the insect happened to die, and they are depletive.

SOURCE: Schultheiss, P. & Cheng, K. (2013). Finding food: outbound searching behavior in the Australian desert ant *Melophorus bagoti*. *Behavioral Ecology* 24(1): 128-35.

---

2 **Now use the criteria below to evaluate the three extracts in Task 1.2.**

   a Are ideas from the source text attributed using appropriate in-text references?

   b Are any direct quotations correctly presented and attributed?

   c Is the language from the source text appropriately paraphrased (if not a quotation)?

Citations (5) Introducing citations

Most writers use a range of structures to introduce citations, to fit with the meaning, flow, and emphasis of the text. Using a variety of structures will improve the sophistication of your writing.

Verbs Choose a verb to report the idea of the author you are citing, and select one which appropriately reflects their argument.

- Using a **reporting verb** in an active form, typically in a present tense, is a common way of putting focus on the author(s):
  argue, highlight, note, observe, suggest, warn
  Fourcassié and Traniello (1994) **suggest** *two possible extrinsic mechanisms.*

- Evidence from research is reported using active verbs, typically in the past simple:
  confirmed, demonstrated, found, showed, studied, tested, used
  Later work by Mewaldt (1964) **confirmed** *the navigational ability in adult migrants.*

- Different reporting verbs tend to be followed by specific language patterns:
  Smith **argues / explains / states that** *…*
  This approach **is shown to** *have two weaknesses …*
  Smith **suggests** *two possible reasons (= noun phrase) …*
  Smith **suggests** *focusing on (= -ing form) …*

Nouns Use nouns, which describe specific ideas or work, to introduce citations:
argument, explanation, claim, definition, theory, model

- author focus:
  Whitehead and Dahlgren (1991) use a **definition** *of health inequalities which …*

- content focus:
  One **explanation** *of health inequalities is … (Whitehead & Dahlgren, 1991).*

TASK 4 Varying reporting structures

1 Choose the best verb to use with the noun in bold.

1 Bussières (1994) *put / proposed / did* a **model** of water import in tomato fruit.

2 Funding agencies are *placing / giving / making* increasing **emphasis** on cross-disciplinary approaches to research questions.

3 Charles Darwin *created / made / developed* the modern **theory** of evolution.

4 He also *made / did / took* detailed **observations** of the behaviour of primates.

5 This model *makes / provides / puts* a general **explanation** of erosion.

6 Observers *gave / did / proposed* differing **descriptions** of the initial earth tremors.

7 Merrick (1988:3) *offers / makes / puts* the following **definition** of demographics …

8 Coleman (1991) *presented / did / placed* a further **argument** for this approach.

2 Use meaning and language patterns to match 1–6 with a–f.

1 Males with better memory abilities were **found / shown**

2 Holt (2001) **explains / describes / illustrates**

3 Morgan and Moss (1965) **argued**

4 As long ago as the 1970s, scientists were **warning**

5 The report (Jacobs, 2002) **emphasizes / highlights / stresses**

6 Ormerod *et al.* (2009) **noted / observed**

a **for** an ecological approach, drawing parallels between communities.

b **to have** larger home ranges.

c **the importance** of aquatic ecosystem health for fisheries.

d **of** the possible adverse effects of ozone depletion.

e **how** plants' particular characteristics affect their dispersal potential.

f **that** conserving the habitat of one endangered species increased biodiversity.

TASK 5 Citing accurately from sources

1 **Work in pairs. Write a sentence including a citation from each of Texts 3–5. Follow the guidelines below.**

Example: *Thorup* et al. *(2010) explain that, whilst small enough tags have now been developed to track the movements of small migratory birds, satellite technology is not yet accurate enough to establish a global tracking system.*

Guidelines for writing citations

1 Read the source extract carefully and check the meaning of any unknown words.
2 Explain the extract to your partner without looking back at the text. This will help you to express the main ideas in your own words. Note down any useful synonyms or phrases.
3 Decide whether to cite details from the extract or a main idea.
4 Choose an appropriate style of citation: quotation, paraphrase or summary, and author-content or content-author focus.
5 Choose an appropriate reporting structure to introduce the idea.
6 Add short comments including interpretation or evaluation where possible.
7 Use the source details to write an in-text reference using author-date conventions.
8 Check that your sentence is correctly attributed and does not constitute plagiarism.

TEXT 3

The size of satellite tags is constantly decreasing and within the next decade we are likely to be able to track globally the migrations of even the smallest songbirds. Despite this development of tags, it is doubtful whether currently available satellites can accomplish the task in the foreseeable future. Furthermore, other technologies, such as cell phones, might prove more promising. When such a global small-animal tracking system is operational, a large-scale collaboration between research groups will hopefully enable a quantum step forward in our understanding of bird migration.

SOURCE: Thorup, K., Holland, A., Tøttrup, A., & Wikelski, M. (2010). p.320. Understanding the migratory orientation program of birds: extending laboratory studies to study free-flying migrants in a natural setting. *Integrative & Comparative Biology*, 50 (3): 315–322.

TEXT 4

In our experiments, ant foragers readily learnt the location of a renewable food source, and displayed a systematic search for it when removed. This search path was centered on the previous food location and was made up of loops of varying size; this looping structure repeatedly brought the ant back close to the target area. Interestingly, the type of food previously available at that location had an effect on the behavior of ants.

SOURCE: Schultheiss, P. & Cheng, K. (2013). Finding food: outbound searching behavior in the Australian desert ant *Melophorus bagoti Behavioral Ecology* 24(1): 128–35.

TEXT 5

Although honey bees use temperature defensively in response to both disease and predators, they are truly the masters at controlling the temperature within a hive. By contracting muscles to heat the colony and fanning wings to cool the colony, honey bees maintain colony temperatures throughout the year. Here we report on heat-shielding – a recently identified mechanism used to help maintain constant colony temperature. To reduce the transfer of heat from outside to inside the hive, worker bees shield the comb from the external heat source by positioning themselves on the hot interior region of the hive's walls. Data gathered indicate that heat-shielding is a behavior performed by young bees to preferentially protect older developing brood.

SOURCE: Starks, P., Johnson, R., Siegel, A., & Decelle, M. (2005). Heat shielding: a task for youngsters *Behavioral Ecology* 16(1): 128–32.

2 **Exchange your citations with another pair. Evaluate the citations based on the guidelines above and give feedback.**

TASK 6 Citing from secondary sources

1 **Read Text 6, student guidelines, and explain the following concepts.**

primary source   secondary source   misrepresentation

TEXT 6

Books are a frequently used source of information. These are invariably derived from other (primary) sources that are referenced in the book. If you have not read these primary sources you need to make this clear in your reference, for example, (Sokal & Rohlf, 1981, as cited in Holmes *et al.*, 2006). This is particularly important, as the authors of the book may have misunderstood the original report and misrepresented the findings. If you have not read the original source, you will not know this, but the error will appear to be yours and not that of the author of the book, unless you make it clear that you have read only the book and not the primary source.

SOURCE: Holmes, D., Moody, P., & Dine, D. (2011). p.393. *Research Methods for the Biosciences* (2nd ed.). Oxford: Oxford University Press.

2 **Complete the in-text references for sources 1–3.**

Example: **You read:** Whelan & Maitre (2010) – The conceptual foundations of this
approach can be found in Townsend's (1979) definition of poverty as …
Your in-text reference: *(Townsend, 1979, as quoted in Whelan & Maître, 2010)*

1 **You read:** Whelan & Maître (2010) – Fahey (2007) argues for the development of
an EU-wide measure …
Your in-text reference: (*as cited in*   )

2 **You read:** Anxo *et al.* (2007) – Reductions in average annual working hours have
also been achieved (Bosch *et al.*, 1994).
Your in-text reference: (   )

3 **You read:** Bainbridge, Goc, & Tynan (2011) – According to Sorensen (2007),
'Every day millions of people choose to watch …'
Your in-text reference: (   )

TASK 7 Identifying, recording, and using references in writing

1 **Add missing stages a–d to the table.**

a Check that full reference details for any citations in your essay are in your reference list.

b Record accurately all the reference details of any source you read.

c Include an in-text reference with any citations in your text.

d Search for key words or phrases using a search engine such as Google Scholar.

Researching and using references

#	
1	Identify key words associated with your topic; note down a variety of synonyms.
2	
3	Evaluate the relevance of sources by skimming abstracts, introductions, and section headings.
4	Read sources that are most relevant to your topic in more detail.
5	
6	Make notes in your own words as you read about any points that are relevant to your topic.
7	Choose a quote, or write a paraphrase or summary of the point you want to cite.
8	
9	Check any citations in your text against the original source for accuracy and plagiarism.
10	

2 **Work in groups. Compare answers and discuss the questions.**

1 Which steps do you think are a) always essential and b) will vary from person to person or depend on your task / topic? Why?

2 Which of these steps do you do already? Which are new to you?

3 **What problems do you think you might encounter as part of the process of researching, recording, and using sources? Suggest possible solutions.**

At the start of a series of lectures, it is common to describe the historical **context**; introducing key names, important work, ideas, and theories that have shaped thinking in the field. Recognizing references to key writers and understanding how they fit into the discipline is important in developing a full understanding of your subject. Lecturers may not give full reference details during the lecture; they may be on a handout or slide, or on the reading list for the course, or in some cases, they may be so well-known that they are considered to be common knowledge or would be easy to look up.

This module covers:
- Making notes on a chronological sequence
- Recognizing citations and references in lectures

TASK 1 Critical thinking – activating real-world knowledge

1 **You are going to watch an extract from a lecture about trends and cycles in the world economy. Work in groups. Read the introduction below and discuss:**
- what you understand by the expressions in bold (check unknown vocabulary)
- what you know about the global recession of 2009/10
- what you know about previous economic recessions in history.

Lecture introduction

Good morning, my name's Jonathan Michie, I'm Professor of Knowledge Exchange & Innovation at the University of Oxford where I direct their Department for Continuing Education, and I'm President of Kellogg College, which is the university's largest graduate college. I'm going to be talking about the **credit crunch**, the global credit crunch of 2007/8, the subsequent **global recession**, and the continuing economic problems globally and in Europe. So what I'll do briefly is go through five points: firstly, talk about the 2007/8 credit crunch and the global recession in 2009/10 but secondly, put that in the context of the fact that the global economy, over the past 100-150 years, does seem to have gone through **long swings in economic activity** and it may be that we're approaching a new long swing after the past 30 years, that this current **economic crisis** is actually the end of one era and ushering in a new one. Thirdly, what might be done proactively to help create a new era, 20- or 30-year era of development; fourthly, put that into the context of **globalization**, and then finally, say a bit more about an alternative vision for the future.

2 **Categorize the words below according to their meaning. Give reasons for your choices.**

crash   crisis   deficit   depression   development   ~~domestically~~   ~~globally~~
growth   inflation   laissez-faire   ~~nationally~~   orthodoxy   policy   recession
recovery   turbulence   unemployment

Example: *'Globally', 'nationally', and 'domestically' describe the geographical area something applies to.*

TASK 2 Making notes on a chronological sequence

1 ▷5.1 **Professor Michie gives a brief overview of the world economic situation from the 1920s to the present day. Watch Extract 1 and fit the events onto the timeline.**

~~era of laissez-faire~~   global recession   Wall Street Crash & Great Depression
deregulation & 'capitalism unleashed'   establishment of World Bank / IMF
Golden Age of Capitalism & sustained economic growth   end of WWII

2 **Work in threes. Each person choose one period A–C mentioned in the lecture extract and prepare to describe the period using your notes from 1.**

A from the 1920s to 1945   B from 1945 to 1973   C from 1973 to 2009

3 Take turns to describe your period to your group. You should:

1 mention the key events

2 briefly explain how they were connected

3 summarize the character of the whole period.

TASK 3 Recognizing citations in a lecture

1 ▶5.2 In Extract 2, Professor Michie talks about the economist John Maynard Keynes. Watch and make notes on:

1 when Keynes did most of his work

2 the context – the relationship between Britain, France, and Germany then

3 what Keynes said.

2 ▶5.3 Watch Extract 3. Make any notes you can on:

• the main events relating to Keynes's two pamphlets

• the main events relating to Keynes's major publication.

3 Work in pairs. Compare notes, and check transcript 5.3 on page 228.

1 Which reference details (title and date of publication) does the lecturer give for each of Keynes's works?

2 Why doesn't the lecturer give all the details for each publication?

ACADEMIC LANGUAGE   ▸ Language reference page 200

Citations (6) References to people, works, and ideas

It is important to recognize when the work of particular academics or writers is being mentioned, to add to your understanding of thinking in your discipline, and also so that you can refer to the people later, for example, in a seminar. Lecturers may refer to sources in different ways.

• Naming and describing key figures:
Keynes, probably one of the greatest and best-known economists ever ...

• Describing their work:
*... when Keynes wrote **his first famous pamphlet** called* The Economic Consequences of the Peace ...
*And then most famously, in 1936, Keynes published his **major work**,* The General Theory of Employment, Interest, & Money.

• Reporting their ideas. When describing the historical context of a subject, it is common to report ideas using past tense forms:
*Keynes **warned that** that was economically wrong ...*
*Keynes **said that** you can't force people to borrow ...*

TASK 4 Recognizing different styles of spoken citation

1 Look at transcript 5.3 on page 228 again. Find examples of:

• references to Keynes's works

• reporting verbs.

2 ▶5.4 Watch Extract 4, from a different lecture by Dr David Howard. Note down:

1 the famous figures he mentions

2 the publication he talks about

3 the expressions he uses to report the writer's ideas.

3 Find one or more lectures online. As you listen, note down the references to any citations given by the lecturer. If possible, follow these up by locating the source.

Many academic projects involve working as part of a team. The skills needed to work successfully in a team include the ability to discuss, **negotiate** and **allocate** tasks in a clear but friendly way. This may involve making suggestions, raising potential problems, coming to **compromises**, giving feedback, and asking for clarification to avoid misunderstandings.

This module covers:
- Planning and conducting team research
- Preparing and giving a group presentation

TASK 1 Critical thinking – the role of teamwork

1 **Discuss the questions below in A or B groups. During your discussion:**
- ensure that every member of the group contributes
- take brief notes so that you can summarize your discussion later.

Group A

Which of the following academic tasks are most suited to teamwork and which are more appropriate to carry out individually? Give reasons and examples.

1 preparing for a seminar discussion
2 preparing a written assignment, such as an essay
3 a practical research project, such as a scientific experiment or a survey
4 a library-based research project to locate relevant sources for citation
5 preparing a poster presentation
6 preparing for an exam

Group B

Based on your own experience of working as part of a team, which of the following have been most successful and which have caused problems? Give reasons and examples.

1 agreeing on an objective (a topic, plan, etc.)
2 dividing tasks between members of the group
3 dealing with questions, problems, and misunderstandings
4 coordination and communication – arranging meetings, sharing information, etc.
5 meeting deadlines

2 **Present a brief summary of your discussion to another group.**
- One person can present the summary or two or more can present jointly.
- Try to group ideas together rather than going through each point in turn.

TASK 2 Planning a group research project

1 ◀))5.5 **Listen to students planning a group research project. Complete the notes.**

Task	Research a person who ...		
Objective	Present a short ...		
Possible subjects	1 Schrödinger	2	3 ....

2 **Work in pairs. Compare answers and identify which suggestions are rejected and why.**

3 ◀))5.6 **Listen to the last part of the discussion. Answer the questions.**
1 What type of information do they decide to include?
2 How do they decide to allocate research tasks?

Hedging (2) Reaching agreement

Reaching agreement as a group involves making suggestions and supporting them with reasons, highlighting potential problems or limitations, and maintaining a focus on the aim of the task. We often use **minimizing language** to soften suggestions and criticisms, and **maximizing language** to emphasize important points.

Minimizing	Maximizing
Making tentative suggestions: ***It might be*** *easier to explain than quantum mechanics.* ***We could*** *either make a choice now or …* ***Perhaps*** *we should stick with what we've got …*	Making stronger suggestions: *I think **it would be better to** focus on one person from the beginning.* ***I'd go for*** *Stephen Hawking.*
Raising problems: ***Don't you think that*** *a subject like quantum mechanics might be a bit difficult to explain?* ***Aren't we meant to*** *be choosing a historical figure?*	Emphasizing important points: ***Remember we need to*** *present this in a really clear way.* ***It's important we don't*** *get bogged down in technical details.*

Erwin Schrödinger

Guglielmo Marconi

Stephen Hawking

TASK 3 Preparing and giving a group presentation

1 Read transcript 5.5 on page 229. Decide whether expressions 1–10 in bold are maximizing or minimizing language. Identify similar expressions in transcript 5.6.

2 Work in groups. Read the task and aim to reach agreement on:
   - your subject
   - the allocation of research tasks.

   Use a range of maximizing and minimizing language as you negotiate.

> **TASK:** *Research a person who has been influential in an academic discipline.*
>
> **Objective:** *Present a short oral profile of the person.*
>
> **To include:** *relevant biographical information; information about their most important work (publication, theory, research); how their work has contributed to thinking in the discipline*

3 Carry out your research plan.

4 Pool your research and prepare your presentation. Follow the guidelines below.

> **Guidelines for preparing a group presentation**
>
> **Organizing information**
> 1 Pick out the most useful points from your research to match the task.
> 2 Check that your information from different sources matches - are dates / facts the same?
> 3 Decide a logical order to present the information.
> 4 Discuss how to express key ideas clearly to an audience who may not be from the discipline.
>
> **Preparing the presentation**
> 1 Decide who will present which parts.
> 2 Rehearse presenting your profile. Use notes rather than a prepared script.
> 3 Offer each other feedback and make changes as necessary.

5 Present your profile to another group.

5E Vocabulary Lexical patterns

Some words are typically followed by a particular grammatical pattern, such as a verb form (*intend* + *to do, have problems* + *-ing*) or a type of clause (*explain* + *how / why, possible* + *that*). You can check the most typical patterns in a learner's dictionary. Understanding the patterns used with particular words will help to improve the accuracy and flow of your writing.

TASK 1 Recognizing verb + verb patterns

1 Match the sentence halves, thinking about both meaning and grammar.

1 The new regulations **exclude** small firms **from**	a **assessing** the effectiveness of these strategies.
2 Good leaders **motivate** employees	b **to reduce** packaging.
3 These countries have **shifted away from**	c **dividing** the structure into discrete elements.
4 The analysis technique **relies on**	d **to perform at** their best via **supportive** practices.
5 Future research should **focus on**	e **to spread** rapidly.
6 Poor hygiene can **cause** such diseases	f **contracting** NGOs for healthcare delivery.
7 The new regulations **encourage** companies	g **participating** in the market.

2 Compare your answers and identify the patterns in the verb + verb constructions in 1.

3 Add these verbs / verb phrases to one of the categories you identified in 2. Give examples to show how they are used.

benefit from   concentrate on   persist in   invite   permit   persuade

TASK 2 Identifying and using clause patterns

1 Complete sentences 1–8 with an appropriate linking word: *that, how, why,* or *whether*.

1 Some commentators argue .... problems of food security can only be solved by addressing issues of inequality.

2 Any business has to anticipate .... its environment might change in the short, medium, and long term.

3 It is uncertain .... the condition is caused by genetic or environmental factors.

4 This led Malthus to conclude .... populations tend to outgrow their resources.

5 The study identified several key reasons .... internet start-ups failed.

6 It is questionable .... consumers would pay extra for such a service.

7 Many employees were unaware .... there had been a change in the regulations.

8 A questionnaire was used to establish .... different groups viewed the changes.

2 Identify the key word (noun, verb, adjective) + linking word pattern in each sentence, 1–8 and write a different example sentence for each.

Example: argue + that … – *Critics **argue that** the reforms do not go far enough.*

TASK 3 Identifying repeated patterns to decode long sentences

1 In the example below, the verb + verb pattern (*focus on* + *-ing*) is repeated later in the sentence, but without repeating the first verb, *focus*. Identify the repeated patterns following the key words in bold in sentences 1–3.

Example: *A large number of studies have **focused on** identifying optimal search strategies for a diverse array of foraging scenarios, **and also on** finding evidence of these strategies in the movements of naturally foraging animals.*

1 It is **unclear** if the behavior is opportunistic – that is, if any individual will do it – or if the behavior is specific to a class of honey bee workers.

2 Data presented here **suggest** that males avoid heat shielding, that worker bees … are most likely to heat-shield, and that the behavior is very sensitive to context.

3 The migratory orientation program **is considered** to be very important for the survival of individual birds and to have a strong impact on the evolution of migration routes.

ACADEMIC FOCUS: SELECTING AND SUMMARIZING FROM SOURCES

LEARNING OBJECTIVES

This unit covers:

Reading
- Understanding the structure and objectivity of a report
- Using the structure of a report to predict and find information
- Identifying assumptions and asking critical questions about a text

Writing
- Analysing a text for a summary: structure, topic, main points
- Preparing, writing, and evaluating summaries
- Incorporating summaries into a literature review

Listening
- Understanding the main points of a lecture
- Summarizing a key concept from a lecture
- Combining and comparing information from two lectures

Speaking
- Reading and preparing a logical argument for a seminar
- Asking questions about a contribution
- Conducting a seminar discussion and summarizing main points

Vocabulary
- Collocation

Discussion

1 **Work in groups. Discuss how different agents might have** *responsibility* **for dealing with pressing global issues. Give examples from your own experience.**

Example: *Academics have responsibility for helping us to understand problems such as climate change. For example, scientists identified the impact of CFCs on the ozone layer, which led to a reduction in their use.*

Agents (people & groups)
local organizations (e.g. citizens' groups)
national governments
international organizations (e.g. the UN)
academics, researchers, or 'experts'
multinational corporations → Person who makes a lot of money /ثري (donate)
wealthy philanthropists and individuals
NGOs (non-governmental organizations)

Global issues
environmental issues national government / philanthropists multinational
farming and food security national government / individuals
human rights → Basic rights / Right to live NGOs
conflict and political instability disagreements/issue international organization
inequalities in wealth, health, and education national & NGOs, multinational

2 **Decide which of the agents in 1 should have (i) the primary responsibility, and (ii) the least responsibility for formulating policies to help solve these problems. Give reasons and examples.** academics researchers

Coupe = انقلاب
(قلب _ إن) Revolution → has a philosophy
(مرد _ن) Revolt → they don't know what happen next

Reading Reports
objective
subjective

The main purpose of research reports is to summarize a piece of research, to offer interpretation, and to make recommendations for future work. Reports are particularly associated with **STEM subjects** (science, technology, engineering, and medicine), law, and social sciences (e.g. economics). Reports are written for a clearly defined purpose and audience. They tend to follow a conventional structure, which typically moves from background information, through a literature (or research) review, to the research itself, followed by interpretation and evaluation. You need to be able to read and understand a report, identify any assumptions and how it relates to a wider context, and respond critically to content.

traditionally used ≠ unconventional

Previous blieve
This module covers:

- Understanding the structure and objectivity of a report
- Using the structure of a report to predict and find information
- Identifying assumptions and asking critical questions about a text

Vegan → don't eat any animals products   Statins → drugs which reduce levels of body fats, cholestrol ,——.

TASK 1 Understanding the structure of a report

1 **What are the main purposes of a research report? Choose from the list and say why.**

to add to human knowledge   to entertain   to explain
to inform   to persuade   to present an argument

2 **Match purposes a–f to the six completed section headings in the table.**

a to restate the main findings and discussion points

b to summarize the findings of the research

c to give background information and a rationale for the research

d to describe how the research was carried out

e to list the sources used in the report

f to give an overview of the whole report including its conclusion

Structure of a research report

Section heading	Purpose of section
1 Abstract	f
2 *introduction*	
3 *literature review*	
4 Background	c
5 Method	d
6 Results	b
7 *discussion*	
8 *Recommendations*	
9 Conclusion	a
10 *appendix*	
11 References	e

3 **Add the other section headings to the table in 2. Identify their purpose and complete the table.**

overview of the relevant research

Appendix   Discussion   Introduction   Literature review   Recommendations *suggestions for future*
table of content   *brif background*
                                            why I'm going to do
4 **Work in pairs. Decide which sections involve some kind of summary.**

Example: *The abstract is a brief summary of the whole report, including the results and conclusion.*

5 **Quickly read Text 1, the abstract of a report. Which section in the table in 2 does each paragraph 1–4 summarize?**

6 **Which sections of a report are mainly *objective*? Why? Which are more *subjective*?**

Low-emission vehicle adoption in a UK local authority fleet: economic barriers and air quality benefits

Abstract

1 Local air quality was one of the main stimulants for low carbon vehicle development during the 1990s. Issues of national fuel security and global air quality (climate change) have added pressure for their development, stimulating schemes to facilitate their deployment in the UK. In this case study, Coventry City Council aimed to adopt an in-house fleet of electric and hybrid-electric vehicles to replace business mileage paid for in employee's private vehicles.

2 This study made comparisons between the proposed vehicle technologies, in terms of costs and air quality, over projected scenarios of typical use.

3 The study found that under 2009 conditions, the electric and hybrid fleet could not compete on cost with the current business model because of untested assumptions, but certain emissions were significantly reduced >50%. Climate change gas emissions were most drastically reduced where electric vehicles were adopted because the electricity supply was generated by renewable energy sources. The study identified the key cost barriers and benefits to adoption of low-emission vehicles in current conditions in the Coventry fleet.

4 Low-emission vehicles achieved significant air pollution-associated health cost and atmospheric emission reductions per vehicle, and widespread adoption in cities could deliver significant change.

TEXT 1

SOURCE: Cruickshank, S. & Kendall, M. (2012). Low-emission vehicle adoption in a UK local authority fleet: economic barriers and air quality benefits. *International Journal of Low-Carbon Technologies*, 7 (1): 16–22.

GLOSSARY

Coventry City Council the local government of a city in the UK

ACADEMIC LANGUAGE

Style (2) Expressing objectivity

Reports, especially scientific reports, typically use **objective** language in order to focus on the procedure and findings rather than on the people doing the action. Objective language is typical of scientific writing, where the focus is on procedures and results. Look out for

- an abstract noun as the subject of the sentence:
  The study identified the key cost barriers and benefits to adoption of low-emission vehicles.
- passive verb forms, often used with inanimate subjects:
  Climate change gas emissions **were** most drastically **reduced** where electric vehicles **were adopted** because the electricity supply **was generated** by renewable energy sources.

Impersonal *it* and *there* structures are also used to express objectivity:

- **It became clear that** lease costs for electric vehicles significantly influenced the cost-effectiveness of the vehicles.

TASK 2 Identifying objective language in a report

1 Read the report extract and put the verbs in brackets into the active or passive.

The air pollution emission impacts of introducing low carbon vehicles compared with mileage by employee's private vehicles [1]................... (examine). The same scenarios of mixed Mitsubishi MiEV and Toyota Prius [2]................... (examine), compared with emissions calculated for a 4-year-old Ford Focus representing the conventional fleet. The emissions of selected pollutants [3]................... (present) and [4]................... (compare). Figure 1 [5]................... (show) that oxide of nitrogen (NOx) emissions from low emission vehicles [6]................... (be) significantly lower in comparison with emissions produced from the 4-year-old Focus using equivalent mileage. The electric vehicles [7]................... (perform) particularly well, as NOx emissions per kilometre [8]................... (report) as negligible. A similar pattern [9]................... (emerge) for carbon monoxide (CO) emissions in Figure 2. The electric and hybrid-electric vehicles [10]................... (reduce) emissions by 75% in 2008-09 over a 5-year projection.

(SOURCE: as Text 1)

2 Compare answers, and discuss why an active or passive form is used in each case.

TASK 3 Comparing and contrasting report abstracts

1 Texts 1 and 2 are abstracts from reports published in the *International Journal of Low-Carbon Technologies*. Read Text 2 and complete the table below.

	Text 1	Text 2
Context	UK city council - adoption of low-emission vehicle fleet	
Aim		To present the results of a case study of algal biodiesel and evaluate its competitiveness
Conclusion	Low-emission vehicles achieved reduced air pollution and health benefits	

TEXT 2

Algal biodiesel production from power plant exhaust and its potential to replace petrodiesel and reduce greenhouse gas emissions

Abstract
The production of biofuels and other products from algae is a technology that is rapidly developing. This paper presents an overview of algae, its benefits over other biofuel sources and the technology involved in producing algal biofuel. The case study in this report looks at the potential of algal biodiesel, produced using power plant exhaust, to replace our current petrodiesel supply and consequently reduce greenhouse gas emissions. The results suggest that using 60% of all coal and gas power plants would allow this new fuel source to replace petrodiesel entirely and thus reduce greenhouse gas emissions by ~5%. The challenge at the present is to improve the efficiency of algal fuel production technology so as to lower the cost of algal biodiesel and thereby make it commercially competitive with petrodiesel. Researchers are currently developing various means of accomplishing this and successful commercialization is anticipated by 2018.

SOURCE: Hundt, K. & Reddy, B.V. (2011). Algal biodiesel production from power plant exhaust and its potential to replace petrodiesel and reduce greenhouse gas emissions. *International Journal of Low-Carbon Technologies*, 6 (4): 294-298.

GLOSSARY

algae *(n)* very simple plants, such as seaweed, that have no real leaves, stems, or roots, and that grow in or near water

biofuel *(n)* fuel made from plant or animal sources and used in engines

2 Work in pairs. Choose one abstract each and recheck the table in 3.1. Take turns to present the context, aim, and conclusion of your abstract without referring to the table.

3 Which abstract do you think presents the key information most clearly? Why?

TASK 4 Using report structure to find information

1 Which points would you expect to be included in the full report for Text 2?
- evidence and arguments for the development of algae diesel
- points in support of other (i.e. non-algal) alternative energy technologies
- a comparison of different types of algae
- an analysis of the cost of algae biodiesel compared to conventional diesel
- a comparison of carbon emissions by various types of fuel

2 Work in pairs. Discuss how you reached your choices. Add any further points.

3 Read the outline of the Text 2 report opposite. Match extracts a–e to sections 1–5.
   a In conclusion, two important points can be made with regard to algal biofuel.
   b The wide variety of algal species offers researchers a lot of options for culturing algae in a wide variety of environments.
   c The content of the initial literature review and the results of the case study both indicate that algal biodiesel has enormous potential as a future fuel source.
   d This paper explores the production of biofuel from algae, its benefits, and future potential.
   e To determine the amount of algal biodiesel that can be produced from power plant exhaust, it is simplest to begin with 1 kg of CO_2.

4 Read Text 3, the conclusion of the report. Compare the information in the abstract (Text 2) and the conclusion (Text 3). Identify repeated and new information.

TEXT 3

Conclusion

In conclusion, two important points can be made with regard to algal biofuel. The first is that algae shows great potential as a biofuel source with several major advantages over other sources. Some of them are: low impact on land use and the food chain; ability to utilise waste streams for nutrients; rapid growth rate and high oil content. Due to the positive characteristics of algae and an abundant supply of power plant emissions, algal biofuel has the potential to be produced on a scale large enough to entirely replace petrodiesel and thereby reduce global greenhouse gas emissions by around 4–5%.

Second, algal biofuel production technology is still somewhat new and uneconomical. The efficiency of growth, harvesting and processing systems must be further improved before the technology can be commercialized. As a result, many researchers and companies are currently developing ways to make this technology more economical. It is forecasted that algal biodiesel will become competitive with petrodiesel by 2020.

(SOURCE: as Text 2)

5 How effectively does reading the abstract and the conclusion give an overview of the main ideas in this report? Which section would you read next to find out more?

TASK 5 Critical thinking – identifying assumptions in a text

1 Whilst reports appear to present objective 'facts', writers frequently make assumptions which can affect the credibility of their conclusion. Which of these ideas from Text 1 on page 089 is a *finding* based on the authors' research and which is an *assumption*?
a Vehicle emissions contribute to climate change.
b The use of electric vehicles reduces gas emissions.

2 Read Text 1 again. Which *two* of the following assumptions are also made?
1 Coventry City Council viewed low carbon emission vehicles as desirable.
2 Local councils are responsible for reducing carbon emissions.
3 People's health can be badly affected by emissions from conventional vehicles.

3 Which assumptions 1–3 do the authors of Text 3 make to support their conclusion?
1 Major investment in algae production technology is being made.
2 There are no currently unforeseen environmental threats by mass-production of algae.
3 The general public will eventually understand and accept this new technology.

4 Decide which assumptions in Texts 1 and 3 are reasonable or open to question.

TASK 6 Asking critical questions about a text

1 Quickly read Text 4, the abstract to a report. Make notes on:
- the context
- the aim of the report
- whether the conclusion is stated in the abstract.

Aviation and climate change: a global sectored approach is the need of the hour

TEXT 4

Abstract

The ªIntergovernmental Panel on Climate Change has estimated that ᵇill-effects of carbon emissions will grow to ᶜ5% by 2050. Although ICAO had initially endorsed the idea of the emissions trading system to meet CO_2 emission reduction objectives, prospects for a comprehensive global agreement ᵈappear to be distant, and a multi-faceted approach is required with a strong commitment from all stakeholders. ᵉOther options could be the usage of carbon neutral fuels, coming from biomass, algae and most recently the usage of CO_2 in the air and water in the atmosphere, and then ᶠthe Fischer Tropsche process to combine the H_2 and CO_2 together to produce oil (Louise and Paul, Aviation and climate change. *House of Commons Library*, 2008).

SOURCE: Banu, S. (2012). Aviation and climate change: a global sectored approach is the need of the hour. *International Journal of Low-Carbon Technologies*, 7 (2): 137-142.

---

2 Look at the circled parts of Text 4. Match items a–f to critical questions 1–6.
1 **What are some examples** of negative effects of carbon emissions?
2 **How** was this figure calculated?
3 **What** is this process, exactly?
4 **When** did the IPCC comment on carbon emissions?
5 **Who says** that an agreement on CO_2 emissions reduction is still far off?
6 **What sort** of options?

3 Write similar critical questions about Texts 1 and 2.

4 Present your critical questions and explain why you asked them.

TASK 7 Independent research – searching for reports

1 Decide how far you agree with statements 1–5.
1 Report abstracts are useful in determining the relevance of a report to a question.
2 Report abstracts offer a comprehensive yet concise overview of a report, including its rationale, context, aims, main perspectives, and conclusion.
3 The Discussion section has balanced, comprehensive, and rigorous content.
4 The Conclusion provides a summary of the main points plus interpretation and recommendations.
5 Citing one or two relevant reports in an essay is sufficient, reliable support for the argument.

2 Search for at least three further report or journal abstracts on a subject related to your discipline. Read these texts and note down the structure of each text.

3 Read the statements in 1 again. Make any changes as a result of your reading.

Writing Summaries

Summarizing is a key skill in academic writing that demonstrates that you have understood and effectively processed ideas from your reading. You may include a summary of a theory or argument that is the main focus of your text; you may use shorter summaries of various sources as part of a literature or research review; you may include a short summary of one source to cite as evidence for a particular point. When you are reading, it is important to identify and note down the topic and main points of a source text; you can use the abstract of an article to identify the structure of the text and find the main points. It is essential to reference summarized material in your writing.

This module covers:

- Analysing a text for a summary: structure, topic, main points
- Preparing, writing, and evaluating summaries
- Incorporating summaries into a literature review

TASK 1 Identifying topic and main points for a summary

1 Work in groups. Discuss the questions.

1 Note down reasons in support of and against buying the following types of food:

- locally-produced food
- organic food
- specific brands of food.

2 How much more (%) would you be willing to pay for each of the above types of food versus basic unbranded food?

3 Are farmers' markets (i.e. markets where farmers sell their produce directly to the public) popular in your country? What reasons can you think of for buying food there?

2 Read Text 1. Make notes on the topic, context, and main point.

Consumer preferences for local production and other value-added label claims for a processed food product

TEXT 1

Abstract

Using stated preference data from Kentucky and Ohio, USA, we estimate consumer willingness-to-pay for varieties of a processed food product (blackberry jam) that are differentiated with respect to their local production labelling and a series of other value-added claims. Results show that consumers were willing to pay more for the product indicating locally produced, produced in their state or in a well-identified multi-state region. Consumers were willing to purchase organic products, although there might be some confusion as to the meaning of the organic logo. Our results also supported the notion that consumers are willing to support small family farms.

Results and discussion

[...] We also included an interaction term to test whether the consumer was more likely to select a product produced in the region of the state in which they live. This parameter estimate was highly insignificant. Thus, consumers in this experiment did not particularly value products of their own region any more than those from another region (in the same state as they live) or bearing no production location information. Conversely, this result shows that where consumers live may not be a determinant for differences across people in our sample on how they react towards the origin of a product. Although past studies have found consumers are willing to pay for various labels indicating locally grown processed products across the world (e.g. Scarpa, Philippidis & Spalatro (2005); James, Rickard, & Rossman (2009), few have considered the multiple levels of local labelling. Darby et al. (2008) and Ernst & Darby (2008) are notable exceptions, where the authors found consumers are willing to pay for several different levels of local labelling including a 'nearby' label, a State Proud label and a country origin label. However, the product considered in these studies was fresh. Results from this research confirm that consumers are willing to pay for various indications of 'locally produced' for a processed product.

SOURCE: Wuyang Hu, W., Batte, M., Woods, T., & Ernst, S. (2012). Consumer preferences for local production and other value-added label claims for a processed food product. *European Review of Agricultural Economics*, 39 (3): 489-510.

TASK 2 Preparing, writing, and evaluating a summary

1 Read the guidelines below. Choose the appropriate missing stage: a, b, or c.

   a Copy down sentences from the text to use in your summary.

   (b) Select and note down the main points from the source text.

   c Add your own evaluation of the material.

Guidelines for writing a summary

1 Select an appropriate source text to suit your purpose.

2 Read the source text for basic understanding and to evaluate its relevance.

3 ....

4 Summarize the selected material using your own words.

5 Check your summary for accuracy and completeness.

---

2 Read Checklist J on page 212. Which three points relate mainly to content? Which three relate mainly to language?

3 Use your notes in Task 1.2 and the guidelines in 1 to write a short summary of Text 1 on page 093. Include a reference to the source text in your summary.

   Example: *Hu, Batte, Woods, and Ernst (2012) investigated ...*

4 Read and evaluate each other's summaries using Checklist J.

TASK 3 Analysing the structure of a text for a summary

1 Put the features of an introduction to a research report, a–e, into a logical order.

   a a brief review of other literature or research in the area

   b an outline of the chosen area of research, including any definitions

   c a statement to gain the reader's interest

   d a statement of the aims of the research, the main findings, and the structure and organization of the report

   e an identification of a 'gap' in the existing research, and why this research area is important

2 Read Text 2, the introduction to a report. Match features a–e in 1 to sections 1–5.

TEXT 2

Going local: exploring consumer behavior and motivations for direct food purchases

1 Perhaps the greatest evidence of momentum in the local food movement is the recognition of 'locavores' as the 2007 word of the year by the New Oxford American Dictionary. **2** Defined as 'a local resident who tries to eat only food grown or produced within a 100-mile radius', the term identifies the growing ranks of environmentally and edibility-conscious consumers who deliberately seek out locally produced food and beverages. **3** Moreover, the market has witnessed considerable growth in the numbers of farmers using direct marketing strategies, a doubling of US farmers' markets over the past decade, and strong growth in Community Supported Agriculture organizations (CSAs), in which shareholders directly pay farmers for a proportion of output (USDA Ag Census, 2002; USDA AMS, 2008; Lass et al., 2003). Furthermore, national media outlets, including *Time*, have dubbed 'Local the New Organic' (Cloud, 2007). **4** However, despite the apparent growth in demand for local foods, there has been a paucity of research results regarding the motivation of consumers to seek out and pay a premium for local produce offerings, the role of direct markets in consumer shopping choices, and buying profiles of consumers who frequent direct channels (Brown, 2002; Zepeda & Li, 2006).

    5 In this article, we summarize much of the authors' research on preferences of direct consumers of fresh produce in the context of a theoretical model regarding product and source choice. A particular focus is how local source and product attribution may connect with perceived private and public good dimensions of such choices. In addition, we present a newly developed analysis of willingness to pay (WTP) for the 'local' attribute, which suggests heterogeneity in the interpretations of the public good dimension of the attribute across consumers who shop at direct markets with differing frequencies.

SOURCE: Thilmany, D., Bond, C.A., & Bond, J.K. (2008). Going local: exploring consumer behavior and motivations for direct food purchases. *American Journal of Agricultural Economics*, 90 (5): 1303–1309.

TASK 4 Analysing and evaluating a student summary

1 **Read a student's summary of Text 2. Put features** a–d **in the order in which they appear in the summary.**

   a main focus of the source text (i.e. Text 2)

   b the results and implications of the research described in the source text

   c statement of the topic and reference to the source text

   d background and literature review

> In their article on consumer behaviour, Thilmany, Bond, and Bond (2008) present their research into the buying habits of consumers of locally-produced food. Thilmany, Bond, and Bond focus particularly on 'locavores', defined as 'a local resident who tries to eat only food grown or produced within a 100-mile radius'. The authors note the strong growth of local food markets in the US, particularly farmers' markets, but cite the limited research into why consumers locate local food products which they are prepared to pay more for, and they propose a new concept of 'willingness to pay' (WTP). Their research findings indicate that there are considerable variations in buyers' habits and attitudes, particularly in terms of how buyers view the particular qualities of products and how much they are prepared to pay.
>
> **Reference**
> Thilmany, D., Bond, C.A., & Bond, J.K. (2008). Going local: exploring consumer behavior and motivations for direct food purchases. *American Journal of Agricultural Economics*, 90 (5): 1303-1309.

2 **Which features of the source text in Task 3.1 do not appear in the summary? Why?**

3 **The language in black in the summary could be used in a summary on almost any topic. For each part of the summary, identify what type of information could replace the blue text.**

   Example: *In their article on* [topic of article], [name(s) of author(s)] [date of source publication] *present their research into* [area of research].

4 **Find these words / phrases underlined in Text 2.**

   seek out   paucity of research   product   perceived   willingness to pay
   attribute   heterogeneity

   1 Which are changed to synonyms in the student summary?

   2 Why are two words / phrases not changed? Choose a, b, or c.

      a it is a technical term

      b there is no synonym for it

      c one word is better than a paraphrase

5 **Work in pairs. Discuss and evaluate the student summary using Checklist J.**

> **Checklist J** Evaluation criteria for a summary
>
> Is the summary ...
> 1 **contextualized?** Does it give a reference to the source text(s)?
> 2 **complete?** Does it include the main points of the text(s), but not supporting points, details, and examples?
> 3 **correct?** Is it closely based on the source text(s) and does not contain any new material?
> 4 **concise?** Is it as brief as possible?
> 5 **clear?** Is it easy to understand?
> 6 **creative?** Does it use some technical terms in the text(s) but mainly the summary writer's original language?

Checklists:
page 209

1 Read Text 3, the conclusion of a report, and the notes on paragraph 1. Make notes on the topic and main point(s) in paragraphs 2 and 3.

TEXT 3

Conclusion

1 From case studies of a number of farmers' markets both rural and urban, and in three states from the east to west coasts, Gillespie *et al.* (2007) concluded that farmers' markets are the 'keystones' for rebuilding local food systems. By making local food more visible in public spaces, they educate customers on the potential for and seasonal limits of local food. The authors found that farmers' markets encourage the production of a greater diversity of food products, which would be needed for a more localized food system. This greater diversity attracts a greater variety of shoppers as well as helping to strengthen local farm operations. In addition, farmers' markets serve as business incubators that then 'increase the density of local food networks and relations' (Gillespie *et al.*, 2007), an important development to expand the reach of local food markets. The authors' final point is that the economic interactions that take place at farmers' markets are combined with a variety of social interactions that make the markets valued community institutions. Thus, the variety of impacts of farmers' markets documented in the literature presented here combine to create the basis for the emergence of new local food systems.

2 It is too early to tell what long-run changes the newer and more unusual CSA model will bring, although CSA farms will probably never be more than a small part of the food system. There appear to be farmer financial problems that need to be worked out and adjustments made by consumers. Ostrom (2007) believes that these consumer changes will be the most important because, 'as they eat, they gain opportunities to increase their understanding of food, the challenges faced by farmers, the needs of the environment, and the potential role informed citizens can play in reshaping food and economic systems'. More research on the many aspects of CSA is obviously needed.

3 This article addressed much of the research on the various impacts of farmers' markets that has been conducted since Brown's (2002) farmers' market research review and also examined research on the impacts of CSA on consumers and producers. Additional research on the impacts of farmers' markets and CSA farms that we did not consider might examine their ecological impacts. For example, how many acres at risk for development have been kept in agricultural production due to these local markets? Are farmers who use farmers' markets or CSA more or less likely than their counterparts to adopt water and soil conservation practices? Research that examines the relationships between selling into a local food system and the impact on the local and regional environment would give a more complete picture of the impacts of local markets.

SOURCE: Brown, C. & Miller, S. (2008). The impacts of local markets: a review of research on farmers' markets and Community Supported Agriculture (CSA). *American Journal of Agricultural Economics*, 90 (5): 1298-1302.

Paragraph 1:
research on farmers' markets in the USA → shows they benefit diversity and help develop localization

Paragraph 2:

Paragraph 3:

2 Use your notes to write a summary of about 100 words. Follow the guidelines in Task 2.1.

3 Reduce the length of your research summary to about 30–40 words by prioritizing only the essential conclusion of the text.

4 Work in pairs. Discuss when you might use a 100-word research summary and when a shorter, more concise summary would be used.

ACADEMIC LANGUAGE   ▸Language reference page 200 1.6

Citations (7) Reference reminder language

As part of a longer text, a summary needs to contain reference reminder language. These structures help ensure that the reader is clear about the source of the ideas in the text.

• A range of structures built around verbs can be used:

*Brown and Miller (2008) say ... / **go on to** argue that ... / **continue by** suggesting that ... / **add** / **conclude** that ...*

• Alternatively, for variation, a content focus can be used:

***They** conclude by stating that ... (Brown & Miller, 2008).*

***Their research** / **This study** shows that ... (Brown & Miller, 2008).*

To avoid accidental plagiarism, check that each time you include ideas summarized from a source in your writing, you also include a reference or reference reminder within the sentence.

TASK 6 Referencing in summaries

◀ In Text 3, the writers summarize the work of Gillespie *et al*. The first mention is highlighted. Identify examples of reference reminder language in paragraph 1.

TASK 7 Incorporating summaries into a literature review

1 One reason for writing a summary is to incorporate it into a longer text, such as a literature review. Analyse the rewritten student summary below as follows:

  1 Look again at the student summary in Task 4. Then read the version below, which has been rewritten for a literature review.

  2 Compare and identify the changes – rephrasing, deletions, and additions.

  3 Suggest reasons for these changes.

Consumer attitudes to buying local food

Literature review

Thilmany, Bond, and Bond (2008) have conducted research into the buying habits of consumers of locally-produced food. They note the strong growth of local food markets in the US, particularly farmers' markets, but cite the limited research into why consumers locate local food products which they are prepared to pay more for. Thilmany, Bond, and Bond (2008) also propose a new concept of 'willingness to pay' (WTP). Their research findings indicate that there are considerable variations in buyers' habits and attitudes, particularly in terms of how buyers view the particular qualities of products and how much they are prepared to pay (*ibid*.).

Reference

Thilmany, D., Bond, C.A., & Bond, J.K. (2008). Going local: exploring consumer behavior and motivations for direct food purchases. *American Journal of Agricultural Economics*, 90 (5): 1303-1309.

2 Write part of the literature review on 'Consumer attitudes to buying local food', incorporating ideas from *all three texts* in this module.

  1 Look again at the two summaries you have written in Tasks 2 and 5 and select the most important, interesting, and relevant material.

  2 Decide how to introduce the summarized material.

    Example: *This section offers an overview of recent research in the area of consumer attitudes to buying local food, with a particular focus on the US.*

  3 Write about 150 words incorporating ideas of your own **plus** the student summaries.

  4 Make sure you include **reference reminder language** to make it clear that the material is from another source and not your own.

3 Evaluate your summary, and one by another student, using Checklist J on page 095.

TASK 8 Independent research – summarizing a longer text

1 Write a summary of an academic article or report in your discipline following the steps below.

  1 Search for and read a number of abstracts.

  2 Select one article based on the most interesting and relevant abstract.

  3 Make notes on the main points while reading the introduction, results / discussion, and conclusion.

  4 Write a summary as part of a literature review, based on your notes.

2 Compare with at least one other summary. Evaluate using Checklist J.

Lectures often present detailed information on a new topic. Parts of these lectures may be **expository**, which means the material is informative, descriptive and explanatory rather than evaluative. You need to work out quickly the structure and organization of the lecture, and note down the main information presented. You may find it useful to process this material into a summary which you can use later in your writing and speaking.

This module covers:

- Understanding the main points of a lecture
- Summarizing a key concept from a lecture
- Combining and comparing information from two lectures

TASK 1 Preparing to listen to lectures

1 Work in groups. Say what you know about the items below related to the United Nations (the UN).

- year of, and reason for, its foundation
- purpose and responsibilities
- number of members
- UN Councils such as the UN Human Rights Council (HRC) and the UN Security Council
- the Universal Declaration of Human Rights (UDHR)
- the Universal Periodic Review (UPR)
- UNESCO (United Nations Educational, Scientific, and Cultural Organization); UNHCR (United Nations High Commissioner for Refugees); International Court of Justice; WHO (World Health Organization); ASEAN (Association of Southeast Asian Nations)

2 Study Slide 1, which represents how the main bodies within the UN are related. Discuss what the *circle*, the *triangle*, and the *rectangle* represent in this diagram.

3 You are going to watch extracts from two lectures on the UN. Look at introductory Slides 2 and 3, and predict which specific points in 1 you think each lecture will cover.

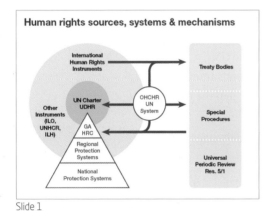

Slide 1

The United Nations Human Rights Machinery:
The Human Rights Council and the UPR

Dr Nazila Ghanea
University of Oxford

Slide 2

The United Nations and International Security

Professor Richard Caplan
Professor of International Relations
University of Oxford

Slide 3

TASK 2 Understanding a lecture introduction

1 ▷6.1 Watch Extract 1, the introduction to Dr Nazila Ghanea's lecture. Note down:

a the two main points from Task 1.1 that her lecture will cover — human rights Concil

b the two types of UN human rights mechanisms — treaty / charter

c any points that she states the lecture will *not* cover. — treaty bodies / local and regional and nation

2 Work in pairs. Compare notes. What extra details can you add to your description of Slide 1 (Task 1.2)?

health organization

TASK 3 Summarizing a key concept from a lecture

1 Work in pairs. Use the prompts to make five *What ...?*, *How ...?* or *When ...?* questions about information in Dr Ghanea's lecture on the Universal Periodic Review (UPR).

① the UPR ④ the objectives of the UPR ③ the UPR system
② a review of the member states ⑤ the content of the review

Example: 1 *What is the UPR?* ② *when are UPR reviewed?*

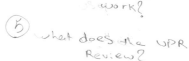

① when UN council meet?
③ what are the objectives of UPR?
④ how does UPR system work?
⑤ what does the UPR Review?

2 ▶6.2 Compare questions. Then watch Extract 2 and focus on the main points. Note answers to the five questions in 1.

3 Use your lecture notes to write a paragraph of about 150 words summarizing the main points about the UPR. Check transcript 6.2 on page 230 if necessary.

4 ▶6.3 Watch Extract 3 and note down Dr Ghanea's three closing remarks.

5 Write a sentence explaining why the UPR 'has great potential to promote and protect human rights in the darkest corners of the world'.

TASK 4 Understanding the main points of a lecture section

1 ▶6.4 Watch Extract 4, the introduction of Professor Richard Caplan's lecture. Take notes on the main points he makes about the UN.

Basic facts about the UN: ....

The role / purpose of the UN: ....

The make-up of the UN: ....

The aim of the lecture: ....

2 Use your notes to briefly summarize the lecture introduction under the headings in 1.

3 ▶6.5 Watch part of Extract 4 again. Explain the lecturer's statement in your own words.

'It's not the UN itself that bears responsibility, but rather, the UN's member states.'

4 ▶6.6 Work in threes. Choose two topics each from the six in the diagram. Watch Extract 5 and note down points related to your two chosen topics.

5 Take turns to summarize the main points from your notes to the group. Use the transcripts on page 231 to clarify any points as necessary.

international security
responsibilities
UN charter
PEACEKEEPING
operations & cost
definition
purpose

TASK 5 Comparing information from two lectures

1 Use your notes from both lectures to check and complete the information in Task 1.1. Add the source of your answers in brackets.

Example: *Year of foundation: 1945 (Ghanea)*

2 Work in pairs. Combine your notes to write a summary of one lecture extract (1–5).

3 Read at least two other summaries, and evaluate them using Checklist J on page 095.

4 Work in groups. Discuss the points in Task 1.1 and decide what you have learned from the two lectures.

5 In your groups, evaluate the two lectures using Checklist C on page 209.

You need to prepare for seminar discussions, so that you have something to say and some material to cite. Lectures and related texts provide supporting material, which you need to respond to and evaluate, using questions such as: Is the argument **valid** and relevant? Is the text **biased**? How do the ideas in the text relate to the specific question being discussed in the seminar? You can ask similar questions in response to other students' contributions in the seminar. At the end of a discussion, you should aim to summarize the points made, and achieve a **resolution** (i.e. come to some conclusions, and reach a consensus).

This module covers:
- Reading and preparing a logical argument for a seminar
- Asking questions about a contribution
- Conducting a seminar discussion and summarizing main points

TASK 1 Reading to prepare for a seminar

1 Read Text 1 and check key terms. As you read, make brief notes on the main points.

The responsibility to protect

TEXT 1

The Responsibility to Protect, the 2001 report of the International Commission on Intervention and State Sovereignty (ICISS), attempted to resolve the tension between the competing claims of sovereignty and human rights by building a new consensus around the principles that should govern the protection of endangered peoples. The principle of responsibility to protect was adopted by the UN General Assembly at the 2005 World Summit, a move described as 'a revolution ... in international affairs' by one commentator (Lindberg, 2005). But what is the 'responsibility to protect', how was it adopted, and what does it mean for the future of humanitarian intervention?

The commission argued that states have the primary responsibility to protect their citizens. When they are unable or unwilling to do so, or when they deliberately terrorize their citizens, 'the principle of non-intervention yields to the international responsibility to protect' (ICISS, 2001: xi). The report broadens this responsibility to encompass not only the responsibility to react to humanitarian crises but also the responsibility to prevent such crises and the 'responsibility to rebuild' failed and tyrannical states. This reframing of the debate away from the question of whether states have a right of intervention towards the question of where responsibility rests for protecting endangered peoples formed the basis of an attempt to generate a new international political consensus supporting what the ICISS report calls 'intervention for human protection purposes' (ICISS, 2001: xiii).

SOURCE: Baylis, J., Smith, S., & Owens, P. (2008). p.535. *The Globalization of World Politics* (4th ed.). Oxford: Oxford University Press.

2 Work in pairs. Based on your reading and notes, identify the writers' conclusions and evaluation. Support these with evidence from the text.

3 In your pairs: A read Text 2 on page 217; B read Text 3 on page 215. Follow the same procedure as with Text 1. Prepare to present the information in your text.

4 Summarize your text to your partner. Ask and answer clarification questions.

TASK 2 Preparing a logical argument for a seminar

1 You are going to participate in a seminar discussion on the question below. Prepare relevant points to introduce in the seminar. Use your notes from 6C and the arguments in the reading texts in this module, together with your own ideas.

DISCUSSION: *Who should be responsible for dealing with threats such as conflict, natural disasters, and disputes? Consider the roles of the following agents:*
- *the UN, including its bodies (e.g. The Human Rights Council, UNICEF)*
- *NGOs (e.g. Médecins Sans Frontières, Oxfam)*
- *sovereign states and their individual governments*
- *business / corporations (e.g. security companies, law firms, etc.)*
- *individuals, e.g. through charitable donations.*

2 **Build up your argument, including material logically supporting the following points.**

1 the specific roles, if any, for each agent

2 the leadership of the action plan – who would have overall responsibility and accountability

3 difficulties with your suggested approach, and suggestions for overcoming these.

ACADEMIC LANGUAGE

Asking critical questions Questioning the logic of a contribution

When participating in a seminar discussion, you need to clarify and question the sense and relevance of the contributions of other students.

Questions should arise from specific contributions in the discussion:

I'm sorry, but how does that idea relate to international security?

You seem to be saying that private corporations have a role to play in peacekeeping;

does this mean that they should participate alongside national security forces?

OK, but what about the role of sovereign states in this process?

To point out weaknesses in an argument, you can use questions such as:

Do you think that argument is valid?

Perhaps you need to consider the implications of that suggestion – wouldn't it lead to disagreement between organizations?

Wouldn't that approach be limited to regional rather than international conflicts?

OK, but there's a problem with / drawback to that argument …

TASK 3 Asking questions about a contribution

1 ◄))6.7 **Listen to four seminar contributions in response to the discussion question in Task 2. Write down one critical question for each, either asking for clarification or pointing out a weakness.**

2 **Work in pairs. Compare questions. Identify the type of question and the language used.**

TASK 4 Conducting a seminar discussion

1 **Work in groups. Conduct a discussion based on the question in Task 2. Follow the guidelines below.**

Guidelines for conducting a seminar discussion (2)

1 Nominate one student to take brief notes on the main points during the seminar.

2 Be individually responsible for sticking to the question closely; avoid irrelevant contributions.

3 Build up arguments by following on from other participants' contributions.

4 Ask critical questions in order to stimulate the discussion and to make sure all points are supported by evidence.

5 Ensure all participants have a fair opportunity to contribute.

6 Aim to reach a resolution.

TASK 5 Summarizing the main points of a discussion

1 **Review the notes taken during the seminar and write a group summary of the main contributions of the participants.**

2 **Exchange and read other groups' summaries.**

Vocabulary Collocation

Collocation refers to patterns of words which typically go together, involving different combinations of nouns, verbs, adjectives, adverbs or grammatical words such as prepositions. Some collocations are common across contexts (*make a mistake*), some are more typical of academic writing (*a strong correlation, assert one's rights*), and others are specific to particular disciplines (*strict liability* - law, *clear an airway* - medicine). Using typical collocations in your writing will help you develop a more natural academic style.

TASK 1 Recognizing collocations in a text

1 **Identify the collocations that appear with the words in bold in the text extract.**

   Example: *have* + a right; a right + *of sth*

   > This reframing of the debate away from the question of whether states have a **right** of intervention towards the question of where **responsibility** rests for protecting endangered peoples formed the **basis** of an attempt to generate a new international political **consensus** supporting what the ICISS report calls 'intervention for human protection purposes'.

2 **Add one or two more collocations that can go with each of the words identified in 1.**

   Example: *human* + rights

3 **In groups, share your collocations and categorize them by type (e.g. verb + noun, adjective + noun). Check any you are not sure about in a dictionary.**

TASK 2 Identifying academic & discipline-specific collocations

1 **Identify the collocations in each phrase, then complete the other information.**

	Collocation(s)	Type	Field/Discipline
1	*a strong correlation between the two variables*	1 adjective + noun (*strong correlation*) 2 noun + preposition (*correlation between*)	statistical analysis / academic research
2	*women were asserting their rights as citizens*		law, social sciences
3	*infection is acquired through human contact*		
4	*an adverse impact on the individual*		
5	*issues of corporate responsibility*		
6	*statistical analyses were performed*		
7	*the high species diversity found in the tropics*		
8	*creating a complex network of social contacts*		

2 **In small groups, compare your answers and identify which collocations are:**
   - used across several disciplines and relevant to most students
   - relevant to your own discipline area.

3 **Identify which of the collocates of the noun *principle* below are more typical of a specific discipline, and which are used across many disciplines.**

basic constitutional ethical general legal	principle	+ of +	democracy energy conservation equality self-determination

4 **Build similar collocation diagrams for the following academic words.**

   challenge (*noun*) evidence (*noun*) apparent (*adj.*) conduct (*verb*)

5 **Use an academic search engine (e.g. *Google Scholar*) to search for the words in 4 and investigate common collocations by looking at the phrases they appear in repeatedly.**

   1 Did you come across the same collocations you proposed in 4?

   2 Which collocations were common across disciplines? Which were mainly in one discipline?

UNIT 7 Data

LEARNING OBJECTIVES

This unit covers:

Reading
- Evaluating data sources and asking critical questions about data
- Recognizing stance and subtle evaluation in an expository text
- Comparing perspective and stance across texts

Writing
- Interpreting data in visual form and writing a commentary
- Decoding and constructing complex noun phrases

Listening
- Understanding visual data in a presentation
- Distinguishing between evidence and evaluation
- Critically evaluating a presentation

Speaking
- Planning, researching, and rehearsing a short presentation of visual data
- Evaluating performance: format, description, interpretation, and stance

Vocabulary
- Being specific

Research project (1)
- Choosing a topic

Discussion

1 **Work in groups. Describe what you know about the characteristics of these research methods.**

   Example: *A case study involves examining in detail a person or group (i.e. a 'case').*

   case study   census   field work   focus group   interview   laboratory experiment   questionnaire

2 **Which methods in 1 are *quantitative* (the data can be measured), which are *qualitative* (the data can't be measured), and which are *both*?**

   Example: *Questionnaires can be quantitative (e.g. multiple-choice answers), or qualitative (e.g. longer answers).*

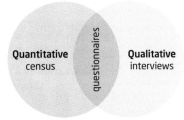

3 **Describe research methods to investigate these areas. Are they *quantitative* or *qualitative*?**
   - engineering – testing the strength of a bridge design
   - economics – factors affecting property prices in an area
   - medicine – attitudes to online health information among health professionals
   - history – determining the age of an archaeological find

Expository texts mainly present information – they describe and explain things. However, the presentation of apparently objective **data** is influenced by the writer's stance. The writer is usually arguing from certain *perspectives* (e.g. economic) and a *stance* (supporting, critical, etc.), and presents the data to support these. You need to ask critical questions: How reliable is the source of the data? Why did the writer choose this source and not others? Which facts do they emphasize and which do they downplay or ignore? Exposition is typically followed by **interpretation** and evaluation: What does the data show? What is significant, and why? What are the implications for the wider context? Recognizing the different stages and functions enables you to differentiate between fact (objective) and interpretation / evaluation (subjective) in a text, and to compare across texts.

This module covers:
- Evaluating data sources and asking critical questions about data
- Recognizing stance and subtle evaluation in an expository text
- Comparing perspective and stance across texts

TASK 1 Critical thinking – evaluating data sources

1 **Work in groups. Which data sources a–e would be most useful to investigate the level of crime in a country? Decide one advantage and disadvantage of each.**
   a statistics from courts about the number of people convicted of criminal offences
   b statistics about the number of crimes reported to the police
   c interviews with victims of crime
   d surveys of the general public about their experience of crime
   e newspaper reports of crime

2 **Compare with the class. Explain which sources you have chosen, and why.**

TASK 2 Identifying purpose and main points

1 **Quickly read Text 1 and complete the notes.**
   Genre: ....

   Date of publication: ....

   Audience: ....

   Topic of this chapter: *crime statistics* ....

   Topic of this section: ....

   Main purpose of this section: ....

2 **According to Text 1, which two sets of data feed into the official statistics on crime? Why are two sets now used rather than just one?**

3 **You are going to write 100 words explaining the British Crime Survey (BCS).**
   1 Read Text 1 again and note down three or four key words / phrases in each paragraph which describe the main points about the BCS, including its history and function.
   2 Without looking at Text 1, use your notes to write your text.

4 **Work in pairs. Compare texts. Did you include the same points? Give reasons for what you included and left out.**

The new orthodoxy? The British Crime Survey

TEXT 1

1 It has already been mentioned that the 'official crime statistics' no longer contain only offences recorded by the police. Since 2002, the main annual statistical publication (renamed *Crime in England and Wales*) has also included large amounts of data from the British Crime Survey. This decision was not taken lightly: the BCS had been running for over 20 years before the change occurred. However, over that period it had established itself as a well-respected alternative source of information about crime levels and trends, and for the Home Office to continue to publish its results separately from the police figures risked it taking on the appearance of a 'rival' set of official statistics. By bringing them together, it was hoped to show that the two data sets were complementary rather than in competition, and jointly provided a richer and more 'complete' picture of crime than previously. In the section, we look briefly at the origins of the BCS and its development over time, then explore similarities and differences vis-à-vis police recorded crime. We also look at some of the limitations of the BCS and the critiques that have been made of it.

2 The first BCS was conducted in 1982 and its results published the following year (Hough & Mayhew, 1983). It was not a new concept: victimization surveys had been conducted in the United States since the late 1960s, and Sparks, Genn, and Dodd (1977) had already undertaken an experimental survey in London. Like these earlier surveys, the BCS was born out of curiosity about the size of the 'dark figure' of crime – i.e. unreported and/or unrecorded offences. The main rationale was that, by asking representative samples of members of the public to describe crimes committed against them within the past 12 months, the vagaries of reporting and recording behaviour are neatly avoided, and the responses can be grossed up to produce a 'fuller' (and arguably more reliable) picture than the recorded crime statistics of the incidence of certain types of offence (Mayhew & Hough, 1988). It was also timely in that it was introduced in a period of rising concern about crime victims, and provided valuable data about their experiences. Over the years, it has grown steadily in prominence and status, being repeated bi-annually from 1991 and annually from 2000/1. Since 2000/1, it has also been sufficiently large (now 46,000 interviews a year) to allow analysis at police force as well as national level.

3 The basic format of the survey, and the framework of presenting the results, have changed little over the years. One person over 16 from each household in the sample is randomly selected to answer the questions. Using the Core Victimization Module, the interviewer first establishes whether this person, or anyone else in the household, has been the victim of any of a specified list of vehicle- or property-related crimes (described to them in ordinary language) within the past 12 months; and secondly, whether the respondent him/herself has been the victim of a 'personal crime' (mainly assault) over the same period. If any positive answers are received, further details of each incident are recorded – up to a maximum of five for any type of offence – on a 'victim form'. The results are analysed and grossed up to produce estimated national totals of both broad types of incidents – described as 'household' and 'personal' crimes – based on calculations using, respectively, the total number of households and the total adult population in England and Wales.

SOURCE: Maguire, M. (2012). pp.218–221. *'Criminal statistics and the construction of crime'* in Maguire, M., Morgan, R., & Reiner, R. (eds.). *The Oxford Handbook of Criminology* (5th ed.). Oxford: Oxford University Press.

TASK 3 Quickly identifying writer's stance

1 **Improving your reading speed is an important skill for dealing with long academic texts. Use the words / phrases below to complete the guidelines.**

details, such as figures / tables   heading   in-text references   italics   topic sentences

Guidelines for identifying a writer's stance

1 Use any questions in the .... to help you focus on the main idea. As you read each paragraph, ask yourself how the question is being answered.

2 At this stage, ignore:
   a ....
   b ....
   c unknown words that you don't need for understanding the main idea.

3 Try to understand the writer's emphasis. Focus on:
   d ....
   e any .... used by the writer for emphasis.
   f key words or phrases that are repeated through the text.

2 Read Text 2, which follows on from Text 1. Time yourself to see how quickly you can identify the main ideas. Follow the guidelines in 1 on page 105.

A fuller picture of crime?

TEXT 2

5 Table 8.2 shows the estimates of the extent of 'BCS crime' that were calculated from the results of the survey in 2010/11. If one compares the overall picture painted by these figures with that derived from police records (Table 8.1, earlier), the two most obvious differences are that the crime categories included are different; and the overall estimated total of 'BCS crime' (9,180,000 offences) is more than double that of police recorded crime.

6 Neither of these differences is surprising, but their implications need some discussion. The first point to emphasize is that the BCS has never set out to cover all kinds of crime recorded by the police. As its designers pointed out at the outset (Hough & Mayhew, 1985: ch.1), public surveys are more suited to gleaning information about some types of incident than others. What it has always aimed to produce first and foremost is a measure of *household and personal crimes against adults* (and, indeed, not all types of these). Thus the annual estimate of 'BCS crime' does not include crimes against commercial or corporate victims, fraudulent offences, sexual offences, or consensual crimes such as the possession of or dealing in drugs, nor does it (at the time of writing) include crimes against children under 16. [...] 'BCS crime' continues to be based only on the Core Victimization Module, which has changed little since the 1980s. This is partly because some of the other available data are considered less reliable, but mainly because (like the long-term 'series' produced from police statistics) one of the aims of the BCS has been to make reliable year-on-year comparisons and track long-term trends in victimization levels.

Broadly comparable with police figures:

	Number (to nearest 1,000)	Per cent
Violence	2,203,000	23
Vandalism	2,156,000	22
Vehicle-related theft	1,189,000	12
Burglary	745,000	8
Theft from person	563,000	6
Bicycle theft	526,000	5

Not comparable:

Other household theft	1,244,000	13
Other theft personal property	993,000	10
Total	**9,618,000**	**100**

Source: Adapted from Chaplin *et al.* (2011). *Crime in England and Wales 2010/11*. London: Home Office.

Table 8.2 Estimated totals of offences in England and Wales, 2010/11, as derived from the British Crime Survey

7 It is also clear, *vice versa*, that not all 'crimes' included in the BCS estimates would have been identified and recorded as criminal offences if they had been reported to the police. The survey gathers information on large numbers of (overwhelmingly minor) personal and household thefts which do not map sufficiently onto police definitions of crime for any direct comparisons to be made.

8 The above differences mean that one cannot simply compare the two overall totals (9.6 million BCS crimes, 4.2 million police-recorded crimes) and conclude that the BCS shows that there is 'a little over twice as much crime' as the official records suggest: this would not be comparing like with like. There are, however, some specific offence categories where meaningful comparisons are possible, once some statistical adjustments have been made. Combined together, these form what is known as the *comparable subset* (see Home Office, 2011: 17–18). Although the fit is not perfect, this allows fair comparisons between about three quarters of the estimated total of BCS crimes and just under half of all crimes recorded by the police. Most of the BCS crimes in the first five categories shown in Table 8.2 are included in the comparable subset, while 'other household thefts' and 'other thefts of personal property' are excluded. *Within this subset*, the BCS clearly does provide a 'fuller' picture than the equivalent police figures. Since the BCS was first conducted, the results have systematically indicated that *victims are aware of between three and four times more offences of these particular kinds than appear in the police-recorded statistics.* [...]

9 In short, BCS crime, like recorded crime, is to some extent an arbitrarily constructed aggregation of disparate types of offence: both include some offences in the count, and omit others. It is therefore a serious misunderstanding to regard the BCS as offering a full picture of 'crime in England and Wales'. Indeed, looked at as a whole, it does not necessarily present a fuller - or indeed 'truer' - picture than that provided by the recorded crime statistics, simply a different one: it is fuller in some important respects (notably the inclusion of unrecorded and unreported offences), but less full in others (notably the exclusion of consensual crimes, crimes against organizations, and crimes against children under 16). It is only in relation to certain well-defined individual offence types, or to the 'comparable subset', that it can safely be said to provide a fuller picture than the police figures - though even then, questions remain about how accurately it reflects the nature and scale of the behaviour in question.

SOURCE: Maguire, M. (2012). pp.218–221. 'Criminal statistics and the construction of crime' in Maguire, M., Morgan, R., & Reiner, R. (eds.). *The Oxford Handbook of Criminology* (5th ed.). Oxford: Oxford University Press.

Use the information in Text 2. Complete the table with *yes* or *no*.

		Police-recorded crime statistics	British Crime Survey
1	has the highest total number of offences		
2	includes all categories of crime		
3	includes violence, vandalism, vehicle theft (incl. bicycles), burglary, and theft from person		
4	focuses mainly on adult and personal crimes		
5	includes consensual crimes and sexual offences		
6	contains regularly updated categories of crime		
7	includes mainly minor crimes		

4 **Does the BCS provide a fuller picture of crime? Focus on the main idea in Text 2. Which statement 1–3 best reflects the writer's stance?**

1 The BCS provides a more complete picture of crime than recorded crime statistics.

2 The BCS does not cover all types of crime, but it helps to provide a more complete picture of certain types of crime.

3 Recorded crime statistics provide a more complete picture than the BCS data.

5 **Based on the information in Text 2, briefly summarize the writer's main conclusions relating to the use of police recorded crime statistics and BCS statistics. Include the strengths and weaknesses of these two measures of crime.**

ACADEMIC LANGUAGE ▸Language reference page 205 6.3

Evaluation (1) Adverbials

Adjectives are commonly used to express evaluation, e.g. **obvious** differences, the fit is **not perfect** (see page 063). Adverbials can also be used to make a subtle evaluative comment, especially one that shows the writer's stance.

Notice the effect of adverbs and adverbials in the following pairs of sentences from Text 2. The writer uses them to emphasize what they feel is important, support their argument, and/or interpret the data:

1 *What it [= the BCS] aims to produce is a measure of household and personal crimes against adults.*

2 *What it has **always** aimed to produce **first and foremost** is a measure of household and personal crimes against adults.*

1 *The survey gathers information on large numbers of personal and household thefts which do not map onto police definitions of crime and so are not useful for making direct comparisons.*

2 *The survey gathers information on large numbers of (**overwhelmingly** minor) personal and household thefts which do **not** map **sufficiently** onto police definitions of crime for any direct comparisons to be made.*

1 *Looked at as a whole, it does not present a fuller picture than provided by the recorded crime statistics, but a different one.*

2 ***Indeed**, looked at as a whole, it does **not necessarily** present a fuller ... picture than that provided by the recorded crime statistics, **simply** a different one.*

TASK 4 Recognizing subtle evaluation

1 **Explain the change in emphasis in sentences 1–5 depending on the adverbial used.**

1 The findings of this survey *simply / apparently / to some extent* reflect differences in personal preferences.

2 Work in this area *clearly / consistently / convincingly* demonstrates a relationship between health status and economic inequality.

3 These two factors are *not necessarily related / completely unrelated / apparently unrelated.*

4 Studies have *overwhelmingly / largely / obviously* failed to find evidence to support the claim.

5 Existing legislation does not *adequately / fully / systematically* address the realities of identity theft.

TASK 5 Asking critical questions about data

1 The writer of Text 1 on page 105 suggests that the BCS data can be useful despite its limitations. Based on what you have read:

   1 to what extent do you agree that the BCS provides a fuller picture of crime than recorded crime statistics alone?

   2 to what extent do the arguments in Texts 1 and 2 match your ideas in Task 1?

2 Complete the critical questions below to find out more about the topic. Refer to Checklist K questions 1–4 on page 212 to check your ideas.

   Example: *How significant are the crimes not covered by the BCS?*

Why does the writer say / believe .... ?

Why is / are .... not mentioned in this text?

How reliable is / are .... ?

How accurately do /does the writer .... ?

How significant is / are .... ?

TASK 6 Comparing perspective and stance across texts

1 Quickly read Text 3. Note down the *genre, audience,* and *purpose* of the text, and the main *perspectives* in the text.

How well do victim surveys count?

TEXT 3

The victim survey count

Victim surveys have a number of methodological limitations that affect the reliability of their counts.

...

Household victim surveys come nowhere near close to measuring all 'crime'. They leave aside victimization of children, as we have seen. Crimes against commercial and public sector targets are omitted, as well as victimless crimes such as drug possession. Homicide is obviously not counted, since no victim is available. And it is difficult to cover fraud, since many people will not be aware they have been victimized.

...

No sample survey represents the population adequately. Household sampling frames exclude those in communal establishments. (They form about 2 per cent of the UK population, so bear in mind that they would not make much difference to national estimates.) They also exclude groups such as the homeless, who may have higher victimization rates than others.

...

There is a set of specific limitations in asking people to remember victimization incidents and locate them accurately in time. One concern is whether victimization that is repetitive in nature can be readily located in time as discrete and definitionally tidy events. This bears in particular on domestic and sexual violence, as well as on many other forms of harassment.

SOURCE: Mayhew, P. (2008). pp.245–246. 'Researching the state of crime' in King, R. & Wincup, E. (eds.). *Doing Research on Crime and Justice* (2nd ed.). Oxford: Oxford University Press.

---

2 Write one sentence summarizing the writer's *stance* in relation to crime victim surveys.

3 List the points made by the writer against victim surveys. Which of these were also mentioned in Texts 1 / 2?

4 Work in groups. Compare your answers to 1, 2, and 3. Discuss how Texts 1 / 2 and Text 3 are similar and how they differ in terms of how they approach the topic. Take into account the type of publication, audience, and purpose.

5 Discuss how the *perspectives* chosen by the two writers affect their *stance.*

   • How different is the stance of each writer?

   • What do you think might be included in the rest of the chapter?

   • If the writers met for a discussion about victim surveys, would they agree or disagree?

Many academic writing tasks involve incorporating data or **statistics** from published sources, and possibly from your own research. Incorporating data into a piece of writing involves not just inserting **graphs** and charts, but also commenting on the data. This **commentary** may involve explaining the relevance of the data to the overall aim or thesis of the text, highlighting significant, interesting, or surprising features of the data, and then interpreting and evaluating it in terms of the wider context.

This module covers:
- Interpreting data in visual form and writing a commentary
- Decoding and constructing complex noun phrases

TASK 1 Understanding data in visual form

1 **You are going to read an extract from an article entitled *The international ban on ivory sales and its effects on elephant poaching in Africa*. Discuss, giving reasons:**
   - what overall effect you would expect a ban on ivory sales to have on elephant poaching
   - what type of data you think the article might present.

2 **Read Text 1. Answer the questions.**
   1 This is Figure 2 – what data do you think will have been shown in Figure 1?
   2 What period does the data cover and why is this period significant?
   3 What other information do you need to fully understand the graph?
   4 How many countries is the data collected from?
   5 What does 'NA' mean next to one of the points on the graph curve?
   6 Does the data show the trend you might expect in this context? Why (not)?

TEXT 1

The international ban on ivory sales and its effects on elephant poaching in Africa

Post-ban population changes

Figure 2 shows the changes in Africa's elephant populations for the post-ban period for 36 of the 37 elephant range states.[4] The data again take the shape of a sigmoidal or S-shaped curve, with some countries having gained elephants, while the population of others continued to decline. The range for this data set extends between a loss of **just over** 60,000 elephants (DRC) and a gain of **nearly** 125,000 animals (Botswana).

Figure 2: Elephant population changes by African country (1989–2007)
Arranged from greatest losses to greatest gains

[4] Eritrea was excluded because of insufficient data.

SOURCE: Lemieux, A. & Clarke, R. (2009). pp.459–460. The international ban on ivory sales and its effects on elephant poaching in Africa. *British Journal of Criminology*, 49(4): 451–471.

---

3 **What is the purpose of the paragraph above the graph?**
   a a detailed description of the data in the graph
   b a general summary of what the graph shows
   c an interpretation of what the graph shows

1 **Read Text 2, which follows the graph in Text 1. Identify the three sentences which summarize the three conclusions drawn from the graph data.**

TEXT 2

Three conclusions can be drawn from the data in Figure 2. First, it appears the ban helped to increase the overall number of elephants in Africa by about 140,000 between 1989 and 2007. Eighteen countries had increases in their populations post-ban, one third of which added more than 10,000 animals each. Two of the countries, Kenya (5) and Tanzania (2), are particularly important, as they suffered greatly from poaching in pre-ban years. Second, the ban has been effective at slowing the off-take of elephants from some countries that have continued to lose them. Thus, the loss of 60,000 elephants in the DRC (1) between 1989 and 2007 was one-fifth of the number of elephants lost in the DRC during the pre-ban period. Third, the international ban has not yet benefited every African country. As in the pre-ban years, a few countries are accounting for much of the total loss on the continent. In fact, since 1989, nearly 180,000 elephants were lost in 17 countries with declining populations; 110,000 of these were lost in the DRC (1) and Congo (34) combined. The other three countries accounting for a large proportion of elephant losses are the Central African Republic (6), Zambia (4) and Angola (21). Much like the unregulated ivory markets, elephant loss was concentrated in Central Africa. This region lost more than 130,000 elephants in the post-ban years. Only two of the seven countries saw population increases, which amounted to a total of about 4,000 elephants. The following sections will argue this is the result of the continued presence of unregulated ivory markets within and near these countries.

SOURCE: Lemieux, A. & Clarke, R. (2009). pp.459–460. The international ban on ivory sales and its effects on elephant poaching in Africa. *British Journal of Criminology*, 49(4): 451–471.

2 **Quickly read Text 2 again and find examples of:**

1 highlighting significant features / trends in the data
2 suggesting reasons for some of the specific features / trends in the data
3 drawing overall conclusions from the data
4 comparing this data to the previous data set (in Figure 1)
5 giving specific figures to support points
6 linking to wider analysis of the situation.

ACADEMIC LANGUAGE
▸Language reference page 206

Noun phrases (3) Multiple postmodifiers

In academic writing, you can make it clearer what you are referring to by describing a main or **head noun** in more detail:

> There have been **changes** … – Changes in what? When? Where? How? Why?

Long noun phrases are a concise way of specifying exactly what you are referring to. In such noun phrases, the head noun is typically followed by one or more phrases, known as *postmodifiers*, which describe and define it. Postmodifiers can be prepositional phrases, relative clauses, or a combination of both.

• **head noun** + one or more prepositional phrases:

> the **changes** in Africa's elephant populations for the post-ban period for 36 of the 37 elephant range states

• quantifier / determiner + **head noun** + non-finite clause (= in which the <u>main verb</u> is not in a tense / modal form, but in a non-finite form, i.e. participle (*-ing* / *-ed*) or *to* … form):

> one-fifth of the number of **elephants** <u>lost</u> in the DRC during the pre-ban period

• **head noun** + prepositional phrase(s) + finite clause (= relative clause in which the <u>main verb</u> is in a tense / modal form)

> the **off-take** of elephants from some countries that <u>have continued</u> to lose them

TASK 3 Decoding and constructing long noun phrases

1 **Work in pairs. For each long noun phrase 1–4:**
- identify the head noun
- break the phrase down into parts, as in the example
- explain what kind of information each phrase gives about the head noun.

speed / size of decline   *head noun*   *decline in what*   *non-defining relative clause showing reason for decline*

Example: *a sharp **decline** in the African elephant population, which resulted from widespread poaching for ivory in the previous decade*

reason for poaching   *when*   *extent of poaching*

1 a case study of abalone poaching in South Africa and its impact on fisheries management
2 ex situ conservation status of an endangered Yangtze finless porpoise population as measured from microsatellites
3 the conservation management implications of potential augmentation of the wild population with immigrants from the captive population
4 a criterion to evaluate the effectiveness of several conservation measures that have been undertaken or proposed for the American lobster fishery in Newfoundland

2 **Make four noun phrases to describe data or statistics, using words from the list and adding any extra words. Use structures including prepositional phrases and relative and non-finite clauses.**

decline   development   global   individual   natural   percentage
population   proportion   region   rise   society   technology

Example: *the **proportion** of the **population** of the **region** with access to internet **technology***

TASK 4 Writing a data commentary – the data

1 **Look at Figure 1. Make brief notes about the main points. Cover:**
- the overall topic
- the specific data sets
- the most noticeable features / trends.

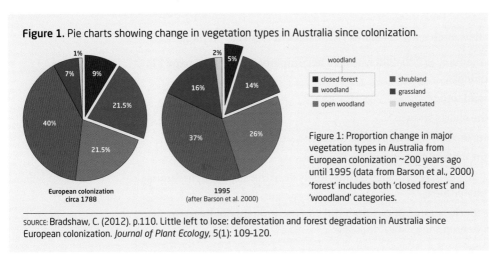

Figure 1. Pie charts showing change in vegetation types in Australia since colonization.

Legend: closed forest, woodland, open woodland, shrubland, grassland, unvegetated

European colonization circa 1788
1995 (after Barson et al. 2000)

Figure 1: Proportion change in major vegetation types in Australia from European colonization ~200 years ago until 1995 (data from Barson et al., 2000) 'forest' includes both 'closed forest' and 'woodland' categories.

SOURCE: Bradshaw, C. (2012). p.110. Little left to lose: deforestation and forest degradation in Australia since European colonization. *Journal of Plant Ecology*, 5(1): 109–120.

2 **Write four sentences describing noticeable features or trends in the data.**

3 **Compare sentences in pairs and discuss:**
- what you understand by the different categories in the data (*shrubland*, etc.)
- why you chose specific features or trends
- possible reasons for these features or trends.

1 **Read Texts 3–5, which include discussions about the topic in Task 4 from different sources. Make notes about:**
   - the possible reasons for the features and/or trends you noted above
   - the possible effects of these trends
   - the wider context.

TEXT 3

Land clearance in Australia, as elsewhere in the world, is driven by the inexorably increasing human population and demand for socio-economic development. Land clearing has focused on better soils because of cultural traditions in agriculture, and society's recognition of the importance of 'good' soils to a nation's development. As a result, from 1861 to the end of the nineteenth century, large areas were extensively cleared and potentially commercial forests were destroyed.

SOURCE: Braithwaite, L.W. (1996). Conservation of arboreal herbivores: the Australian scene. *Australian Journal of Ecology*, 21: 21-30.

TEXT 4

It is worrisome in its own right that Australia has been subjected to such broadscale deforestation when, in global terms, the country had little forest cover to begin with. What is perhaps more distressing is that much of the remaining vegetation is highly fragmented, disturbed or ecologically compromised (Gill & Williams, 1996), to the point where many plant and animal species have already gone extinct or are in immediate danger of extinction (Lindenmayer, 2007; Norton, 1996).

SOURCE: Bradshaw, C. (2012). p.114. Little left to lose: deforestation and forest degradation in Australia since European colonization. *Journal of Plant Ecology*, 5(1): 109-120.

TEXT 5

Asia currently has the greatest concentration of areas of rapid land-cover changes, and dryland degradation in particular. The Amazon basin remains a major hotspot of tropical deforestation. Rapid cropland increase, often associated with large-scale deforestation, is prominent in south-east Asia. Forest degradation in Siberia, mostly related to logging activities, is increasing rapidly. Many of the most populated and rapidly changing cities are found in the tropics.

SOURCE: Lepers, E., Lambin, E.F., Janetos, A.C., DeFries, R., Achard, F., Ramankutty, N., & Scholes, R.J. (2005). p.122. A synthesis of information on rapid land-cover change for the period 1981-2000. *BioScience*, 55: 115-24.

2 **Work in groups. Discuss how each extract relates to the data in Figure 1 on page 111.**

3 **Work alone. Write a commentary of 200–250 words to accompany Figure 1 on page 111. Include the following elements.**
   - Introduce the background topic.
   - Briefly describe what the charts show.
   - Highlight the interesting features / trends in the data (two or three points only).
   - Suggest possible reasons for features / trends in the data.
   - Evaluate the data. Note any effects, and give a short analysis of the situation, including implications for the wider context.
   - Give in-text references for the source of any material you use (you do not need to include a bibliography or reference list for this task).

Structure the text in the way that best expresses the key ideas; you do not have to follow the order above.

TASK 6 Proofreading and editing your writing

1 Proofread your text from Task 5, looking out for the following.

- **noun phrases**
  Have you used noun phrases to describe the data concisely and exactly?

- **hedging / evaluation**
  Have you used appropriate hedging language, e.g. *may, seem, potentially* (see **3B** on page 045) in your interpretation and evaluative comments?

- **in-text references**
  Have you correctly attributed any sources?

2 Work in pairs. Exchange texts and give constructive feedback on the points below. Comment on positive features as well as pointing out things which could be improved.

1 Does the text fulfil the brief (including all the points in Task 5.3)?

2 Is the language clear and accurate so that it does not misrepresent the information?

3 Is information from sources correctly referenced?

3 Use ideas from your partner to help you edit your text before submitting your final draft.

TASK 7 Independent research – visual data across disciplines

1 Find at least three examples of texts in books or journal articles from your own discipline that contain visual data (graphs, tables, diagrams, etc.). If possible, make a copy or printout of the relevant page.

2 For each text, note down:

- the source of the data (e.g. the author's own research data, official statistics, etc.)

- how the visual is referred to in the accompanying text (search for the word *figure, table*, etc.).
  Examples: *Figure 4 presents ...; It can be seen from Table 2 that ...*

3 Compare in class. Which of the following visuals did you find? Add any others.

bar chart   diagram   flow chart   graph   histogram   map   pie chart   table

4 Discuss any similarities and differences you found between disciplines in terms of:

- the type of visuals

- the type and sources of data

- the way the visuals were referred to in the text.

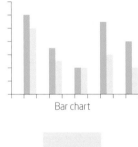

Bar chart

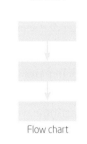

Flow chart

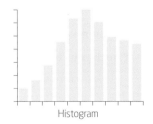

Histogram

Presentations by other students or visiting speakers often cover the findings of their research or some aspect of their area of specialization. Oral presentations often involve objective evidence in the form of facts or data, along with the speaker's own interpretation and evaluation. It is important to distinguish the speaker's evaluative comments in order to see how their ideas fit in with your own and with other sources, such as from your reading. By preparing critical questions as you listen, you will be ready to participate in a question and answer session or discussion at the end of the presentation.

This module covers:
- Understanding visual data in a presentation
- Distinguishing between evidence and evaluation
- Critically evaluating a presentation

TASK 1 Understanding visual data in a presentation   *blurd & clear*

1 Work in groups. You are going to watch a presentation entitled *Work–life balance in the modern labour market*. Discuss:
- what you understand by the term *work–life balance*
- what type of factual evidence or data the speaker might present on this topic.

2 ▶7.1 Watch Extract 1, the introduction to the presentation. Complete the outline structure of the presentation.

Part 1	average ...working hours... & general trends in ..labour market..
Part 2	'extensification' = pressure to ..work outsk office hours..

3 ▶7.2 Watch Extract 2, the first part of the presentation. Note the main points made for each slide. (Note that the presenter returns to an earlier slide to make further points.)

Slide 1: Average hours in the UK

Slide 2: Different sectors of the economy

Slide 3: Part-time working

4 Answer the questions about Extract 2.
1 Choose the statement which best describes how the speaker uses the data.
   a to show evidence of a change in working hours that affects work–life balance
   b to provide general background information about working hours in the UK
   c to illustrate how more people are choosing to work in sectors with shorter hours
2 What two variables affect the 'average working hours' statistics?

5 From your notes and memory, note down information relating to the points below. Watch Extract 2 again if necessary.

longer   same
shorter increase
   the construction sector   the manufacturing sector *decreas longer*
increase
   the service sector   agriculture *decrees*
increase
   part-time working   the 1990s recession → *number of partime people like fulltime increase*
   it mean bad economical situation

6 Work in pairs. Discuss how the points in 5 relate to:
- changes in the make-up of the UK economy
- part-time working.

7 To what extent does this section of the presentation focus on:
1 description and explanation of the data
2 interpretation and evaluation of the data?

Check your answers in transcript 7.2 on page 232.

TASK 2 Critical thinking – looking beyond the data

1 **Work in pairs. Look at Slide 3, about part-time working. Discuss:**

   1 the connection between the economic recession from 2008 onwards and the trend shown in the graph

   2 the possible effects on part-time workers wanting to work full-time from each of the following perspectives: economic, social, cultural, psychological.

2 **Ask critical questions about the data presented so far. Complete the questions below, and add at least one more question. Refer to Checklist K questions 5–10 on page 212 to check your ideas.**

   Example: How is the data *collected? Does it refer to contracted hours or actual hours worked?*

   • How is the data ...?

   • Has the presenter offered sufficient evidence to ...?

   • Is the evidence the most ...?

   • Does the evidence logically ...?

   • Has the presenter accurately interpreted ...?

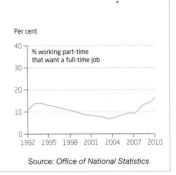

Part-time working

1992 onwards
Share of employment working part-time increasing

Part-time wanting full-time
Was around 14% following 1990s recession

In 2011 stood at 16% or around 1 in every 6 working part-time

Per cent

% working part-time that want a full-time job

40
30
20
10
0

1992 1995 1998 2001 2004 2007 2010

Source: *Office of National Statistics*

Slide 3

TASK 3 Distinguishing between evidence and evaluation

1 ▶7.3 **Watch Extract 3, the second part of the presentation. Use the headings on Slide 4 to make notes about the main points.**

2 **Work in pairs. Describe one example given in the presentation for each of the four bullet points in Slide 4.**

   Example: *For the first point, the speaker mentions families who live in cramped city centre apartments because the parents feel pressure to live near the centre for their job.*

3 **Look at transcript 7.3 on page 232. Answer the questions.**

   1 What source(s) of evidence does the speaker mention?

   2 What points does the speaker use the evidence to support?

4 **Match the three colours of the sections in transcript 7.3 to functions 1–3:**

   1 speaker's own comment and evaluation – ....

   2 supporting evidence from a stated source – ....

   3 supporting evidence, no source given – ....

Work-life balance in the modern labour market

Pratt & Jarvis (2006)
San Francisco new media study

• a flexible & mobile workforce
• 'overflow' & the role of new technologies
• 'intensification' > 'extensification'
• 'balance model' > 'depletion model'

Slide 4

TASK 4 Critically evaluating the content of a presentation

1 **Discuss in groups. To what extent is the data in Extract 2 relevant to the main topic?**

2 **How strong is the evidence presented in Extract 3?**

   a Is the San Francisco study relevant to the UK or elsewhere?

   b Is it acceptable to use evidence in a presentation without giving a source (e.g. the study about BlackBerry users)?

Oral presentations are part of the learning and assessment process in many universities. Their purpose is to help you improve and demonstrate your understanding of a topic, and to express ideas in your own words. Rather than just present a list of learnt 'facts' you should demonstrate your ability to interpret and evaluate information, and to put it into context. When you are presenting data you need to give enough information for your audience to understand the data and its relevance to the topic, without explaining every detail.

This module covers:

- Planning, researching, and rehearsing a short presentation of visual data
- Evaluating performance: format, description, interpretation, and stance

TASK 1 Critical thinking – evaluating the role of visual data

1 **Work in groups. Reflect on your own experiences of presenting. Discuss the importance of points a–e. Give examples from your subject area.**

a The data you choose will depend on your audience (e.g. expert or non-expert).

b Choose straightforward rather than complex graphics with a lot of detail.

c Give the source of all data, graphs, or charts on your slide.

d Describe what the axes refer to on a graph or chart, and the measurements used.

e Show how the data relates to the main topic or to the point you're making.

> Example: a – *I'm studying Economics. With economists, I'd use a chart showing the GDP of different countries; for a general audience, I'd explain what 'GDP' means.*

TASK 2 Planning and researching a short presentation

1 **You are going to give a short individual presentation. Read the Task and the guidelines.**

> **TASK:** *Give a five-minute presentation on a topic related to your subject area. It should be focused around a dataset presented in a visual (graph, chart, or table).*

Guidelines for giving a data presentation

1 Use a small number of slides (e.g. up to four), including a title slide and the visual itself.

2 Talk about the data from one (or two) specific perspective(s), and/or in relation to a particular question or issue.

3 Provide some background to the topic and put the data into context.

4 Include explanation of the data, interpretation, evaluation and your own stance.

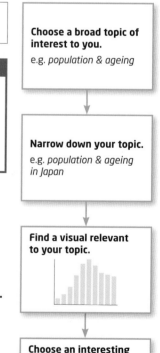

Choose a broad topic of interest to you.
e.g. *population & ageing*

Narrow down your topic.
e.g. *population & ageing in Japan*

Find a visual relevant to your topic.

Choose an interesting perspective on your topic.
e.g. *Japan's ageing population and its effect on the labour market*

2 **Choose a topic. Use the flowchart. Work in groups to discuss your initial ideas, then narrow them down.**

3 **Research your topic. Work alone on your chosen topic, using Checklist L on page 212 to find sources. Scan your sources for charts, graphs, or tables that present data. Decide which data to present.**

4 **Develop your material. Think about how you will do more than simply describe the data.**

1 Write down:

- **perspectives** to cover (social, economic, business, etc.)
- the **problem** or **issue**
  > Example: *With an ageing population, will people be forced to retire later?*
- your **stance**
  > Example: *As people live longer, the pension bill will become unaffordable, so later retirement will be unavoidable.*

2 Make brief notes under the following headings:
  introduction & **background** to topic   link to **wider context**
  presentation & **explanation** of data   your **stance** & **concluding comments**
  interpretation & **evaluation** of data

TASK 3 Rehearsing your presentation

1 Work in pairs. Informally present what you have so far: explain why you have chosen your topic and dataset, what perspective(s) to cover, and the stance you plan to take.

2 Ask your partner questions to clarify anything that you don't understand.

  Example: *When was this data published?*

ACADEMIC LANGUAGE

Signposting (3) Referring to visual data

When you include visual data as part of a presentation, make clear to your audience
- the overall topic and source of the data:
  __I have here some statistics on__ working hours __from__ the Office of National Statistics.
  __These figures are from__ the latest statistics __on__ ... __published by__ the government.
- what the visual shows in general terms:
  __This first graph shows how__ working hours have changed from 1992 to 2011.
  __This graph shows the relationship between__ ...
  So __every row in this table corresponds to__ ...
- the key trend or feature you want to highlight:
  __Looking at this next graph, we can see that__ the share of total employment that is part-time has been steadily increasing.
  __I want to focus your attention on this column__ here.
  __This table tells us something interesting about__ how ...

TASK 4 Presenting visual data

1 Look at the transcripts of the presentation in 7C on pages 231–232. Note any other useful expressions used to present visual data.

2 Prepare your five-minute presentation. Follow the steps below.
  - Use the information and ideas from Tasks 2 and 3. (You may not be able to include everything.)
  - Prepare your slides and rehearse your presentation to check the timing.
  - To help you remember your main points, prepare clear notes (e.g. next to a printout of your visuals, or each point on a small card), but not a detailed script.

3 Take turns to give your presentation to the class.

TASK 5 Evaluating performance

1 Think about the other presentations. Which students were particularly effective in these areas? Give examples.

  Presentation structure   Linking to wider context / issues
  Introduction and background   Evaluation and expression of stance
  Description of visual data   Format and clarity of slides
  Interpretation of data   Timing

2 Look at Checklist I on page 211. Note any other relevant criteria for evaluating presentations.

3 Think about your own performance. Choose at least two areas that you achieved successfully, and two areas that you need to work on before your next presentation.

1 In academic writing, it is important to specify exact details to your reader. Categorize the words in bold in sentences 1–9 in terms of their function:
a time or frequency
b the source of data
c method of data selection / analysis.

1 The **year-on-year** increase in global oil demand amounted to 3.1 per cent.

2 Many demographic studies are **based on** official census statistics.

3 Data is **derived from** a national survey conducted in 2012.

4 The results were **adjusted for** age and gender.

5 The 85 volunteers were **randomly selected** from a pool of 498 individuals between the ages of 45 and 64.

6 These **discrete** events can, however, be viewed as part of a **long-term** trend.

7 From the **available** data it is not possible to make further distinctions in terms of educational level.

8 **According to** the latest figures from the World Bank, the country's GDP grew at an average **annual** rate of 2.4 per cent.

9 Patients were **excluded from** the study if they were under the age of 18 years.

2 Choose four of the words or phrases in sentences 1–9 and use each in a new sentence describing data from this unit. Change the form of the words if necessary.

Example: *Crimes against children are currently **excluded from** the British Crime Survey data.*

7F Research Project (1)

Choosing a topic

What is a research project?

You are going to research, plan, and write up a project of 2,000–2,500 words based on a topic from your own discipline or area of interest. The aim of this research project is to find and read academic books and journals focusing on a specific topic or research question. You will then develop a working title around which to plan and write an extended piece of written work, based on your research and combining your own ideas with citations from sources.

Check with your tutor whether there are any specifications in terms of:

a word limit   c format
b deadline   d other criteria

Choose a topic that:

• **you are interested in.** You will spend a lot of time working with the topic and if you get bored, your motivation will drop.

• **you already know something about, but would like to learn more about.** If you choose a topic you have already studied in detail, there will be no new research to do; if you choose a topic you know nothing about, it may be difficult to assimilate all the new information.

• **you will be able to research.** You may not be able to find enough sources if your topic is too specialized, too focused on a specific context, or too new.

TO DO Stage 1: Initial research phase

Discuss your topic ideas with your tutor and other students. Search for two or three sources (academic books or journal articles) for your topic. How easy or difficult it is to find relevant sources will tell you how practical your topic may be to research. You may decide to completely change or slightly alter your topic at this stage.

UNIT 8 Influence

ACADEMIC FOCUS: CAUSE, EFFECT, AND ASSOCIATION

LEARNING OBJECTIVES

This unit covers:

Reading
- Identifying cause, effect, and association connections in a complex text
- Recognizing confident and tentative connections
- Exploring evaluation across texts

Writing
- Expressing cause and effect relationships coherently
- Researching, planning, and writing a cause and effect essay

Listening
- Reading a pre-lecture handout to prepare for a lecture
- Listening for facts, association, and evaluation

Speaking
- Gathering evidence for a seminar discussion
- Defending your argument using justifying and evaluation language

Vocabulary
- Word formation (1)

Research project (2)
- Establishing a working title

Discussion

1   **Work in groups. Look at the list. Discuss the factors that influence these things during a lifetime. Give examples.**

   Example: general health – *A person might be more or less healthy at different points depending on diet or exercise. Health is also influenced by genetic factors, which don't change.*

   - general health
   - physical fitness
   - general knowledge
   - subject knowledge
   - the local environment
   - society

2   **List factors from your discussion in 1 which are:**

   causes   effects   associations

   Examples: *An unbalanced diet may be one cause of poor general health.*
   Low income is often associated with poor health.

Academic texts frequently present, discuss, and evaluate complex connections. Phenomena can be connected by cause and effect relations and other, less strong, associations. In order to understand a text correctly, you need to accurately identify connections - **causes**, **effects**, and **associations** - between the phenomena in the text. As writers may present causes and effects in any order, you need to be familiar with the language used, e.g. verb phrases like *affect, result in, may be influenced by*. Writers typically evaluate connections, for instance by expressing their likelihood or seriousness.

This module covers:

- Identifying cause, effect, and association connections in a complex text
- Recognizing confident and tentative connections
- Exploring evaluation across texts

TASK 1 Identifying connections in a text

1 **Work in groups. Discuss how these factors can be connected through cause, effect, or association.**

   disease   height   household income   hygiene   number of children per family   overcrowding

   Example: *The number of children per family could affect household income, because ... / although ...*

2 **Read Text 1, the abstract of an article, and complete the notes.**

   Title / date of publication: *The effects on stature of poverty, family size, and birth order:* ....
   British children in the 1930s; pub. 2010 ....

   Genre, Audience, Purpose: ....

   Aim of research: ....

   Background and context of research: *original data is from Britain in 1937–9; analysis in* ....
   article is recent, 2010 ....

   Perspectives: ....

   Main findings: ....

The effects on stature of poverty, family size, and birth order: British children in the 1930s

TEXT 1

Abstract

This article examines the effects of socio-economic conditions on the standardized heights and body mass index (BMI) of children in interwar Britain, using the Boyd Orr cohort, a survey of predominantly poor families taken in 1937-9. We examine the trade-off between child quality (in the form of health outcomes) and the number of children in the family. We find that birth order and family size have negative effects on the heights of children, but not on their BMI. Household income *per capita* positively influences height but, even after accounting for this, the number of children in the family has a negative effect on height. This latter effect is closely associated with overcrowding and with the degree of cleanliness or hygiene in the household, which conditions exposure to factors predisposing to disease. We also analyse follow-up data, which indicates that the effects of family size on height persisted into adulthood.

SOURCE: Hatton, T.J. & Martin, R.M. (2010). The effects on stature of poverty, family size, and birth order: British children in the 1930s. *Oxford Economic Papers*, 62(1): 157-184.

GLOSSARY

cohort *(n)* a group of people who share a common feature

per capita *(adj / adv)* (from Latin) for each person

3 **Based on the information in Text 1, draw a diagram showing connections between the factors in the list in 1.**

4 Describe connections made in Text 1 using the verbs below.

  1 cause → effect: cause(s)   lead(s) to   result(s) in   bring(s) about

  2 effect → cause: is / are caused by   result(s) from

  3 association: is / are (typically) associated with
                 influence(s)
                 is / are / may be influenced by

5 Are there any factors in the list in 1 which are *not* connected?

TASK 2 Preparing to read a complex text

1 Quickly read Text 2, the conclusion of Text 1. Match main topics a–c to
  paragraphs 1–3.

  a The underlying factors influencing child health

  b The continuing effects of poor child health

  c The main causes of poor child health

TEXT 2

Conclusion

1 This paper contributes to the debate on the determinants of child quality using a unique dataset from 1930s Britain. It focuses on child health, as reflected by standardized height and BMI, in a sample of relatively poor households. [i] We find that **birth order and the number of children** both have **strong negative effects on height** but not on BMI. These results are consistent with **an interpretation that stresses the consequences of resource dilution within the household**. [ii] **The development literature** often interprets height as reflecting **enduring deprivation** (as it is cumulative) while BMI is typically associated with **short-run privations**. On that interpretation, the effects measured here capture the longer-term effects, which are likely to have prevailed throughout the childhood of those in the survey.

2 A question less often posed is whether there is a negative family size beyond that of simply diluting family income *per capita*, and if so, what channels of influence it represents. Our answer to the first question is that the number of children does have an independent negative effect and one that appears to be associated with the degree of crowding within the household. Our answer to the second question is suggestive rather than definitive. We find that the degree of cleanliness is important, a variable that is likely to be associated with the standard of hygiene and thus with the disease environment within the household. This in turn is negatively associated with the degree of crowding in the household and positively with income *per capita*. Better quality housing seems to reduce the effect of crowding on height, presumably through its effects on hygiene. [iii] Thus the two key channels through which **the number of children in a family affects the health status of children** is directly through **the reduction on food intake** and more indirectly through **the effect of crowding via the level of hygiene on the incidence of disease**.

3 Finally, there is evidence that these effects observed for children in the 1930s persisted into adulthood. Although our evidence here is less precise, it appears that poverty, family size and housing conditions influenced the height and the health of those who were prime-age adults in the early postwar period. These findings are consistent with other evidence showing that childhood height is a marker for bio-physiological processes that can affect future health. Reduced height is associated with increased risk of heart disease and stroke, the major causes of death in this cohort.

SOURCE: as Text 1

---

2 Note down any new information in the conclusion compared to the abstract (Text 1).

3 Work in pairs. Explain sentences (i)–(iii) highlighted in Text 2 in your own words.
  Focus on the noun phrases in bold. Refer to the context, and use a dictionary.

4 Compare explanations with other students. Discuss how you dealt with complex
  grammar and vocabulary. Why do the authors use this kind of language?

TASK 3 Identifying connections in a text

1 Look at the table below, and focus on the underlined factors in Text 2 paragraphs 1 and 2 on page 121. Complete the table to show the connections between factors.

	Factor 1	Factor 2	Connection
1	birth order & no. of children	height	negative effect
2	birth order & no. of children	BMI	no effect
3	enduring deprivation		association
4	short-run privations		association
5	hygiene	cleanliness	
6		disease	
7	degree of household crowding		
8	better quality housing		
9		child health status	cause → effect
10	reduced food intake	child health status	

2 Read paragraph 3 of Text 2 again and identify at least two connections between factors in childhood and adult health.

ACADEMIC LANGUAGE   ▸Language reference pages 202, 203, 205

Connection (1) Confident and tentative interpretations

When academic writers express connections, it is important that they make it clear how strong those connections are and how confident they are about their interpretation of the data.

Strong cause and effect For a strong cause and effect connection, supported by evidence, such as the statistical analysis of research data, the connection can be expressed confidently:

*We find that birth order and the number of children both **have strong negative effects on** height but not on BMI.*

Clear association Sometimes evidence points to factors that are clearly associated, but do not constitute a direct cause and effect relationship. These connections can also be expressed confidently, using expressions such as *associated with, influenced by, an important factor in*, etc.:

*Reduced height is **associated with** increased risk of heart disease and stroke.*

Tentative interpretation of connections Where the evidence is less conclusive, writers show their degree of confidence in their interpretation using hedging language:

*Better quality housing **seems to** reduce the effect of crowding on height, **presumably** through its effects on hygiene.*

***Although our evidence here is less precise, it appears that** poverty, family size and housing conditions **influenced** the height and the health of those who were prime-age adults in the early postwar period.*

TASK 4 Recognizing confident and tentative interpretation

1 For each sentence, decide the type of connection and whether the interpretation is confident or tentative. Identify the connection language.

1 Thus family income and demographics affect the overall size of children as reflected in height.

2 These results support the idea that health is influenced not only by food intake but also by the disease environment.

3 Repeated infection may have a cumulative effect on height, particularly when food supply is limited.

4 These trends are often associated with rising income and nutrition, improving public sanitation and better housing conditions, and possibly better medical conditions and school environments.

5 Previous studies of the Boyd Orr cohort indicate that there is a strong correlation between measures such as height and leg length observed during childhood and the same measures observed in adulthood.

2 In the sentences in 1, decide whether the writers are expressing their own interpretations of the data or those of others.

3 Look back at Text 2 on page 121 and identify examples of language expressing:

a cause–effect connection

b association

c tentative interpretation.

4 Select three or four connections from the table in 3.1 and express them in sentences using a range of connection language.

Example: *Hatton and Martin (2010) report that birth order and number of children in a family have a strong negative effect on children's height.*

TASK 5 Understanding complex connection language in a text

1 Read Text 3 and make notes about key information. Use the headings in Task 1.2.

TEXT 3

Family influences and parenting

Families are **a potent influence both on** a child's genetic constitution **and**, as we have seen in the last section, **on** their health and related behaviour. The family **also** constitutes a child's immediate social network **and** has **a vital influence on** the development of socio-emotional health **and** wellbeing.

Family size and structure

Until fairly recently, epidemiological studies of **the influence of** families **on** children's growth and development have concentrated on easily measurable **determinants** such as family size and structure. In industrialized countries, **both of these factors** have changed dramatically over the last century, and these changes have had **a major influence on** the way children are looked after.

Large family size is a distinctive feature in most low-income countries and has been the focus of much aid and education by industrialized countries. These efforts have often been ineffective, and there is now a much better understanding of how reproductive decisions are taken. **The key factors in** reducing family size in developing countries **are** increasing income (**so that** children are not seen as an economic necessity), educating women, **and** making contraceptive advice available throughout the health service. Countries such as Kerala (a state of Southern India) and Sri Lanka, which have focused on **these factors**, have had remarkable success in reducing fertility. Family size and short birth interval are **important predictors of** nutritional status, but far more of the earth's resources are used by the small families of the industrialized countries rather than the large families of the poor world. The average family size in the UK is now 1.9 children, meaning that only children are now more common and large siblingships are rare. However, the latter are a risk factor for poverty in the developed as well as in the developing world.

Partly as a result of changing gender attitudes and expectations, **which have given** women greater financial independence, marital breakdown is now very common. Forty per cent of first marriages end in divorce, and in England and Wales in 2007, nearly one in four children (a total of 2,672,000 dependent children) lived in lone-parent families, over 90% of which are headed by the mother. More than one in ten dependent children (1,284,000) live in a step-family (ONS). The latter **are more prone to** break down than first-time marriages, so many children move in and out of different family structures throughout their childhood. While these changes create problems for many children, for some they **may be a source of** resilience. Becoming a single parent **is almost inevitably associated with** a drop in family income, and marital breakdown is **therefore an important cause of** childhood poverty.

SOURCE: Blair, M., Stewart-Brown, S., Waterston, T., & Crowther, R. (2010). p.59. *Child Public Health* (2nd ed.). Oxford: Oxford University Press.

GLOSSARY

epidemiological *(adj)* related to the scientific study of the spread and control of disease

2 List all the factors mentioned in Text 3 which can influence developmental outcome.

Example: *poverty*

3 **Work in pairs. Respond to and discuss the following points made in the first half of Text 3. Give reasons and examples to support your position.**

1 The family has a vital influence on the development of a child's socio-emotional health.

2 Changes in family size and structure in industrialized countries have had a major influence on the way children are looked after.

3 Educating women in developing countries is a key factor in reducing family size.

4 Far more of the earth's resources are used by small families in industrialized countries than by large families in the poor world.

4 **Select one or two points in the rest of the text that you find interesting. Quickly compare responses.**

5 **Put the bold connection language in Text 3 into the following categories.**

1	Connecting a cause to an effect / introducing an effect	*Families are **a potent influence both on** a child's genetic constitution **and on** their health and related behaviour.*
2	Connecting an effect to a cause / introducing a cause	***The key factors in** reducing family size in developing countries are increasing income …*
3	Expressing an association	*Large siblingships are **a risk factor for** poverty.*

6 **Compare answers. Decide whether each item in 5 is confident or tentative.**

Example: *'a potent influence … on' expresses a cause–effect connection confidently*

TASK 6 Critical thinking – exploring evaluation across texts

1 **Work in pairs. Select and organize information from Texts 1–3 on the theme of *poverty*.**

Cover:

• connections between poverty and other factors (causes, effects, associations)

• references to source text(s)

• authors' evaluations of connection, e.g. *remarkable success* (Text 3).

2 **Work in groups. Choose one of the themes below, and follow the procedure in 1. Use your preferred note-taking technique. Prepare to present your findings.**

child health   diet and nutrition   family size

3 **Take turns to present your chosen theme based on your notes.**

4 **Critically respond to the authors' evaluations. Discuss the questions.**

1 Is the evaluation based on convincing evidence?

2 Which perspective(s) inform the evaluation (e.g. medical, cultural, western)?

3 Is the evaluation generalizable across different cultures and contexts, e.g. does it apply in so-called developing and developed countries?

4 How far do you agree with the authors' evaluations of connection? Why?

8B Writing Cause and effect essays

Essays are frequently based on a discussion of causes and effects. An essay may be weighted more towards causes, or effects, or may balance both. The cause and effect material can be embedded in a complex structure, for example, an examination of the causes of a problem, followed by a discussion of possible solutions. Where cause and effect connection is not certain, you may have to speculate on the present or past connection (*This may result from …* / *may have resulted from …*). You need to include evaluation, integrated throughout the essay or 'blocked' in a paragraph (usually) before the conclusion. When writing about cause and effect, you need to ensure coherence by making the connections clear using cause and effect language.

This module covers:
- Expressing cause and effect relationships coherently
- Researching, planning, and writing a cause and effect essay

TASK 1 Speculating on cause and effect relationships

1 **Work in pairs. Note down at least three possible causes for scenarios 1–5.**

Example: 1 *This child might be feeling stressed as a result of workload, or might have had a negative experience of talking about problems at home, or …*

1 A 13-year-old child has become withdrawn, returning from school every day clearly unhappy but reluctant to speak to anyone.

2 Despite being a below-average school student, a 40-year-old has achieved great academic success.

3 A cancer patient believed to be in remission has recently not been responding to treatment.

4 A promising student has just done surprisingly badly in their exams.

5 Despite increasing economic development in some countries, unhappiness and depression appear to be increasing.

2 **Think of possible *effects* for the scenarios in 1.**

Example: 4 *The child may eventually refuse to go to school, or …*

3 **Think about the causes and effects you have identified. Answer the questions.**

1 How strong is the connection between cause and effect?
2 How serious / widespread is the effect?
3 Will the situation get better / worse? Why?
4 Could the effect be / have been avoided? How?

4 **Use the following diagrams expressing cause and effect connections to illustrate examples from this task. Which diagram do you prefer?**

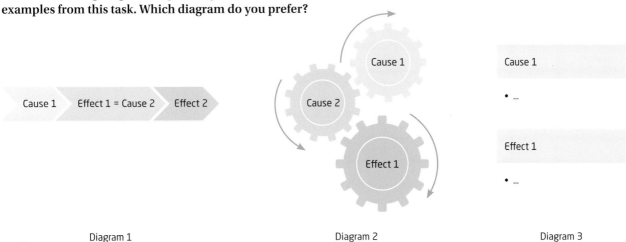

Diagram 1   Diagram 2   Diagram 3

TASK 2 Writing a cause-effect and evaluation paragraph

1 Read the paragraph from a student essay. Which scenario in Task 1 does it relate to?

> [1]There are a number of possible causes of educational underachievement. [2]A symptom of such underachievement might be a promising student doing badly in her exams. [3]The student's poor marks may result from her own behaviour. [4]She might have become demotivated and not worked hard enough, or she might have developed emotional problems as a result of her relationships with her friends and family. [5]Alternatively, there may be another reason for her underachievement which is essentially beyond her control, because she has been bullied, for example. [6]A different category of explanation for her academic failure could be medical: in cases of Attention Deficit / Hyperactivity Disorder (ADHD), young people 'who show symptoms of inattention, hyperactivity, and impulsivity with or without formal diagnoses of ADHD also show poor academic and educational outcomes' (Loe & Feldman, 2007: p.643). [7]While any of these causes may have led to the student's underachievement, the effects are likely to be similar, whether loss of confidence or a negative cycle of failure and lowered expectations. [8]However, one poor set of exam results does not necessarily mean permanent failure; therefore it is never too late to change a pattern of behaviour.
>
> **Reference**
> Loe, I.M. & Feldman, H. (2007). Academic and educational outcomes of children with ADHD. *Journal of Pediatric Psychology*, 32(6): 643-654.

2 Note down all the different possible causes given in the paragraph in 1.

3 Sentence 1 states the topic of the paragraph. Decide how each sentence 2–8 builds on the topic. Does it:

speculate on possible cause(s)?   speculate on possible effect(s)?
give an example?   evaluate?

4 What kind of interpretation and evaluation does the writer give: tentative, neutral, or confident? Identify the language used.

5 Read the paragraph again. Identify examples of cause and effect language. Decide whether each item is confident or tentative.

6 Look back at your ideas in Task 1 for a different scenario. Write a paragraph summarizing the main points you discussed.

TASK 3 Exploring cause and effect essay structures

1 Work in pairs. Look at the four example essay structures. Match them to outline plans a–d opposite.

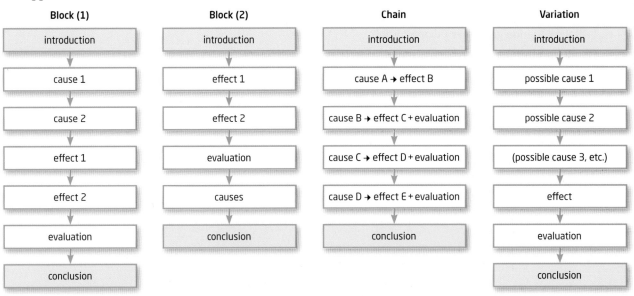

Block (1)	Block (2)	Chain	Variation
introduction	introduction	introduction	introduction
cause 1	effect 1	cause A → effect B	possible cause 1
cause 2	effect 2	cause B → effect C + evaluation	possible cause 2
effect 1	evaluation	cause C → effect D + evaluation	(possible cause 3, etc.)
effect 2	causes	cause D → effect E + evaluation	effect
evaluation	conclusion	conclusion	evaluation
conclusion			conclusion

2 Compare answers. Discuss the differences between the essay structures in terms of:

a the main emphasis   c which are most / least widely applicable and why.

b the balance of content

Example: *Block (2) emphasizes the effects; Variation gives more space to the causes.*

a *Chain*

TITLE: *Discuss the relationship between child poverty and health.*

Introduction
Poverty & poor housing → poor hygiene
Poor hygiene → disease environment (+ evaluation)
Disease environment → poor child health & development (+ evaluation)
Poor child health & development → risk factors for heart disease & stroke in later life (+ evaluation)
Conclusion Implications for policy: focus on child poverty, esp. housing → lower health & welfare costs.

c

TITLE: *To what extent have the recent changes in UK examinations led to a decline in standards?*

Introduction
Easier exams & more coursework = 'dumbing down'
Generally improved standards of teaching & education
Statistics show continued increase in school exam grades & higher % university entrants
Two stances: 1) dumbing down 2) standards improving
Conclusion Improvement can't only be due to better teaching – important that exam standards do not drop.

b

TITLE: *Discuss the causes of stress on modern children.*

Introduction
More pressure on students to get higher grades in 'competitive' school system
Increased peer pressure to keep up with latest trends & gadgets
Children tired, stressed & burnt out
Parents pressured to buy gadgets → increased debt in poor families
Reflects changes in society & social pressures generally
Conclusion Children need to enjoy childhood. Suggestions for change.

d

TITLE: *Discuss the effects of an increased % of students going on to higher education in the UK.*

Introduction
Positive: – less elitist, more social mobility – greater range of courses
Negative: – 'dumbing down' of courses – a university degree has less value
Important for universities to balance greater participation with maintaining standards
Increase in school-leaving grades; financial pressure on unis to expand student nos.
Conclusion Ref to other countries → implications for UK unis in global education market.

ACADEMIC LANGUAGE ▸ Language reference pages 202, 203, 205

Connection (2) Expressing cause and effect coherently

Cause and effect **connections** can be expressed using a range of nouns, verbs, and other expressions. You may need to try several possibilities to find the construction that expresses a connection most accurately and coherently. You may also want to include **speculative** or **hedging language** to show your degree of confidence.

Nouns used to express

- a **cause** - *cause, reason, source, explanation, root*:
  There are a number of **possible reasons** for educational underachievement.

- an **effect** - *effect, result, consequence, outcome, impact*:
  The **effects** are **likely to be** similar.

Verbs used to express

- a **cause → effect** connection - *cause, affect, lead to, result in, bring about, prompt*:
  Any of these causes **may have led to** the student's underachievement.

- an **effect → cause** connection - *result from, originate from, derive from, stem from*:
  A student's poor marks **may stem from** her own behaviour.

The passive form of verbs can often be used to express an **effect → cause** connection:

A student's poor marks **could be caused by** her own behaviour.

Other expressions used to signal

- a **cause → effect** relationship - *therefore, accordingly, thus, so that*:
  Therefore it is never too late to change a pattern of behaviour.

- an **effect → cause** relationship - *as a result of, due to, because (of), on account of, owing to*:
  She **might have** developed emotional problems **as a result of** her relationships with her family.
  Her underachievement was **partly because** she was bullied at school.

TASK 4 Using cause and effect structures

1 Join 1–6 with a–f using an expression from the list.

because   can be caused by   can sometimes result in
is one possible effect of   owing to   typically leads to

1 A poor diet in childhood	a a low-calorie diet.
2 The clinical trial failed	b repeated exposure to amplified music.
3 Lack of energy	c health problems in later life.
4 Unemployment and poverty	d dehydration or stress.
5 Musicians can develop hearing problems	e the incorrect dosage was given.
6 Headaches	f serious social problems and even crime.

2 Which word / phrase in each set has a different meaning?

1 cause, impact, influence, reason, source

2 association, consequence, effect, outcome, result

3 can lead to, could bring about, may account for, may cause, might result in

4 consequently, moreover, so, therefore, thus

5 as, because, for, since, so that

6 as a result of, because of, due to, in relation to, owing to

3 Rewrite the sentences in 1 using suitable language items from 2. Make any minor changes.

Example: 1 *A poor diet in childhood* **can lead to** *health problems in later life.*

TASK 5 Analysing a cause and effect essay

1 Work in pairs. Read the essay title and the student's initial notes below. Discuss how to organize the notes using a suitable essay structure from Task 3.

> **TITLE:** *Identify two major causes of underachievement in education. What effects might these have on children's future lives?*

Opening statement: the case of an underachieving student / child from literature / film

Key term: 'underachievement' – define

Background and context: money, funding, expectations, poor teaching, poor facilities, other disruptive students, poor parenting, school curriculum

Key factors:
- parental background (Triventi, 2011)
- migration? (Wu *et al.*, 2010)
- dedication / ability to study independently
- health, mental well-being – depression
- ADHD (Loe & Feldman, 2007)
- distractions, e.g. relationships

Effects: vicious circle of underachievement, poor job, low self-esteem and self-confidence

Conclusion: the most important are expectations and parents, although mental health is significant; poor facilities are not that important

Food for thought: these causes can become cyclical, resulting in the student's own children repeating the same cycle

References
Loe, I.M. & Feldman, H. (2007). Academic and educational outcomes of children with ADHD. *Journal of Pediatric Psychology*, 32(6): 643-654.
Triventi, M. (2011). Stratification in higher education and its relationship with social inequality: a comparative study of 11 European countries. *European Sociological Review*.
Wu, Q., Palinkas, L.A., & He, X. (2010). An ecological examination of social capital effects on the academic achievement of Chinese migrant children. *British Journal of Social Work*, 40(8): 2578-2597.

2 Read the student's cause and effect essay on page 218–9. Identify which essay structure in Task 3.1 it most closely follows and any ways in which it differs.

3 Which points from the initial notes were *not* used in the final essay? Discuss why.

4 Match sections 1–10 in the student's essay with functions a–j below.

Example: 1 = *h – opening statement to gain the reader's interest*

a   acknowledgement of limitations

b   conclusion

c   definition of key term in title

d   discussion of possible clinical psychological causes

e   discussion of possible socio-economic causes

f   discussion of possible personal psychological causes

g   effects

h   opening statement to gain the reader's interest

i   reference to the wider context

j   thesis statement

5 Identify specific examples of evaluation in the essay. Where is the evaluation expressed?

TASK 6 Refining and focusing the title of an essay

1 You are going to write a cause and effect essay. Work alone or with students from a similar academic discipline. Focus on the theme of 'influence' and select a topic related to your current or future study.

2 Refine and focus your title using the stages below.

1   Narrow down and contextualize the subject matter, e.g. by limiting it to a geographical place, historical time, and/or social context.

2   Decide on the causes and effects in your essay.

3   Formulate a working title for your essay. Express this as a statement or a question.

Example: Topic: *languages – influences on languages except English / last 50 years*
Causes: *digitization, …*
Effects: *language of internet is English …*
Working title: *A discussion of the effects of the digitization of literature on languages apart from English. OR What are the main effects of the digitization of literature on languages apart from English?*

TASK 7 Researching and planning a cause and effect essay

1 Research your topic.

1   Search for two or three academic sources for your essay to meet the needs of your title.

2   Examine the cause and effect connections from different perspectives.

3   Make notes and develop evidence and examples to support your argument.

4   Carefully note down reference details for all sources.

2 Plan your essay using an appropriate structure and Checklist G on page 210.

TASK 8 Writing and evaluating a cause and effect essay

1 Write your essay, aiming for 1,000 words. Follow your preferred writing process based on the stages in 1B Task 3 on page 014.

2 Check your use of cause and effect language. Make sure it correctly expresses the causes and effects and appropriate certainty or tentativeness.

Example: (confident) *the major cause of x is y → a probable cause of x is y → y may / can result in x* (tentative)

3 Critically evaluate your essay using Checklist H on page 210. Check that the cause and effect connections are coherent.

Lecturers frequently present and discuss cause and effect connections in the past, present, or future. In many contexts it can be difficult to establish a clear cause and effect connection between two phenomena, therefore the connection is likely to be an association instead. Depending on the subject matter and context, the amount of speculation and degree of certainty can vary. You need to listen closely to the lecturer's presentation of different phenomena and choice of language to accurately identify how they are connected.

This module covers:

- Reading a pre-lecture handout to prepare for a lecture
- Listening for facts, association, and evaluation

TASK 1 Preparing – reading a pre-lecture handout

1 You are going to watch part of a medical lecture on strokes. Quickly read the pre-lecture handout on page 220, and note down the *genre*, *audience*, and *purpose*.

2 Read the handout again in detail, and label sections a–f.
- background information
- causes
- definition
- people affected
- symptoms, process, and diagnosis
- specialist information

3 Match the words in the list with definitions 1–6.

diagnosis .... impact .... prevention .... prognosis .... risk .... symptom ....

1 the powerful effect that sth has on sb / sth
2 the act of discovering or identifying the exact cause of an illness or problem
3 a change in your body or mind that shows that you are not healthy
4 the act of stopping sth bad from happening
5 the possibility of something bad happening in the future
6 an opinion, based on medical experience, of the likely development of an illness

TASK 2 Listening for essential factual information

1 ▷8.1 Look at Slide 1 and watch Extract 1. Make notes on the aims and content of the lecture.

2 Which points in Slide 1 have you already read about in the pre-lecture handout?

3 ▷8.2 Look at Slide 2. Then watch Extract 2 and note down the facts and figures given in the lecture. Listen *both* for the numbers *and* note what they refer to.

Example: / 2 seconds – worldwide sb has stroke

4 Compare answers. Express the information in full spoken form.

Example: Every two seconds, worldwide, somebody has a stroke.

5 ▷8.3 Look at the definitions of the following terms highlighted in the pre-lecture handout. Watch Extract 3 and compare the lecturer's definitions of the terms.
- stroke
- ischaemic stroke
- brain haemorrhage (haemorrhagic stroke)

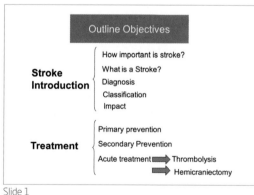

Slide 1

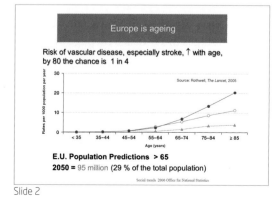

Slide 2

Connection (3) Association, speculation, and degree of certainty

In many contexts, cause and effect connections are not certain, and may be expressed more cautiously as associations. Listen for tentative expressions which indicate the speaker's degree of confidence in terms of possibility, frequency, probability, etc., especially using a **modal verb + main verb** and adverbs.

- Possibility:
  Blood vessels are involved, not necessarily a neurological event, where brain tissue ***may be involved***.
  Examination is obviously important in terms of … the risk factors that cause the stroke, or potentially cause the stroke, for example, problems with the carotid artery with narrowing or stenosis, subsequently ***can result in*** *increased stroke risk.*
- Frequency / probability:
  Migraine ***can*** *rarely* ***present*** *with stroke-like symptoms.*
  Things that strokes ***can*** *mimic are … usually secondary to blood pressure problems …*
- Tentative speculation:
  Perhaps because of the association between stroke and old age … it has not had the profile of other perhaps less serious or rarer disorders.

TASK 3 Listening for association and evaluation

1 **Work in pairs. Predict how the following items might be connected.**

reducing smoking   rehabilitation   treating blood pressure   improving diet
promoting exercise   stroke prevention   risk of subsequent strokes
high blood pressure   taking aspirin   diabetes

2 ▷8.4 **Watch Extract 4 and check your predictions. Listen for any evaluation from the lecturer.**

3 **Identify the lecturer's evaluation of the following items in relation to stroke.**
  - reducing smoking, treating blood pressure, improving diet, and promoting exercise
  - aspirin
  - rehabilitation

4 **Compare answers and complete any missing information. Use your notes to write a paragraph expressing the connections in Extract 4 of the lecture.**

TASK 4 Reprocessing information from a lecture

1 **Work in pairs. Each choose one topic below. Take turns to present the information, based on the pre-lecture handout, the lecture transcript, and your notes on the lecture.**
  - technical and medical information about strokes
  - ways of preventing strokes

Collaborating with other students to develop an argument or strategy in preparation for a seminar can be very useful. You can discuss your responses to texts that you have read, and bring together key connections. You also need to formulate arguments which you can then use in a seminar. In some seminars, you may have to present a **case**, i.e. a coherent set of arguments which support a strategy. It is usually advisable to prepare a case by working closely with other students.

This module covers:

- Gathering evidence for a seminar discussion
- Defending your argument using justifying and evaluation language

TASK 1 Reading to gather evidence for a seminar discussion

1 Read Text 1, the summary of a research article published in a medical journal. Make brief notes on the *aims*, *main results*, and *recommendations* of the research.

TEXT 1

Effect of physical inactivity on major non-communicable diseases worldwide: an analysis of burden of disease and life expectancy

SUMMARY

Background

Strong evidence shows that physical inactivity increases the risk of many adverse health conditions, including major non-communicable diseases such as coronary heart disease, type 2 diabetes, and breast and colon cancers, and shortens life expectancy. Because much of the world's population is inactive, this link presents a major public health issue. We aimed to quantify the effect of physical inactivity on these major non-communicable diseases by estimating how much disease could be averted if inactive people were to become active, and to estimate gain in life expectancy at the population level.

Methods

For our analysis of burden of disease, we calculated population attributable fractions (PAFs) associated with physical inactivity using conservative assumptions for each of the major non-communicable diseases, by country, to estimate how much disease could be averted if physical inactivity were eliminated. We used life-table analysis to estimate gains in life expectancy of the population.

Findings

Worldwide, we estimate that physical inactivity causes 6% (ranging from 3.2% in south-east Asia to 7.8% in the eastern Mediterranean region) of the burden of disease from coronary heart disease, 7% (range 3.9%–9.6%) of type 2 diabetes, 10% (range 5.6%–14.1%) of breast cancer, and 10% (range 5.7%–13.8%) of colon cancer. Inactivity causes 9% (range 5.1%–12.5%) of premature mortality, or more than 5.3 million of the 57 million deaths that occurred worldwide in 2008. If inactivity were not eliminated, but decreased instead by 10% or 25%, more than 533,000 and more than 1.3 million deaths, respectively, could be averted every year. We estimated that elimination of physical inactivity would increase the life expectancy of the world's population by 0.68% (range 0.41%–0.95%) years.

Interpretation

Physical inactivity has a major health effect worldwide. Decrease in or removal of this unhealthy behaviour could improve health substantially.

Funding

None.

SOURCE: Lee, I.M., Shiroma, E.J., Lobelo, F., Puska, P., Blair, S.N., & Katzmarzyk, P.T. (2012). Effect of physical inactivity on major non-communicable diseases worldwide: an analysis of burden of disease and life expectancy. *The Lancet*. (Digital Object Identifier: 10.1016/S0140-6736(08)61345-8), accessed 18th July 2012.

2 Note down information in Text 1 which could be useful for promoting the value of physical activity.

ACADEMIC LANGUAGE

Evaluation (2) Defending your argument

When presenting a case, you need to defend and justify the points you make, in order to convince your listeners of the strengths of your argument. You can do this by using **justifying language** which introduces the reasons for your choice, together with **evaluative language** to indicate your stance:

*Programmes like this reach the target groups, **as** they're based in their local community.*
*We **believe** education is **especially effective because** it targets the root of the problem.*
***There are two main reasons why** this is a **convincing** strategy ...*
***The reason why** such campaigns often prove **successful** is ...*
*Its national reach **means that** this kind of system is **workable** and **cost-effective**.*
*Such initiatives **can clearly be justified on** educational **grounds** as well as ...*
***Our rationale for this** is ...*

TASK 2 Preparing a case for a seminar discussion

1 You are going to prepare a case for a seminar discussion around the following topic.

> **DISCUSSION:** *What are the best strategies for promoting physical activity in this country?*

Study the possible strategies for promoting physical activity. Think of a benefit for each.

Example: *Health education in schools can promote physical activity before children develop bad habits, and prevent problems later.*

Strategies for promoting the value of physical activity	Benefits
Local • Volunteers reaching target groups through local organizations • Subsidized or free membership of gyms and swimming pools in your area	
National • Education through schools following a national curriculum • National government warnings on unhealthy foods and tobacco	
Global • Major public health campaigns conducted by global organizations (e.g. the WHO) • Encouraging participation in sport through international events	

2 Add at least one idea of your own for each group in 1. Then choose one strategy from each group and decide why it would be the most effective.

3 Work in pairs. Take turns to present and justify your strategies. Take account of:
   • the typical culture and mindset of the population in your chosen country
   • the challenges of reaching the target group.

4 Decide how your two strategies might work together. Agree a joint approach.

5 Work with another pair.
   1 Take turns to present, justify, and defend your strategies.
   2 Evaluate each other's selection and presentation of strategies.
   3 Reach a consensus on which *two* strategies to adopt for your joint case.

TASK 3 Presenting a case and reaching consensus

1 Join with another group. Discuss the cases you have prepared in response to the discussion question in Task 2.
   1 Take turns to present each case, based on the two chosen strategies.
   2 Allow a short question and answer stage for each mini-presentation.
   3 Reach a whole-group consensus by means of either a final discussion or a vote.

2 In your groups from Task 2.5, write a paragraph summarizing the final decision.

3 Read all the summaries and vote for the most persuasive one.

1 **Understanding how words are formed can help you to work out the meaning of new words you encounter. Group these words from the unit according to how they are formed, using prefixes or compounds (words joined together).**

bio-physiological breakdown dataset follow-up inadequate intake interwar layman non-communicable outcome overcrowding postwar socio-economic trade-off unhealthy well-being

Example: *breakdown*, *follow-up*, and *trade-off* are all nouns formed from phrasal verbs by adding the verb and particle together

2 **In groups, compare and explain your classifications. Together, add at least one more word to each group.**

Example: *breakdown, follow-up, trade-off + takeover*

3 **Identify which fields or disciplines these perspective adjectives are associated with. Add at least two more similar adjectives to the list.**

a neurolinguistic

b biomechanical

c microelectronic

d sociopolitical

e geophysical

8F Research Project (2)

Establishing a working title

What is a working title?

A working title is usually in the form of a noun phrase or a short question that captures the specific topic you plan to research and write about. Your working title will guide the next stage of your research and the planning of your project.

- If your title is **too narrow**, you may struggle to find enough sources. You should not rely on just one or two sources for your project.

  Example: *Micro-credit schemes aimed at women to encourage rural development in South India.*

- If your title is **too broad**, your project may be too vague and lack a clear argument and structure.

  Examples: *The role of technology in language teaching. How effective are TV campaigns in improving public health?*

Narrow your topic by:

- **focusing on a geographical area.** You could focus on one particular country or compare the situation in two different countries. Bear in mind that it may be difficult to find sources *in English* about some countries.

- **focusing on a particular group of people, companies, etc.** Again, remember that there may not be enough available material if you choose a very small group.

- **using *wh*- questions:** *Which area of public health? What type of technology?*

> **TO DO** Stage 2: Main research phase
>
> When you have narrowed down your topic, you can start to do the main part of your research. Use the research guidelines, Checklist L on page 212, to search for relevant material and make notes. You may find that some topics are less interesting and new topics may come up: adjust your working title, based on your research.

UNIT 9 Variation

ACADEMIC FOCUS: EVALUATION AND CRITICAL RESPONSE

LEARNING OBJECTIVES

Reading
- Evaluating types of source
- Recognizing narrative in source texts
- Identifying writing style, levels of formality, and marked language

Writing
- Recognizing, responding to, and expressing evaluation
- Writing a critical response to a text

Listening
- Techniques for dealing with different lecture styles
- Using lecture notes and slides effectively

Speaking
- Preparing an oral summary and evaluation of a text
- Participating in a seminar discussion and incorporating examples

Vocabulary
- Idioms in academic writing

Research project (3)
- Making an outline plan

Discussion

1 **Work in groups. Think about varieties of English used around the world. Discuss the questions.**
   - In which countries is English a) the main language, b) an official language, c) a common *lingua franca*?
   - What is the status and usage of English in your home country?
   - Give examples of differences between varieties of English (e.g. pronunciation).

2 **Which varieties of English do these words come from? Use a dictionary to check.**

   bairn   biltong   color   lakh   sidewalk   sook

3 **Compare the genres in the list and discuss how the language might vary.**

   an academic journal
   a popular science magazine (e.g. *National Geographic)*
   an email between students
   a lab report
   a social science PhD thesis
   a student essay
   a textbook

When researching a topic, you need to be aware of different types of sources, how reliable they are, and when to use them. Academic textbooks are generally considered to be reliable because they have been carefully checked, and journal articles are **peer-reviewed**, i.e. critically evaluated by academics in the same discipline. You should treat other sources with caution. **Popular academic texts** for a non-expert audience may provide background reading, but may not be appropriate to cite as evidence. Non-academic sources such as journalistic texts may be relevant to cite a recent example. Academic blogs and other online forums may be useful for keeping up-to-date, and may have links to journal articles.

This module covers:

- Evaluating types of source
- Recognizing narrative in source texts
- Identifying writing style, levels of formality, and marked language

TASK 1 Critical thinking – evaluating types of source

1 **Match sources 1–6 from the area of social anthropology with genres a–f.**

Sources

1 Empson, R. (2011) *Harnessing Fortune: Personhood, Memory, and Place in Mongolia.* Oxford: Oxford University Press.

2 Lavenda, R. & Schultz, E. (2012). *Anthropology: What Does It Mean To Be Human?* Oxford: Oxford University Press.

3 Monaghan, J. & Just, P. (2000). *Social and Cultural Anthropology: A Very Short Introduction.* Oxford: Oxford University Press.

4 Shea, N. (2010) 'Africa's Last Frontier' in *National Geographic magazine*, March 2010.

5 'Anthropology' http://en.wikipedia.org/wiki/Anthropology, accessed 16th January 2013.

6 Singer, A. (2008) 'Anthropology on television'. ASA *Globalog* website of Association of Social Anthropologists http://blog.theasa.org/?p=107.

Genres

a an undergraduate textbook

b a monograph

c a popular book aimed at a general audience

d an online encyclopaedia written by members of the public

e an academic blog

f a journalistic article

GLOSSARY

monograph *(n)* a detailed study of a specialized academic subject, usually in the form of a short book

2 **Work in groups. Classify the sources in 1 as *academic*, *popular academic*, or *non-academic*. Give reasons.**

3 **Discuss how you would (or would not) use the sources in 1:**

- to cite in an essay
- to cite in a seminar discussion
- as background reading to help you understand a topic
- to keep up-to-date with ideas in the area.

TASK 2 Recognizing narrative in source texts

1 Read Texts 1–3, focusing especially on the outlined *narrative* or story sections. As you read, make notes under headings a–c.

  a the location / host culture

  b the 'outsider(s)'

  c the cultural difference / practice

2 Work in groups. Choose one of the texts to read in more detail. Discuss the questions.

  1 What impression do you get of the culture described – what picture do you have in your mind of the people, the location, and their way of life?

  2 How familiar or strange does the cultural practice described seem to you – can you draw any parallels from your own experience?

  3 In your own words, summarize the key concept described in the part of the text *after* the narrative.

Why do cultural differences matter?

TEXT 1

The same objects, actions, or events frequently mean different things to people with different cultures. In fact, what counts as an object or event in one tradition may not be recognized as such in another. This powerful lesson of anthropology was illustrated by the experience of some Peace Corps volunteers working in southern Africa.

> In the early 1970s, the Peace Corps office in Botswana was concerned by the number of volunteers who seemed to be 'burned out'; failing in their assignments, leaving the assigned villages, and increasingly hostile to their Tswana hosts. The Peace Corps asked American anthropologist Hoyt Alverson, who was familiar with Tswana culture and society, for advice. Alverson (1977) discovered that one major problem the Peace Corps volunteers were having involved exactly this issue of similar actions having very different meanings. The volunteers complained that the Tswana would never leave them alone. Whenever they tried to get away and sit by themselves for a few minutes to have some private time, one or more Tswana would quickly join them. This made the Americans angry. From their perspective, everyone is entitled to a certain amount of privacy and time alone. To the Tswana, however, human life is social life; the only people who want to be alone are witches and the insane. Because these young Americans did not seem to be either, the Tswana who saw them sitting alone naturally assumed that there had been a breakdown in hospitality and the volunteers would welcome some company. Here, one behaviour – a person walking out into a field and sitting by himself or herself – had two very different meanings.

From this example, we can see that human experience is inherently ambiguous. Even within a single cultural tradition, the meaning of an object or an action may differ, depending on the context. Quoting philosopher Gilbert Ryle, anthropologist Clifford Geertz (1973: 6) noted that there is a world of difference between a wink and a blink, as anyone who has ever mistaken one for the other has undoubtedly learnt. To resolve the ambiguity, experience must be interpreted, and human beings regularly turn to their own cultural traditions in search of an interpretation that makes sense. They do this daily as they go about life among others with whom they share traditions. Serious misunderstandings may arise, however, when individuals confront the same ambiguous situation without realizing that their cultural ground rules differ.

What is ethnocentrism?
Ethnocentrism is the term anthropologists use to describe the opinion that one's own way of life is natural or correct, indeed the only way of being fully human. Ethnocentrism is one solution to the inevitable tension when people with different cultural backgrounds come into contact. It reduces the other way of life to a version of one's own. Sometimes we correctly identify meaningful areas of cultural overlap. At other times, we are shocked by the differences we encounter. We may conclude that if our way is right, then their way can only be wrong. (Of course, from their perspective, our way of life may seem to be a distortion of theirs.)

SOURCE: Lavenda, R. & Schultz, E. (2012). pp.220–221. *Anthropology: what does it mean to be human?* Oxford: Oxford University Press.

Vessels of harnessed fortune

It was late spring, but the morning air was cold. There had been a hard frost overnight and I found it hard to get out of bed. Mornings meant helping Delgermaa set the fire and milk the cows before we let the calves out for the day, or gave the cattle hay, and then settled down for tea and soda bread with fresh cream and jam. This morning was different. Outside, Delgermaa and I shouted instructions to each other as we struggled to corral the bull calf into a small pen. As soon as it was in, Delgermaa climbed nimbly into the enclosure and approached the animal. Our movements in the morning had become so familiar that I hardly noticed when she bent over and swiftly wiped the inside of her coat over its muzzle. She repeated this action and then pulled out a pair of scissors and cut off a small handful of hair from the young animal's tail. She tied this into a loose knot before placing it inside her pocket. Her actions were quick and it would have been easy to miss them, but I later learnt that they had to be performed before she handed over the animal to the men who had come to collect it. The money from its sale would go towards her daughter's university fees, its meat would go to people in the district centre or to the markets of Ulaanbaatar. The tuft of tail hair remained in the house. [...]

In this chapter I focus on practices involved in harnessing fortune for households. These practices permeated many activities for countryside and district centre households as people worked to secure the prosperity and wellbeing of their families. In trying to understand what is meant by fortune, I compare this concept to the Polynesian concept of '*mana*', and the Japanese practice of 'beckoning luck'. Shifting ideas of fortune are also traced in relation to different historical periods. By focusing on various actions involved in 'harnessing fortune' (*hishig hürteh*), from livestock to mountain ceremonies, certain features come to the fore. This leads me to consider not so much what fortune is, but how it is made to appear through the various practices in which it is attended.

SOURCE: Empson, R. (2011). pp. 67-69. *Harnessing Fortune: Personhood, Memory, and Place in Mongolia.* Oxford: Oxford University Press.

Ñañuu María gets hit by lightning: people and their selves

While on a visit to Nuyoo in 1994, John visited Ñañuu María Lopez, who had provided him with meals when he had first visited Nuyoo a decade earlier. By this time she was quite old and John asked her how she was doing. She replied that she had been sick for several months owing to a terrible burn she had received. Thinking her house had caught fire, John immediately asked after the other members of her family, who, she said, were fine; what had happened was, she had been hit by lightning while out in the fields. Later on John commented on this chance event and María's miraculous survival to her neighbours, who professed to know nothing about her being hit by lightning. One young man, however, who knew something about the incident, jumped in and said he knew that she had been asleep in her house when the lightning struck; it was her 'animal' (*kiti nuvi*) which had been hit by the bolt.

The Mixtec, like other Mesoamerican people, believe that living things that come into the world at the same time are fundamentally linked to one another. An animal and a human born at the same moment will thus share life experiences, are often said to have a single soul, and will, at times, share a consciousness. This latter most often occurs through dreams, which may be interpreted as the world seen through the eyes of one's 'coessential' animals (so labelled because the animals and their human counterparts are essentially linked). In Ñañuu María's case her *kiti nuvi* is a small, playful, furry creature called a coati (this had been determined years beforehand through divination and because like the coati she had a special liking for bananas). It was on one of its nocturnal journeys that the coati had been hit by lightning.

The idea of the coessential animal is something that to us seems a bit far-fetched. But the Mixtec case is far from unique, and ethnographers report many examples of traditions that hold that things not physically attached to the body are an intimate part of the self. For the Mixtec, the concept of the coessential animal is at least as complex and comprehensive as the *id* or *superego*, and has no less basis in empirical science: it explains good and bad luck, sudden and even deadly illnesses, the nature of dreams, and even why some individuals have more wealth and power than others, since those with big, ferocious animals such as jaguars stand higher in the social hierarchy than those with small, innocuous animals such as rabbits.

SOURCE: Monaghan, J. & Just, P. (2000). pp.131-132. *Social and Cultural Anthropology: A Very Short Introduction.* Oxford: Oxford University Press.

GLOSSARY

Nuyoo a town in south-west Mexico

Which statement, a or b, best describes the function of the *narrative* in each of the three texts?

a The narrative serves as an example to support the explanation of a general theory or concept.

b The narrative describes the main focus of research and then is linked to more general theories.

Present a brief summary of your group's discussion on each text to the class. What are the key differences between the text types you have looked at? Explain why these differences exist.

Give examples of narrative accounts in your own discipline, i.e. types of writing that might involve a first person (*I / we*) or third person (*he / she*) description of events.

   Example: *In health science, you might have to write a report of a work placement, a bit like a diary, describing your experience and what you learnt from it.*

TASK 3 Identifying different writing styles

1 Work in pairs to compare extracts A–E. Which language features are *more formal / specialized* and which are *more informal / for a non-expert audience*? Consider:

- vocabulary
- sentence length and grammatical construction
- use of personal / impersonal language.

A **Ethnocentrism** is the term anthropologists use to describe the opinion that one's own way of life is natural or correct, indeed the only way of being fully human.

   SOURCE: Lavenda & Schultz (2012), anthropology textbook

B By focusing on various actions involved in 'harnessing fortune' (*hishig hürteh*), from livestock to mountain ceremonies, certain features come to the fore. This leads me to consider not so much what fortune is, but how it is made to appear through the various practices in which it is attended.

   SOURCE: Empson (2011), academic monograph

C The idea of the coessential animal is something that to us seems a bit far-fetched.

   SOURCE: Monaghan & Just (2000), popular introduction to anthropology

D For generations the tribes of the Omo were shielded from the outside world by mountains, savanna, and by Ethiopia's unique status as the only African nation never to have been colonized by Europeans. In the late 1960s and '70s, anthropologists began recognizing what that meant – people living near the river had largely escaped the colonial blundering and conflict that shredded other societies.

   SOURCE: Shea (2010), *National Geographic* magazine

E The recent plethora of 'tribal' reality shows favours entertainment at the expense of education, while the indigenously-produced films favoured by anthropologists (at least, the ones I have seen) are heavily weighted towards the informative end of the spectrum.

   SOURCE: Course (2008), anthropology blog post

Style (3) Marked language

Academic writing is relatively formal in style. However, texts written for a general audience, such as magazines, popular books, or websites, may use more informal expressions and/or colourful, descriptive, or idiomatic language to appeal to non-academic readers.

- from a popular academic anthropology book, *jump in* (v) = informal, meaning 'interrupt':
  *One young man **jumped in** and said …*
- from an article in *National Geographic* magazine, *serpentine* (adj) = literary, meaning 'curving like a snake':
  *Near the Kenyan border the river carves **serpentine** oxbows …*

Expert academic writers sometimes used **marked** language; language that is not in the style of the genre and so stands out as different. This may be as part of a narrative describing an event or scene:

- from Text 2, *nimbly* (adv) = descriptive, meaning 'moving quickly and easily':
  *Delgermaa climbed **nimbly** into the enclosure.*

You need to recognize marked language so that you do not use it inappropriately in your own writing. Informal, journalistic, or colourful words or expressions can sound awkward in a student essay.

Sometimes academic writers acknowledge their use of marked language by putting it in quotation marks.

- from Text 1, *burned out* (phr v) = informal, meaning 'very tired from too much work':
  *the number of volunteers who seemed to be **'burned out'***

If you want to use an interesting, but possibly marked, expression from your reading, it is better to include it in quotation marks.

TASK 4 Recognizing levels of formality and marked language

1   Look at the list below. Match pairs of words or phrases with similar meanings.

a bit   blunder   broke   clear up   deplete   envelop   error   far-fetched
implausible   insolvent   miss out   nimbly   omit   resolve   somewhat
surround   swiftly   use up

Example: *far-fetched – implausible (= difficult to believe)*

2   For each pair, categorize the words / phrases as:
- typically academic – formal or neutral
- marked in academic writing – informal or literary.

Example: *far-fetched = quite informal; implausible = neutral*

TASK 5 Independent research – recognizing writing styles

1   Find at least three texts of different genres within your discipline, in print or online. Try to find an example of a narrative.

2   Some disciplines, such as Law and Medicine, are dominated by formal, impersonal language. Others involve a mix of writing styles used in different genres. Looking at your three texts, note to what degree they vary in terms of writing style.

3   Report your findings to the class. Discuss the different genres and any differences between disciplines.

It is common across disciplines to write a **critical response**, sometimes called a **critique** or a **review**. In such an assignment, you may be asked to critically evaluate a method, a technique or practice, a theory or argument, a text, or a piece of research. A critical response is an evaluative judgement which is based on your academic understanding of the topic and common academic **norms** and principles, rather than your unsupported personal opinion. It might address strengths and weaknesses of precision (*accurately measures*), extent (*does not fully explain*), consistency (*contradictory results*), or usefulness (*an effective method*).

This module covers:

- Recognizing, responding to, and expressing evaluation
- Writing a critical response to a text

TASK 1 Recognizing types of evaluation

1 Work in pairs. Read extracts A–E from student writing, which all contain evaluation. For each extract, decide:

- **Discipline:** Which discipline is the student studying?
- **Topic:** What topic is being discussed? (e.g. a technique, a method, a theory, an argument)
- **Stance:** What is the writer's stance? (e.g. supportive, critical, expressing limitations)

> A **Whilst** both tools have **significant uses** in the design process, they **remain a guide**, and their findings **should not be treated as absolute**. All computational simulation models **have to make assumptions** that are **not entirely consistent with** the real world.

> B The use of non-synthetic pesticides should be a last resort, because it can impact beneficial insects and have a significant effect on the environment. This is **not fully in line with** the principles of organic farming.

> C Proponents of section 34 would argue that an innocent defendant will have nothing to hide, and would suffer no ill effects from having conversations with his legal advisor examined. This **does not account for** the multitude of reasons an innocent defendant might have for not wanting the contents of a confidential dialogue revealed in open court.

> D By using this specific case study, the author puts forward **a useful model** that can **easily be applied to** other businesses.

> E Because the concept of decommodification is based on labour markets, women **can only really** be included in Esping-Anderson's analysis if they are in formal employment. Women's needs, **however**, in terms of state support, **are most likely to be** based around unequal household and caring responsibilities.

2 **Focus on the language in bold in extracts A–E. In each extract, which category 1–5 below is the writer evaluating?**

Example: *In Text A, the writer is evaluating **extent** (Whilst ... remain a guide)*
*and **consistency** (not entirely consistent).*

1 precision (how accurate something is)
2 extent (the degree to which something is true)
3 basis (how strong the basis for something is)
4 consistency (how regular and reliable something is)
5 usefulness (how practical and workable something is)

3 Choose the best category in 2 for the evaluative words and phrases in the list.

assumption   compatible   comprehensive   conjecture   consistent with
effective   error   exactly   limited   presuppose   reliability   sufficient

Example: assumption = *category 3 – connected to the **basis** of something. If you make*
an assumption, this means that the basis is not certain, but assumed.

4 Which words in 3 are largely used for a) negative, b) positive evaluation?
How can their opposites be expressed?

Example: compatible – *largely positive*   opposite – *incompatible / not compatible*

TASK 2 Identifying and responding to a writer's evaluation

1 Text 1 describes reasons why it can be difficult to change people's eating habits.
Read the first paragraph and write a sentence paraphrasing each reason 1–5.

Example: 1 *There are many different influences on people's ideas about food: society,*
family, personal experience, the media.

Food likes and their relative importance in human eating behavior: review and preliminary suggestions for health promotion

TEXT 1

1 **Although** many people are interested in developing healthier eating patterns, nutritional interventions **do not always succeed in** bringing about behavioral change. The difficulty of changing eating habits has been related to [1] the multiple roots of people's ideas about food (e.g. the society's 'food ideology', the family environment, personal experience and the media), [2] conflicts between intrinsic and extrinsic values (i.e. liking on the short term and health consequences on the long term) characterizing dietary advice, [3] the gradual development (instead of immediate appearance) of diet-related health problems, [4] the requirement of long-term changes in habitual food intake for risk reduction and disease prevention through nutritional means, and [5] the less than obvious physical feedback of some dietary changes (Glanz & Mullis, 1988; Wardle, 1993; Wardle & Solomons, 1994).

2 Basically, two broad intervention strategies exist to alter eating behavior. One strategy focuses on individual problem awareness and personal motivation and skills, the other on providing context stimuli intended to direct food choice. **The effectiveness of** these programmes **can be questioned**. Because food (dis)likes **appear of major importance** to eating behavior and learning mechanisms are responsible for their development and change, **effectiveness of** interventions **may be increased by** special emphasis on these two elements.

SOURCE: Eertmans, A., Baeyens, F., & Van den Bergh, O. (2001). Food likes and their relative importance in human eating behavior: review and preliminary suggestions for health promotion. *Health Education Research*, 16(4): 443-456.

2 Read paragraph 2, which reviews health promotion strategies. Note which *two* of the following are existing strategies for promoting healthy eating, according to the text.

a raising individual awareness about healthy eating

b providing direct encouragement for people to opt for healthy food

c recognizing that individual food preferences are crucial to eating behaviour

3 Note down examples of healthy eating campaigns that use the techniques mentioned in the text. (Think about your experience / your country / another country.)

4 Look at the first and last sentences (highlighted) in Text 1, especially the evaluative language in bold. Decide the main focus of the writers' evaluation.

a the precision of the health promotion strategies   c the consistency of the strategies

b the usefulness of the strategies

5 Work in pairs.

1 Compare your answers to 1–4 and summarize in your own words why the authors believe that current strategies are ineffective.

2 To what extent do you agree with this evaluation? Refer to any campaigns you noted in 3.

Evaluation (3) Confident and tentative language

You may express evaluative comments **confidently**, especially those based on clear evidence:

*Current techniques **do not account for** sampling variability.*

*The data shows that interventions **were not sufficient** to overcome negative effects.*

However, you will often want to express your degree of confidence more **tentatively**, using hedging language so that you don't over-generalize and leave yourself open to counter-criticism.

- How sure am I that this is true or correct? Use *perhaps, possibly, potentially, can / may / might, appear / seem to*, etc.:

  *Because food (dis)likes **appear** of major importance to eating behavior … effectiveness of interventions **may be increased by** …*

  *Stem cell therapy offers a **potentially** powerful treatment for inherited disorders.*

- To what extent is this true? Use *largely, partially, mostly, to a (limited / certain) extent*, etc.:

  ***To some extent**, therefore, this finding contradicts the main hypothesis.*

- Is this always true in every case? Use *sometimes, often, generally, tend to*, etc.:

  *Nutritional interventions **do not always succeed in** bringing about behavioral change.*

As well as modals and adverbials, vocabulary choice can reflect your degree of confidence. Compare:

*The effectiveness of these programmes … **can be questioned** / **is sometimes disputed** / **has been heavily criticized**.*

TASK 3 Expressing evaluation confidently and tentatively

1 Order each set of words 1–6 from most confident to most tentative.

Example: *attack, criticize, dispute, question*

    ←————————————→

    confident   tentative

1 aid, contribute to, enable, ensure (verbs)

2 alter, modify, revolutionize, transform (verbs)

3 indicate, prove, show, suggest (verbs)

4 beneficial, desirable, invaluable, useful (adjectives)

5 adverse, detrimental, devastating, harmful (adjectives)

6 hostility, opposition, reservation, resistance (nouns)

2 For each set, write a sentence in which you can substitute two words in the set.

Example: *This important publication **aids** / **contributes to** our understanding of the topic.*

3 Read the two student texts, A and B, evaluating healthy eating campaigns. For each text, identify:

- the writer's stance
- evaluative language
- confident or tentative evaluation.

A The process of school food reform in the UK was dramatically accelerated by the 2005 campaign by celebrity chef Jamie Oliver to encourage healthy eating among children by ensuring that only healthy lunches were served in school canteens. Despite some initial resistance from children and some parents, these reforms have undoubtedly made a significant contribution to the promotion of healthy eating habits from an early age, and thanks to support from government and education authorities, the momentum of the initial campaign has been sustained.

B The '5-a-day' programme, aimed at encouraging greater consumption of fresh fruit and vegetables, which has operated in various forms across the world, may have raised public awareness of the benefits of healthy eating. However, the effectiveness of this message seems to be contradicted by other emerging trends in eating habits. With a growing proportion of the food we consume now coming from pre-prepared and away-from-home sources such as take-aways, rather than being cooked at home from fresh ingredients, many people apparently have limited control over their intake of fresh vegetables. Fried potatoes, for example, account for 35% of away-from-home vegetable consumption (Stewart & Blisard, 2008).

4 Write a short paragraph similar to the student texts in 3, describing and evaluating a healthy eating campaign (or other health promotion initiative) that you are familiar with. Make sure:

- you include appropriate evaluative language
- you use confident or tentative language that reflects your stance.

5 Work in pairs and exchange texts. Identify your partner's use of evaluative language and stance, and decide how clearly expressed these are.

TASK 4 Responding critically to a text

1 Work in groups. You are going to read Text 2, about variation in individual food preferences, i.e. foods that different people like or dislike. Discuss how the following factors might influence people's food preferences.

advertising   biological factors   cultural background   exposure to foods   family
genetic factors   health education   personal experience   social transmission   taste

Example: *Although health education might influence your food choices to some extent, it is unlikely to fundamentally change which foods you like and dislike.*

2 Quickly read Text 2 and identify which three of the factors in 1 are mentioned.

TEXT 2

One of the strongest environmental influences on food preference is taste. This can affect an individual's likes and dislikes from the earliest stages of life; the maternal diet can influence the child *in utero*. In a series of studies at the Monell Chemical Senses Center, USA, Julie Mennella and her colleagues demonstrated this phenomenon by assigning pregnant women who were planning to breastfeed to one of three groups. Women were asked to drink carrot juice regularly either in the last trimester of pregnancy, while breastfeeding, or not at all. Babies born to the mothers in either of the carrot juice groups had less negative responses to carrots during weaning, and were perceived to like them more by their mothers than babies of mothers in the control group (Mennella *et al.*, 2001). Similar results have been documented in rats, dogs, sheep, rabbits and piglets.

Evidence for the ability of exposure to promote liking for certain foods has been building over the past three decades. Surveys in children of food consumption and preferences have linked early taste experiences to subsequent food acceptance (Cooke *et al.*, 2004), which is consistent with an exposure effect. Experimental studies have also shown that exposure increases liking and acceptance in animals, children (Sullivan & Birch, 1990) and adults (Pliner *et al.*, 1993). One study that compared children's acceptance of three varieties of a new food – plain, salted or sugared tofu – showed that children preferred whichever variety they had been exposed to earlier (Sullivan & Birch, 1990).

These findings have been replicated in the outside world. In one study, school children were randomly divided into three groups: exposure to the food (red pepper), exposure plus reward, or no exposure. After eight days, the children exposed to red pepper had significantly increased their liking and intake of it, compared with the control group (Wardle *et al.*, 2003b). The same effects were achieved when the intervention was delivered by mothers who had been taught exposure feeding techniques. When offered a vegetable that they had initially disliked, children in the experimental group showed a greater increase in liking and intake after 14 days than those in the control groups, who had received no treatment or had been given leaflets about healthy eating (Wardle *et al.*, 2003a).

In animals, food preferences are thought to be socially transmitted: the sight of members of their own species eating, or even the smell of food on their breath can encourage consumption. In one study, lambs were exposed to three treatments: they ate a new food with their mother, observed her doing so but were unable to eat it themselves, or the mother ate the food out of their sight. Lambs that were with their mother while she was eating showed a stronger preference for the food in a subsequent test, even if they had not eaten the food themselves (Saint-Dizier *et al.*, 2007).

These modelling effects have also been observed in humans. In one study, children drank different flavours of new drinks while watching a video of a model expressing a like or dislike of the same drink (Baeyens *et al.*, 1996). The children were found to prefer the flavour that the model had liked. This suggests that in the home, if parents, or better still peers, show that they like a food, the child will be more inclined to taste and accept it.

SOURCE: Wardle, J. & Cooke, L. (2010). One man's meat is another man's poison. *EMBO reports*, 11: 816–821.

Read Text 2 again in detail. Complete the table with information about the three factors influencing food preference.

	Factor	Evidence from studies	Foods tested in studies
1	taste	Mennella *et al.*, 2001	carrot juice
2			tofu red pepper
3		Saint-Dizier *et al.*, 2007	

4 Work in groups. Evaluate the main ideas put forward in Text 2.

1 Evaluate the **accuracy** and **relevance** of the seven studies in relation to the points made in the text.

2 Assess the extent to which the conclusions drawn from the studies can be **applied** more generally.

3 Assess the implications of the findings and how **useful** they are.

TASK 5 Writing a critical response to a text

1 Write a critical response to Text 2. Write one or two paragraphs. Follow the guidelines below.

Guidelines for writing a critical response

1 Decide on your overall stance: supporting, critical, or a mix of the two.
2 Assume that your audience has not read the original text; briefly summarize the topic and main points from the text before you add your evaluative comments.
3 Refer to the text where necessary, e.g. *Wardle & Cooke (2010) argue that* ….
4 Include the points you most agree with from the group discussion in Task 4.4.
5 Choose only the points you think are the most interesting or significant; you do not need to include all the details in the source text.
6 Finish with a brief overall evaluative comment on the whole text.

2 When you have finished, use Checklist M to evaluate your writing. Edit your text in the light of your answers.

CHECKLIST M Evaluation criteria for a critical response

Does your writing:

1	present a clear stance?	Yes / No
2	present an organized, coherent flow of ideas?	Yes / No
3	clearly but concisely explain main points from the text?	Yes / No
4	link evaluative comments to the points from the text?	Yes / No
5	use appropriate evaluative language?	Yes / No
6	use appropriate language to express confident or tentative evaluation?	Yes / No

Checklists:
page 209

Listening Lectures (7)

Lecture styles can vary significantly between disciplines and individual lecturers. You might find yourself in a large lecture theatre with the lecturer talking for an hour or more with very little interaction with the audience; alternatively lectures may be in smaller groups where the lecturer involves the audience through questions. Many lecturers use visuals such as PowerPoint slides and video, and may make these available to students before or after the lecture, either online or as printed handouts. Adopting a variety of techniques for dealing with different styles will help you to make the most of this part of your studies.

This module covers:
- Techniques for dealing with different lecture styles
- Using lecture notes and slides effectively

TASK 1 Evaluating different lecture styles

1 **Work in groups. Discuss how the factors below affect your response to a lecture.**

Lecturer's voice
- accent
- speed
- volume
- pausing to allow comprehension

Lecturer's style
- body language
- eye contact
- attitude and enthusiasm
- practical demonstrations

Visuals
- bullet points
- diagrams
- pictures
- video
- availability of slides before / after the lecture

Interaction
- audience size
- lecturer–students questions and tasks
- student–student discussion

Dr Kathleen Quinlan

2 **You are going to watch three extracts from different lectures. Look at the lecture titles and predict the discipline and the general topic of each lecture.**
   1 Making the most of higher education in English-speaking countries – *education*
   2 The forgotten Prime Minister – ....
   3 A romp through the philosophy of mind – ....

3 ▷9.1–9.3 **Watch the three lecture extracts.**
   1 Make notes under the four headings in **1**. Focus on the style of the lecture rather than the content.
   2 After each extract, work in pairs and compare notes. Look for points of agreement.

Professor Angus Hawkins

4 **In your groups, compare the styles of the three lectures using your notes. Discuss which of the lectures you preferred, referring to the following criteria. Give reasons.**
   1 how easy it is to follow and understand
   2 how interesting and engaging it is
   3 how memorable the content is

5 **Compare your ideas with the class.**

Professor Marianne Talbot

TASK 2 Techniques for dealing with different lecture styles

1 **Match techniques 1–8 for dealing with lectures in English with one or more possible benefits a–f. Some benefits apply to more than one technique.**

1 Watch lectures in English online, for example, via *TED.com*, *YouTube*, *iTunes U*

2 Carefully read the titles of lectures and any information you are given in advance

3 Do any suggested background reading before a lecture

4 Note down questions about any points you do not understand during a lecture

5 Make audio recordings of lectures you attend, to listen to later

6 Type up your lecture notes after each lecture

7 Download the lecturer's slides where they are available, before or after the lecture

8 Form a study network with other students; compare notes and discuss the lecture

a to review any points you missed or didn't understand.

b to ask for clarification at the end of the lecture or in a tutorial.

c to get used to listening to different accents and speaking styles.

d to make sure you understand the topic and key vocabulary.

e to help you process the information from the lecture and keep a record for revision.

f to maximize opportunities for interaction and clarification.

2 **Which techniques in 1 are best suited to dealing with the three different lecture styles you have just watched? Explain why (not).**

3 **Work in groups. Discuss how the techniques could help you to get the most out of lectures in English. Note down advantages and potential problems for each.**

Example: *A potential problem with making audio recordings is that you won't realistically have time to listen back to all your lectures.*

TASK 3 Using lecture notes and slides effectively

1 **Work in pairs. Look at the slide from Extract 1 and take turns to explain what you can remember from the lecture about each bullet point.**

2 ▷9.1 **Watch Extract 1 again and add your own notes to the information on the slide.**

3 **Compare notes and discuss:**

1 which bullet points were not covered in this extract

2 whether you both wrote down similar information

3 how you chose what to write and how to write it

4 to what extent you think lecturer's slides / your own notes are most useful

5 whether your notes would be clear if you came back to them several weeks later.

> The *process* of university learning in English-speaking universities
>
> - Reading
> - Listening (actively)
> - Writing
> - Laboratories or practical experiences
> - Discussion
> - Debate
> - Critique
> - Questioning
> - Developing and supporting an argument (YOUR argument)
> - Finding your voice and your place in a re-made world

TASK 4 Reflecting on techniques for dealing with lectures

1 **Work with another pair to compare your ideas from Tasks 2 and 3. Compile a list of advice for students about dealing with lectures in English.**

Example: *After a lecture, combine your own notes with the lecturer's slides.*

2 **Present your advice to the class.**

You may be asked to read a text in preparation for a seminar discussion and give a brief summary to the group. This process involves summarizing the key points of the text clearly and concisely, and adding your own response or evaluation by comparing the ideas with your existing knowledge; from your reading or lectures, or from your own experience. You may find you support the arguments in the text, or you may question and criticize, and in these cases, you should be prepared to support your ideas with reasons, evidence, or examples.

This module covers:

- Preparing an oral summary and evaluation of a text
- Participating in a seminar discussion and incorporating examples

TASK 1 Critical thinking – comparing academic cultures

1 ▶9.4 **Watch an extract from the lecture by Dr Kathleen Quinlan. Note any differences that students from other cultures might notice at a British university.**

2 **Work in pairs. Discuss any differences from your own experience.**

3 **Think of other ways in which British academic culture might be different from other cultures you know about. Consider the following points and add others.**

- asking questions
- relationship between students and academic staff
- teamwork and collaborative study

TASK 2 Reading to prepare for a seminar discussion

1 **You are going to take part in a seminar discussion on the following question.**

> **DISCUSSION:** *In what ways and to what extent do differences in academic culture present a challenge to international students at universities in English-speaking countries?*

Divide into two groups, A and B. Each group will read one of two texts on the topic.

2 **Students in group A: read the text on page 221. Students in group B: read the text on page 222. As you read, make notes on:**

1 the main perspective(s) of the text (e.g. education, linguistics)
2 the groups of people it predominantly refers to (e.g. students, specific nationalities)
3 the main issues highlighted and support given
4 implications / suggestions.

3 **Work with other students who read the same text. Identify the key ideas in the text.**

> **ACADEMIC LANGUAGE**
>
> **Discussion** Giving examples
>
> You can explain or support an idea or an argument by using an example from sources (reading or lectures), from general contexts familiar to other participants, or from your own experience.
>
> - Examples from sources:
>   **The example in the text we read** about Americans not using formal titles …
>   **I'm interested in this idea that's come up** several times **about** …
> - General or hypothetical examples:
>   **In Germany, for example**, most students stay in their home town, unlike here, so …
>   **Say** that every student called out when they wanted to ask a question.
> - Personal examples from your own experience:
>   For example, **from my own experience as** a high school teacher in China, …
>   **There was this** researcher that I was collaborating with …

TASK 3 Giving examples

1 🔊 9.5 Listen to two students giving examples to illustrate a point. Note down:
- the type of example(s) they use (from a source, general, or personal)
- the language they use to introduce their example(s).

	Type of example(s)	Language that introduces the example(s)
Student A		*I'm interested in this idea that's come up ... about ...*
Student B		

2 Work in your same-text groups from Task 2. Report specific examples from your text. Use appropriate language from Academic Language on page 148 to introduce the example, giving the source and paraphrasing in your own words.

   Example: *Gallagher gives the example of students from East Asia who tend to feel ...*

3 Look again at the discussion question in Task 2, then discuss your reactions to the text. Use the prompts below. Give examples from your own experience where possible.
- In what ways are the ideas in the text relevant to the discussion question?
- To what extent do you agree with the ideas in the text?
- What criticisms or limitations can you identify?
- Do the ideas match your own experiences?

TASK 4 Preparing an oral summary and evaluation of a text

1 Work in your same-text groups from Task 2. Collaboratively develop an oral summary of the main points of the text. Follow the guidelines below.

> **Guidelines for giving an oral summary of a text**
> 1 Include the name of the authors and the overall topic of the text.
> 2 If the text is reporting on a research project, briefly outline it.
> 3 Explain any key terms or abbreviations clearly from the start.
> 4 Summarize the text in two or three key points.
> 5 Only include examples if they help to explain a key point.

2 Work alone. Decide how to introduce your text in a seminar discussion, and make notes.
- Keep your introduction brief – 1–2 minutes.
- Note ideas from the oral summary in 1.
- Explain how the text relates to the main discussion question. Remember, some group members have not read the same text.
- Include your own brief, evaluative comments using ideas from Task 3.3.

TASK 5 Participating in a seminar discussion

1 Form into mixed groups, e.g. two As and two Bs, for a seminar discussion on the question in Task 2.1. Follow the process below.

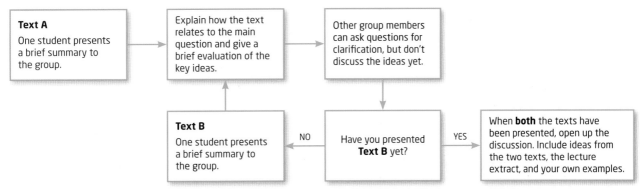

2 Report back to the class on your discussion, picking out two or three key points.

1 Although the more colourful idioms found in conversation or journalism (*raining cats and dogs, once in a blue moon*) are not typical in academic genres, some multi-word expressions are commonly used in academic writing. Explain the meaning of the idioms from this unit highlighted in sentences 1–4.

1 By focusing on various actions involved in 'harnessing fortune', certain features **come to the fore**.

2 Ethnocentrism is one solution to the inevitable tension when people with different cultural backgrounds **come into contact**.

3 … 'Tribal' reality shows favour entertainment **at the expense of** education.

4 **In the same vein**, Ballard (1996: 155) reports an exchange between a politics lecturer in an Australian university and a Japanese student.

2 In pairs, compare your answers and discuss whether each of the idioms always has the same fixed form or whether it can vary. Use a dictionary if necessary.

Example: *I think you can also say 'bring something to the fore'.*

3 Complete sentences 1–6 with one word in each space. Underline the idiom in each case.

1 Each feature may be present to a greater or _____ extent in any individual.

2 These voters tend to vote for the same party _____ matter who the candidate is.

3 Higher levels of rainfall can _____ rise to flooding and landslides.

4 The report paints a disturbing _____ of the state of UK prisons.

5 The ban on smoking in public places _____ into force in England and Wales in 2007.

6 Germany introduced stricter controls and other countries soon followed _____ .

4 In pairs, discuss the meaning and variability of the idioms you identified in 3.

9F Research Project (3)

Making an outline plan

What is an outline plan?

When you have researched your topic, you need to organize your ideas into a coherent structure. This will involve identifying the key themes that have emerged and organizing these into a basic plan with an introduction, three or four main sections, and a conclusion.

Example:

Working title: *Technology in the English language classroom: aid or distraction?*

Introduction: *context and thesis statement*

1. *Technology in English language teaching: brief overview & literature review*
2. *Technology in the classroom*
   a. used by teachers – case study 1: interactive whiteboards – uses & evaluation
   b. used by students – case study 2: electronic dictionaries – uses & evaluation
3. *Discussion: technology as an aid to learning or a distraction?*

Conclusion: *summary, 'answer', limitations, the future*

Organize your ideas by:

- **choosing two or three main themes.** Focus on the themes which fit together. You may have to drop some interesting points at this stage.

- **grouping themes into a logical structure.** Consider whether any typical academic text structures, such as cause and effect (8B), comparison (4B), or problem-solution (10B), fit your topic.

- **trying to achieve a balance.** Bear in mind especially the balance between description, evaluation and discussion. Make notes about your critical response to what you read to form the evaluative element of your project.

TO DO Stage 3: Planning phase

When you are happy with your outline plan, you can start adding detail.

- Add more detailed notes about what to include in each section.
- Note down references from your research so far to support your points in each section.
- Delete any sections that do not fit logically, or for which you do not have enough material.
- Identify any gaps where you may need to do more research.

UNIT 10 Globalization

ACADEMIC FOCUS: PROBLEMS, SOLUTIONS, AND EVALUATION

LEARNING OBJECTIVES

This unit covers:

Reading
- Identifying problems, solutions, and evaluation in different texts
- Working out meaning in complex sentences
- Recognizing the perspective and stance of writers and readers

Writing
- Defining problems, proposing and evaluating solutions
- Incorporating voice in an essay
- Planning and writing a problem–solution essay

Listening
- Reading a conference presentation abstract to predict content
- Recognizing known and new information
- Evaluating the summary of a presentation

Speaking
- Pre- to post-presentation planning
- Working towards script independence
- Giving and evaluating a presentation

Vocabulary
- Sensitive language

Research project (4)
- Writing a first draft

Discussion

1 Work alone. For each headline a–d, note down:
- possible causes
- a more general global issue it exemplifies.

Example: *a) cause – increase in Polish immigrants to UK; issue – changing migration patterns*

a POLISH BECOMES ENGLAND'S SECOND LANGUAGE

b MALDIVES ISLAND PARADISE THREATENED BY SEA LEVEL RISES

c RICE HARVEST FAILS IN THAILAND

d BRAZIL LEADS 'OBESITY EPIDEMIC' IN DEVELOPING WORLD

2 Work in groups. Discuss examples of specific problems associated with the global issues you identified in 1.

Example: *A large influx of new migrants to a country can have trouble integrating, and they can also be vulnerable to exploitation.*

3 Focus on one issue. Decide on two or three problems and draw up a list of possible solutions. Divide your solutions into 'local' and 'global'.

4 Present your problems and solutions to the class. Evaluate each solution using the following criteria – is it ...?

cost-effective   culturally acceptable   politically viable
practical   sustainable

Academic texts frequently follow a problem-solution-evaluation pattern. They typically include information about context, description and analysis of the problem(s), existing or proposed solutions, and evaluation integrated at each stage or at the end. You need to identify the context, problems, solutions, and evaluation, and also which ideas are the writer's own and which are from other sources (citations). Such texts tend to deal with controversial issues, and writers are influenced by their own perspective (e.g. Western) and stance. Your response will also be affected by your perspective in relation to the topic.

This module covers:

- Identifying problems, solutions, and evaluation in different texts
- Working out meaning in complex sentences
- Recognizing the perspective and stance of writers and readers

TASK 1 Identifying problems and solutions in a text

1 **Work in pairs. You are going to read a text about the phenomena of *brain drain* and *brain gain* in a global economy. Discuss the possible meaning of these two terms.**

2 **Read Text 1 and take notes on:**
   - the context / situation (time, place, people involved)
   - the problem(s) identified in the text
   - the solutions proposed.

TEXT 1

Promoting the return of international students: examples of three programmes

When individuals who have acquired higher education abroad return home, they often come back not only with a higher level of education, but also with various human capital assets that are not easily obtainable at home. These may include language skills, technical know-how, and a network of business relationships that may lead to new opportunities, to name a few. The return of skilled labour is therefore an important asset for economic development. Often, however, we observe that those individuals who migrate as students, or as temporary workers, do not return home. The ever-increasing number of skilled emigrants, as well as the increase in the number of students studying abroad, is raising concerns of brain drain for developing nations. The emigrants may find better employment opportunities in the host country. But this may be to the detriment of growth and development in the source country. Individual emigrants will typically choose to return home if and only if doing so is their best course of action.

Preventing outflows of workers and students is not easy. It also prevents the acquisition by these individuals, and to some extent by the source country, of knowledge available abroad. In fact, from a policy point of view, and at least in the short run, promoting emigration by workers and students (the latter probably more than the former) in order to acquire higher levels of education and skills may very well be a cost-efficient way to improve the quality of domestic human capital, as opposed to establishing, say, universities or research institutes in the source country.

In this section, we focus on the following policy challenge: how could a government in a source country make the best of the fact that students want to go, or are already going, abroad? Our approach is practical, as we provide a review of three programmes that have been implemented in Latin American countries in order to minimize brain drain, or maximize brain gain. The first programme is implemented by the *Consejo Nacional de Ciencia y Tecnologia* (CONACYT hereafter) in Mexico. The programme has a repatriating component for scientists (i.e. recent PhDs). CONACYT also implements a separate initiative, called the *Sistema Nacional de Investigatores*, in order to provide higher pay for productive researchers, in order to make it more attractive for them to remain at home (and, more generally, in order to encourage their research productivity). The second programme is Colombia's COLFUTURO, whereby a contract is signed with students going abroad. The students receive a stipend that allows them to pay for part of their studies, but in return they must come back home after the completion of their study. [...] Finally, we also review the experience of Colombia's network, an example of a diaspora programme. In this third programme, the objective is to build bridges between those undertaking research at home and Colombian nationals residing in the US, for example, in universities.

SOURCE: Angel-Urdinola, D.F., Takeno, T., and Wodon, Q. (2008). pp.185-186. 'Student migration to the United States and brain circulation: Issues, empirical results, and programmes in Latin America' in Solimano, A. (ed.) *The International Mobility of Talent.* Oxford: Oxford University Press.

3 Identify language in Text 1 that introduces problems and solutions.

Problems	Solutions
… is raising concerns of …	*(programmes) … to minimize …*

4 Write a brief summary (100–120 words) of the key problem and the three solutions described in Text 1. Paraphrase the ideas using language *not* used in the original text.

TASK 2 Identifying evaluation in a problem–solution text

1 Quickly read the first paragraph of Text 2 and find:

a a definition of *global commons*

b seven examples of global commons issues mentioned in the text.

Global commons

TEXT 2

As we welcome the projected 2 billion new global citizens between now and 2050 (the equivalent of two new Indias), it will become increasingly clear that a positive relationship between globalization and development depends on the effective management of the global commons. By global commons, we mean fragile global resources that are important to large numbers of countries. The issue of global commons management is not necessarily or primarily economic, although the financial crisis demonstrated the extent to which global management of economic systems is vital and how the existing institutional framework is unfit for this purpose. Important emerging global commons issues include climate change, fisheries, water resources, food security, pandemic threats, biodiversity, and human security. Each poses a difficult public policy problem in its own right.

A first best approach to managing global commons issues is via multilateral agreements. These are not easy to reach, but successes in the area of multilateral environmental agreements (MEAs) suggest that difficulties can indeed be overcome. As emphasized by Buchanan *et al.* (2009), this is an issue of global cooperation in which 'parochialism interacts with globalization'. If we are to overcome parochialism to achieve global cooperation, it is necessary that the threats of non-cooperation be made explicit, that any significant economic losses inherent in cooperation be addressed, and that successful models in one area (e.g. trade or the environment) be used in other areas.

In the area of climate change, for example, Schelling (2009) rightly pointed out that the developing world is likely to experience the most significant potential damage. Addressing this potential damage will require some form of international cooperation to both protect vulnerable people and help to restructure the emerging energy systems in the developing world itself. It is likely that solving emerging food security issues will be contingent on international cooperation on climate change, as well as reinvigorating the Consultative Group on International Agricultural Research (CGIAR), ignored for too long under the assumption that the food security issue had been 'solved'.

With regard to pandemic threats, the oft-forgotten case of the 'Great Influenza' of 1918 stands as a cautionary tale. A similar outbreak in the modern era could result in the death of hundreds of millions, health deprivation on a vast scale. Responding to such a threat relies on the work of the World Health Organization, with a budget of only that of a single, modern university hospital. This is insufficient preparation.

The global commons agenda is admittedly huge and perhaps overwhelming. The daunting nature of the task cannot be an excuse for inaction, however. If it is, history will not look kindly on the current generation.

SOURCE: Goldin, I. & Reinert. K. (2012). pp.41–42. *Globalization for Development: Meeting New Challenges*. Oxford: Oxford University Press.

2 Read the rest of Text 2 and make notes about four problems and solutions relating to the global commons you listed in 1b.

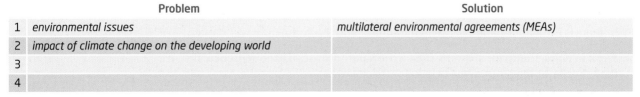

	Problem	Solution
1	*environmental issues*	*multilateral environmental agreements (MEAs)*
2	*impact of climate change on the developing world*	
3		
4		

3 Identify examples of *evaluative language* in Text 2. In each instance, decide whether it evaluates:

a a problem   b a solution   c other writers' ideas.

Example: 'not easy to reach' – *refers to multilateral agreements = evaluation of a solution*

4 Work in pairs and compare findings. Decide whether each evaluation in 3 is more *tentative* or *confident*.

5 Compare Text 1 and Text 2, focusing on the authors' evaluation. Discuss possible reasons for any differences in style.

ACADEMIC LANGUAGE   ▸Language reference page 206

Sentence patterns (1) Identifying subject + verb to work out meaning

Information-rich academic texts often pack a lot of detail into a single, long sentence. Decoding a complex sentence involves identifying the subject (typically a long noun phrase) and the main verb.

● It may be helpful to reduce a sentence to its basic elements (subject + verb, etc.), in order to understand the key idea, i.e. subject, **head noun** in subject, verb:

*With regard to pandemic threats, the oft-forgotten **case** of the 'Great Influenza' of 1918 stands as a cautionary tale.*

= This case stands as a cautionary tale.

*The ever increasing **number** of skilled emigrants, as well as the increase in the number of students studying abroad, is raising concerns of brain drain for developing nations.*

= The increasing number of skilled emigrants is raising concerns.

● The head noun may be an *-ing* form:

*In fact, from a policy point of view, and at least in the short run, **promoting** emigration by workers and students (the latter probably more than the former) in order to acquire higher levels of education and skills may very well be a cost-efficient way to improve the quality of domestic human capital ...*

= Promoting this emigration may be a cost efficient way to improve domestic human capital.

TASK 3 Working out meaning in complex sentences

1 Identify the subject of each highlighted verb in sentences 1–4. Underline the head nouns.

1 Estimates based on panel data for fifty countries over the period 1990–99 provide some limited evidence on brain drain or gain.

2 In a process more akin to 'brain circulation' than 'brain drain', these US-educated engineers and entrepreneurs, aided by the lowered transaction costs associated with digitization, are transferring technical and institutional know-how between distant regional economies faster and more flexibly than most large corporations.

3 The interdependency of socio-ecological systems and the increased reach of human activity have led to major political and scientific challenges in the governance of environmental resources.

4 The global environmental processes commencing from the Stockholm Summit of 1972, the Rio Summit of 1992, and the Rio and non-Rio conventions of climate change, biodiversity, ozone depletion, the Basel Convention, and the POPS (Persistent Organic Pollutants) Convention offer many lessons on how to manage global goods.

2 In sentences 1–4, the head noun is separated from the main verb. In each case, is this because:

a the subject is a long noun phrase with the head near the beginning?

b there is extra information between the subject and the verb?

3 Work in pairs. Compare answers, then write a paraphrase of each sentence in 1. Are they shorter or longer than the originals? Discuss why.

Example: 1 *There is some evidence available on brain drain and gain in data from the 1990s on fifty countries.*

TASK 4 Recognizing the influence of perspective in texts

Work in groups. Read the book cover and discuss:

- the most likely intended audience for the book
- the stance of the writers in relation to globalization
- how the background of writers and audience might influence the ideas in the book.

2 **Quickly read Text 3 and identify the main purpose, a or b. Give reasons.**

a to provide a striking example that introduces discussion of a more general topic

b to give background context for a more detailed discussion of a specific situation

3 **Read Text 3 again and identify at least two *problems* highlighted in the text. For each one, identify any *solution(s)* and *evaluation* given.**

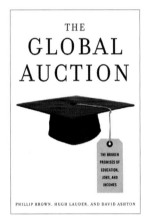

TEXT 3

CHAPTER THREE
Knowledge Wars

Having been to China and been aware of what's going on there, the speed at which the high skills work is being developed is something of a threat I think, and something of a shock ... totally gone is the comfort of, it's just low wage jobs and cheap labor.
– Head of Education Policy, American Industrial Trade Association

The multinational companies are our schools.
– A leading Chinese economist

In southern China, an entire island has been developed into a Higher Education Mega City, with its metro line connecting it to the city of Guangzhou. It is home to 10 universities with 120,000 students and the potential to accommodate another 80,000 students, with 20,000 faculty and 50,000 support staff. It took only 18 months to construct, and includes state-of-the-art information technology (IT) and science labs, world-class libraries, an Olympic-standard stadium and sports facilities. In addition, there are more than 50 research centers in fields ranging from engineering, medicine, IT, and advanced manufacturing, to business management.

The sheer speed and scale of the project demonstrates China's ambition to create a world-class workforce. Expansion plans are also being repeated across emerging economies, with major financial investments in countries like India, Russia, Brazil, Hungary, Lithuania, Ukraine, and the United Arab Emirates. In Saudi Arabia, the King Abdullah University of Science and Technology has an endowment fund of over $10 billion, with ambitious plans to join the ranks of the world's leading universities. All of this presents a major challenge to the idea that the knowledge wars would remain restricted to head nations in North America, Western Europe, and Japan.

Although leading-edge knowledge was supposed to trickle down to emerging economies traveling the evolutionary path to development, in reality it has taken the form of a tsunami of ideas, knowledge, and technologies flooding over national borders. This has contributed to a massive increase in the global supply of college-educated workers armed with the latest scientific ideas, software applications, and management techniques, along with the lingua franca of economic globalization, English.

The explosion in the global supply of college-educated workers is, however, only part of the story. Increasing the supply of educated workers rarely generates the kinds of learning and business innovation necessary for competitiveness. Unlike the pundits of neoliberalism, who assume the supply of human capital creates its own demand in the job market, policy makers in China understood that more is required if investments in education are to translate into economic gain. China has not only expanded its education system, but actively tried to link it to national economic development. Here, Western universities and companies have played a key role in taking best practice to emerging countries, offering a crash course in what it takes to globally compete on brainpower.

SOURCE: Brown, P., Lauder, H., & Ashton, D. (2011). pp.29–30. *The Global Auction: the broken promises of education, jobs, and incomes.* New York: Oxford University Press.

4 **Briefly discuss how the background of the writers influenced the ideas in Text 3. Did it match your suggestions in 1?**

1 Read Text 4, from the same chapter, and identify *problems*, *solutions*, and *evaluation*.

TEXT 4

Engineering the future: the focus on science, engineering, and technology in Asia

When we look behind the headline figures of educational expansion around the globe, it's important to consider what subjects are being studied in pursuit of a college diploma. In America, the rhetoric of 'learning is earning' led to the view that it does not matter what is studied, because interesting well-paid jobs are available across the economy. But no matter how a knowledge economy is defined, it is difficult to produce an account that does not include the centrality of science and technology, given that these are major fields of innovation.

If America has been engaged in an act of 'unilateral educational disarmament', it stems from large numbers of students attracted to celebrity careers and the lure of big prize-winners at the top of industries like finance, law, business, fashion, and media. This has been reinforced by proponents of the knowledge economy who portrayed manufacturing as part of yesterday's economy, overtaken by knowledge economy jobs in financial services and other creative industries. In response, talented students turned their backs on what are viewed as less exciting or financially rewarding careers in science, technology, engineering, or math (STEM subjects). Even before the financial crash, the governor of the Bank of England, Mervyn King, was sufficiently concerned to speak out against the social and educational distortions caused by inequalities in material wealth, working conditions, and cultural prestige in the financial markets in London, which applied equally to Wall Street. 'I do think it is rather unattractive that so many young people, when contemplating careers, look at the compensation packages available in the City and think ... it is the only place to work in. It shouldn't be. It should be one of the places, but not the only one.'

In the early 1970s, there were four times more bachelor's degrees awarded to American students studying engineering than communication and journalism. This picture dramatically changed as more students now graduate in journalism or related programs than engineering. The picture of mathematics and statistics is especially perilous because, although the number of students in colleges and universities significantly increased, those studying mathematics and statistics fell from 24,801 to 14,770 during the same period, representing a fraction of the bachelor's degrees awarded in psychology (18,134) or business (318,042). In the United Kingdom, we find a similar picture. There are now twice as many students studying business and administration than engineering and technology. Even in computing, a discipline that stands at the heart of high-tech industry, there has been a significant decline. The number of students studying computing fell by 22 percent between 2003 and 2006, a decline of more than 30,000 students, which may reflect concerns about future employment prospects as high-skill computing jobs are offshored. [...]

In Asia, the study of science, technology, and engineering is viewed as crucial to national economic development and the route to a worthwhile career, in the way a liberal arts degree is in North America. We were made aware of this during a visit to a high-achieving school in Singapore in the late 1990s. Students told us how mathematics was the core subject, because it offered the flexibility to take different routes into higher education and the job market. This was reinforced by a strong steer from government based on the view that you could make a manager out of an engineer, but you couldn't make an engineer out of a manager.

The Singapore government has relaxed this approach as it strives to diversify its economy. But the focus on science, technology, and engineering remains a major facet of the educational explosion across Asia. When we compare national differences in the proportion of students studying engineering for their first degree, the scale of the transformation in the global distribution of expertise in key areas of the knowledge economy becomes obvious. In China, around 37 percent of students are studying engineering compared to 27 percent in South Korea, 22 percent in Germany, 7 percent in the United Kingdom, and 5 percent in the United States.

SOURCE: as Text 3

2 **Work in groups and discuss:**

a the writers' stance towards student discipline choices in the US (and the UK) and in Asian countries

b evidence the writers use to support their stance

c assumptions that underlie the writers' arguments

d examples of evaluation that are *explicit* (clearly expressed in the text) and *implicit* (that you understand, but which are not directly expressed).

TASK 6 Critical thinking – responding to texts

1 Work in groups. Discuss the main factors influencing your decisions about what and where to study. How do these relate to the ideas in this module? Consider:
- personal strengths and interests
- social influences: from family, teachers, and wider society
- the education system and curriculum you followed in school
- future career prospects
- financial incentives: grants, scholarships, job prospects, etc.

2 Choose at least three examples of evaluation in Texts 3 and 4. How far do you agree with the authors? Support your stance with examples from your own experience.

3 Discuss the question below and prepare to present your answer, with examples.

To what extent does your own perspective and stance on a topic influence your response to a text?

4 Choose one person from the group to summarize your answer.

TASK 7 Synthesizing material from texts to use in a discussion

1 Work alone. You are going to discuss one of the following statements. Select the one you most agree with and note down some initial points to support it.
- a International agreements and national government intervention are needed in order to limit the negative effects of 'brain drain' in certain countries.
- b The increasing global mobility of students is a long-term solution to the problem of global commons such as the allocation of scarce water supplies.

2 Prepare for the discussion by identifying material in Texts 1–4 in this module which relates to the statement you chose in 1.

3 Work in groups with students who chose the same statement. Discuss your responses, drawing on the material in the texts to support your argument. Choose one student to note down the main ideas.

4 Evaluate the content of your discussion in 3. Use your notes and the criteria below.
- 1 Have the arguments been supported by relevant source material from Texts 1–4?
- 2 Have further examples and explanation been offered to support the arguments?
- 3 Has the argument reached a conclusion or resolution?

In a problem-solution essay, you will present a situation leading to a problem, speculate on causes, then propose and evaluate solutions. Your essay should flow logically from one point to the next, using appropriate language. You need to critically evaluate the problem(s) and solution(s) you propose. Evaluation is subjective – it reflects your own perspective and stance on an issue – so this is an important area where you can develop your own **voice**, so that your audience has the sense that they are reading an original piece of work.

This module covers:
- Defining problems, proposing and evaluating solutions
- Incorporating voice in an essay
- Planning and writing a problem-solution essay

TASK 1 Defining problems

1 **Work in groups. Read the situation and decide which problem presents the most serious challenge a) globally, b) in your country. Give reasons and examples.**

Situation

The provision of education, particularly in tertiary contexts, is becoming increasingly globalized. This trend towards globalization is characterized by more internationalized and standardized curricula (particularly in business and STEM subjects), increasing movement of students to other countries to study, and the use of English as the medium of instruction.

Potential problems
- international study can be very expensive for students
- key sectors of education could become controlled by multinational organizations
- students whose first language is not English may be at a disadvantage
- minority languages might be marginalized if not used for academic purposes

2 **Use the list below, and think of more problems arising from the situation in 1.**

career and professional   culture   national identity   personal and family

3 **Evaluate each problem you have identified using questions 1–5.**
1 How likely is the problem to happen?
2 What effects might there be as a result?
3 How potentially widespread is the problem, e.g. very localized or global?
4 How difficult would it be to find solutions to the problem?
5 Is the problem widely understood, and is it being addressed? If so, who by?

4 **Collaboratively summarize the problems you discussed, and your evaluation.**

TASK 2 Proposing and evaluating solutions

1 **In your groups, select one of the problems you discussed in Task 1. Note down possible solutions from two different perspectives (e.g. geographical, political).**

2 **Evaluate your solutions. How likely are they to work? What results might you see?**

Example: Problem: International study can be very expensive for students.
            Solution: *The cost can be met through a long-term loan, which can be paid back after graduation.*
            Evaluation: *This is a risky option, as students may not find a well-paid job.*

Evaluation (4) Collocation and connotation

A **connotation** is a cultural or emotional association which affects the meaning of a word or phrase. When evaluating, you can emphasize or downplay something by selecting and/or combining words and phrases to express a range of connotations. Compare:

- *a significant problem, a serious challenge* – serious, negative connotations
- *a relevant issue, one possible challenge* – largely neutral
- *a minor problem, an interesting challenge* – less serious or more optimistic connotations

Some nouns, e.g. *crisis, emergency, disaster,* always have a serious, negative connotation; they suggest that something very bad has already happened.

Selecting **collocations** with specific connotations will refine your meaning. You can adjust the connotation through your choice of noun, adjective, or adverb to express a more positive or negative, approving or disapproving, optimistic or pessimistic, tentative or confident evaluation. Notice the changes of meaning here:

> *Finding suitably qualified English teachers is clearly one of the **key issues** for English-medium universities in non-English-speaking countries.*

> *Finding suitably qualified English teachers is already a very **real issue** for many English-medium universities in non-English-speaking countries.*

> *Finding suitably qualified English teachers can sometimes be a **contentious issue** for English-medium universities in some non-English-speaking countries.*

TASK 3 Refining your evaluations

1 **Make collocations using an adjective / adverb plus a noun / verb from the table below. Add a determiner where necessary.**

Examples: *a significant problem, successfully tackle*

Adjectives and adverbs		Nouns and verbs
1 significant, considerable, serious, minor	a	problem, crisis, challenge
2 quick, simple, practical, possible, definitive	b	solution, fix, answer
3 adverse, positive, serious, potential, little	c	outcome, impact, repercussion
4 directly, successfully, effectively, explicitly	d	address, tackle, confront
5 easily, efficiently, largely, completely	e	solve, overcome, alleviate
6 potentially, seriously, adversely, primarily	f	affect, threaten, attack

2 **Describe your phrases in 1. Use the following ideas:**

- positive or negative
- approving or disapproving
- optimistic or pessimistic
- tentative or confident

Example: *'a significant problem' is quite negative and pessimistic*
'successfully tackle' sounds fairly confident

3 **Choose the best combinations from the table to describe problems and solutions you discussed in Tasks 1 and 2.**

Example: *The spread of English-medium universities could have **potentially serious repercussions** for minority languages.*

1 Read the essay plan below. Work in pairs and discuss the points for each paragraph. Make notes about evaluation that could be included.

> **TITLE:** *What can be done to address the challenges facing minority languages in today's globalized tertiary education sector?*

Essay plan

Introduction

With English becoming increasingly established as the *lingua franca* of the globalized economy (Brown, Lauder, & Ashton, 2011), it is perhaps unsurprising that there has been an accompanying increase in English-medium tertiary education across the globe. The prevalence of English in academic contexts, however, poses a potential threat to minority languages, defined here as those with fewer than 10 million speakers, which are being 'squeezed out' of the curriculum, creating what some see as an English 'monoculture'. This essay focuses on the case of Scandinavian languages and in particular Swedish, with very few subjects now taught through the medium of Swedish at university level. It explores the tensions between market forces pushing students and educators in the direction of English, and social, cultural, and political pressures to prevent local languages and cultures being allowed to decline. It goes on to evaluate the effectiveness of supporting minority languages through intervention at a national and international level.

Body paragraph 1 - description and overview of the **situation** and **problem** in a specific context
- English 'monoculture'
  - introduce concept and causes of monoculture - university rankings & performance indicators based on international publications, dominated by English
- Scandinavia
  - a well-established case of the 'increasing monoculture' of English
  - minority languages - English taught from early age
  - few subjects taught in local language (mainly literature & history)
- Rest of world
  - brief overview of other global regions affected by similar problems

Body paragraph 2 - **solution 1** with integrated evaluation
- national strategy to encourage local languages
  - governmental (Swedish) / intergovernmental (Scandinavian / EU) strategy incl. new laws to protect minority languages & subsidize tertiary teaching in these languages
  - price differentiation - levy on English-medium courses to cross-subsidize courses in Swedish, etc.
  - use of open-source, online channels to publish academic papers in local languages

Body paragraph 3 - **solution 2** with integrated evaluation
- UN intervention
  - UNESCO programmes and initiatives to promote mother tongue-based education
  - new, binding international agreements on the use of languages in education for all member states

2 Based on your discussion in 1, summarize your stance on the issue in the essay title in *one* sentence.

3 Write a short conclusion (100–150 words) using Checklist E on page 210 to structure your paragraph. Remember to:
- bear in mind your stance and evaluative comments in making your voice clear
- use hedging language to avoid over-confident comments and over-generalization.

4 Exchange your conclusion with another student. Give feedback on:
- how clearly their voice comes across
- how effectively their conclusion fits in with the rest of the essay.

TASK 5 Planning a problem–solution essay

1 You are going to write a problem–solution essay. Work in pairs. Read the essay title and note down problems that university education might be facing.

> **TITLE:** *University education is facing unprecedented challenges in the face of increasing globalization. Which challenges are most serious, and how can they be addressed?*

2 Consider how the following might be relevant to the topic. Add any extra points to your ideas in 1.

- qualifications and curriculums
- academic publications
- university rankings
- different academic cultures and norms

3 Plan your essay. Work through the stages below.

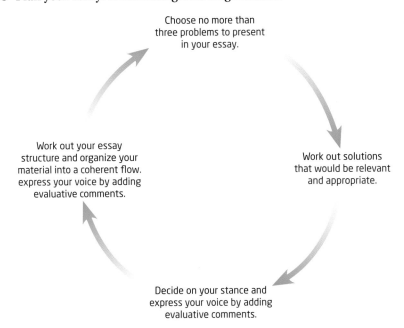

Choose no more than three problems to present in your essay.

Work out solutions that would be relevant and appropriate.

Decide on your stance and express your voice by adding evaluative comments.

Work out your essay structure and organize your material into a coherent flow. express your voice by adding evaluative comments.

4 Decide what further material you need to complete your essay. Write a short list of points to research.

TASK 6 Drafting to refine voice and flow

1 Write a first draft of a 1,000-word essay using material from Task 5.

  1 Write an outline plan. Choose a suitable structure, e.g. problem + solution + solution (as Task 4), or problem–solution, problem–solution.

  2 Refine your plan individually or collaboratively to achieve a logical flow.

  3 Write a first draft of your essay, incorporating your own voice via evaluation.

  4 Exchange first drafts and give critical feedback using Checklist H on page 210.

2 Write the final draft of your essay, incorporating changes from feedback.

3 Note down 'next steps' to work on for your next essay.

  Example: *Remember to include hedging language in evaluative comments to avoid making over-generalizations.*

Presentations can be within a familiar context such as a university course, or more public, e.g. at an academic or professional conference. Presenters have to submit their title and abstract in advance, and these are published in the conference programme. The presentation may give the results of research, an interim 'work in progress' report, or new thinking on a topic. Presentations at conferences are expected to offer something new, rather than simply be a description of, for example, a theory. A summary of the presentation may be written up for inclusion in the **conference proceedings** – a post-event publication which can reach a wider audience.

This module covers:

- Reading a conference presentation abstract to predict content
- Recognizing known and new information
- Evaluating the summary of a presentation

TASK 1 Reading a presentation abstract to predict content

1 Read the abstract of a presentation and identify the main problems and solutions that the presenter expects to cover.

TITLE: *The global pharmaceutical market today: confronting the challenges*

Abstract

This presentation focuses on current challenges facing the global pharmaceutical market, and offers possible solutions. Characterized by widespread monopolies, poorly-informed consumers, limited competition, and highly variable demand, the global pharmaceutical market is currently imperfect and imbalanced. Given extreme variations in pharmaceutical expenditure across different income countries and rising per capita expenditure, solutions need to involve both governments and private providers, and address the financing of medicines through policies such as the increased use of generic products to reduce costs. Through strategic planning in public financing, health insurance, and user fees, the pharmaceutical market can achieve a better balance.

---

2 Find examples of evaluation in the abstract. Identify the evaluative language.

  1 Is it confident or tentative?

  2 What is the presenter's stance on the main issue?

3 Based on this title and abstract, what type of audience would the presentation attract?

TASK 2 Listening to and evaluating a presentation

1 ▶10.1 Watch the presentation and make notes on:
- Situation (background and wider context)
- Problems
- Solutions
- Evaluation at each stage.

2 Work in pairs and compare notes. Add any points you missed.

3 Watch the presentation again and evaluate it using criteria 1–5. Compare responses.

  1 Did the presenter follow the abstract closely?

  2 Was the content relevant and sufficient to achieve the aims set out in the abstract?

  3 Was the research clearly cited and relevant to the presentation aims?

  4 Was the delivery effective? Consider language, pronunciation, fluency, and manner.

  5 Did the presenter use visuals effectively?

4 Write down questions you would like to ask the presenter.

ACADEMIC LANGUAGE

Sentence patterns (2) Known and new information

When listening, it is important to recognize information you already know, and information which is new and adds to your understanding of the topic. This will help you to make effective notes and link ideas from different parts of your studies.

English sentences typically start with known information; this may be the topic of the text or presentation, or it may be something already mentioned earlier. This known information introduces the new information, which is presented at the end, and often contains evaluation:

The pharmaceutical market is not a perfect market where supply perfectly matches demand.

↑
Topic of the presentation

I'd like to look at public financing, health insurance, and user fees. As far as public financing is concerned, this finance is mainly raised through taxation.

↑
mentioned before

If several pieces of information are presented in a sentence, useful background information (which may or may not be new to the reader / listener) may be given in the middle:

The WHO is the world's most visible global health organization, with a 193-country membership, which means it operates at both a global and a local level.

TASK 3 Recognizing known and new information

1 **Identify why the highlighted information in sentences a, c, and e below is 'known' to the audience.**

1 It can be seen in the visuals.

2 It is general knowledge / common sense.

3 It has been mentioned before in the presentation.

a The WHO is the world's most visible global health organization, with a 193-country membership, which means it operates at both a global and local level.

b This global reach means that they are able to collect data from more countries than any other organization.

c As we can see, this table shows the private and government per capita expenditure on pharmaceuticals in1990 and 2000.

d First, private expenditure on pharmaceuticals outweighs government expenditure in all income categories ...

e Most parties agree that medicine costs need to be kept down, so national governments have a key role to play in drawing up principled lists of cost-effective medicines.

f Governments can use their buying power to negotiate with the manufacturer on prices.

g They can do this effectively by comparing the medicines with others on the market.

2 **For each sentence a–g, identify:**

1 known / background information and why it can be described as 'known'

2 new information.

TASK 4 Evaluating the summary of a presentation

1 **Read the presentation summary on page 223. Evaluate it using questions 1–6.**

1 Does the summary include all the main points of the presentation?

2 Is the summary well-structured and does it present the information clearly?

3 Are all the technical terms and acronyms explained?

4 Are the language and style appropriate for the genre, audience, and purpose?

5 Are the references given in the summary accurately presented?

6 Is the material in the abstract, presentation, and summary coherent?

Delivering a presentation gives you the opportunity to both inform and challenge your audience. Presentations are often used to propose and evaluate solutions to a problem. Start by reading around the topic and carrying out research. You need to select and refine the material, then structure and practise the presentation. You should aim for a certain amount of **script independence**, i.e. being able to deliver your presentation without reading it from a script. You may have the opportunity to write up the presentation for wider circulation in a publication.

This module covers:
- Pre- to post-presentation planning
- Working towards script independence
- Giving and evaluating a presentation

TASK 1 Advice on giving a presentation

1 Match the stages in the list to advice on giving a presentation 1–8.

abstract   content   delivery   practice   post-presentation   research   ~~topic~~   visuals

1	_topic_	decide the title and aims of the presentation
2		do background reading and find sources to support your main points
3		include enough, but not too much, material to meet the presentation aims
4		prepare slides to support key points in the presentation
5		rehearse the presentation in front of other people and get critical feedback
6		write a short summary of the presentation aims for your audience
7		aim for a fluent delivery, with varied pace and some script independence
8		write up a summary of the presentation

2 Work in groups. Divide up the stages in 1 and think of more advice for each. Present back to your group.

Example: *During the practice stage, you should anticipate audience questions and prepare responses.*

3 Rate the advice below from 1 (important) to 5 (not important). Add ideas of your own.

Pronunciation, vocabulary, and grammar for presentations
- Notice, and keep a record of, useful language chunks and expressions.
- Memorize sentences / text to use at specific points in the presentation.
- Work with a colleague on language, focusing particularly on accuracy.
- Play fluency games, e.g. speak for one minute on a topic without hesitation.
- Record sections of the presentation to analyse stress, rhythm, and intonation.
- ...

TASK 2 Pre- to post-presentation planning

1 You are going to give a presentation. Prepare using the following stages to guide you.

> **PRESENTATION ACTIVITY:** *Prepare a ten-minute presentation on a problem linked to globalization.*

Topic and title
- Choose a topic which you are interested in and know something about, e.g. aviation.
- Consider how globalization has raised new challenges in this area.
  Example: *More international travel means increased traffic at major hub airports.*
- Narrow down your topic by focusing on a specific problem, e.g. congestion at London Heathrow Airport.
- Give your presentation a working title: a statement or a question.
  Example: *What is the best solution for relieving congestion at London's major hub airport?*

Research and content

- Bring together the information you already have, and search for new information on the topic.
- Focus on information about problems and solutions (existing or proposed).
- Check that information is relevant to your working title; adapt your title as necessary.

Structure

- Work with your material to build a coherent presentation. Select only what is relevant.
- Plan the introduction, giving the rationale for your presentation and an overview of the situation.
- Formulate main points for the body of your presentation.
- Decide how to organize problems, solutions, and evaluation – in separate sections or integrated.
- Prepare a brief conclusion, summing up your main points and including overall evaluative comments.

Visuals

- Prepare clear visuals and images on slides or posters to support your material.
- Include limited text: a few words / bullet points per slide.
- Include references for any citations on the relevant slide and/or at the end of the presentation.

Language

- Select about five key pieces of information that you plan to present. Formulate sentences to express these. (See Academic Language box on page 163 for effective ways to include multiple points in one sentence.)
- Write out what you plan to say in the *first* and the *last* minute of your presentation.

Practice

- Practise your presentation using ideas from Task 1, working towards script independence.
- Anticipate questions, and ask other students to ask you questions. Prepare responses.

Abstract

- Write a 100-word abstract for your finalized presentation.

TASK 3 Working towards script independence

1 Work in pairs. Read the following methods of achieving script independence in a presentation, and decide what would work best for you. Compare answers.

a Use small cue cards with the main points presented in bullet points or visual form with different colours.

b Print out your slides annotated with your main points, to serve as visual prompts.

c Repeatedly practise your presentation content until you feel you know it.

d With others, take turns to give short sections of your presentation. Comment on how the information is presented.

e With others, practise your delivery. Focus on stress, rhythm, intonation, pace, and variety.

f Practise memorizing your main points using techniques like studying your script, chanting, and repetition.

g Think of a narrative or story to link your main points together.

TASK 4 Giving and evaluating a presentation

1 Give out copies of your abstract for other students to read in advance. Take turns to give your presentations.

2 While watching other presentations, evaluate them using Checklist I on page 211.

3 Draw up a whole-class action plan of areas to work on in future presentations.

1 **Academic study often touches on socially or culturally sensitive topics. Choosing appropriate vocabulary to set the right tone and avoid causing offence is very important. In pairs, compare the vocabulary choices highlighted in extracts 1–3.**

> 1 Ward *et al.* (1958) were the first to draw attention to the high incidence of viral hepatitis among **mentally retarded patients** (Szmuness, Pick & Prince, 1970; 51–52).

> 2 Though it is recognized that the presence of a **mentally handicapped child** may be a source of stress for a family, less is known about precisely which impairments are particularly stressful (Quine & Pahl, 1985; 501).

> 3 The programme, launched in 2003, works with local authorities to develop systems of self-directed support for **people with learning difficulties** (Parvaneh, Moran & Glendinning, 2009; 920).

2 **Suggest reasons for the different vocabulary in extracts 1–3. What implications does this have for your own reading and writing?**

3 **Discuss the different possible connotations and uses of the sets of words and phrases a–d.**

a crippled, handicapped, disabled

b an old lady, an elderly woman, older women

c a poor country, a Third World country, a developing country

d a child from a poor family, children from deprived areas, children from disadvantaged backgrounds

4 **Compare your answers and discuss how usage might differ if you are:**

- talking about a figure or place in literature, art, or history
- referring to specific individuals (e.g. subjects in a study) or a more general group.

10F Research Project (4)

Writing a first draft

What is a first draft?

Your **first draft** is a complete version of your text, not just notes or an outline. However, you will probably make changes to it later, based on your own proofreading and feedback from your tutor. This will produce a **final draft** which you will submit for assessment. In order to complete an extended piece of writing, make a **study plan** to help you structure your time.

To manage your time:

- **divide your project into stages and allocate time for each stage.** Don't spend too long on one stage; if you go past the allocated time, move on to the next stage.
- **do the most difficult work when your concentration is highest.** If you are struggling with a difficult section, move on to something simpler and come back to it later.

- **review the next day.** When you are working closely on something, it is difficult to evaluate your writing objectively. If you come back to it the next day, you are more likely to spot errors or inconsistencies.

TO DO Stage 4: Main writing phase

Some writers start at the introduction and work through to the conclusion. Others prefer to work on different sections of their project and put them together at the end. Whichever method you choose, make sure you:

- always keep in mind your title, thesis or research question, and consider how each point, example, paragraph or section is linked to this
- use headings and subheadings to help structure your writing
- keep an eye on your word count – it can be helpful to allocate an approximate number of words for each section
- keep a list of full references for any citations you include for your bibliography – it will be much more difficult to go back and search for them again later.

UNIT 11 Observation

ACADEMIC FOCUS: CHRONOLOGY – CASE STUDY AND PROCESS

LEARNING OBJECTIVES

This unit covers:

Reading
- Understanding case studies
- Using generic language to express relationships
- Taking detailed notes to use for writing

Writing
- Analysing types of process and identifying evaluation
- Writing a description of a process based on notes from reading and research

Listening
- Using visuals to understand and explain key concepts
- Taking notes on multiple related processes

Speaking
- Analysing a process text and developing material to use in a discussion
- Participating in a seminar discussion

Vocabulary
- Word formation (2)

Research project (5)
- Making a clear argument

Discussion

1 **Work in groups. Think of examples of what researchers can observe in different disciplines.**

   Example: *In psychology, researchers observe their subjects in a range of settings, e.g. people doing role plays, or how animals behave.*

2 **How is observation necessary in the following disciplines? What differences are there across disciplines?**

   business   computer science   history of art   languages
   law   mathematics   pharmacology   *other ...?*

   Example: *In Languages, researchers observe people learning another language in order to understand patterns and propose theories about how people learn.*

3 **Think about the disciplines you have discussed. How can observation be involved in both *qualitative* and *quantitative* research?**

   Example: Languages – *Researchers interview the subjects about how they feel when making mistakes (qualitative). They systematically record the types of mistake (quantitative).*

4 **Think of examples of observation in the following processes.**
   - the development of a new drug
   - the growth of an emerging market economy
   - shifting power relations in a multinational corporation
   - creating a new app

Case studies present detailed research in a specific context (people in a company headquarters, an event like an election, etc.) which may be generalizable across other contexts. Case studies are a key genre describing chronology (time and sequence). Researchers study a context over an extended period of time, using a range of research methods (observation, questionnaires, etc.). You may read the original source of a case study written up in a journal, or a reported version cited in another text. You need to understand the context and aim(s) of the research; the methods used, the main findings, and the conclusion and evaluation, and record these clearly in notes for later use.

This module covers:

- Understanding case studies
- Using generic language to express relationships
- Taking detailed notes to use for writing

TASK 1 Understanding the case study genre

1 **Work in groups. Read the definition of 'case study' and decide which research aim** 1–5 **would be *least suited* to this approach. Give reasons.**

Research aims

1 to determine the extent to which one multinational bank's employee attitudes to corruption vary across different countries

2 to trace the language development of a postgraduate student studying in an overseas university during their degree programme

3 to study the impact of the 2011 tsunami on coastal settlements in Pacific countries

4 to formulate a new beauty product to reduce the visual effects of facial wrinkles

5 to document the social practices of high-status males in one Kenyan village

case study *noun* A research design that entails the detailed and intensive analysis of a single case. The term is sometimes extended to include the study of just two or three cases for comparative purposes.

2 **Read Text 1, from a textbook on research methods. Complete the notes.**

Genre; Audience; Purpose	*extract from university textbook; aimed at students of business; to present an initial overview of case study design and research*
Definition of case study	
Types of case	
Selected examples	

Case study design

TEXT 1

The basic case study entails the detailed and intensive analysis of a single case. As Stake (1995) observes, case study research is concerned with the complexity and particular nature of the case in question. The case study approach is a very popular and widely used research design in business research (Eisenhardt & Graebner, 2007), and some of the best-known studies in business and management research are based on this design. A case can be:

- *a single organization,* such as Pettigrew's (1985) research at Imperial Chemical Industries (ICI), Joanne Martin's (1992) study of organizational culture at 'OxCo', a high-technology industry company based in California, or Born's (2004) study of managerialism in the BBC
- *a single location,* such as a factory, production site, or office building – for example, Pollert's (1981) research in a tobacco factory, Linstead's (1985) study of humour in a bakery, or Milkman's (1997) investigation of an automobile assembly plant
- *a person,* as in Marshall's (1995) study of women managers, where each woman constitutes a separate case – such studies are characterized as using the life history or biographical approach
- *a single event,* such as the NASA space shuttle Challenger disaster in 1986 (Vaughan, 1990) or the events surrounding a pipeline accident in Canada (Gephart, 1993).

SOURCE: Bryman, A. & Bell, E. (2011). pp.59–60. *Business Research Methods* (3rd ed.). Oxford: Oxford University Press.

3 **Match the four types of case in Text 1 with four of the research aims in 1.**

4 **Note down the following, then compare:**

1 what you now know about case studies having read Text 1

2 at least three things you *want to know.*

Example: *How did the researchers carry out the different types of case study?*

TASK 2 Using a glossary to understand detail in a text

1 Read Text 2, which follows on from Text 1. Identify points in the text which answer your *want to know* points from Task 1.4. Ignore unknown language at this stage.

What is a case?

TEXT 2

The most common use of the term associates the case study with a geographical location, such as a workplace or organization. What distinguishes a case study from other research designs is the focus on a bounded situation or system, an entity with a purpose and functioning parts. The emphasis tends to be upon intensive examination of the setting. There is a tendency to associate case studies with qualitative research, but such an identification is not appropriate. It is certainly true that exponents of the case study design often favour qualitative methods, such as participant observation and unstructured interviewing, because these methods are viewed as particularly helpful in the generation of an intensive, detailed examination of a case. Knights and McCabe (1997) suggest that the case study provides a vehicle through which several qualitative methods can be combined, thereby avoiding too great a reliance on one single approach. In their study of quality management in a UK retail bank, they were able to combine participant observation with semi-structured interviewing and documentary data collection of company reports, Total Quality Management (TQM) guides, and newsletters. They suggest that the findings from the case study can only be used to identify insights into why so many quality management programmes have failed. However, case studies are frequently sites for the employment of both quantitative and qualitative research. Indeed, within business research, the dominance of positivism has meant that the way that case studies are conducted has been heavily influenced by this epistemological tradition. For example, Lee (1999) reports that qualitative research that is published in American journals tends to cite the work of Yin (1984), who adopts a relatively narrow view of case study research (Lee, Collier, & Cullen 2007). In some instances, when an investigation is based exclusively upon quantitative research, it can be difficult to determine whether it is better described as a case study or as a cross-sectional research design. The same point can often be made about case studies based upon qualitative research.

With a case study, the case is an object of interest in its own right, and the researcher aims to provide an in-depth elucidation of it. Unless a distinction of this or some other kind is drawn, it becomes impossible to distinguish the case study as a special research design, because almost any kind of research can be construed as a case study. However, it also needs to be appreciated that, when specific research illustrations are examined, they can exhibit features of more than one research design. However, for some case study researchers, cases are selected in order to represent a population, and, in such cases, more formal sampling is required. What distinguishes a case study is that the researcher is usually concerned to elucidate the unique features of the case. This is known as an *ideographic* approach. Research designs like the cross-sectional design are known as *nomothetic*, in that they are concerned with generating statements that apply regardless of time and place.

Stake (1995) suggests that the selection of cases should be based first and foremost on the anticipation of the opportunity to learn. Researchers should, therefore, choose cases where they expect learning will be greatest. He distinguishes between three different types of case study. Intrinsic cases are undertaken primarily to gain insight into the particularities of a situation, rather than to gain insight into other cases or generic issues. Instrumental case studies are those that focus on using the case as a means of understanding a broader issue or allowing generalizations to be challenged. Finally, there is the category of multiple or collective cases that are undertaken jointly to explore a general phenomenon. Stake (2005) notes, however, that the boundaries between these three types of case study are often blurred.

SOURCE: as Text 1 p.60

2 Compare answers to 1. Which *want to know* questions are still unanswered?

3 Read Text 2 on page 169 again in detail. Refer to the Glossary from the same book below as you read, to understand the technical content.

GLOSSARY

cross-sectional design A *research design* that entails the collection of data on more than one case (usually quite a lot more than one) and at a single point in time in order to collect a body of quantitative and qualitative data in connection with two or more variables (usually many more than two), which are then examined to detect patterns of association.

epistemological A theory of knowledge. It is particularly employed in this book to refer to a stance on what should pass as acceptable knowledge. See *positivism*, *realism*, and *interpretivism*.

participant observation Research in which the researcher immerses him or herself in a social setting for an extended period of time, observing behaviour, listening to what is said in conversations both between others and with the fieldworker, and asking questions. Participant observation usually includes interviewing key informants and studying documents, and as such is difficult to distinguish from *ethnography*. In this book, participant observation is employed to refer to the specifically observational aspect of ethnography.

population The universe of units from which a *sample* is to be selected.

positivism An *epistemological* position that advocates the application of the methods of the natural sciences to the study of social reality and beyond.

qualitative research Qualitative research usually emphasizes words rather than quantification in the collection and analysis of data. As a *research strategy* it is *inductivist*, *constructivist*, and *interpretivist*, but qualitative researchers do not always subscribe to all three of these features. Compare with *quantitative research*.

quantitative research Quantitative research usually emphasizes quantification in the collection and analysis of data. As a *research strategy* it is *deductivist* and *objectivist* and incorporates a natural science model of the research process (in particular, one influenced by *positivism*), but quantitative researchers do not always subscribe to all three of these features. Compare with *qualitative research*.

SOURCE: as Text 1 pp.713-717

4 Discuss how far the Glossary was helpful to your understanding of Text 2.

5 Select other technical terms from the text that you would like to know more about. Follow the guidelines below.

Guidelines for using a Glossary

1 Is it essential to my understanding of another term (e.g. in order to understand *epistemological* do I also need to understand *positivism*)? → **look it up now**

2 Is it interesting but non-essential to my understanding of the text? → **look it up later**

3 Is it peripheral and unnecessary to my understanding of the text? → **do not look it up**

ACADEMIC LANGUAGE ▸Language reference page 201 2.5

Cohesion (2) Expressing relationships using generic language

A text typically states the main topic at the start, then introduces related ideas using a range of generic structures such as verbs (e.g. *associate X with Y, distinguish X from Y*), nouns (e.g. *the emphasis, a tendency*) and other language, (e.g. *through which ...*).

The opening section of Text 2 illustrates how the writer uses **generic language** to repeatedly connect the main topic to new information (such as its characteristics or relations to other things):

What is a case?

The most common use of the term **associates** the case study **with** a geographical location, **such as** a workplace or organization. What **distinguishes** a case study **from** other research designs **is the focus on** a bounded situation or system, an entity with a purpose and functioning parts. **The emphasis tends to be upon** intensive examination of the setting. **There is a tendency to associate** case studies **with** qualitative research, but **such an identification** is not appropriate ... the case study **provides** a vehicle **through which** several qualitative methods **can be combined**, ...

Identifying the main topic + **generic language** + new information helps you to follow relationships in the text and take effective notes:

Case study

- *associated with geographical location*
- *focuses on 'a bounded situation or system ...'*

TASK 3 Using generic language to express relationships

1 **Complete the text using the expressions in the list.**

based on   can allow   has emphasized the importance of   involves
is relatively little used in   ~~represents~~   Such a   that is typically used to
therefore   through which

What is longitudinal design?

The longitudinal design [1] _represents_ a distinct form of research design [2] ....
map change in business and management research. Pettigrew (1990) [3] ....
longitudinal study in understanding organizations as a way of providing data on the mechanisms and
processes [4] .... changes are created. [5] .... 'contextualist'
research design [6] .... drawing on 'phenomena at vertical and horizontal levels of
analysis and the interconnections between those levels through time' (1990: 269). However, partly
because of the time and cost involved, longitudinal design [7] .... business and
management research. In the form in which it is typically found, it is usually an extension of social
survey research [8] .... self-completion questionnaire or structured interview
research within a cross-sectional design. Consequently, in terms of reliability, replication, and validity,
the longitudinal design is little different from cross-sectional research. However, a longitudinal design
[9] .... some insight into the time order of variables and [10] ....
may be more able to allow causal inferences to be made.

SOURCE: Bryman, A. & Bell, E. (2011). pp.57-8. _Business Research Methods_ (3rd ed.). Oxford: Oxford University Press.

---

2 **Use two different styles to highlight the parts of the text in 1 which refer to
a) the main topic, b) to its characteristics / related features.**

Example: _The longitudinal design represents a distinct form of research design that is
typically used to map change in business and management research._

TASK 4 Making detailed notes to use for writing

1 **Write detailed notes on Texts 1 and 2 for a later writing task. Use your preferred style
(annotating the text, using headings and bullet points, etc.).**

Example: _Case studies_
            SOURCE: _Bryman, A. & Bell, E. (2011). pp.59–60. Business Research Methods
            (3rd ed.). Oxford: Oxford University Press._
            • _Key characteristics:_
              – _associated with geographical location, e.g. workplace / organization_
              – _focus on 'bounded situation or system, an entity with a purpose and
                functioning parts' (p.60), i.e. a case is clearly defined and limited_
              – _associated with qualitative research, but quantitative methods are
                also used_
              – _..._

2 **Choose one specific point in your notes, and write a one-sentence summary.**

Example: _Key characteristics of case studies include an association with a clearly defined
            geographical location, and a tendency to involve mainly quantitative research._

1 Case study researchers often need to capture (i.e. collect and record) data. Work in pairs. Think of different ways of capturing data about a company.

Example: *Researchers can capture data by observing selected company employees at work.*

2 Read Text 3, a summary of a case study from a textbook. Compare the data capture methods you noted in 1 with those in the text. Build up a more complete list.

Research in focus

TEXT 3

General Motors capture data

It comes as a surprise to many people in Britain to find out that Vauxhall is known to many people under a different name: General Motors. General Motors began life in 1908 and grew to such an extent that it could make many impressive claims for its position as a motor vehicle producer. At one point, it was the largest corporation ever in the USA, in terms of its revenues as a percentage of GDP; in 1984, General Motors (GM) was the largest manufacturing company in the world. There are other superlatives: it was named one of the 100 Best Companies for Working Mothers by *Working Mothers* magazine in 2004.

In the UK of the 1980s, GM companies were providing employment to well over 27,000 people, under many different company names. These included AC Spark Plug, Bedford, Delco, Fisher Body, Packard Electric, Saginaw, and Vauxhall. A research study was initiated to investigate the likely benefits of identifying these companies and their products more closely with General Motors.

Clear and detailed objectives were formulated by the client in collaboration with the appointed advertising and public relations group, Charles Barker. These satisfied the rather complicated market situation at the time. A research agency, the British Market Research Bureau, was appointed to carry out the study in 1983. The objectives were articulated as: '*To provide information on awareness of General Motors and attitudes to the Corporation and its constituent operating companies in Great Britain and Ireland in order: to serve as input into the thinking about the determination of corporate strategy; to serve as a baseline against which to monitor change in the position and understanding of the organisation over time; and to assess the impact of corporate communications.*'

The method proposed, and adopted, was split into three phases: a qualitative phase; a pilot stage; then quantitative surveys. The detailed approach is listed below, clearly showing how different types of data capture were used to address the objectives:

Phase I Qualitative This stage involved twenty group discussions with the general public, mostly motorists and with people living in the area of GM plants, and over fifty in-depth interviews with various audiences as follows (the numbers interviewed are shown in brackets): vehicle dealerships (10); fleet operators (10); repair managers (5); motor insurance specialists (2); pressure groups who were pro- and anti-motoring (5); senior civil servants and MPs (6); motoring press (5); general press and TV (5); trade union leaders (4); suppliers (5).

Phase II Pilot surveys Once quantitative questionnaires were developed, they were tested with the general public, local audiences, fleet operators, dealers, and employees.

Phase III Quantitative surveys This stage involved representative samples for several populations, as follows (sample sizes are shown in brackets). These were with the UK general public (1,232), the general public in Northern Ireland (250), the general public in Eire (258), and motorist over-sampling took place for all of these general publics. Employees of General Motors were interviewed (889), as were people living within the catchment areas of six main GM plants in the UK (619). Fleet operators for both cars and commercial vehicles were interviewed (274), as were dealers and repairers (274). Additionally, a sample of very large fleet operators was interviewed with a semi-structured questionnaire (31). Opinion formers, such as key business leaders located locally, were interviewed using semi-structured questionnaires (60) and a 'City panel' provided valuable input (100). Image was measured on such things as: 'the sort of car I'd like to own'; reliability; range; durability; and individuality.

The research concluded successfully and provided much information: for example, where respondents knew more about Vauxhall and particularly those who knew of the American parentage, there was evidence of a better view of the company and of its products. The study led to considerable repositioning of GM promotions through brochures, signage, internal communications, and more. A second survey took place three years after the first in order to see the changes in perceptions by the target audiences.

Compiled by Nigel Bradley 2009. SOURCES: Fountain, E., Parker, I., & Samuels, J. (1986). 'The contribution of research to General Motors' corporate strategy in the UK' in *Journal of the Market Research Society*, 28:25–42.

SOURCE: Bradley, N. (2010). pp.125–126. *Marketing Research* (2nd ed.). Oxford: Oxford University Press.

3 Choose a different note-taking style from the one you used in Task 4. Take notes on the following main points in Text 3.

- the context of the research
- the aim of the research
- the implications of the research
- the main findings, conclusion, and evaluation

4 Use your notes from 5.2 and 5.3 to write an 80-word summary of the research aims, methods, results, and implications of the research described in Text 3.

TASK 6 Evaluating and applying information on case studies

1 Compare your notes on Texts 2 and 3. Which note-taking style do you find most effective? Why?

2 Work in pairs. Identify what you have learned in this module about case study research methods. Identify any limitations of case studies.

3 Draw up a group list of possible ways to learn more about case studies. Come up with an action plan for how to do this.

You may need to include descriptions of processes in longer texts such as research essays and reports. A description of a process typically involves a chronological sequence, for example, a natural process (e.g. coastal erosion), a human-driven process (e.g. urbanization), or a combination of the two (e.g. wine-making, where humans harness a natural process like fermentation). It may not be described in order from start to finish; it may start from a key event and then refer back and forward to previous and future events in order to explain causes and effects. In complex descriptions, you need to make clear how different stages are related.

This module covers:

- Analysing types of process and identifying evaluation
- Writing a description of a process based on notes from reading and research

TASK 1 Analysing and describing types of process

1 Work in pairs. Think about processes 1–8 and complete the table. The first is done as an example.

Process	One-off	Recurrent	Natural	Human-driven	Local	Global
1 photosynthesis		✓	✓			✓
2 desertification						
3 the global financial crisis of 2007-8						
4 passing a new law in a specific country						
5 building employee trust in a company						
6 industrialization in post-war Japan						
7 designing a new public space						
8 research and development of a new drug						

2 Choose one process from the table in 1, and represent its main stages in a timeline, flow chart, or cycle. Make sure the stages are clearly signalled.

3 Work in threes. Take turns to present your process.

Example: *The process of photosynthesis involves firstly …*

TASK 2 Analysing a process and identifying evaluation

1 Work in groups. Share any information you know about the 2007–8 global financial crisis. Use the key words and prompts below to help you.

THE 2007–8 GLOBAL FINANCIAL CRISIS

Key words

- debt • financial (de)regulation • recession • sub-prime lending

Prompts

- its background and context
- how it compares with previous global financial crises
- how and why the crisis developed
- its effects, from various perspectives

2 Organize your information from 1 into chronological order using a process visual (timeline, flowchart, etc.) to illustrate your points.

3 Quickly read Text 1. Notice the *genre*, *audience*, and *purpose* of the text, and identify your points from 1 and 2. Do they occur in the same order in Text 1? Did you state any point not given in the text, and vice versa?

The global financial crisis

1 The global financial crisis (GFC) that began in 2007–08 was the biggest shock to the capitalist economy since the Great Depression that originated in 1929. The crash in asset values, particularly share market values, sent shock waves through the global economy. An economic recession developed in many nations, with falling incomes and rising unemployment.

2 The warning signs of the coming crash became evident during the emergence of the 'sub-prime crisis' in the United States in 2007. The egregious business practices of a range of financial institutions were the immediate cause of the problem. The financial institutions had been making loans to low-income people wishing to buy houses: these were known as 'sub-prime' loans because there was a relatively high probability that the borrowers would default. Indeed, both borrowers and lenders would become losers when the US housing price bubble burst and prices started to fall.

3 A devastating transmission process ensued. The problem of mortgage defaults spread because the debts had been repackaged as securities called 'collateralised debt obligations'. Other banks, companies, and governments had bought the securities, believing them to be less risky than proved to be the case. The false confidence was partly because inappropriate reassurances were given by the big credit ratings agencies, Moody's, and Standard and Poor's. Holding mortgage-backed securities came to be recognized as a much more hazardous process than those ratings agencies had indicated.

4 When the extent of the actual risks was revealed, financial institutions wanted to sell these mortgage-backed securities. As in any market, when there are lots of sellers but few buyers, prices inevitably fall. The stock market values of the institutions themselves also fell, because they were holding securities that were worth less (if not completely worthless). With the collapse of some of these major financial institutions, particularly in the US and the UK, a financial crisis emerged.

5 So what originated as a sub-prime crisis of largely US origin became generalised as a global financial crash. The long period of economic growth shuddered to an end, as it inevitably had to sooner or later. The growth of the 1990s and early 2000s had been based on debt-fuelled consumerism, speculation, and the quest for unlimited capital gains, rather than sound finance and sustainable economic production.

6 Not even government bailouts following the onset of the GFC were able to restore the confidence necessary for the failing financial institutions to resume normal trading with each other. The downturn spread from speculative financial markets to the 'real' economy in which goods and services are produced, leading to the onset of a severe and prolonged global recession in many countries.

7 Not surprisingly, economists have been divided over how to analyse what fundamentally caused the GFC and what policy responses are appropriate. A common theme in political economic analyses has been that neoliberal economic ideas and policies facilitated the creation of such a crisis-prone situation. Certainly the GFC was a major blow to the claims of mainstream economists that 'free markets' would produce continually efficient outcomes. We need to recognise that economic instability is rife, perhaps even endemic, in the capitalist system. The role of the state in crisis management and the creation of more long-term stability becomes a particularly contentious issue in these circumstances.

SOURCE: Stilwell, F. (2012). pp.30–31. *Political Economy: The Contest of Economic Ideas* (3rd ed.). Oxford: Oxford University Press.

GLOSSARY

default *(n & v)* failure to do sth that must be done by law, especially paying a debt

neoliberal *(adj)* relating to belief in a global free market, without government regulation, with businesses run for profit by private owners

---

4 **Text 1 is part of the textbook chapter *Political economic challenges*. Decide which *one* section heading is *least* likely to appear in the same chapter, and why.**

a Financial instability   c Political systems
b Unemployment   d Environmental stress

5 **Read Text 1 again in detail. For each paragraph, identify one or two key stages in the global financial crisis. Make notes and add any evaluation by the writer.**

Example:

Para.	Stage in the process	Evaluation
1	*2007-8 global financial crisis began*	*biggest economic shock since 1929 Great Depression*
	crash in asset values	*sent shock waves through global economy*
2	*US sub-prime crisis emerged*	

6 **Work in pairs. Compare notes and work out the actual chronological order of the events.**

Chronology language Expressing events in time using verbs, nouns, and adverbials

Writers of chronology texts need to contextualize the events in time. Notice how this is done through verb forms and adverbials in Text 1:

> *The global financial crisis (GFC) that began in 2007-08 was the biggest shock to the capitalist economy since the Great Depression that originated in 1929 …*

> *An economic recession developed in many nations, with falling incomes and rising unemployment.*

> *The financial institutions had been making loans to low-income people wishing to buy houses: … Indeed, both borrowers and lenders would become losers when the US housing price bubble burst and prices started to fall.*

Verbs

- Use the past simple to express a sequence of events, e.g. *began …, started …*
- Describe a 'backstory' of events which happened **earlier** with more complex verb forms, e.g. *had been making* expresses an earlier event already in progress at that time. (past perfect progressive)
- Use modal verb *would* to express an event in the past which happened **after** the other events, e.g. *would become.*

Adverbials

To add variety, instead of using verb tenses, use adverbials to express a sequence of events. Compare:

> 1 *Incomes fell and unemployment rose, as an economic recession developed.*

> 2 *An economic recession developed, with falling incomes and rising unemployment.*

Nouns

- 'Nominalization', i.e. converting verbs to nouns, is a common tendency in academic writing, e.g. *borrow ➔ borrowers*. These forms enable you to avoid stating something fairly obvious in a simplistic way (i.e. *people borrowed money*), and may reduce word count. Using a nominalized form also enables you to choose your emphasis. Compare:

> 1 *The problem was caused by the egregious business practices of a range of financial institutions. (focuses on the problem)*

> 2 *The egregious business practices of a range of financial institutions were the cause of the problem. (focuses on the business practices)*

TASK 3 Using chronology language

1 Write equivalent forms for the extracts from Text 1.

	Verb-based form	Nominalized form	Adverbial
1	Asset values crashed	The crash in asset values	with crashing asset values
2	sent shock waves through the global economy	global economic shock waves	sending shock waves through the global economy
3	An economic recession developed		
4			with falling incomes and rising unemployment
5		the warning signs of the coming crash	
6		the emergence of the 'sub-prime crisis'	
7	the US housing price bubble burst and prices started to fall		

2 Underline the <u>events</u> in sentences 1–3 from Text 1, and rewrite them using equivalent forms.

Example: <u>*The crash in asset values*</u>, *particularly share market values, <u>sent shock waves through the global economy</u>.*

       a   *The crash in asset values, particularly share market values, resulted in global economic shock waves.*

       b   *Asset values crashed, particularly share market values, sending shock waves through the global economy.*

   1   The warning signs of the coming crash became evident during the emergence of the 'sub-prime crisis' in the United States in 2007.

   2   The financial institutions had been making loans to low-income people wishing to buy houses.

   3   Both borrowers and lenders would become losers when the US housing price bubble burst and prices started to fall.

3 Compare and evaluate your texts. What makes a text effective?

TASK 4 Describing a process based on notes from reading

1 Write a 100–150 word description of the global financial crisis of 2007–8 based on your notes from Task 2. Use only your notes and do *not* refer to the original text. Use a range of language structures to achieve your desired focus for each stage of the crisis.

2 Compare your text with Text 1 on page 175. For any differences in focus and form, describe the effect the differences have.

3 Exchange texts and offer specific points for improvement for the other text(s) you read.

TASK 5 Researching and writing a description of a process

1 You are going to write a description of a process based on an aspect of your discipline / a discipline you are familiar with. Follow the guidelines below.

Guidelines for writing a description of a process

   1   Decide on a specific process to focus on. Look back at Task 1 for possible examples.

   2   A description of a process is typically part of a longer text. Sketch out the wider context.

   3   Decide on the precise name of the process, making sure it is clear and can 'stand alone'.

   4   Make initial notes on the main stages in the process, based on what you already know.

   5   Formulate specific points to research, based on gaps or shortcomings in your knowledge.

---

2 Research the points you identified in 1 using the resources available to you. Use Checklist L on page 212 to guide you.

3 Use your notes and material to write a plan based around a process visual.

4 Write a first draft. Incorporate your own evaluation into your description. While / After writing, check your draft using Checklist H on page 210.

TASK 6 Evaluating a written text

1 Work in groups and exchange texts.

   1   For each text you read, extract the key stages in the process and represent these visually.

   2   Note down any instances where the information is not clearly presented and contextualized.

   3   Give evaluative feedback to the writer of the text, including positive points (e.g. clearly contextualized points; language) and specific points to clarify.

11C Listening Lectures (8)

In many contexts, lecturers include detailed descriptions of a chronological sequence, such as a case study or process. The lecturer may explain any technical content with supporting visuals, which you can use to help you understand. You need to notice the lecturer's evaluation of the material, which may be integrated throughout the lecture or given towards the end.

This module covers:
- Using visuals to understand and explain key concepts
- Taking notes on multiple related processes

TASK 1 Using visuals to understand and explain key concepts

1   Work in pairs. You are going to watch the first part of a lecture entitled *An introduction to community ecology* by Dr Kerry Lock. Discuss and note down essential information relating to the points below.
- the meaning / definition of *ecology*
- the potential scope of ecology
- key terms associated with ecology, e.g. *organism*
- examples of an ecological community

2   ▷11.1 Turn to Checklist C on page 209. Watch Extract 1 of the lecture and use part A to make notes about general information on the lecture.

3   Take turns to explain the following concepts based on your notes about key terms and definitions in 2. Refer to lecture slides 1–3 opposite to illustrate your explanations.
- abiotic factors
- populations, habitats, and communities
- ecological niches and niche separation

TASK 2 Taking notes on multiple related processes

1   Ecological processes 1–6 are discussed in Extract 2 of the lecture. Before you watch, work out the meaning of the terms (e.g. *mutual* = affecting two things equally) and study slides 4–9 opposite. Describe what you think the stages of each process are.

1 community structure	4 predation	
2 energy transfer	5 parasitism	
3 herbivory	6 mutualism	

2   You're going to make notes on the ecological processes in 1 in order to explain them in groups. Read the list of listening techniques. Select one or more appropriate techniques to use as you watch the next part of the lecture.

Before listening
- Discuss the topic and predict possible content before listening
- Prepare for a lecture by reading a relevant textbook chapter or pre-lecture handout

While listening
- Build your notes around slides and headings
- Link the content of your notes to the signposting language in the lecture
- Make notes on a chronological sequence, perhaps using a timeline
- Make notes relating only to specific points, e.g. main points, perspectives
- Connect essential elements in the lecture, e.g. causes, problems, stages in a process
- Focus on citations in the lecture
- Focus on language, e.g. identifying and working out meanings of key terms
- Use your own range of abbreviations, symbols, and visuals

Following up listening

- Evaluate the lecturer's delivery (e.g. using Checklist C part B on page 209)
- Evaluate the content of the lecture (e.g. using Checklist C part C on page 209)
- Summarize part or all of the lecture in writing or to explain / present to others
- Compare and combine the information in two or more lectures on a similar topic

Slide 1

What is a Community?

An assemblage of 2 or more of such populations is a community.

Structurally complex sward

Slide 2

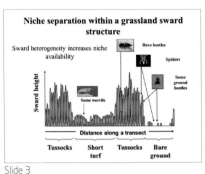

Niche separation within a grassland sward structure

Slide 3

How are Communities structured?

- Species richness
- Relative abundances of species
- Physical characteristics of the organisms
- Trophic relationships among interacting populations within a community

Slide 4

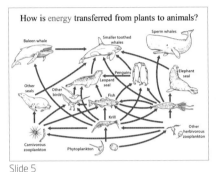
How is energy transferred from plants to animals?

Slide 5

Herbivory

A consumer-resource interaction involving the consumption of plants or plant parts.

Slide 6

Predation

Interaction whereby the predator kills and eats the other species, the prey.

Slide 7

Parasitism

•Symbiotic interaction in which a parasite derives its nourishment from a host, which is harmed in the process.

•Hemi-parasitic plant
Rhinanthus minor (Yellow Rattle)

Slide 8

Mutualism

Large Blue Butterfly
(*Glaucopsyche arion*)

Red ant
(*Myrmica sabuleti*)

Thomas, JA, Simcox, DJ, Clarke, RT (2009) Successful Conservation of a Threatened Maculinea Butterfly. Science 325, 80-83.

Slide 9

3 ▶11.2 Watch Extract 2 and make notes using your chosen technique.

4 ▶11.3 Watch Extract 3. Listen for and note down the main evaluative comments made by the lecturer relating to eco-systems and ecological processes.

5 Take turns to present one ecological process from the lecture, based on your notes.

6 Evaluate each other's performance using Checklist C part B on page 209.

TASK 3 Assessing personal progress in listening

1 Look again at the listening techniques in Task 2.2. Evaluate your progress in listening to lectures by marking the techniques using the scale 1–4 below.

++ 1 I am very comfortable and familiar with this technique.

+ 2 I am usually reasonably successful with this technique.

– 3 I have made some progress in using this technique, but I need more practice.

– – 4 I still find this technique quite challenging.

2 Compare responses. Which techniques work best for you, and why?

You may need to read chronological source texts – process descriptions and case studies, sometimes as part of a longer text – to prepare for a seminar discussion. You need to critically evaluate the text, and decide how the issues in the text relate to your own studies (i.e. the specific module or topic you are studying) or research interests. You can then consider further issues from your own experience and other sources. This preparation process enables you to bring appropriate material into the seminar that is informed by your own reading and thought.

This module covers:

- Analysing a process text and developing material to use in a discussion
- Participating in a seminar discussion

TASK 1 Analysing a process text to prepare for a discussion

1 **You are going to participate in a discussion on processes of change in cities.**
   To start preparing, think of at least two specific examples of such change, and
   note the perspectives.

   Example: *In London, wealthy overseas buyers have driven up house prices, leading to an*
   increasingly diverse demographic mix in some areas. – Perspectives: financial,
   economic, ethnic, cultural, geographical

2 **Read Text 1 and note down points relating to your chosen perspectives in 1.**
   Which other perspectives are covered in the text?

Introduction

TEXT 1

The city that lost its soul

In the early years of the twenty-first century, New York City lost its soul. Some people doubt that the city ever had a soul, because New York has grown by shedding its past, tearing down old neighborhoods and erecting new ones in their place, usually in a bare-faced struggle for financial gain. Others just shrug because today, all big cities are erasing their gritty, bricks-and-mortar history to build a shiny vision of the future. Beijing, Shanghai, and other Chinese cities are clearing out the narrow, rundown alleys in their center, removing longtime residents to the distant edges of town, and replacing small, old houses with expensive apartments and new skyscrapers of spectacular design. Liverpool and Bilbao have torn down their abandoned waterfronts and turned aging docks and warehouses into modern art museums. In London, Paris, and New York, artists and gentrifiers move into old immigrant areas, praising the working class bars and take-out joints but overwhelming them with new cafés and boutiques, which are soon followed by brand-name chain stores. A universal rhetoric of upscale growth, based on both the economic power of capital and the state and the cultural power of the media and consumer tastes, is driving these changes and exposing a conflict between city dwellers' desire for authentic origins – a traditional, mythical desire for roots – and their new beginnings: the continuous reinvention of communities.

To speak of a city being authentic at all may seem absurd. Especially in a global capital like New York, neither people nor buildings have a chance to accumulate the patina of age. Most residents are not born there, neither do they live in the same house for generations, and the physical fabric of the city is constantly changing around them. In fact, all over the world, 'Manhattanization' signifies everything in a city that is *not* thought to be authentic: high-rise buildings that grow taller every year, dense crowds where no one knows your name, high prices for inferior living conditions, and intense competition to be in style. Lately, though, authenticity has taken on a different meaning that has little to do with origins and a lot to do with style. The concept has migrated from a quality of people to a quality of things, and most recently to a quality of experiences. *Time* magazine named authenticity one of the ten most important ideas of 2007, partly because of the promotional campaign of two marketing gurus, James H. Gilmore and B. Joseph Pine II, whose work emphasizes this journey from things to experience, and partly because of the anxiety fuelled by social theorists such as Walter Benjamin and Jean Baudrillard, who say that through technology, imitation of novelty, and the normal hype of consumer culture, experience is increasingly seduced by appearances. Viewed through either of these lenses, a city is authentic if it can create the experience of origins. This is done by preserving historic buildings and districts, encouraging the development of small-scale boutiques and cafés, and branding neighborhoods in terms of distinctive cultural identities.

SOURCE: Zukin, S. (2010). pp.1–3. *Naked city: the death and life of authentic urban places.* New York: Oxford University Press.

3 Note down the stages in Text 1 which relate to the on-going process of change in a city. Note possible perspectives relating to these processes.

Example: *knocking down old buildings and replacing them with new ones – Perspectives: architectural, aesthetic, cultural, economic, commercial, political*

4 Identify the author's evaluation of the stages in 3, and the language which conveys this.

Example: knocking down old buildings and replacing them with new ones – *The author's choice of language shows she is critical: '**shedding** its past, **tearing down** old neighborhoods, a **bare-faced** struggle for financial gain'*

5 Represent the stages in Text 1 using a process visual. Present it to other students.

TASK 2 Developing material to use in a discussion

1 Choose a city you are familiar with and would like to speak about.

1 Which specific points of change in Task 1.3 are also applicable to this city? How significant are they?

2 Think of other points you could make about the current process of change in your chosen city. Which perspectives do they relate to?

3 Organize your material so that you are ready to present it informally. Prepare an informal process visual.

2 Work in groups. Prepare for the whole-class seminar discussion in Task 3.

1 Take turns to present your city.

2 Together identify issues which apply generally across the different cities.

3 Agree a focus for your group contribution to the seminar, based on one or more of the issues in 2.1. Express this as a question:

Example: *Should old buildings in a city be preserved for future generations regardless of current pressures for redevelopment?*

4 Choose different students to be a) the group leader, b) the note-taker, c) the feedback reporter. The feedback reporter will note down points relating to content and language.

TASK 3 Participating in a seminar

1 Conduct a whole-class seminar on the process of change in cities.

- Nominate a student to chair the discussion.
- Group leaders: Present your question.
- Chair: Write up all the groups' questions. Select the first question, and manage the discussion. Guide the seminar participants to reach majority agreement on an answer to each question. Aim to cover all the questions in the time available.
- Group note-takers: After each question has been discussed, summarize the main points.

2 Review the seminar.

- Feedback reporters: Offer points relating to content and language.
- Seminar participants: Offer further feedback and discuss advice for improvement.

1 **Categorize the words from the unit into three groups, a–c.**

a referring to a process

b referring to a quality or characteristic

c referring to a person or actor

accumulate authenticity borrower complexity distinctive facilitate generalize identification instability Manhattanization motorist participant promotion respondent theorist transmission

2 **Recognizing common word formation patterns can help you to work out the meaning of new words you encounter in your reading (such as *Manhattanization*). In pairs, compare your categories and identify which suffixes (word endings) are used:**

- to express each of the general concepts a–c
- with particular word forms (nouns, verbs, adjectives).

3 **Add as many words as possible to the table below. Note that not all positions can be filled and not all words use the suffixes above.**

Process		Quality/Characteristic	Person/Actor
participate	participation	participatory	participant
investigate			
	competition		
		responsive	
	extension		
generate			
		collaborative	
			producer
		stable/stability	

Making a clear argument

What is an argument?

The writing-up of a research project should be organized around an argument that links all aspects of the process, from introduction and thesis, through literature review and the presentation of the main points, to the discussion and conclusion. Too often, students make a series of points without asking what the contribution of those points is to the overall argument that they are trying to present. Ask yourself: 'What is the key point or message that I want my readers to take away with them when they have finished reading my work?' If you cannot answer that simple question satisfactorily (and it may be worth trying it out on others), you almost certainly do not have an argument.

ADAPTED FROM: Bryman, A. (2012). p.687. *Social Research Methods (4th ed.)*. Oxford: Oxford University Press.

Achieve coherence and cohesion by:

- **deleting irrelevant material.** It is difficult to delete something that you have spent a long time writing, but sometimes it can improve the overall text.

- **making connections more explicit.** Sometimes adding an extra sentence, a linking paragraph or just a few words will make the relevance of a particular point or example clearer.

- **reworking your introduction and conclusion.** Your introduction plays a vital role in establishing your main argument. Your conclusion brings everything together at the end. Sometimes your ideas develop as you write and you may need to go back and alter your introduction in the light of these changes.

TO DO Stage 5: Refining your first draft

Now you have your rough first draft down on paper, reread the whole project, checking for **coherence** (i.e. that your argument is clear and your points link together logically) and **cohesion** (i.e. that your language makes this clear to your reader). Add, delete, or make changes before you submit your first draft to your tutor for feedback.

ACADEMIC FOCUS: RESEARCH AND REPORTING

LEARNING OBJECTIVES

This unit covers:

Reading
- Establishing reading purpose
- Employing appropriate reading techniques
- Reporting on reading in spoken and written form

Writing
- Using feedback to edit a text for language accuracy
- Developing a personal proofreading checklist
- Acting on feedback to finalize a text

Listening
- Matching note-taking technique to purpose of listening
- Using lecture notes to prepare for a presentation

Speaking
- Planning a research presentation – understanding the task
- Considering your audience
- Preparing and giving a research presentation

Vocabulary
- Review and research

Research project (6)
- Finalizing your work

Discussion

1 Work in groups. Think of one example of a piece of research you have come across (e.g. in reading, from a presentation). Make brief notes about:
   - the discipline (e.g. *geography*)
   - the aim (e.g. *to measure melting of the polar ice caps*)
   - the research methods (e.g. *satellite measurements and computer modelling*)
   - the results (e.g. *the rate at which the polar ice caps are melting each summer*)
   - the implications (e.g. *potential effects on global sea levels & climate patterns*).

2 Take turns to describe your research example. Compare the different methods you have identified.

3 Share what you know about the following aspects of research methodology. Take turns to explain, and add to other students' explanations.

   answering research questions
   combining multiple research studies   gathering data
   literature review   randomization   research ethics
   research processes and outcomes   selecting a sample
   selecting search terms

4 Discuss which research methods you expect to use in your future studies. Give reasons.

Throughout this course you have used techniques to navigate books and journal articles, to choose which texts to read, and which parts of a long text to focus on. You have studied how to understand the genre, audience, and purpose of a text, pick out the main points, identify supporting evidence, and recognize the writer's perspective and stance. A final key principle is always to consider why you are reading: Do you want to better understand a concept or a writer's arguments? Are you going to use material from your reading in your own work, such as an essay, a literature review, a presentation, or a discussion? Keeping a clear purpose in your mind will help you to focus on what is important in the text and use your time efficiently.

This module covers:
- Establishing reading purpose
- Employing appropriate reading techniques
- Reporting on reading in spoken and written form

TASK 1 Critical thinking – establishing reading purpose

1 **Work in pairs. Read the description below of the activity that you will be working on in this module. Decide your purpose for reading your text.**

> **READING ACTIVITY:** *Compare and contrast research methods across disciplines, using examples drawn from reading.*
>
> **Reading** Read one of three texts about an academic research method.
>
> **Reporting** In groups, take turns to briefly report to the group on the research methods described in your text.
>
> **Discussion** Discuss the following:
> - similarities and differences between the research methods in your texts
> - how far the methods in each of the texts are relevant across disciplines
> - research methods that are common across disciplines or that are restricted to certain areas (e.g. the sciences).
>
> **Summary** Collaboratively summarize your discussion, either as a short written summary, or as a presentation. Include reference information in an appropriate form. Cover:
> - similarities and differences in research methods across disciplines
> - examples drawn from your reading where appropriate.

2 **How did you decide your 'reading purpose'? Draw a visual, such as a table with headings for notes, to show what you will look for as you read. Compare with another pair.**

TASK 2 Employing appropriate reading techniques

> **Reading** Read one of three texts about an academic research method.

1 **Identify reading techniques that might be useful for the activity in Task 1, bearing in mind your purpose for reading.**

   1 Look back through the previous Reading modules in the book to identify which techniques might be useful for this task (e.g. **2A** Tasks 1, 2, …)

   2 Look at the Checklists on page 209–210 and note any points to use when reading.

      Example: *Consider the examples given in the texts: where and what type (Checklist F)*

2 **Work in threes. Allocate one text each, 1, 2, or 3. Spend no more than five minutes reading your text.**

   - Use different techniques as you read, in order to focus on different information.
   - Make notes using headings that are relevant to your purpose for the task.

3 **Organize your notes. Reread any sections of the text as necessary, and prepare to report on your text to your group of three.**

Populations

> **Key points** The term *population* has a number of meanings. In statistics, a population is all the items that are the subject of your research.

There are several different definitions for the word **population**. In ecology, the term means the individuals that can be observed within an identifiably discrete group; for example, the number of individuals in a wood, river, or city. In genetics, a population usually means the grouping in which all the individuals of a particular species mate at random. When you are using statistics to analyse your data, the term population is used in yet another way.

> **Example 1.1 The effects of the introduction of new individuals on behaviour in an established herd of wildebeest** An undergraduate had links with a local safari park and was interested in the changes in behaviour of animals when new individuals were introduced into an established herd.

In example 1.1, the statistical population would be all the wildebeest in the population at the safari park. You might argue that safari park conditions are sufficiently similar that the statistical population might be extended to all safari park populations of wildebeest. However, it would be difficult to argue the case for extending the statistical population to all wildebeest including those in the wild.

The statistical population reflects your aim. Sometimes a statistical population will be the same as an ecological population. For example, if your aim was to investigate the characteristics of individuals of one species within a wood, then the ecological population and the statistical population are the same. However, if your aim was to examine the characteristics of a particular species worldwide, then the statistical population will be all the individuals of that species on the planet. The ecological population will still be the group of individuals of that species in each wood.

Identifying the statistical population is of great importance to your work. Any hypothesis testing revolves around the statistical population. Similarly, when you come to discuss your results you will automatically apply your findings to the statistical population. For example, having studied the wildebeest behaviour (example 1.1), the student presented some suggestions on management of such populations. She needed to make it clear in her report whether her recommendations were just for the safari park she studied, for safari parks in general, or for the management of all wildebeest. The previous consideration of the 'statistical population' meant she was sure where her results could be justly applied.

Sample

> **Key points** It is common practice to sample from your statistical population. It is usual to try to obtain a representative sample. This can be achieved in a number of ways (random, systematic, and random stratified).

It is often not possible to study the whole statistical population because of practical and economic constraints. The testing procedure may also be destructive and you may therefore wish to limit your investigation. For example, if you wanted to carry out taste testing on cheese and onion crisps, it would not help the factory managers if you tasted all the crisps. Usually a subset of the population is examined. This is the **sample**. For example, in the investigation into the effect on heart rate of football and non-football fans when watching live and recorded matches, the student might study only five Manchester United football supporters and one of their non-football fan friends. But is this a representative sample?

SOURCE: Holmes, D., Moody, P., & Dine, D. (2011). pp.4–8. *Research Methods for the Biosciences* (2nd ed.). Oxford: Oxford University Press.

Why choose focus groups as a method of enquiry?

All research focuses on establishing new knowledge and is a prospective, systematic form of enquiry. Since **qualitative research** is an inductive approach, the intent is exploration and the questions are open-ended. The focus group method sits neatly within this framework. Focus groups can be used in many ways. The box below summarises the purposes of focus groups.

Purposes of focus groups
- assessing needs
- describing contexts
- eliciting knowledge, attitudes, and beliefs on a group basis
- evaluating health care interventions
- exploring knowledge, attitudes, and beliefs
- generating hypotheses
- elucidating quantitative study findings

When planning and conducting research, it is important to consider the feasibility of selecting an appropriate methodology. The collective perspective and the capacity to capture multiple participants' views in a single interview setting make focus groups a prudent use of limited research resources (Gibbs, 1997; Madriz, 2000; Vogt *et al.*, 2004). Ideally, focus groups consist of 5-15 participants. This size is recommended to allow all participants to contribute and achieve cohesion within the group. However, the size of a focus group can vary depending on the research topic and social context of the participants (Hennink, 2007; Liamputtong, 2009 in press).

According to Gibbs (1997), the interaction among participants is the novelty of the focus group method. Hence focus groups are useful in obtaining information on perceptions, insights, attitudes, experiences and beliefs (Davidson *et al.*, 2003; Liamputtong in press). Focus groups are also useful in obtaining unique subjective perspectives, particularly as they pertain to collectives or groups. This collective perspective is achieved by creating an opportunity for group members to stimulate each other to comment and question. For example, an investigation was undertaken of how nurses working in cardiology and respiratory clinical areas viewed end-of-life and palliative care in the acute care setting. As nursing care is a collaborative activity, this group perspective was important. Advantages of focus groups are that the group dynamic can yield useful information that individual data collection does not provide, particularly when exploring collective views. As in the example given above, health care delivery is dependent on the attitudes of professional groups and therefore this collective viewpoint is as important to obtain as an individual one (Davidson *et al.*, 2003; Willis *et al.*, 2009).

The focus group method also allows access to research participants who may find individual interviews intimidating, or where it may not be culturally appropriate to interview individuals alone (Madriz, 2000; Liamputtong, 2010). Focus groups can also be useful in gaining insight into a topic that may be more difficult to gather through other data collection methods. For example, in individuals who have limited literacy or language, focus groups can provide an excellent vehicle for accessing marginalised and vulnerable groups (Liamputtong, 2007). Focus groups are particularly suggested in studying under-represented and marginalised populations such as women and those who are not part of the mainstream culture, and are particularly suited for research investigating cultural perspectives (Halcomb *et al.*, 2007; Liamputtong, 2007, 2010). [...]

Risks associated with the focus group method are that they can be susceptible to moderator bias and that there is the potential for discussion to be dominated by a minority. Yet these risks can be minimised with effective planning, such as the critical analysis of audiotapes to assess the moderator's role and other forms of ensuring the integrity of qualitative data (Morgan, 1998). The focus group method does not allow for in-depth information at the individual level and therefore if this is the intention of the research other methods should be employed. The strongly contextual aspects of focus groups means that the information is not representative of other groups and therefore the ability to generalise findings is limited (Morgan, 1998).

SOURCE: Davidson, P., Halcomb, E., & Gholizadeh, L. (2010). pp.62–64. 'Focus groups in health research' in Liamputtong, P. (Ed.), *Research methods in health: foundations for evidence-based practice*. Oxford: Oxford University Press.

The Hawthorne effect

TEXT 3

The effect of the experimenter or the fact of being studied on the subject is commonly referred to as the '**Hawthorne effect**'. This phrase was coined as a result of the series of interlinked investigations carried out during the late 1920s and early 1930s at the Hawthorne works of the Western Electric Company in the USA (Roethlisberger & Dickson, 1939).

One phase of the investigations entailed a group of women carrying out manual tasks being taken away from their department and working in a separate room. The aim of the study was to discover how changes in the number and duration of rest pauses, in length of the working day, in heating and lighting, and so on affected productivity, as this quotation from the study illustrates:

> First, the amount of light was increased regularly day by day, and the girls were asked each day how they liked the change. As the light was increased, the girls told the investigator that they liked the brighter lights. Then for a day or two the investigator allowed the girls to see the electrician come and change the light bulbs. In reality, the electrician merely took out bulbs of a given size and inserted bulbs of the same size, without in any way changing the amount of light. The girls, thinking that the light was still being 'stepped up' day by day, commented favourably about the increase of light. After a few days of this, the experimenter started to decrease the intensity of light, keeping the girls informed of the change and soliciting their reaction. After a period of this day-by-day decrease in illumination, he again allowed the girls to see the electrician change the bulbs without really changing the intensity of illumination. Again the girls gave answers that were to be expected, in that they said the 'lesser' light was not so pleasant to work under as the brighter light. The production did not change at any stage of the experiment. (Roethlisberger & Dickson, 1939: 17)

However, as the study went on, it was found that productivity *did* increase, irrespective of the changes that were being introduced. Eventually it was recognized that the women were responding to the positive attention and special treatment they were receiving. The researchers concluded that increases in worker productivity were due not to any changes in the conditions of the working environment, but instead to the favourable circumstances that the experimental arrangement had produced. While this finding did much to stimulate the 'human-relations' approach to the study of work, by pointing to the potential advantages of providing people with psycho-social support in the workplace, it also neatly demonstrates that experimental arrangements may induce an effect over and above the intentions of the investigator. This has been referred to, more generally, as the 'experimenter effect', where the researcher creates a bias in the data through participation in the research situation or by inadvertently communicating his or her preferred research outcome.

SOURCE: Bryman, A. & Bell, E. (2011). p.50. *Business Research Methods* (3rd ed.). Oxford: Oxford University Press.

TASK 3 Reporting on and discussing reading texts

Reporting In your groups, take turns to briefly report on the research methods described in your text.

Discussion Discuss the following:
- similarities and differences between the research methods in your texts
- how far the methods in each of the texts are relevant across disciplines
- research methods that are common across disciplines or that are restricted to certain areas, such as the sciences.

1 In your threes, report on and discuss your reading. Ask clarification questions. Ensure that at least one person makes notes on the main points of your discussion.

2 Using your notes, agree on two or three general points to emerge from your discussion.

TASK 4 Summarizing a discussion of reading

> **Summary** Collaboratively summarize your discussion, either as a short written summary, or as a presentation. Include reference information in an appropriate form. Cover:
> - similarities and differences in research methods across disciplines
> - examples drawn from your reading where appropriate.

1 **In your threes, prepare a description and comparison of research methods across different disciplines. Use the notes from your discussion in Task 3. Choose either a written summary (up to 500 words), or a spoken presentation (about five minutes).**

Written summary

- Include a short introductory paragraph, two or three main body paragraphs with clear headings, and a short conclusion.
- Incorporate accurate in-text references plus a References section.

Spoken presentation

- Work out and divide up the stages in the presentation; allocate different people to present these.
- Prepare simple visuals. Include only essential information such as section headings / aims – present the details orally.

2 **Working as a team, check and redraft your summary / presentation until you are all happy with it. Refer to the appropriate Checklist I or J on pages 211–212.**

3 **Exchange your summaries or give your presentations across groups.**

TASK 5 Designing a strategy to improve reading skills

1 **Decide which of the following skills related to reading you a) have most improved since the beginning of the course, b) want to improve further.**

Reading skills

- effectively researching, locating, and selecting appropriate sources to read
- achieving an appropriate reading speed for your purpose
- efficiently navigating the text, identifying the main points and the writer's stance
- making effective notes while reading
- accurately keeping track of references, both the sources themselves and those cited within the sources
- reporting in your own texts on what you've read, using your own language
- subsequently recalling the main points in specific texts days / weeks / months later

2 **Work in groups and compare answers to 1. Suggest and note down ways of improving specific reading skills.**

3 **Set yourself individual goals to improve your reading skills. Include:**
- **What:** the specific skill(s) in 1 that you have identified to improve (and why)
- **How:** an effective way of improving this skill, based on suggestions in 2
- **When:** the dates by which you plan to achieve these goals (in x days / weeks / months)

Example: **What:** *improve my reading speed – I spend too long looking up every unknown word. I need to just focus on the main points.*
How: *timing myself when I read, setting time limits and keeping a record of reading times*
When: *read at least five texts a week for the next four weeks*

Longer academic writing projects (extended essays, dissertations, research proposals) involve research and reading, drafting, feedback, and redrafting in order to refine the clarity and impact of your work, and to finalize content, organization, flow, and language. First you may be asked to submit a proposal, a draft title or an outline to a tutor for initial discussion. You may then submit a first draft and receive feedback in written form or orally during a tutorial, before submitting further drafts, and then the final draft of your writing for assessment. Responding to feedback is essential in arriving at the best possible final text.

This module covers:

- Using feedback to edit a text for language accuracy
- Developing a personal proofreading checklist
- Acting on feedback to finalize a text

TASK 1 Critical thinking – evaluating writing skills

1 Complete the table to evaluate your writing.

		Always	Usually	Sometimes	Never
1	I can identify areas for reading and research relevant to my writing project.				
2	I can locate sufficient, appropriate sources to feed into the content.				
3	I can critically respond to what I read, and select and synthesize sources.				
4	I can plan my written text with logical sections and a clear argument.				
5	I can incorporate sources logically and reference this cited material.				
6	I can use sophisticated and accurate language to express my ideas.				
7	I can understand and respond effectively to feedback on my writing.				
8	Other people can read my written text and fully understand it.				

2 Find at least three examples of your own recent written work that has been submitted to a tutor. Look at their feedback comments including any corrections, and note down which of the following areas have been highlighted. Add further areas as necessary.

- language issues
- structure, organization, or length
- use of sources and references
- content – e.g. answering the question, balance of description vs. evaluation
- flow, cohesion, and voice

3 Work in pairs. Compare findings to 1 and 2, and discuss the points.

- which areas you have made progress on in writing and research through this course
- areas still needing further work
- whether you have persistent problem areas that repeatedly come up in feedback
- which feedback comments have been most useful to you, and why
- whether any of the feedback was unclear / confusing and why

4 Based on your discussion, set yourself one or more individual goals to improve your writing and research skills in the future. Include the following points.

- **What:** the specific writing skills that you have identified to improve
- **How:** an effective way of improving this skill
- **When:** the dates by which you plan to achieve these goals: (in x days / weeks / months)

TASK 2 Using feedback to edit a text for language accuracy

1 Read a paragraph from the literature review section of a student essay. Using the language tutor's comments, correct the language errors highlighted.

Punctuation in abbreviation - full stop and italics

Uncountable noun

Collocation with 'task'? - verb choice

Word order / sentence construction?

+ article

This needs a determiner - check the original quotation

Word form?

Prefix?

across ...?... lifetime

According to Abutalebi [1] et al (2009: 9) [2] 'bilingual brain is a special brain' and there [3] are some evidences that demonstrate that. For example, higher activity has been found in memory and other areas of the brain when someone is [4] developing a multilingual task (ibid). Other studies suggest that [5] it exists a control structure unique in bilinguals that let them choose the right language to use, because both languages are always [6] actives in the brain, and this fact improves [7] bilingual's attention and cognitive control, giving them the ability to solve problems in [8] no-verbal tasks as well as verbal ones (Bialystok et al, 2004, Costa et al., 2007). Further still, this superior stimulation of the brain across [9] lifetime is thought to be good protection against cognitive decline due to aging (Bialystok, 2009).

2 Work in groups, and compare corrections. Where your suggestions differ, decide whether more than one alternative is possible.

3 Read two more sentences from the same essay. Correct any language errors.

1 It is essential to make a difference between early bilingual, who learn two languages at the same time, and late bilingual, who learn a second language once the first is known.

2 Considerably more work will need to be done to determine how the human brain works, although 'neuroscience of multilingualism' (Abutalebi et al, 2009) is a growing field.

4 What type of language errors is this student making consistently? Suggest how she could systematically check her future writing to avoid similar issues.

TASK 3 Developing a personal proofreading checklist

1 Make your own proofreading checklist of common language issues, based on feedback on your previous writing. You could include:

- general language areas: *spelling, punctuation, ...*
- specific areas of grammar: *articles before nouns, sentence structure issues (e.g. subject-verb agreement), ...*
- specific areas of vocabulary: *uncountable nouns (research, evidence), ...*

2 It can be difficult to spot errors in your own writing. Work in groups and discuss how you can use the tools and techniques below to systematically check your writing. Add other ideas.

computer spell-check   computer 'find' facility   copies of source material
a dictionary / thesaurus   peer review / feedback   reading aloud

Example: *If your tutor highlights a problem with a specific word, use your computer's 'find' facility to search for all examples of that word in your text and check you haven't made the same mistake each time.*

3 Briefly compare with the class. Which techniques seem most useful?

TASK 4 Checking citations and references

1 **Look at student essay extracts a–c and their original source texts. These students have made errors in their citations or in-text references. Check the students' work against the original sources and identify the errors.**

a   Marsden, Hayden, Fox, Furness, Bulman, and Desholm (2009) conducted one of the few comparative studies to look at bird movement both before and after the construction of a wind farm.

     Little is known of the effects of wind farms on bird populations because of a lack of pre- and post-construction comparative studies […]. Application of the BACI (before–after–control–impact) method is advocated as the gold standard for study design in the context of wind farms, but is rarely feasible with time or monetary constraints and a lack of legislative necessity. We present here an unusual dataset recording bird-movement data before and after the construction of an offshore wind farm, in an area of dense migratory movements.

     SOURCE: Masden, E. A., Haydon, D. T., Fox, A. D., Furness, R. W., Bullman, R., & Desholm, M. (2009). p.749. Barriers to movement: impacts of wind farms on migrating birds. *ICES Journal of Marine Science*, 66: 746-753.

b   Whilst the economic burden of an ageing population is a cause for concern in many developed countries, research suggests that in OECD countries falling fertility rates will lead to a greater proportion of working-age people within the population, encouraging economic growth and offsetting increases in the older age group (Bloom, D., 2010).

     In most non-OECD countries, declining fertility rates will cause labour-force-to-population ratios to rise as the shrinking share of young people will more than offset the skewing of adults towards the older ages. These factors suggest that population ageing will not significantly impede the pace of economic growth in developing countries.

     SOURCE: Bloom, D., Canning, D., & Fink, G. (2010). p.583. Implications of population ageing for economic growth. *Oxford Review of Economic Policy*, 26(4): 583-612.

c   In the modern world, we have traded unique species of animals, such as Spix's macaw and the Chinese freshwater dolphin, for convenient gadgets such as the iPhone. Heal (2012) states 'we have build up our intellectual and physical capital while at the same time we have run down our natural capital'.

Spix's macaw

     … we have built up our intellectual and physical capital massively while at the same time we have run down our natural capital. We have lost forests, rangelands, and quite a number of species, but we have gained cures for common diseases, acquired central heating and air conditioning, domestic appliances, cell phones, laptops, and the Internet. We have traded Spix's macaw, the Chinese freshwater dolphin (the Baiji), and other unique species for the iPhone and other (not so unique) gadgets.

     SOURCE: Heal, G. (2012). p.154. Reflections – defining and measuring sustainability. *Review of Environmental Economics and Policy*, 6(1): 147-163.

Chinese freshwater dolphin

2 **Edit essay extracts a–c, correcting the errors.**

3 **Work in pairs and compare answers. Evaluate the essay extracts and decide whether any constitute plagiarism, and why.**

1 Read a paragraph from a student essay on the shopping habits of Chinese tourists in
   Japan. Read the subject tutor's feedback comments and categorize them according
   to the areas in Task 1.2 on page 189, i.e. language; structure and organization; use of
   sources; content; flow, cohesion, and voice.

2.2 A profile of Chinese leisure tourists

Since the start of the Visit Japan Project in 2004, the Japanese Tourist
Authority (JTA) has surveyed consumption trend of foreign tourists.
These surveys reveal some interesting figures regarding Chinese leisure
tourists and their consumption behaviour. Over the period, 51.4 per cent of   *Which period?*
Chinese tourists came to Japan for leisure and their average expenditure
on shopping during their trip was 95,239 Japanese Yen per person, the
highest for any nationality and twice the overall average (JTA, 2010). The
survey also found that many Chinese tourists (65.2%) were attracted to
luxury retail outlets such as prestige department stores. In their study
of Taiwanese tourists, Mok and Iverson (2000 cited in Lehto *et al.* 2004,
p.321) describes how shopping abroad fulfilled an important cultural role

Grammar?

in 'maintaining social relationships through the giving of gifts'. Although
the Taiwanese context is slightly different, the same cultural ideas may be
true for the current wave of tourists from the Chinese mainland. However,
there is an unanswered question why Chinese tourists prefer high-end,

*An awkward sentence
grammatically.*

more expensive stores than other retail shops in Japan. Moeran, B. (1983),   *Reference format.*
in his study into the habits of Japanese tourists, identified that they did not
just buy souvenirs as a reminder of their travel, but as a status symbol that
comes from having been abroad. He pointed out that they placed particular
importance on the country of origin of their souvenirs, as an indicator of
their ability to purchase the goods in their country of origin (ibid). At that
time, Japan was a 'bubble economy', an economic situation similar to that
in contemporary China. Thus, it seems that Chinese tourists may be drawn

*A good point, but
explain a little more
how the economic
context might affect
cultural attitudes.*

to Japanese Department stores for their 'Made in Japan' products, gift-
wrapped in original logo paper, which verifies their status as authentic
Japanese goods.

*Lots of good ideas here, but all lumped into one long paragraph. Try splitting your
two main points into separate paragraphs:*

*1 Chinese tourists spending more than other groups – why (Taiwan study, gift-
    giving culture)*

*2 Choice of department stores – prestige branded goods – Japan study – bubble
    economy*

2 Write an improved draft of the paragraph based on a) the subject tutor's feedback,
   particularly the advice on paragraph structure at the end of the essay, b) any changes
   to language and organization you can identify.

3 Work in pairs and compare improved drafts. Discuss which points of feedback were
   easiest to act on and which you found more difficult. Give reasons.

TASK 6 Redrafting a written text

1 Select part of a text you have written (1–2 pages) and produce a final draft.
Follow the guidelines below.

> ### Guidelines for writing a final draft
>
> 1 Work on 'deeper structure' first, i.e. structure and organization of the text, paragraphing.
> 2 Work on language, including 'surface' errors such as spelling. In addition, find ways of improving sentences which do not flow well.
> 3 Check all citations, in-text references, and References section entries for accuracy.
> 4 Carry out a final read-through of the redrafted text to spot any errors missed.

2 Work in pairs. Exchange texts and read critically to identify any errors.

TASK 7 Independent research – writing assessment

1 Many universities provide information online to help students with their writing.
Work in pairs. Read the criteria below from the University of Oxford Department of
Continuing Education website. Make sure you understand each point.

Learning support

> Bookmarking tools

> Citation tools

> Information sources

> Searching online

> A guide to producing coursework

Planning and writing an essay

Producing other forms of written work

Presenting your written work

<u>Submission of assignments</u>

Seeking further help

Assessment criteria

The following criteria are used to assess assignments for credit:

Knowledge and understanding   Rating

- shows understanding of the requirements of the assignment   ....
- displays knowledge of subject matter   ....
- demonstrates understanding of relevant ideas, contexts, issues, and relationships   ....

Selection and analysis

- selects appropriate ideas, evidence, data, techniques   ....
- evaluates evidence / analyses data or sources used to support argument or justify conclusion   ....

Organization and structure

- structures assignment according to the conventions of the discipline   ....
- develops a logical and coherent argument   ....
- shows ability to organize ideas, evidence, data, to support argument   ....

Communication and presentation

- uses language and/or tables, graphs, etc., effectively to communicate ideas   ....
- provides references and reading list.   ....

2 For each point above, rate yourself from 1–4 according to how well you can now
achieve this aim.

1 = very unsure
2 = some ideas but more information needed
3 = basically able
4 = very confident

3 Search for similar information on the website of your own institution or one you hope
to attend. Rate yourself using the scale in 2 for any new criteria.

Your aims and objectives in attending lectures will vary depending on your course and what stage you have reached in it. At the start of a course, understanding the key terms and concepts in your subject may be the focus for your listening and note-taking. As you learn more, you will need to link the ideas you hear in lectures with what you have read or discussed elsewhere, and you will listen for material relevant to specific assignments or research topics in which you are interested. You need to go into each lecture thinking about how it might fit in to your existing knowledge, what you hope to get out of it, and which note-taking techniques will be most relevant to identify what you need from a continuous lecture extract.

This module covers:
- Matching note-taking technique to purpose of listening
- Using lecture notes to prepare for a presentation

TASK 1 Preparing to listen – note-taking and purpose

1 You are going to watch a continuous lecture extract entitled *A brief introduction to social science research methods*, which will mention a number of terms / concepts related to research methods. Look at introductory lecture slide 1 and relate the questions to terms from the list.

   Example: What are we trying to find out? = *answering research questions*

   literature review
   combining multiple research studies
   selecting search terms
   research ethics
   gathering data
   research processes and outcomes
   randomization
   answering research questions
   selecting a sample

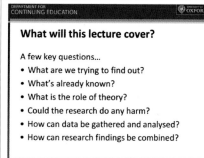

Slide 1

2 After you have watched the lecture extract, you will give a short oral presentation. Read the presentation activity. Then decide which listening and note-taking technique(s) you will use to prepare effectively. Refer to Checklist N on page 213 for ideas.

> **PRESENTATION ACTIVITY:** *Prepare a two-minute presentation on a description of an aspect of social science research.*

Topic Based on your lecture notes, confirm the main topics, and select one aspect of social science research covered by the lecturer (e.g. a literature review).

Expanding your notes Go through your notes and identify relevant points to use in your presentation. Process the material into a coherent description of the topic.

Key concepts Check you understand the key concepts introduced in the lecture, and find a way of explaining them; use the lecturer's definition, find a published definition, or come up with your own explanation.

Examples Where possible, add examples from your own academic experience to illustrate your presentation.

Practice Plan and briefly practise your presentation; keep to the time limit.

TASK 2 Noting relevant information from a long extract

◀ ▶12.1 **Watch the extract and while listening:**

- listen for the main topics (e.g. literature review)
- make sufficient notes for each topic to build up material for your presentation
- listen for key concepts and technical terms, and the lecturer's explanation of these.

ACADEMIC LANGUAGE

Style (4) Informal and idiomatic language

Some lecturers may use more formal academic and technical language, while others may employ informal, idiomatic, conversational language, even when explaining serious topics. Informal language may be a matter of personal style. However, it may be used when explaining a familiar concept in the lecturer's discipline, and/or to make the explanations of technical concepts more accessible. Noticing and understanding such language can help you to decode the lecturer's explanations more easily.

Study these examples:

__You know__, they __just kind of__ went into the library, __picked anything up__ off the shelf, __just kind of had a quick look__ …

Obviously that then __begs the question of__ how we would combine this research …

It takes multiple studies, __coming at it__ from different perspectives.

__OK, well so we've sorted all that out__, we know what humanity is …

The research literature __is littered with__ examples of that.

Researchers have __cut corners__, under pressure to publish, under pressure to produce results and I'm afraid, plagiarism and falsification of results, plagiarism being where __you rip off__ somebody else's work and present it as your own and falsification, where you __literally just stick in__ the numbers that suit you.

OK, so let's go onto __some of the nitty gritty__ about the kind of data we might need to gather.

TASK 3 Using lecture notes to prepare for a presentation

1 Work in groups. Divide up the main topics of the lecture, one (or two) per student.

2 Prepare your presentation. Follow the procedure in Task 1.2.

TASK 4 Discussing and extending ideas from a lecture

1 Take turns to deliver your presentations. Refer to how your ideas link to or overlap with the other speakers where relevant.

2 Following the presentations, continue the discussion. Consider how to relate the different approaches to your own discipline, and any limitations and practical implications. Give examples from your own experience where possible.

A central activity in academic speaking is presenting your own research - results or work in progress - and it is essential to consider your audience, who may not be as familiar with your topic as you are, or from the same discipline. You need to make your topic / research question clear from the beginning and give enough background information to put your research into context. The content and approach should be more accessible to a non-expert audience than most written work; however, your presentation should be suitably academic, including references to the literature, research data and theory where relevant, and your own findings, discussion, and evaluation. You need to find an appropriate balance between offering a brief overview of the research, and explaining the whole project in detail.

This module covers:
- Planning a research presentation - understanding the task
- Considering your audience
- Preparing and giving a research presentation

TASK 1 Understanding the presentation task

1 **You are going to give a research presentation following the procedure below. Read the presentation activity and decide on the topic of your presentation.**

> **PRESENTATION ACTIVITY:** *Give an individual presentation based on a research project.*
>
> **Topic** *Either* 1 Give a presentation based on the research project you have been writing through this course.
>   *Or* 2 Base your presentation on another piece of research-based writing you have completed, such as the 'cause and effect' essay in Unit 8.
>
> You can present a summary of your whole project or focus on one aspect / section.
>
> **Format** Give a 10–15 minute presentation to the class, using appropriate visual aids. Take questions from the audience at the end.

2 **A 10–15 minute presentation does not allow time to cover a 2,000-word+ research project in detail. Look at your own chosen piece of research writing, focusing especially on the main sections and/or headings. Note down:**
- *either* the approach you intend to take to presenting your work in summary
- *or* two different approaches you could take to presenting one aspect of your work.

3 **Prepare at least two questions to ask your tutor about the presentation. These can be about practical issues or about the content / topic.**

Example: *Do we have to prepare visuals for our presentation?*
Can I just talk about the case study part of my project?

TASK 2 Considering your audience

1 ◀))12.2 **Listen to Extract 1, two students talking about giving a presentation. For each student, note how they tried to make their presentation relevant or interesting to their audience.**

2 **Consider your own presentation and audience and place them on the scale below.**

Project topic

of general interest ◀————————————————▶ specialized / technical

Audience knowledge about my topic / discipline

familiar ◀————————————————▶ unfamiliar

Work in pairs and discuss the piece of work you will present. Use the other student as your 'audience'. Make notes as you talk, to review before you finalize your presentation later.

1 Take turns to explain your topic informally.

2 Discuss ideas for making your presentation accessible, relevant, and interesting to your audience.

3 Find ways of explaining technical terms and concepts that may be unfamiliar.

4 Ask and answer questions about any points that are not clear.

ACADEMIC LANGUAGE

Introducing a topic Giving reasons and examples

The introduction of your presentation is important in gaining your audience's interest and establishing your topic. One way to introduce your topic is to give your reasons for choosing it.

- Personal / professional reasons:
  In my home country ... is a serious issue / a significant problem.
  In my work as ..., / From my work in ..., I frequently come across ...
- Significance / relevance of the topic:
  The latest research shows that ... is becoming ...
  You may have heard in the news recently that ...

You can also start with an interesting example or illustration:
  Some of you may be familiar with ...
  I'd like / I want(ed) to start with an example which shows how ...

TASK 3 Preparing and giving a research presentation

1 ◀)) 12.3 **Listen to Extract 2, two short extracts from student presentations. Note down their reasons for choosing their topic.**

2 **In your pairs from Task 2, discuss ways you can each introduce your presentation, either by giving reasons for your choice of topic, or by using an example.**

3 **Review your informal presentations in Task 2.3, looking back at your feedback notes. Choose one or two areas in which you would like to improve your performance.**

4 **Prepare your presentation. Refer to Checklist I on page 211.**

5 **Give your presentation to the class.**

TASK 4 Critical thinking - learning from experience

1 **Work in groups. Discuss your presentations.**
- Take turns to say what you think worked well in your presentation and what you would do differently next time.
- Review the points for improvement you identified in Task 3.3.
- Give other students feedback on their performance, using Checklist I on page 211.
- Pick out positive points as well as areas for improvement.

2 **As a class, make a list of the best points from the presentations you have seen that you would like to use yourself in future.**

Example: *Leisa's diagrams were really clear and simple, and helped me understand the topic. I think sometimes it's better to present ideas visually rather than just having lots of text.*

1 Choose three words from the list to research and analyse from one of the following perspectives a–e. Use a dictionary, look back through this book, or explore their usage via internet searches or other online tools.

assumption   authority   backward   consume   demonstrate devote   establishment   exclusion   industrialized   insight insufficient   interaction   label   reliable   revolutionary   significant

a general and specialized uses

b synonyms and antonyms

c collocation (words which are typically used together)

d word formation (prefixes, suffixes, and compounds)

e connotation (emotive, negative, or sensitive language)

2 Work in groups and take turns to present what you have found.

12F Research Project (6)

Finalizing your work

How do I prepare my final draft for submission?

Having worked through any feedback from your tutor and edited your final draft (see 12B), there are some final checks you need to go through in order to prepare your project for submission and assessment. Check the particular requirements you need to follow, either in any guidelines or handbook published for your course, or ask your tutor.

To finalize your project, check:

- **whether you have kept to the word limit.**
- **whether you need to include an abstract.** An abstract is usually written at the end of a project and is a brief summary of the main points and conclusions.
- **what form your bibliography or reference list should take.** Check that any sources cited in your project have correct in-text references and full reference details are given in your bibliography. A bibliography is typically presented in alphabetical order by the family name of the first author of each source.
- **that any tables or diagrams are correctly labelled.** Give the source where appropriate. References for graphs, diagrams or tables you have used should be included in the bibliography. If you have created your own graphs or tables, the source of any data should be stated and a reference given.
- **what format your project should be presented in.** It is common practice to use a large, clear font and double spacing. If your project is to be submitted as a hard copy (on paper), you should print on one side of the page.
- **whether you need a contents page and page numbers.** This should be the final thing you do, as page numbers may change during editing.
- **whether you need a cover page.** This might include details such as the project title, your name, the date, your tutor's name, your course or group, etc.

Glossary

Words and phrases describing common academic terms covered in this book.

Abstract the text at the beginning of an academic article which summarizes the whole article; abstracts are also available and searchable separately

Allocate to give each person in a group a share of sth or a particular task to do

Analysis detailed examination of information or statistics, especially the results of research, in order to understand and classify it

Application the practical use of sth, especially the results of research

Argument a written or spoken discussion based on reason, logic, and evidence; an argument can be the main argument or a supporting argument

Association a connection between two things where one is affected or influenced by the other in some way

Audience all the people who read or might read a particular book or article, or attend a lecture or presentation

Biased showing a tendency to favour a particular perspective or point of view; not presenting all sides of sth fairly

Bibliography a list of sources (books, articles, etc.) used in writing a text; a bibliography typically appears at the end of the text and shows the full details of the author(s), date, title and publication

Case a set of arguments and evidence intended to persuade others

Case study a detailed study of a particular situation, person, or group, especially over a period of time

Citation a summary, paraphrase, or quotation which is from a source text

Coherence how a text is connected in terms of meaning and ideas

Cohesion how a text is connected in terms of meaning and language

Collaboratively working together as a group

Commentary a written description or explanation of sth, e.g. a graph or diagram

Compromise an agreement between two people or groups in which each changes their position so as to reach a **resolution**

Conclusion the part of a written or spoken text which sums up the main argument of the whole text, usually the end of the text

Conference proceedings a written report of the presentations given at a conference, which can be read by a wider audience

Context the background or situation surrounding sth which helps you to understand it better

Critical questions questions you ask about the information in a text or presentation to test how reliable or accurate it is

Critical response a written or spoken **evaluation** of a text, giving a subjective, evidence-based assessment of the ideas in the text; a critical response can include positive comments and/or criticisms (also known as a **critique** or **review**)

Critique a written or spoken **evaluation** of a text, giving a subjective, evidence-based assessment of the ideas in the text; a critique can include positive comments and/or criticisms (also known as a **critical response** or **review**)

Data information or **statistics** collected and examined as part of a research study

Definition an explanation of the exact meaning of a word or phrase, especially a term used in a particular context

Delivery the way a speaker gives a lecture or presentation, including the speed, volume and clarity of their speech

Discursive writing involving discussion of an issue or question

Evaluation the writer's subjective, evidence-based response to an idea in the text

Evidence facts, information or statistics which show that a particular statement or argument is true or valid

Expository explaining or describing sth

Genre a particular style or form of written or spoken text with its own special features; a textbook, a **journal article** and a report are all genres

Graph a diagram showing the relationship between two (or more) sets of numbers

Handout printed information given to people attending a lecture or presentation

Implication the likely consequences of sth; what effects the results of research might have in the real world

In-text reference information in a text showing the source of any citations; in-text references consist of the authors' name and the date of the source, or a number, which are linked to the full reference details in the **bibliography** or reference list

Interpretation explanation of the possible meaning of sth, e.g. the results of research

Journal article a written text, typically following a set structure, which is published in an academic journal

Learning style the way that an individual prefers to study

Limitation the points that were not covered in a piece of writing or a research project, due to restrictions on time, space, etc., which affect how full and complete the conclusions can be

Literature what has been written, in academic books, **journal articles**, etc., about a particular topic

Literature review a written text, typically part of a longer piece of writing, which provides an overview of what has already been written about a particular topic or what research has already been done in the area

Navigate to find your way around sth, e.g. a book, to find the information you need

Negotiate to discuss sth in order to reach an agreement, taking different opinions into account

Norm behaviour or a way of doing sth which is typical or accepted within a particular context

Objective based only on facts and evidence, not influenced by personal judgements

Paraphrase a piece of text which expresses similar ideas to another text of similar length, but using different language

Peer-reviewed articles written for academic journals are usually reviewed by other academics in the field (the writer's *peers*) before they are accepted for publication; this ensures a level of quality and reliability

Perspective a mainly objective way of viewing sth, e.g. *From a medical perspective …*

Plagiarism the use of someone else's work in your own writing without acknowledgment; plagiarism can involve using the exact words or the ideas of someone else without a correct reference or submitting work for assessment that you have submitted before (self-plagiarism)

Popular academic text a book on an academic subject that has been written for general, non-academic readers, e.g. a popular science or psychology book

Position a way of viewing sth which is mainly subjective but based on evidence; you can take a position on an issue and argue in support of or against it

Prediction a statement about what you think may happen in the future, based on evidence

Primary research research that involves collecting new data, from experiments, measurement, observation, interviews, etc. (see also **secondary research**)

Purpose what a piece of writing aims to achieve, e.g., to describe or explain sth, to discuss an issue, to evaluate sth, etc.

Quotation a **citation** which uses the exact words of the original source

Rationale the reasons for doing sth in a particular way, e.g. the reasons for choosing a topic or taking a particular approach

References section a list of sources (books, articles, etc.) used in writing a text; a references section typically appears at the end of the text and shows the full details of the author(s), date, title and publication

Research findings the results of academic research

Resolution a situation in which agreement has been reached about the answer to a question, the solution to a problem or how to deal with sth

Responding reacting to new information you read or hear by asking questions, making comments, etc.

Review a written or spoken **evaluation** of a text, giving a subjective, evidence-based assessment of the ideas in the text; a review can include positive comments and/or criticisms (also known as a **critical response** or **critique**)

Scope the range of ideas that a text, a presentation or a piece of research deals with

Script independence the ability to give a presentation without reading from or memorizing a prepared script

Secondary research research that is based on reading about what others have already researched and written about, rather than conducting **primary research** yourself

Seminar a class in which a small group of students and a teacher discuss a topic

Stance a way of viewing sth which is mainly subjective but based on evidence, and connected to an **argument**

Statistics information collected about sth in the form of numbers

STEM subjects acronym for Science, Technology, Engineering, and Maths

Subjective based on personal judgements; in an academic context these judgements are typically informed by evidence and reading rather than personal opinion

Summary a short text which expresses the main argument(s) of a longer text

Thesis the main point which you argue for and support with evidence in a piece of writing, typically expressed in a **thesis statement** in the introduction; your thesis reflects your **stance**

Thesis statement the part of a text which briefly expresses some or all of the following: purpose, aims, rationale, stance, limitations, organization

Valid based on what is logical or true

Academic language reference

1 Citation, referencing, reporting, referring to sources

There are various ways of referring to material from other sources.

1.1 Content focus

This focuses on the content (the main message or material) rather than the author(s) whose ideas are being reported. The reference is usually placed in the middle of the content, or at the end, e.g.

*One useful analysis of human motivation (**Maslow 1970**) suggests that we have a hierarchy of needs.*

*Numerous academic studies have used this framework to show that differences in technological approaches account for the early success of wind turbine manufacturers in some countries and not others (**Heymann 1998; Est 1999; Karnøe, Kristensen, and Anderson 1999; Johnson and Jacobsson 2000; Garud and Karnøe 2003; Boon 2008**).*

1.2 Author focus

This focuses on the author, or authors, rather than the content. The author's name is placed before the content, and the year of publication is given in brackets directly following, e.g.

*As emphasized by **Buchanan et al. (2009)**, this is an issue of global cooperation …*

For clarity, the author can be introduced at the start of the sentence, with the full reference placed at the end, e.g.

***Paul Gipe** – a well-known wind energy pioneer – wrote in the mid-1990s, 'From the deserts of California to …' (**Gipe 1995**).*

1.3 Reporting verbs and structures

A wide range of reporting verbs and structures can be used to report other writers' ideas. Typical reporting verbs include *argue, believe, claim, contend, describe, discuss, explain, illustrate, maintain, note, observe, point out, say, state, suggest*, e.g.

*Axel Bruns (cited in Sorensen 2007) **claims that** what we are seeing with YouTube and Wikipedia is …*

*Carl Bernstein, veteran journalist of Watergate fame (cited in Stockwell 2004) **maintains that** the problem with news and news journalism today is …*

According to can be used to refer to an external source of information or evidence, e.g. ***According to** Sorensen (2007), 'Every day millions of people choose …*

1.4 Referring to an argument, idea, or theory

Sometimes you may want to refer to a particular piece of work by one or more persons, rather than the person themselves. Useful nouns include *analysis, argument, claim, definition, explanation, model, theory*, e.g.
***Maslow's theory** also does not really give a detailed picture of the workings of needs.*

If you want to refer to information from a graphic such as a table, put the reference to this either before or after the content, e.g.

***Table 8.2 shows** the estimates of the extent of 'BCS crime.'*

*Partly as a result of changing gender attitudes and expectations (**Table 3.4**) …*

1.5 Quotation, paraphrase, and summary

a Quotation: using the original language of the source (a direct quotation). To do this, use quotation marks. The reference, including the page number where appropriate, needs to be given directly before or after the quotation, e.g.
***Pettigrew (1990)** has emphasized such a 'contextualist' research design involves drawing on 'phenomena at vertical and horizontal levels of analysis and the interconnections between those levels through time' (**1990: 269**).*

b Paraphrase: expressing the same idea from a source, but using the writer's own words (vocabulary and grammar), e.g.
***Ostrom (2007)** believes that these consumer changes will be the most important.*

c Summary: the cited material is expressed in the writer's own words, and integrated into the rest of the text. It includes the main points of an argument, idea, or theory, but not the detail.

1.6 Reference reminder language

With longer citations of several lines, or repeated citations from the same source, it is sometimes useful to remind the reader about the author. You can do this by repeating their name or using reference reminder language, such as *Brown and Miller (2008)* **continue by saying / go on to say (that) / also conclude (that)** …

The following example shows multiple repetitions of the author's name throughout the paragraph:
*One useful analysis of human motivation (**Maslow, 1970**) suggests that we have a hierarchy of needs … Only when these are satisfied are we able to worry about the next level – which **Maslow** described as the safety needs … **Maslow** completes his pyramid of needs with …*

1.7 Indirect references

References to sources that are not directly cited, but may be useful to the reader, can be included either in an in-text reference, or in a footnote, e.g.

*Although the question of nature walks is still being debated (**see for example** Edwards 2011; James et al., 2011) …*

*The ontogeny of a honey bee worker takes it through a series of tasks (**for review, see** Jassim et al., 2000).*

2 Cohesion

Cohesion refers to the ways in which the different meanings in a text are linked. A cohesive text presents the different items in the text in such a way that the meaning is clear and unambiguous.

2.1 Pronouns and determiners

Pronouns (e.g. *he, it, them*) and determiners (e.g. *the, one, such, the other, this, that, these, those*) usually refer back to something already mentioned, e.g.

Wind power advocates frequently employ this framework and argue that the industry's global development is inevitable, given that it is driven by continuous technological advances.

They can also refer forward, e.g.

*Basically, **two** broad intervention strategies exist to alter eating behavior. **One** strategy focuses on individual problem awareness and personal motivation and skills, **the other** on providing context stimuli intended to direct food choice.*

2.2 Related words and synonyms

Writers use different techniques such as synonyms, related words / phrases, and paraphrasing to avoid too much repetition of the same key word or phrase. In the following example, not all the highlighted items are identical in meaning, but they all refer to the basic idea of consumers buying local food:

*Perhaps the greatest evidence of momentum in **the local food movement** is the recognition of '**Locavores**' as the 2007 word of the year by the New Oxford American Dictionary. Defined as '**a local resident who tries to eat only food grown or produced within a 100-mile radius**,' the term identifies the growing ranks of **environmentally and edibility-conscious consumers who deliberately seek out locally produced food and beverages**. ... However, despite the apparent **growth in demand for local foods**, there has been a paucity of research results regarding **the motivation of consumers to seek out and pay a premium for local produce offerings**, the role of **direct markets in consumer shopping choices**, and **buying profiles of consumers who frequent direct channels.***

Example of synonyms: *food / produce*

Examples of related words / phrases: *consumer / resident; local food / local produce / locally produced food and beverages*

Example of paraphrasing: *local food – food grown or produced within a 100-mile radius*

2.3 Cohesive noun phrases

Cohesive noun phrases refer back to one or more earlier sentences in a text. They typically consist of a **determiner** (e.g. *this, these, such*) plus a **noun** (e.g. *issue, process, challenge*), and sometimes a **modifying adjective** (e.g. *important, interesting*). They can either reuse key language in the earlier sentence(s), or introduce new language, e.g.

*The authors found that farmers' markets encourage the production of a greater diversity of food products, which would be needed for a more localized food system. **This greater diversity** attracts ...* (reuses key language)

It has already been mentioned that the 'official crime statistics' no longer contain only offences recorded by the police. Since 2002, the main annual statistical publication

*(renamed Crime in England and Wales) has also included large amounts of data from the British Crime Survey. **This decision** was ...* (introduces new language, labelling the ideas expressed in the previous sentences as *This decision*).

2.4 Linking adverbials

Linking adverbials are words or phrases that connect two (or more) ideas in a text to show an important relationship, such as a contrast or conclusion.

a To sequence items in a list or add information, e.g. ***Firstly**, drugs harm an individual; **secondly**, drugs harm those ...; **In addition**, farmers' markets serve as business incubators ...; **Moreover**, the market has witnessed considerable growth in the numbers of farmers using direct marketing strategies.*

b To conclude or summarize, e.g. ***In conclusion**, two important points can be made; **In summary**, motivation is an interaction of influences ...*

c To rephrase, e.g. ***In other words**, the author's insights ...*

d To give an example, e.g. ***For example**, California was the leading US wind energy producer in 2005.*

e To introduce a result, e.g. ***As a result**, many researchers and companies are ...*

f To indicate inference, e.g. *It is **therefore** a serious misunderstanding ...*

g To indicate contrast or concession, e.g. ***However**, as Guio (2005) observes ...; This success was made more likely due to superior, **though** completely legal, equipment ...*

h To show transition or provide contextualization, e.g. ***In this chapter** I focus on ... ; statements that apply **regardless of** time and place; Case studies will receive attention **in Chapter 25**.*

2.5 Generic language

Generic language can be found in texts from any academic discipline. It connects the main topic of a text to related ideas that the writer wishes to discuss. The topic and related ideas are the **content** of the text (i.e. information, ideas, evaluation). The generic language provides a **structure** for the content, and is made up of 'chunks,' mainly based on nouns and verbs.

In the following example, the topic is highlighted in yellow, and the related ideas in blue. The rest of the text is made up of **generic language**: *Humour **is associated with** creativity at work. **The analysis provides evidence that** humour **not only contributes to** the construction of effective workplace relationships (the creative use of relational humour), **but may also** stimulate intellectual activity **of direct relevance to** the achievement of workplace objectives (the use of humour to foster workplace creativity). **The analysis suggests that the first category is** pervasive **and** examples abound throughout our data set, **whilst** humour **associated with** workplace creativity **is** less frequent **and tends to** characterize some communities of practice more than others.*

2.6 Other types of cohesion: interaction and direction

a Interaction – the writer sometimes includes the reader by addressing them directly, e.g. *From this example, **we** can see that human experience is …*

b Direction – the writer uses an imperative form to direct the reader to information elsewhere in the text, e.g. *While these changes create problems for many children, (**see below**) …*

3 Comparison and contrast

Comparisons between two or more items or ideas are frequent in written and spoken academic texts. In general, comparative forms (e.g. *easier, more detailed*) are much more frequently used than superlative forms (e.g. *the greatest, the most common*).

3.1 Comparative adjectives and adverbs

The following comparative structures are used to express comparison between two or more items.

a adjective with *-er + than*, e.g. *A group is **smarter than** your individual.*

b *more/less* + adjective/adverb + *than*, e.g. *It is **more difficult** to find a fact illustrating reaction to a speech than simply to take a stab at summing up that reaction yourself; Infotainment … is engaging, informing and entertaining the public **far more effectively than** the traditional news outlets.*

c *as* + adjective/adverb + *as*, e.g. *Not all facts are **as straightforward as** a name.*

d *so* + adjective/adverb + *that*, e.g. *Our movements had become **so familiar that** I hardly noticed …*

e *too* + adjective/adverb + *to*, e.g. *Others are **too common to** ignore; Interpretation **too often** leads to guesswork and subjectivity.*

f adjective/adverb + *enough* + *to*-clause, e.g. *Algal biofuel has the potential to be produced on a scale **large enough to** entirely replace petrodiesel.*

3.2 Other language to express similarity and contrast

a Language for expressing similarity includes *Similarly, In the same way, Likewise,* e.g.
***Similarly**, when you come to discuss your results you will automatically apply your findings to the statistical population.*

b Language for expressing contrast includes *Conversely, In contrast, On the other hand,* e.g.
***Conversely**, this result shows that where consumers live may not be a determinant for differences across people.*

c Subordinators like *while* and *although* can also be used to show contrast, e.g.
***While** Maslow's theory makes good intuitive sense, a number of objections have been made to it; **Although** it can affect people of all ages, it is most common in old age.*

3.3 Comparison and evaluation

Writers frequently use comparative structures, including superlatives (e.g. *the strongest*), to express part of their evaluation, e.g.

*Volume 2 **has more to offer** and **is**, as mentioned above, **better constructed** in my view.* (Comparative forms – the writer adds the phrase *in my view* to express the personal nature of the evaluation.)

*Recent studies show the United Kingdom has **the strongest**, **most dependable**, and **most convenient** onshore winds, **as well as the highest** offshore wind potential.* (Superlative forms.)

4 Connection: cause, effect, and association

Cause and effect connections are frequent in academic writing, and the relationship between two or more items needs to be made very clear. The writer can choose to put the **cause** first, then introduce an effect: *This variability **causes** many problems.* Alternatively, if the topic of the text is an **effect**, this would then come first, e.g. *Five per cent of strokes **are caused by** a condition called subarachnoid haemorrhage.* The category of cause, effect, and association also includes reason, result, and connection.

A Cause → effect

You can use a wide range of structures to express cause and effect connections, i.e. to state a cause first in a sentence, and then introduce an effect.

4.1 Nouns / noun phrases

You can use only the cause and effect noun, or build up a longer noun phrase based on the cause and effect noun (underlined) to express evaluation, e.g. the importance or seriousness of the cause, e.g.

*Marital breakdown is therefore **an important <u>cause</u> of** childhood poverty.*

*The average length of career for an American football player is under four years, with injury being **one of the main <u>reasons</u> for** this lack of longevity.*

4.2 Verbs

To express cause → effect, the verb (underlined) is used in the **active** voice, e.g.

*Inactivity **<u>causes</u>** 9% of premature mortality.*

*Differences in technological approaches **<u>account for</u>** the early success of wind turbine manufacturers in some countries and not others.*

Further information can be added using a modal verb (e.g. *can, may*) and/or an adverb (e.g. *also, often*):

*Taste **can <u>affect</u>** an individual's likes and dislikes from the earliest stages of life.*

*Interpretation **too often <u>leads to</u>** guesswork and subjectivity.*

4.3 Adverbials: *as a result, consequently, hence, so, thereby, therefore, thus*

There are a number of adverbials (which may be adverbs or prepositional phrases) which can be used to indicate or introduce an effect, e.g.

__As a result__, from 1861 to the end of the nineteenth century, large areas were extensively cleared and potentially commercial forests were destroyed.

__Consequently__, in terms of reliability, replication, and validity, the longitudinal design is little different from cross-sectional research.

4.4 Subordinators: *so that, so as to*

The subordinators *so that* and *so as to* can be used to introduce an effect or result, e.g.

The key factors in reducing family size in developing countries are increasing income (__so that__ children are not seen as an economic necessity).

The challenge at present is to improve the efficiency of algal fuel production technology __so as to__ lower the cost of algal biodiesel.

4.5 Other expressions

Certain fixed expressions can be used to express similar connections, e.g.

Motivation can be modified by learning, __which means that__ higher mental processes can play a significant role in our understanding of motivation and our responses to it.

Either deprivation or stimulation produce a need state in the organism, __which in turn gives rise to__ a drive to satisfy that need.

B Effect ← cause

A similarly wide range of structures can be used to link an effect to its cause, i.e. to state an effect first in a sentence, and then introduce the cause.

4.6 Nouns / noun phrases

This includes noun phrases based on nouns like: *consequence, effect, outcome, result*, e.g.

This is __the result__ of the continued presence of unregulated ivory markets within and near these countries.

__The results__ of fieldwork thus depend in part upon __the outcomes of__ the unofficial study.

4.7 Verbs

Some verbs are used in the **active** voice to introduce a cause, e.g.

Cross-national variation __results from__ differences in technological approaches.

So what __originated as__ a sub-prime crisis of largely US origin became generalized as a global financial crash.

Some verbs are used in the **passive** voice to introduce a cause, e.g.

It is a disease of the brain (not the heart) and __is caused by__ a blockage or rupture of the essential blood supply.

Verbs in the passive voice can be combined with a modal verb or other hedging language: *can be produced by, is likely to be brought about by, may be attributed to.*

4.8 Subordinators: *as, because, since*

The subordinators *as, because* and *since* are frequently used to introduce causes, e.g.

Nectar from flowers, for example, usually comes in patches, __as__ one plant often has several flowers.

The stock market values of the institutions themselves also fell, __because__ they were holding securities that were worth less.

It is difficult to cover fraud, __since__ many people will not be aware they have been victimized.

4.9 Prepositions: *as a result of, because of, due to, owing to, through*

Complex prepositions (containing two or more words) and some single-word prepositions are frequently used to introduce causes, e.g.

This phrase was coined __as a result of__ the series of interlinked investigations carried out during the late 1920s and early 1930s.

Land clearing has focused on better soils __because of__ cultural traditions in agriculture.

This success was made more likely __due to__ superior, though completely legal, equipment.

She replied that she had been sick for several months __owing to__ a terrible burn she had received.

Better quality housing seems to reduce the effect of crowding on height, presumably __through__ its effects on hygiene.

4.10 Expressing association

An association is a connection that does not necessarily constitute a clear cause and effect relationship. Such associations can be expressed using (*be*) *associated with,* (*have*) *an association with,* (*be*) *connected to,* (*have*) *a connection with, involve,* (*be*) *involved with, link to,* (*be*) *linked to,* e.g.

Humour __is associated with__ creativity at work.

A particular focus is how local source and product attribution __may connect__ with perceived private and public good dimensions of such choices.

… Blood vessels __are involved__, not necessarily a neurological event where brain tissue __may be involved__.

Surveys in children of food consumption and preferences have __linked__ early taste experiences __to__ subsequent food acceptance.

5 Contextualizing language: adverbials

Adverbials function as **clause elements**, and express information relating to *where, when, why,* and *how.* They are widely used in academic texts to contextualize information: for example, to express **circumstance** (situating something in time and place), to express abstract meanings such as reason and condition, to indicate stance and perspective, and to link different ideas in a text.

5.1 Expressing circumstance

The following points relate to the main types of circumstance: place, time, process, connection, and focus. There are three examples for each, which show a prepositional phrase, an adverb, and an adverbial clause.

a Place (distance, direction, position)

*On the graph, you will see that **towards the end of the graph** it goes right up to 10 billion.* (position / direction)

*Physical inactivity has a major health effect **worldwide**.* (distance)

*We had a web portal **where the names of all colleagues were listed**.* (position)

b Time (time relationships, duration, frequency)

*No one foresaw that, **within a couple of years**, media watchers would be talking about an end to the TV era.* (duration)

*The data again take the shape of a sigmoidal or s-shaped curve, with some countries having gained elephants **while the population of others continued to decline**.* (time relationship)

*North Dakota has **frequently** been called the 'Saudi Arabia of wind'.* (frequency)

c Process (how something is done)

*A sample of very large fleet operators was interviewed **with a semi-structured questionnaire**.*

*It has grown **steadily** in prominence and status.*

*It looked **as if none of the colleagues had a doctorate**.*

d Connection (concession, condition, purpose, cause and effect)

The following subordinators are used to express concession: *although, though, even though, while, whilst, whereas*, e.g.
***While** these changes create problems for many children, … for some they may be a source of resilience.*

There are many subordinators to express condition: *if, unless, provided, given that, as long as*, e.g.

***If** the behaviour succeeds, the result is satisfaction; **if** not, frustration.*

***Unless** a distinction of this or some other kind is drawn, it becomes impossible to distinguish the case study as a special research design.*

In order to and *to* + verb (the 'infinitive of purpose') are frequently used to express purpose, e.g. *Most people think about motivation in terms of needs that must be met **to achieve a state of comfort**.*

e Focus (extent, amount, addition, restriction, definition)

*At one point, it was the largest corporation ever in the USA, **in terms of its revenues as a percentage of GDP**.*

***Additionally**, a sample of very large fleet operators was interviewed.*

***Only when these are satisfied** are we able to worry about the next level.*

See **4 Connection: cause, effect, and association**

5.2 Expressing perspective

There are four main adverbial forms used to express perspective.

a Prepositional phrases (phrases that begin with a preposition, e.g. *for, in, on, with, due to, with regard to*)

*Shifting ideas of fortune are also traced **in relation to different historical periods**.*

*With the ever-expanding movement of individuals to all corners of the globe **for the purposes of business, entertainment, education, and economic opportunity**, …*

b Adverbs

*Much of the remaining vegetation is highly fragmented, disturbed or **ecologically** compromised.*

*We are likely to be able to track **globally** the migrations of even the smallest songbirds.*

c Non-finite clauses (where the verb is in the -ed, -ing, or to infinitive form)

*However, the size of a focus group can vary **depending on the research topic and social context of the participants**.*

*As Cortazzi and Jin (1997: 78) say, **speaking particularly of China**, 'A learner's duty is to understand and master what those in authority say.'*

Non-finite verb forms usually use fewer words than finite forms, and can be used to avoid saying when something happened.

d Finite clauses (where the verb is in a tense form)

*There is no doubt that being born in the UK in the 1980s meant that you were more likely to win a cycling gold medal in the Beijing Olympics than **if you had the same genes**, but were born in Morocco.*

Finite verb forms can be used to express specific times, e.g. present or past.

5.3 Multiple adverbials in a sentence

A sentence can contain several adverbials expressing different things, particularly when providing contextualization early in a text. It is important to read such sentences carefully and make sure you understand what each adverbial phrase means. The example sentence below includes stance (*In fact*), perspective (*from a policy point of view*), time (*at least in the short run*), purpose (*in order to acquire higher levels of education and skills*), possibility (*very well*), and contrast (*as opposed to establishing, say, universities or research institutes in the source country*).

***In fact, from a policy point of view** and **at least in the short run**, promoting emigration by workers and students (the latter probably more than the former) **in order to acquire higher levels of education and skills** may **very well** be a cost-efficient way to improve the quality of domestic human capital, **as opposed to establishing, say, universities or research institutes in the source country**.*

5.4 Other contextualizing language

Other structures can also be used to contextualize material in a text.

a Noun phrases to express circumstance, e.g. **Countries such as Kerala (a state of Southern India) and Sri Lanka, which have focused on these factors**, have had remarkable success in reducing fertility.

b Noun phrases to express perspective, e.g. **The technological perspective** argues that the development of new industries is influenced primarily by technological innovations and traditions.

c Verbs to express stance, e.g. *An alternative critique focuses on the fact that low income **fails** to identify those experiencing deprivation.*

d Verbs to link ideas in a text, e.g. *This **leads** me to consider …*

6 Evaluation and stance

You can use a variety of grammatical structures and vocabulary to express your evaluation and stance.

6.1 Adjectives

Examples of positive adjectives include: *attractive, believable, effective, important, significant, sound, useful.* Examples of negative adjectives include: *ineffective, irrational, surprising, unconvincing, unfortunate,* e.g.

*Higher mental processes can play a **significant** role in our understanding of motivation.*

*These efforts have often been **ineffective**.*

6.2 Adverbs

Adverbs that can be used to modify an adjective or adverb in an **adjective phrase** include *a bit, extremely, only, particularly, quite, rather, somewhat, very,* e.g.

*This was **very** unlikely to be the case.*

*These satisfied the **rather** complicated market situation.*

*Two of the countries are **particularly** important; algal biofuel production technology is still **somewhat** new and **uneconomical**.*

6.3 Adverbs and adverbials

a Expressing certainty and doubt

*CSA farms will **probably never** be more than a small part of the food system.*

*Non-research student learning, moreover, can and **no doubt** will, increasingly adopt distance modes.*

*It is **certainly** possible to identify values and practices among …*

b Expressing stance

Interestingly, *the type of food previously available at that location had an effect on the behavior of ants.*

Indeed, *looked at as a whole, it does not **necessarily** present a fuller – or **indeed**, 'truer' – picture than that provided by the recorded crime statistics, **simply** a different one.*

*Volume 2 has more to offer and is, as mentioned above, better constructed **in my view**.*

c Expressing knowledge or understanding

In fact, *all over the world, 'Manhattanization' signifies everything in a city that is not thought to be authentic.* (prepositional phrase)

In some cases, *cognitive appraisals lead individuals to make regulatory decisions.* (prepositional phrase)

6.4 Nouns

Nouns to express evaluation include *challenge, doubt, evidence, importance, possibility, problem, risk, significance, understanding, validity, value,* e.g.

*The **challenge** at the present is to improve the efficiency of algal fuel production technology.*

*The **problem** of mortgage defaults spread …*

6.5 Variations of form

For variety, you can use different forms of the same word to express similar meanings, e.g.

There is no doubt that *the tabloid entertainment style of journalism captures our attention.*

It is doubtful whether *currently available satellites can accomplish the task.*

*There is a world of difference between a wink and a blink, as anyone who has ever mistaken one for the other has **undoubtedly** learnt.*

7 Hedging

Hedging language can be used to 'soften' or 'minimize' your message so that it does not seem absolute, and to avoid presenting ideas or conclusions as facts. It can also be used to distance yourself from a claim or statement, and make it more objective.

a Verbs: *appear, indicate, seem, suggest, tend to,* e.g.

*Much, if not most, of the time, our behaviour **appears to be** mindful, that is, rational and sensible.*

*We also analyse follow-up data, which **indicates that** the effects of family size on height persisted into adulthood.*

*Much of animal behaviour **seems to be** based on four instincts.*

*The analysis **suggests that** the first category is pervasive …*

*Consumers **tend to** be better informed about products like the clothes they buy …*

b Modal verbs: *can, could, may,* e.g.

*Taste **can** affect an individual's likes and dislikes from the earliest stages of life.*

*Widespread adoption in cities **could** deliver significant change.*

*Drugs **may not** be necessary for top performance.*

c Adverbials: *apparently, arguably, relatively,* e.g.

*Many people **apparently** have limited control over their intake of fresh vegetables.*

Arguably, *different cultures approach the notion of altruistic behaviour in different ways.*

*Both countries have a low population density and **relatively** low crime rates …*

d Adverbs used as modifiers: *quite, rather, somewhat*, e.g.

*It turns out the use of polyurethane can be **quite** controversial.*

*These satisfied the **rather** complicated market situation.*

*Second, algal biofuel production technology is still **somewhat** new and uneconomical.*

e *It …* and *There …* structures, e.g.

***It is estimated that** daily inbound traffic would be reduced by 5 per cent in New York …*

***There appear to be** financial problems that need to be worked out.*

***There is evidence that** these effects observed for children in the 1930s persisted into adulthood.*

8 Noun phrases

Noun phrases are most often used as the subject or object in a sentence. They are built round a **head noun**, e.g. *a difficult public policy **problem*** (a *problem* relating to *policy* concerned with *public* issues which is *difficult* to solve). Words can be added before (pre-modifiers) or after (post-modifiers) to modify the **head noun** (i.e. to add to or limit its meaning), e.g. *low **impact** on land use*. The whole noun phrase can be replaced by a pronoun based on the head noun, e.g. *this article* → *it*; *the effects of socio-economic conditions* → *they / them / these*. Noun phrases can be short (one or more words) or long, e.g. ten to twenty words), with longer phrases being both complex and dense in information.

8.1 Noun phrase patterns

Noun phrases follow a number of typical patterns. In the following examples the head noun is in bold. Note how it can be modified before, or after, or both.

a Single noun with or without a determiner, e.g. ***we**; **consumers**; **this purpose**; **some of them**.*

b Adjective(s) + noun, e.g. *The primary **objective**; clear **parallels**; his genial and relaxed **manner**; ordinary living **patterns**.*

c Noun(s) + noun, e.g. *food **sources**; human **behaviour**; consumer **preferences**; no production location **information**.*

d Adjective(s) + noun(s) + noun (a combination of the patterns in **b** and **c**), e.g. *the traditional news **outlets**; local air **quality**; a difficult public policy **problem**; changing gender **attitudes** and **expectations**.*

e Noun + prepositional phrase(s), e.g. *an **interview** with the accused person; The territorial **dynamics** of innovation in China and India.*

f Noun + relative clause, e.g. ***patterns** that looked like instinct; an **author** whose arguments they had used in their assignments* (defining relative clauses); ***Denmark**, which adopted a specific approach to technology* (a non-defining relative clause).

g Noun + prepositional phrase + relative clause, e.g. ***everything** in a city that is not thought to be authentic;*

*a **network** of business relationships that may lead to new opportunities.*

h Noun + non-finite clause (where the main verb is in an *-ing* form, *-ed* form, or *to-* infinitive), e.g. ***time** devoted to housework.*

i A combination of any of the above, e.g. *a fundamental **shift** in the model of consumption that grew out of the industrial revolution; relatively little **research** which focuses on the use of humour among professionals in particular workplaces.*

j Noun + adjective, e.g. *a **cause** greater than self-interest.*

k Noun + appositive (a noun / noun phrase used to identify or rename another noun), e.g. *the **construction** of effective workplace relationships (the creative use of relational humour); two marketing **gurus**, James H. Gilmore and B. Joseph Pine II.*

8.2 Nominalization

Nominalization is where information is presented in a noun or noun phrase rather than a verb or adjective, e.g.

*Fahey (2007) **argues** for the development of an EU-wide measure …* (verb phrase)

→ *Fahey's (2007) **argument** for the development of an EU-wide measure …* (noun phrase)

See **2 Cohesion, 2.3 Cohesive noun phrases**

9 Sentence structure

9.1 Sentence patterns

Sentences in English have up to five **clause elements**. These are a **Subject (S)**, **Verb (V)**, **Object (O)**, **Complement (C)**, and **Adverbial (A)**. Sentences usually follow one of two patterns: subject – verb – object (SVO), or subject – verb – complement (SVC), e.g.

This perspective acknowledges the importance of technological or economic factors. (SVO)

Motivation is an interaction of influences that come from the genetic, biological, cognitive, and social levels. (SVC)

Sentences can also include one or more adverbials, e.g. *In summary, motivation is an interaction of influences that come from the genetic, biological, cognitive, and social levels.* (ASVC)

A **complement** is part of a sentence following verbs like *be, seem, appear,* and *look*. It adds complementary information about the subject. A complement can be:

- an adjective / adjective phrase, e.g. *both countries are quite different*
- a noun phrase, e.g. *Stroke is a disease of the brain*
- a *wh- / that* clause, e.g. *The first point is that algae shows great potential as a biofuel source*
- a prepositional phrase, e.g. *Many plant and animal species are in immediate danger of extinction.*

Adverbials can be added to sentences to provide additional information about context, e.g. time, place, and cause. There are three main types of adverbial:

a Adverbs, e.g. *usually, furthermore*

- Adverbial clauses, e.g. *Because much of the world's population is inactive ...; If the behaviour succeeds ...*
- Prepositional phrases, e.g. *during the 1990s; due to lack of resources*

See **5 Contextualizing language: adverbials**

9.2 Simple, compound, and complex sentences

a Simple sentences consist of one main clause (with any number of adverbials), e.g.
We also analyse follow-up data.

b Compound sentences have two or more main clauses, joined by a coordinator (*and, but, or*), e.g.

*The students receive a stipend that allows them to pay for part of their studies, **but** in return they must come back home after the completion of their study.*

Each clause in a compound sentence can alternatively stand alone as a separate clause.

c Complex sentences have two (or more) clauses, including one main clause and one subordinate clause, e.g. *People working in construction have tended to work the longest hours, with people in the service sector working the shortest hours.* In this example, the main clause comes first, and the subordinate clause second. The order can be reversed to change the focus, e.g. *While people working in the service sector tend to work shorter hours, people working in construction have tended to work the longest hours.* The focus of the sentence in the first version is what *people working in the service sector do*, and in the second version is what *people working in construction do*. Subordinate clauses begin with subordinators such as *although* or *while*, and cannot stand alone.

9.3 Identifying the subject and verb to work out meaning

In some sentences it can be hard to identify the subject and main verb, which in turn makes it hard to work out the meaning. This can be for a number of reasons.

a The subject and verb are separated by one or more adverbials, e.g. *Rapid cropland increase, often associated with large-scale deforestation, is prominent in South-East Asia.*

b There are a number of adverbials at the beginning of a sentence before the subject, e.g.

Consequently, in terms of reliability, replication, and validity, the longitudinal design is little different from cross-sectional research.

c The subject is a complex noun phrase with a relative clause ending in a verb or a noun which is not the head noun, e.g.

One major problem the Peace Corps volunteers were having involved exactly this issue of similar actions having very different meanings. (the verb in the relative clause, *were having*, is directly followed by the main verb in the sentence, *involved*)

Not all 'crimes' included in the BCS estimates would have been identified and recorded as criminal offences if they had been reported to the police. (the subject of the verb *would have been identified* is not the noun *estimates*, but the whole noun phrase built around the head noun *crimes*)

9.4 Known and new information

English tends to start a sentence with known information, and introduce **new information** at the end:

*This paper contributes to the debate **on the determinants of child quality using a unique dataset from 1930s Britain**.*

Another tendency in English is to put longer structures at the end of sentences. Often, these longer structures express new information, so the two tendencies are aligned, e.g.

For our analysis of burden of disease, we calculated population attributable fractions (PAFs) associated with physical inactivity using conservative assumptions for each of the major non-communicable diseases, by country, to estimate how much disease could be averted if physical inactivity were eliminated. (In this example much of the new information is presented using adverbials.)

10 Verbs and modal verbs

Most verbs in written academic texts are in the present simple or past simple, although many tense / aspect combinations are possible. Modal verbs are also frequently used. Progressive and perfect forms are used less often, and perfect progressive forms together, e.g. *have / had been working*, are rare.

10.1 Verb forms expressing present time

Academic texts frequently refer to events that are taking place or are important in the present.

a Facts and general truths, e.g. *Physical inactivity **increases** the risk of many adverse health conditions.* (present simple)

b Habitual events and tendencies, e.g. *Nonetheless, audiences today still often **emerge** with news and current affairs through outlets other than news bulletins.* (present simple active); *BMI **is** typically **associated with** short-run privations.* (present simple passive)

c The current importance of events which took place in the past, e.g. *Several common trends in employment and household transitions over the life course **have emerged** in advanced economies since the 1970s.* (present perfect)

d Ideas from other sources, e.g. *Stockwell (2004: 14) **argues** that reality television 'provides a more intense account of experience than either news or entertainment.'* (present simple)

e Evaluation, e.g. *The writing **is** generally insightful.* (present simple)

f Trends and events currently in progress, e.g. *The size of satellite tags **is** constantly **decreasing**.* (present progressive)

10.2 Modal verbs expressing present time: *may, must, should, will*

a Expressing possibility, e.g. *Researchers have described several mechanisms that **may account for** these effects.* (*may* + infinitive)

b Expressing universal obligation, e.g. *In order to claim recognition as a refugee, individuals **must give** a 'plausible' account of persecution.* (*must* + infinitive)

c Expressing advice, e.g. *Researchers **should**, therefore, **choose** cases where they expect learning will be greatest.* (*should* + infinitive)

d Expressing logical result, e.g. *An animal and a human born at the same moment **will** thus **share** life experiences.* (*will* + infinitive)

e Expressing 'universal' time (past / present / future), e.g. *Athletes **are** always after 'the edge' – knowledge that **will make** the difference between success and failure.* (present simple / *will* + infinitive)

f Speculating about a present situation, e.g. *And it is difficult to cover fraud, since many people **will** not **be** aware they have been victimized.* (*will* + infinitive)

g Generalizing about a present situation, e.g. *Humour **not only contributes to** the construction of effective workplace relationships, **but may also stimulate** intellectual activity of direct relevance to the achievement of workplace objectives.*

10.3 Expressing past time

a Expressing event(s) which took place in the past, e.g. *California **was** the leading US wind energy producer in 2005, although it **was ranked** just seventeenth in wind generation potential.* (past simple active, past simple passive)

b Expressing an event which took place before another event already mentioned, e.g. *By 2011 traditional news outlets **had learnt** their lesson.* (past perfect active); *Bob Woodward and Carl Bernstein of The Washington Post refused to report on any charge until it **had been confirmed** by two sources.* (past simple active, then past perfect passive)

c Expressing chronology / narrating events which took place in the past, e.g. *The egregious business practices of a range of financial institutions [1]**were** the immediate cause of the problem. The financial institutions [2]**had been making** loans to low-income people wishing to buy houses … The problem of mortgage defaults [3]**spread** because the debts [4]**had been repackaged** as securities called 'collateralised debt obligations.' Other banks, companies, and governments [5]**had bought** the securities, believing them to be less risky than [6]**proved** to be the case.* ('Narrative' tenses: 1 & 3 past simple to express an event in the past; 2 past perfect progressive to express an activity already in progress at that time; 4 past perfect passive to express what had already happened to the subject, *debts*; 5 past perfect to express an event which happened before the first event; 6 past simple to express the next event in the sequence, following on from 1.)

d Expressing past habits or states, e.g. *Children **used to go** to school by foot, bicycle, or bus.* (*used to* + verb)

e Expressing past habits (not states), e.g. *The money from its sale **would go** towards her daughter's university fees, its meat **would go** to people in the district centre or to the markets of Ulaanbaatar.*

f Reporting events in the past, e.g. *The volunteers complained that the Tswana **would** never **leave** them alone.*

g Expressing hypothetical or counterfactual events in the past, e.g. *Not all 'crimes' included in the BCS estimates **would have been identified** and **recorded** as criminal offences* (result) *if they **had been reported** to the police* (past condition).

10.4 Expressing attitudes to future time

As the future is never certain, many forms for referring to the future involve speculating, predicting, and expressing varying degrees of certainty. Modal verbs are often used, and structures like *is/are likely to*.

a Stating aims, e.g. *The following sections **will argue** this is the result of the continued presence of unregulated ivory markets within and near these countries.* (*will* + infinitive)

b Predicting (tentative), e.g. *A large-scale collaboration between research groups **will** hopefully **enable** a quantum step forward in our understanding of bird migration.* (*will* + *hopefully* + infinitive)

c Predicting (more confident), e.g. *Graduation, for example, is hard to predict on the basis of biological needs, yet you **will work** hard over a number of years to become university graduates.* (*will* + infinitive)

   It is likely that solving emerging food security issues will be contingent on international cooperation on climate change. (expression built round *likely*)

d Speculating and forecasting, e.g. *It is forecasted that algal biodiesel **will become** competitive with petrodiesel by 2020.* (*will* + infinitive)

e Expressing a future condition with speculation, e.g. *If full variable pricing **were introduced*** (condition), *the reduction **could reach** 13 per cent* (result).

f Speculating about future events, e.g. ***It is too early to tell** what long-run changes the newer and more unusual CSA model **will bring**.*

10.5 Passive voice

The passive voice can be used in academic texts to:

a shift the focus of the text to the item that is having something done to it, e.g. *Goods and services **are produced**.*

b maintain focus on the topic when describing a procedure or method, and/or avoid stating who did the action, e.g. *Assumptions **were defined** and a coding structure **used** to systematically extract a list of assumptions from a series of written determinations. These assumptions **were** then **submitted** to an inductive thematic analysis.* (the topic is *assumptions*, and the **passive forms** express what was 'done' to them)

Checklists

CHECKLIST A Reflecting on reading texts | Unit 1A Task 9

1 What strategies have I learned for navigating and analysing texts?
2 How much of the text(s) can I understand?
3 What aspects of the topic do I understand better after reading the text(s)?
4 What is my personal reaction to the text(s)?
5 How might the text(s) be interpreted in my own culture?
6 What language have I learned that I can now use in my own writing?
7 How can I use elements of the text (content / organization / structure / language) in my own writing?
8 What can I read next and how can I find it?

CHECKLIST B Evaluation criteria for an essay introduction | Unit 1B Task 7

1 Is the introduction closely relevant to the essay question?
2 Does it contain the essential features of an introduction?
3 Is it logically organized?
4 Are the aims and rationale of the essay clearly given?
5 Does it contain appropriate academic language for an essay introduction?
6 Is it the right length (e.g. a 750-word essay may have an introduction of up to 150 words)?

CHECKLIST C Lecture overview | Unit 1C Tasks 2 & 4; Unit 6C Task 5; Unit 11C Tasks 1 & 2

PART A: General information on the lecture

Lecture title: _making the most of higher education_
Lecturer: _Kathleen M. Quinlan, PHD_
Discipline: _education_
Topic / main focus: _education for international students in English-spoken Countries_
Rationale and aims: _why you want to study / what you can expect/ gain specific recommendation strategie_ _what is university learning_ _make the most benefits for enhancing_
Limitations: _differences of studying in English-spoken Countries_
Key terms and definitions:
Supporting information
☐ Pre-reading: _____
☑ Slides: _____
☐ Handouts: _____
☐ Other: _____

(margin note: intraction / paper / pen / take note / answer the question)

PART B: Delivery of the lecture

1 Lecturer's accent and pronunciation: _____
2 Type of delivery (scripted / semi-scripted / spontaneous; speed): _semi-scripted_
3 Use of visuals: _on the right hand side, you'll see a little face ..._
4 Lecturer's questions and interaction with the audience: _what does it mean to learn and how_
5 Other (digressions, humour, points of interest): _experience a word to learn it_

PART C: Content of the lecture

6 Complexity and accessibility of subject matter: _____
7 Audience questions during and after the lecture: _____
8 Knowledge assumed by lecturer; knowledge gained during lecture: _____
9 Language complexity and difficulty, including academic and technical language: _____
10 Lecturer's stance and evaluation of the subject matter: _____
11 Visuals (charts, graphs, tables, pictures, maps, diagrams): _____
12 Questions following the lecture (reading, language, discussion, tasks, websites, resources):

CHECKLIST D Evaluation criteria for a body paragraph Unit 2B Tasks 3 & 5

1 Does the writer state their main argument clearly?
2 Do supporting points flow logically? Give evidence.
3 Are key concepts / terms clearly defined and/or explained? Give evidence.
4 Does the evidence chosen support the main argument? Explain why (not).
5 Does the writer include comment and/or evaluation to make their own stance clear? Give evidence.

CHECKLIST E Evaluation criteria for an essay conclusion Unit 3B Task 6; Unit 10B Task 4

1 Does the conclusion match the thesis statement and the points in the main body?
2 Does the conclusion summarize the main points logically?
3 Does it refer back to findings of research?
4 Is the focus / stance consistent throughout?
5 Does it state any limitations?
6 Does it comment on implications, or offer predictions for future developments?
7 Is there appropriate use of minimizing language?
8 Is the writing cohesive, repeating words or synonyms from the Introduction?

CHECKLIST F Evaluation criteria for information in a source text Unit 4A Task 7

Consider:
1 the context and currency of the texts, i.e. where and when they were published
2 the examples given in the texts: where and what type
3 the interest, relevance, and usefulness for you of the information in the texts
4 how clearly the information in each text is presented
5 the difficulty of the texts, in terms of language, concept, and cultural understanding
6 the application of the texts: how generally / specifically the information and arguments apply.

CHECKLIST G Evaluation criteria for a basic essay plan Unit 4B Task 2; Unit 8B Task 7

1 Does the sequence of body paragraphs follow a coherent (logical) structure?
2 Does each paragraph have a clear topic, expressed in a topic sentence? Is this relevant to the essay question?
3 Are the items in each paragraph relevant to the paragraph topic?
4 Which order of body paragraphs is the most effective? Why?
5 Is there any material in the plan which is not relevant to the essay question?

CHECKLIST H Evaluation criteria for a complete essay Unit 4B Task 8; Unit 8B Task 8; Unit 10B Task 6; Unit 11B Task 5

1 Is there a clear connection between the title of the essay, the thesis statement, and the concluding remarks?
2 Does the conclusion directly address the aim of the essay, by offering a complete or partial answer?
3 Does the essay argument flow logically, particularly from one paragraph to the next?
4 Is all the content in the essay relevant and supportive of the argument?
5 Are all the sources used in the text correctly referenced, complete with a References section (Bibliography) at the end?
6 Is the language of the essay accurate and appropriate for the purpose?

Evaluating a poster presentation (Unit 4C Task 4)

1   Visual: does the poster look attractive, with relevant supporting images?
2   Clarity: is the information presented clearly? Is the poster easy to navigate?
3   Interest: is the information interesting? Do the authors make a good effort to appeal to the audience?
4   Language: is the language straightforward to understand, appropriate, and accurate?
5   Depth: is there sufficient explanation and development of key themes, without excessive detail?

Evaluating presentation preparation, delivery, and questions (Unit 4D Task 5; Unit 10D Task 4)

1   Preparation: has the presenter, in advance:
     - checked the room, decided where to stand, and where to put any notes?
     - assembled any aids (pointer, handouts, etc.)?
     - rehearsed the presentation, with some friends as the audience to ask example questions?
2   Effectiveness: is the information presented clearly and concisely? Is the technology used confidently? Does the presenter keep to the time limit?
3   Content: is the content appropriate, particularly any evaluation offered by the presenter?
4   Visuals: are visuals included, and is there an appropriate balance between visual and spoken information? Can visuals be seen from the back of the room?
5   Rapport (for a group presentation): do the presenters work well together and communicate the topic clearly?
6   Interest: does the presenter make the material engaging for their audience?
7   Language: is the language of the presentation accurate and appropriate in terms of style, sophistication, and choice of words?
8   Body language: is the presenter facing the audience (not the screen), and making eye contact?
9   Performance: is the presenter speaking at a steady pace, with appropriate pauses after making points?
10 Handling questions: does the presenter invite and respond to questions accurately and in sufficient detail? Do they thank the audience at the end?

Evaluating a data presentation (Unit 7D Task 5)

1   Is the presentation clearly structured, including a title slide and a contents slide?
2   Is there an appropriate number of slides?
3   Are the slides clearly designed, with an appropriate amount of information?
4   Is there sufficient background and contextualizing information for the topic?
5   Does the presenter talk about the data from a limited number of perspectives?
6   Does the presenter clearly explain, interpret, and evaluate the data?
7   Does the presenter link the material to wider contexts and issues?
8   Does the presenter clearly express their own stance on the topic?

CHECKLIST J Evaluation criteria for a summary

Unit 6B Tasks 2, 4, 7, & 8; Unit 6C Task 5; Unit 12A Task 4

Is the summary...

1 contextualized? Does it give a reference to the source text(s)?

2 complete? Does it include the main points of the text(s), but not supporting points, details, and examples?

3 correct? Is it closely based on the source text(s) and does not contain any new material?

4 concise? Is it as brief as possible?

5 clear? Is it easy to understand?

6 creative? Does it use some technical terms in the text(s) but mainly the summary writer's original language?

CHECKLIST K Asking critical questions about evidence / data Unit 7A Task 5; Unit 7C Task 2

1 Why does the speaker / writer say / believe...?

2 Why is this point mentioned / not mentioned in the text?

3 How accurate / reliable is the evidence used by the speaker / writer?

4 How significant is the main point / are the implications in the text?

5 How is the data collected? Has it been collected in an appropriate way?

6 Has the speaker / writer offered sufficient evidence to support their claims?

7 Is the evidence the most recently-available and up-to-date?

8 Does the evidence logically support the points being made by the speaker / writer?

9 Has the speaker / writer accurately interpreted the evidence?

10 Does the speaker / writer use all the available information that is relevant to the point?

CHECKLIST L Evaluation criteria for researching a topic Unit 7D Task 2; Unit 11B Task 5

When researching a topic, follow this cyclical process:

1 Read books or articles known to you or recommended by others.

2 Make notes as you read, and note down any key words.

3 Make a note of any references worth following up, including reference details.

4 Generate key words relevant to the research topic.

5 Use the key words to search the library database and/or conduct an online search for relevant sources.

6 Examine titles and abstracts for relevance.

7 Retrieve relevant sources.

8 Go back to point 2 above and repeat.

Does your writing:

1 present a clear stance?

2 present an organized, coherent flow of ideas?

3 clearly but concisely explain main points from the text?

4 link evaluative comments to the points from the text?

5 use appropriate evaluative language?

6 use appropriate language to express confident or tentative evaluation?

Before listening:

1 Discuss the topic and predict possible content before listening.

2 Prepare for a lecture by reading a relevant textbook chapter or pre-lecture handout.

While listening:

3 Build your notes around slides and headings.

4 Link the content of your notes to the signposting language in the lecture.

5 Make notes in a chronological sequence, perhaps using a timeline.

6 Make notes relating only to specific points, e.g. given headings / questions, main points, perspectives, the lecturer's stance.

7 Connect essential elements in the lecture, e.g. causes, problems, stages in a process.

8 Focus on citations in the lecture.

9 Focus on language, e.g. identifying and working out meanings of key terms.

10 Use your own range of abbreviations, symbols, and visuals.

Following up listening:

11 Evaluate the lecturer's delivery (see Checklist C, part B).

12 Discuss and evaluate the content of the lecture (see Checklist C, part C).

13 Summarize part or all of the lecture in writing to explain / present to others.

14 Compare and combine the information in two or more lectures on a similar topic.

CONTENTS

Global Liveability Survey

TEXT 1

Every year, the Economist Intelligence Unit compiles a survey of the world's most liveable cities. It assesses 140 cities worldwide and assigns each one a score for over 30 qualitative and quantitative factors across five broad categories: stability, healthcare, culture and environment, education and infrastructure. In the 2011 survey, cities in Australia and Canada scored highly, taking between them seven of the top ten positions. Both countries have a low population density and relatively low crime rates, which along with other factors, make them attractive places to live. At the opposite end of the list, Harare in Zimbabwe, Port Moresby in Papua New Guinea, and Dhaka, the capital of Bangladesh, ranked lowest.

Most Liveable Cities 2011

1 Melbourne   2 Vienna   3 Vancouver   4 Toronto   5 Calgary
6 Sydney   7 Helsinki   8 Perth   9 Adelaide   10 Auckland

SOURCE: *Global Liveability Survey.*

A corporate alternative to United Nations *ad hoc* military deployments

TEXT 3

Abstract

The history of United Nations peacekeeping is frequently one of failure. The causes are endemic, persistent and unlikely to be remedied. It seems reasonable to consider two ideas in response: whether *ad hoc* peacekeepers might be augmented or even replaced by competent contract labour; and whether well-trained contractors might in future subdue by force those who inflict gross human rights abuses on others. Alternatives to *ad hoc* forces are not new. Nevertheless, theoretical or practical substitutes have not been evaluated alongside the merits of a private corporation supported by a business model. Military contractors are frequently represented as an affront to states' authority. This is misleading. There has never been a clear divide between public and private resources in armed conflict and states have always employed both. There exists no compelling reason in law why the UN should not devise modern contracts that evolve from historically ubiquitous arrangements amongst its members and their more ancient predecessors. Formidable hurdles remain. Nonetheless, the deployment of disciplined, professional contractors under rigorous conditions may offer improvements on present standards of peacekeeping.

SOURCE: Patterson, M. (2008). A Corporate Alternative to United Nations *ad hoc* Military Deployments. *Journal of Conflict Security Law.* 13 (2): 215-232.

(S) "historical arguments"

(3) *(1)* *(2)* *idio*

TEXT 1

Why wage a war on drugs in sport?

Barry Houlihan has summarised the historical arguments used to ban drugs in sport.[13] Firstly, doping harms athletes; secondly, doping is unfair to the athlete's competitors; thirdly, doping undermines sport in society. Contrast this with the arguments against recreational drugs. Firstly, drugs harm an individual; secondly, drugs harm those with whom an individual interacts; thirdly, drugs harm the moral structure of society. There are clear parallels in the first and third arguments. Even the second has resonance. For where a heroin user steals money directly from other people, a steroid doper steals gold medals and fame from other athletes.

(S) counter argument to (1) — *opposite of your idea*

Does sport have a unique nature that makes it easy to legislate without controversy? Sometimes the waters can seem just as muddy. [...] Athletes consciously and continuously put their health at risk without risking the ire of the sporting authorities. In some sports, such as boxing, the risks may be self-evident. However they hold for any contact sport. In fact, it is a rare sport, contact or otherwise, that is not harmful to health at the elite level. Exercise may be good for you; elite sport demonstrably isn't. Waddington and Smith illustrate this point with numerous relevant examples.[14] In the US, for example, the average length of career for an American football player is under four years, with injury being one of the main reasons for this lack of longevity. Between 1997 and 2007 on average, five fatalities per year were directly attributable to American football, the majority of these being high school students.[15] In the round ball version, professional footballers in the UK run a 1,000 times higher risk of injury than other so-called high-risk jobs such as construction and mining,[16] although it has been said that in football, incidents are only rarely life-threatening. [...] A UK House of Commons report in 2007 noted that, while it was difficult to ascertain the precise number of deaths caused by anabolic steroids worldwide, for it to be anywhere near the deaths caused by contact sports it would need to be in the hundreds or even thousands a year; it was suggested this was very unlikely to be the case.[17] [...]

soccer?

Basing a ban merely on drugs being harmful to athletes would of necessity result in elite sport itself being banned. So what about the second argument? Do drugs create an unfair playing field and so harm other non-drug-taking athletes? Previous chapters in this book suggest that, with the right genes and training regimes, drugs may not be necessary for top performance, at least in males. But this is clearly a debatable argument and certainly not true of female athletes. A sense of fairness is a powerful argument for fans who like to know that they are observing an event that is the true test of the athletes themselves. However, emotionally attractive as it is, basing a decision to ban drugs solely to level the playing field does not really stand up to close scrutiny. There are lots of cases where sport is not 'fair'. Athletes are always after 'the edge' – knowledge that will make the difference between success and failure. There is no desire to share this information with others. In most sports, key information is a well-kept secret. Witness the British team that dominated the track cycling medals at the Beijing Olympics in 2008, claiming seven of the ten gold medals on offer. As well as a well-funded and well-oiled support infrastructure, this success was made more likely due to superior, though completely legal, equipment – termed 'technological doping' by its critics.

why ... it fails *E*

There is no doubt that being born in the UK in the 1980s meant that you were more likely to win a cycling gold medal in the Beijing Olympics than if you had the same genes, but were born in Morocco. Is it fair that rich athletes and countries can afford the best equipment?

SOURCE: Cooper, C. (2012). pp.228–230. *Run, Swim, Throw, Cheat: The science behind drugs in sport.* Oxford: Oxford University Press.

Note: Numbers 13–17 ([13], etc.) refer to footnotes in the original text.

Depends on the sport?
Little equipment needed for running – e.g. successful African runners

Key:

1, 2, 3	main arguments
E	Evidence or examples
S	different stances presented
Underlining	points to discuss
Highlighting	useful key language

scouting? very close inspec / get details

Promoting human security

TEXT 2

The role of the international community

[...] Non-governmental organizations contribute to human security in a number of ways: as a source of information and early warning about conflicts, providing a channel for relief operations, often being the first to do so in areas of conflict or natural disaster, and supporting government or UN-sponsored peacebuilding and rehabilitation missions. NGOs also play a central role in promoting sustainable development. A leading NGO with a human security mission is the International Committee of the Red Cross (ICRC). Established in Geneva, it has a unique authority based on the international humanitarian law of the Geneva Conventions to protect the lives and dignity of victims of war and internal violence, including the war-wounded, prisoners, refugees, civilians, and other non-combatants, and to provide them with assistance. Other NGOs include *Médecins Sans Frontières* (emergency medical assistance), Save the Children (protection of children), and Amnesty International (human rights).

SOURCE: Baylis, J., Smith, S. and Owens, P. (2008). *The Globalization of World Politics (4ᵗʰ ed.).* Oxford: Oxford University Press. p.502-3.

GLOSSARY

NGO *(abbr.)* non-governmental organization (a charity, association, etc. that is independent of government and business)

How metro areas rank

TEXT 2

How well an individual, a household, or a family fares in any community can be judged by many criteria. Economists suggest that a household's well-being can be gauged by its consumption of goods and services. In turn, that household's consumption depends on its income. The more it earns, the greater its ability to consume, and thus the greater its economic well-being. Political scientists might suggest that individual well-being, as well as that of the community, is dependent on the quality of political institutions, the level of participation in the democratic process, and the extent to which human rights are guaranteed. Sociologists might rank the well-being of individuals and households on the basis of community cohesion and on the extent of social networks. Across the disciplines, well-being certainly depends on incomes and how they are distributed, but money is not everything. The quality of life in any city or suburb depends on how individuals fare and how they tend to treat each other.

SOURCE: Bluestone, B., Huff Stevenson, M., and Williams, R. (2008) *The Urban Experience: Economics, Society, and Public Policy.* Oxford: Oxford University Press.

Student's cause and effect essay

> **TITLE:** *Identify two major causes of underachievement in education. What effects might these have on children's future lives?*

1 In his novel *Great Expectations* (1861), the English novelist Charles Dickens tells the story of a boy called Pip who was born into a poor blacksmith's family. What transformed Pip's life was being noticed by an unknown patron who subsequently 'invested' in him by mentoring him and paying for his education. This narrative illustrates the importance of expectations in achievement. 2 Underachievement, which refers to students who fail to develop as much of their potential as expected, is remarkably widespread in education today, and can result in a number of serious problems including poor employment prospects. 3 It is more difficult to determine the causes of underachievement. Low expectations are certainly a contributing factor. Many other factors might however bring about underachievement. These may include personal factors such as health and well-being, external factors including school environment and the quality of teaching, as well as other environmental, political and economic issues. 4 This essay investigates two major causes of underachievement, one socio-economic and the other psychological, and assesses their impact on children at secondary school level and beyond.

5 There are a number of possible reasons for underachievement in education. An obvious starting point is the student's socio-economic background. Research into this area indicates that social and economic background does affect a student's performance. For example, research by Triventi (2011) focused on students at tertiary levels who had similar social backgrounds and academic ability. He found that the parents of such students were 'strongly associated with' greater success in tertiary education. Triventi concluded that:

> In particular, students from culturally advantaged families have a higher probability of graduating from the best educational paths in terms of quality and future occupational outcomes. This indicates that none of the equity scenarios described by Hearn (1991) is at work in European higher education. [...]The effects of social background are not completely mediated by previous school achievement, and inequalities are not reversed at the tertiary education level. (Triventi, 2011)

Triventi's important research underlines the important role played by parents in their child's educational achievement. This finding ties in with other work in the political sphere which aims to compensate for underprivileged backgrounds by offering scholarships and other schemes directed at improving students' academic achievement.

6 The other area of crucial importance in any discussion of educational underachievement is the mental and physical health of the individual student. In some respects it can be problematic to accurately measure a student's mental and physical health. However, there are number of widely-recognized disorders which can be diagnosed. One such disorder is Attention Deficit / Hyperactivity Disorder (ADHD). One study, cited in Loe and Feldman (2007), found that students with symptoms of ADHD, regardless of whether or not they were diagnosed as such, were 'far less likely' to graduate from high school and attend university than students without any such symptoms. This finding suggests that the diagnosis of a specific clinical condition can be a predictor of academic success or failure.

7 Setting aside specific conditions, what is critical for all students is their personal or psychological 'mindset', in other words their attitude to education and what they expect to gain from it. This is arguably connected to their socio-economic background because of the likely association between lower socio-economic groups and lower engagement with formal institutions such as schools, and lower expectations generally. Put simply, a teenage boy whose father is unemployed or an unskilled worker is unlikely to aim for a profession which demands higher qualifications, such as a lawyer. Such a goal would seem unattainable. Factors such as the professions of the child's parents are likely to be important contributors to the child's level of ambition. The career ambitions of the child are likely to be aligned with their parents. These career ambitions, in turn, affect the child's subsequent academic success.

8 Major causes of underachievement, then, appear to be the related issues of socio-economic status, and the personal psychological outlook or mental health of the individual. These are both likely to lead to underachievement in the student's education, and subsequently in their career. The first step in the cycle is often below-average attainment in school examinations, with higher education opportunities becoming less favourable. In the longer term, children following this path will probably become parents themselves in families at a similar socio-economic level, whose children will in turn have similarly low expectations. This unfortunate cycle of negative effects is rooted in the child's background and may not be directly connected to the type of school they attend. The main effects of low achievement are negative.

9 In conclusion, this essay has presented the importance of interconnected and sometimes cyclical social, economic and personal factors in educational underachievement. These factors appear to play a major role in how a child progresses through the education system, thus influencing their future life chances. 10 Of course, other factors not explored here, such as the quality or ranking of the individual school that the child attends (see Wu, Palinkas, & He, 2010), may also have a greater or lesser effect. Most crucially though, a child's own expectations determine their success, with low expectations typically bringing about disappointing results. Trying to change this situation is extremely challenging, but a good starting point would be to educate and encourage children to achieve higher goals. Both teachers and parents should foster a culture of 'great expectations'.

References

Loe, I. M.& Feldman, H. (2007). Academic and Educational Outcomes of Children with ADHD. *Journal of Pediatric Psychology*. 32 (6): 643-654.

Triventi, M. (2011). Stratification in Higher Education and Its Relationship with Social Inequality: A Comparative Study of 11 European Countries. *European Sociological Review*.

Wu, Q., Palinkas, L. A., & He, X. (2010). An Ecological Examination of Social Capital Effects on the Academic Achievement of Chinese Migrant Children. *British Journal of Social Work*. 40 (8): 2578-2597.

Unit 3C TASK 4.1 (page 050)

Student A:

As you watch the lecture extract, make notes in the form of key words and phrases on:

- properties of polyurethane swimsuits
- use of polyurethane swimsuits in competitions.

Student B:

As you watch the lecture extract, use the timeline below and make notes using labelled pictures or diagrams to illustrate the key points.

| 2008 | 2009 | 2010 | 2011 | 2012 |

Student C:

As you watch the lecture extract, make notes to help you remember the key points. Use any form of notes you want: headings, bullet points, diagrams, etc. or a mix of these techniques.

Pre-lecture handout

What is stroke?

Key points

a   *Background information*

- Stroke is the third most common cause of death (after heart disease and cancer) in developed countries.
- Stroke is a disease of the brain (not the heart) caused by a blockage or rupture of the essential blood supply.

b   ....

- A transient ischaemic attack (TIA), or 'mini-stroke' is a major warning sign of impending major stroke and needs to be taken seriously.
- 'Brain attack' has been suggested as a useful new name for the first 24 hours of a stroke or TIA.

Stroke has been recognized for thousands of years and is the third most common cause of death in developed countries (after heart attacks and all cancers combined). Although it can affect people of all ages, it is most common in old age. Perhaps because of the association between stroke and old age, or terminal disease, it has not had the profile of other perhaps less serious or rarer disorders and thus is less well known to the general public. However, stroke is so common that most people will know someone who has had a stroke or have a close family member who has had a stroke.

c   ....

[...]

A stroke occurs when the blood supply to the brain is disrupted, and part of the brain stops working. This produces sudden characteristic symptoms ranging from a rapidly fatal illness to a barely perceived loss of sensation on one side of the body. This variability causes many problems! It is hard for the layman to understand what a stroke is (or is not) as there are so many variants. It is also often hard for doctors and nurses to make the correct diagnosis, as many illnesses mimic stroke. Surveys of public knowledge of stroke have shown that this common disorder is not well understood. Many people are not aware that the problem lies within the brain. It is certainly not the same thing as a heart attack, which has quite different symptoms (usually severe chest pain). Stroke is not usually accompanied by severe pain. If pain is present, it is usually a headache and may be a sign that the stroke has been due to a brain haemorrhage.

d   ....

The underlying cause of stroke

e   ....

There are actually two main causes of stroke which, confusingly, can present in exactly the same manner. About 80 per cent of all strokes are due to blockage or occlusion of the blood supply to the brain, usually from a blood clot. Blood clots can develop along a blood vessel or may have travelled along the blood vessel from a source further away. [...] This type of stroke is commonly called ischaemic stroke. The other main pathological cause of stroke is brain haemorrhage, which is caused when a blood vessel in the brain (the cerebral artery) leaks or bursts. This type of stroke is called primary intracerebral haemorrhage. About 15 per cent of strokes are of this type. The final 5 per cent of strokes are caused by a condition called subarachnoid haemorrhage which has a very different presentation, assessment, and treatment from ischaemic stroke and primary intracerebral haemorrhage.

f   ....

SOURCE: Lindley, R. I. (2008). *Stroke*. Oxford: Oxford University Press, pp. 1–2

Text for Student A

This extract is from a study in which academics working as part of international research teams were interviewed about their experiences.

A trip around the world: accommodating geographical, linguistic and cultural diversity in academic research teams

Reasons and benefits of collaboration

As the participants outlined, significant benefits are gained through these collaborations. For some, the very nature of the project itself requires this type of diversity. For example, the data under exploration and its analysis may be housed in different countries or available in different languages, requiring individuals with the necessary access to data and expertise, which may not be available at the home institution. Others indicated that the funding agency requirements dictated participation from other countries. Finally, there was also a realization that a 'group is smarter than your individual'. In other cases, these collaborations provided opportunities to develop skills and to experience new perspectives. One of the European interviewees stated that 'international team work allows you to learn a bit of the language'. For others, they found it 'very exciting to work in such an international context and to get to know different kinds of vision, i.e. not just the [their home country] one.

Challenges

Notwithstanding these benefits, these research teams faced challenges. First, given the diversity within these teams, they faced challenges flowing not only from the language diversity, but also from cultural differences. As one North American stated, 'So, it's not just showing up and speaking Arabic, it's showing up and knowing how to interact with people and dealing with what is a very different culture with different codes and expectations'. One of the Europeans who is collaborating with Europeans and North Americans further found that different countries/cultures had varying perspectives on deadlines with some more oriented to precise delivery as scheduled than others.

Other challenges derive from differences in the level of formality required within different cultures. Some countries and cultures have more formal senses of hierarchy that are expressed through titles and clearly defined communication channels. [...] Further difficulties ensued when individuals from less formal cultures did not use professional titles as required by those in more formal cultures. As one of the Europeans outlined, 'We had a web portal where the names of all colleagues were listed. The Americans were against using titles… I tried to tell the American colleagues that in Germany the title is part of the name. It was nearly an offence for somebody who was Prof. Dr., i.e. a very important man, also a library director, that we called him just [by his first name]. On the other hand, as the Americans didn't want to list the titles it looked as if none of the colleagues had a doctorate'. In many cases, team members experienced frustration and confusion in these situations, particularly when they evaluated these differences as 'strange' and did not follow the culturally required protocol.

SOURCE: Siemens, L. and Burr, E. (2012). A trip around the world: Accommodating geographical, linguistic and cultural diversity in academic research teams. *Literary & Linguistic Computing*, first published online June 25, 2012.

Text for student B

This extract is from the abstract of a journal article reporting research.

Willingness to communicate and cross-cultural adaptation

With the ever-expanding movement of individuals to all corners of the globe for the purposes of business, entertainment, education, economic opportunity, and political asylum, the need to understand and facilitate intercultural contact grows more important every day. This rapid increase in movement across cultural boundaries has brought about the popularized notion of *culture shock* (Oberg 1960), an all-encompassing term for everyday difficulties encountered by immigrants and sojourners (i.e. business people, students, and travelers on extended but finite stints abroad) in their attempts to fit into their new cultural environments. When in this condition, these individuals must make a repeated choice either to persist in interfacing with the host culture or to withdraw from interaction. The choice to communicate in the second language (L2) is, therefore, a crucial aspect in understanding how individuals face these challenges, ultimately determining whether intercultural contact succeeds or breaks down.

Students from East Asia, with their large and growing presence on campuses worldwide, represent an important contingent of sojourners. Despite a large number of these students placing an expressed priority on learning English (Dörnyei et al. 2004), many nonetheless find their stay abroad difficult, and are prone to the same feelings of loneliness, uncertainty, and academic difficulties as their host national counterparts, as well as suffering from additional troubles associated with communication problems and differences in academic culture (Chataway and Berry 1989; Ying 2005). These problems may be compounded by sociocultural values prevalent in China and the greater region, including an intense level of face protection, a sublimation of the individual self, and deference to authority. As played out in the English language classroom, these factors often produce students who are especially reluctant to speak up in English (Wen and Clément 2003). It is within this context of sojourning Chinese students that the current article focuses on the relationship between the willingness to communicate in the second language (L2 WTC; MacIntyre et al. 1998) and the process of cross-cultural adaptation.

SOURCE: Gallagher, H.C. Willingness to Communicate and Cross-cultural Adaptation: L2 Communication and Acculturative Stress as Transaction. *Applied Linguistics*, first published online June 24, 2012.

Conference proceedings summary

The presentation focused on the challenges facing the global pharmaceutical market today, and discussed ways in which these can be addressed. Unlike many markets, the pharmaceutical market is not a perfect market where supply perfectly balances demand. This has led to various imbalances.

The situation regarding global medical expenditure illustrates extreme variations in expenditure in different categories of country: high-, medium-, and low-income countries. Based on figures from the World Health Organization (WHO) from 1990, 2000, and 2006 (WHO, 2011), private expenditure on pharmaceuticals outweighs government per capita expenditure. Total expenditure and per capita pharmaceutical expenditure are increasing rapidly, with the highest increases in middle-income countries and an extremely wide variation between countries with different incomes. In 2005 to 2006 this ranged from $7.61 in low-income countries up to $431.6 in high-income countries. The WHO figures show that while only 16 per cent of the world population currently live in high-income countries, these populations account for over 78 per cent of global medicine expenditure. However, the proportion of total health expenditure which is spent on medicines in low-income countries is higher.

The pharmaceutical market is an unusual type of market for a number of reasons. First, consumers are not particularly well-informed about the medical products they are using, particularly in terms of the quality, safety, efficacy and appropriateness of their medicines. Second, there is limited competition in this market, with a vast number of potential consumers compared with rather few providers. Third, there is the issue of monopoly. Manufacturers create a monopoly through their use of patents, which protect medicines and manufacturing processes from copying by other manufacturers for a fixed number of years. Related to this, there is also brand loyalty, which is achieved through intensive marketing. There have also been many cases of price-fixing by producer cartels in order to keep market prices high. Finally, externalities exist, meaning that treatment for some conditions benefits not only the patient receiving the treatment but also the wider public, who will as a result have a reduced chance of themselves contracting the disease. This analysis shows that the pharmaceutical market is essentially a failed market; it cannot be balanced by the usual laws of supply and demand because of these unique issues.

In trying to address these issues, the financing of medicines plays a critical role in making the market more equitable. For global and local pharmaceutical markets to become more competitive, costs need to be kept down. Governments can play a key role in this through measures such as drawing up principled lists of cost-effective medicines for which people can be reimbursed, and encouraging the use of cheaper generic products. Other policies such as parallel imports and compulsory licencing can also be used to promote competition and reduce prices.

Three key issues also emerge in the management of medical costs: public financing, health insurance, and user fees. Public financing involves raising finance, mainly through taxation. This is beneficial in that medicine supplies can be better selected and targeted to those who need it most. Meanwhile, the cost of payment is shifted to all taxpayers, with those earning higher salaries paying more. Health insurance has an important role to play in many countries. Such schemes, which may be public or private, and compulsory or voluntary, are widespread in most developed countries, but much rarer in developing countries, where medicines account for a large share of total household expenses. Risks include over-prescription, abuse, and fraud, and these schemes require cost control measures. User fees, sometimes supplemented by cost-recovery schemes, are a major cost in developing countries where the private sector is dominant. However, the needs of the poorest are often not met.

In short, the pharmaceutical market is far from perfect, but there are a range of options to improve it, with varying degrees of success.

REFERENCE: The World Medicines Situation, WHO/EDM/PAR.2004.5. cited in Walley, J. & Wright, J. (2010). p.222. *Public Health: an action guide to improving health* (2nd ed.). Oxford: Oxford University Press.

Transcripts

Unit 1

Listening

▶ **1.1** **Extract 1**

Dr Kathleen Quinlan Hello, my name is Kathleen Quinlan, my specialty area is in education. I have a PhD in Educational Psychology from Stanford University, so I'm American, and I have a special focus in my research on learning and teaching and student development and faculty development in higher education. I've taught in Australian, American, and now English universities; I now teach and do research here at the University of Oxford, so I'll be speaking to you from my experience of having worked in universities in those three countries.

We're going to be talking today about 'Making the most of higher education in English-speaking countries'. I've not lived in every single English-speaking country, mind you, but I have, as I said, worked in those three main contexts. You're, I'm assuming that most of you are studying academic English, so I'm assuming that many of you are planning to pursue higher education in a country, in a predominantly, in a predominantly English-speaking country, so that might be the US, it might be the UK, it might be Australia, or Canada, or some other English-speaking country, Ireland. While there are significant differences in these settings, those are beyond the scope of our talk today; rather, I want to talk about some of the fundamental, underlying assumptions that underpin education across those various countries. In any of these settings, you will have the opportunity to create possibilities for yourself, to expand your own choices. You're starting down a path, as this image suggests, and while you may have some visions about what lies ahead, there'll be some surprises as well, you can't predict from here what might lie around the next bend on that journey, and what we would hope then is that you'll be alert to the unexpected, to those possibilities that will arise only through taking that journey. Through this lecture, I'm hoping that you will consider why you want to study in an English-speaking university, I want you to have a better understanding of what you can expect from a liberal university education, and I expect that you will gain some very specific recommendations and actions, strategies for enhancing your overseas education.

To get the most from the lecture, I'd like you to take out a piece of paper and a pen or a pencil, and I'm going to pause at various points during the lecture and ask you a reflection question, and I want you to take a moment at that point, to write down some answers, think about it, just jot down some answers. We won't have an opportunity today with such a large group to get feedback from all of you, but we will have a chance to talk about that in a tutorial setting, so save your answers for that discussion. Doing that will help you though to stay awake – we certainly want you to do that in the late afternoon – and it will also help to keep you focused on what we're talking about today and engage you in thinking about the key points. Once you've had a chance to think about these questions, you'll be better prepared to hear the kinds of responses that I'll be giving to those, some of which are drawn from key literature and key educational ideas, so you can watch for these reflection points – they're in red print on the slides and they have a big red question mark

on them – so that should give you a clue that we're at that point.

While you will get some very practical tips on how to get the most from your university education through this talk, we must first understand the assumptions that underpin higher education, in English-speaking countries. So I'll highlight some key ideas from the field of education and link those key assumptions back historically to its historical roots in Ancient Greece. So the talk will also be theoretical; as a prominent education researcher once said, nothing is as practical as a good theory, so we will have a very practical element, even when we're talking about theory, and of course, by looking at theories of education, you'll get a taster of a typical lecture in the field of education.

So our talk addresses three main questions today: What is university learning? How can you make the most of that educational experience? and What do you want to get out of a university education?

▶ **1.2** **Extract 2**

Dr Kathleen Quinlan So we'll turn to the first one first. [1]**First we need to clarify the meaning of 'university learning', and we need to clarify the meaning of 'learning'. We need to understand what it means from a variety of different theoretical perspectives,** because the same idea or word means different things to different people. We can look at this example: if I say to you 'transportation', that's a quite simple word, a quite simple concept perhaps, and some of you are going to think about planes, some of you are going to envision buses, others of you will think about cars, and some will think about bicycles, and who knows what else you might be thinking when I say 'transportation'.

So the same is true of the word 'learning'. When I say we're going to learn something, you might have quite different pictures about what that means, what it will result in, and how to go about it. [2]**So your first reflection question is very briefly to think about, 'What does it mean to learn something?'** How do you know then if you have learned something? So take just a minute and think about that. … All right, good. [3]**Now let's take a look at some research that outlines a variety of different conceptions of learning that are commonly held, and how those relate to what is expected in universities.** From the literature on learning, we can describe two main conceptions of learning. The first is represented here by this pile of rocks on the left hand side; this is a representation of learning as a quantitative increase in knowledge, so just like the stones in this pile of rocks, it sort of envisions learning as a pile of things, a pile of facts or a pile of theories, accumulated one on top of another. A second major way of looking at learning is to view it as some kind of a change process, as a process of transformation or qualitative change, and the images here suggest that you could look at a tree in a variety of different ways, and that you'll have a changed perception of that tree, as you do so. So in the first picture you might look at a tree and see a branching in different directions, looking up the trunk, but if you take another perspective and you look more closely, then you see something quite different; here you see a close up of the bark of that tree, and if you look even more closely, you'll find a little surprise in here. [4]**On the right hand side, you'll see a little face that looks like a monkey!** So by changing our way

of looking at some-, at things, we can go from seeing a tree right down to seeing the face of a little monkey, so that's quite a difference in perspective. So those are the two main ways of looking at this.

Säl, Säljö, who is a part of a major research group that's had a lot of influence on the way we think about learning and teaching in higher education, he and his colleagues in Gothenburg in Sweden did some research on university students, asking them what their conceptions of learning were, and [5]**he came up with five major conceptions of learning, which can be broken into these two rough categories** we just talked about. So the first three of the conceptions that he noticed were related to seeing learning as a quantitative increase. So at the very lowest levels of that is literally that pile of rocks view, that 'one thing on top of another' accumulation. A second framework for thinking about it is –, a second way of looking at learning is memorizing, so in this view we're seeing learning as a way of, of storing information that can be re-, reproduced later. A third way of looking at it is to see it as acquiring facts, skills, and methods that can be retained and used later, so not just spitting it back out for a test, but actually being able to apply it.

[6]**So I could give you an example from my own experience of viewing learning as a quantitative increase.** When I was in school as a young person, about 12 years old, I'd learned a lot of vocabulary, week after week after week we studied vocabulary, and I tended to think of that as just increasing, adding another word and another word and another word to my repertoire; and we had to memorize those for the tests, and each week we were quizzed, and we had to spell it properly, and we had to describe what the-, what the meaning of it was, and yes, I did some-, I did realize that if I remembered this and retained this, that I could apply it, I could use this vocabulary in my writing, for example, and sometimes I did. So, but still I was still seeing this as a quantitative increase. [7]**Another way of looking at things is a more qualitative change, which is not really what I did with my own vocabulary tests when I was 12 years old,** but I did start to think about it more, start to experience learning as a qualitative change as an adult, for example, when I was studying geological terms. I lived in an area that was formed by glaciers, and I learned some terms that described glacial-, er, glacial landscapes, words like 'esker' and 'kettlepons' and 'errants'-, er 'erratics' rather, and that those, by understanding those words and learning those words and appreciating them and connecting them to the landscapes around me, I could start to see the landscape differently; I could start to see the story of how that landscape was formed. So in this case, I was doing more than just memorizing those words, I was making sense of them, I was abstracting some meaning that connected to my own world, the world around me. So I was be-, by relating these things and making those relationships, I was experiencing learning in a much more qualitative way, I was experiencing a change in my world and my ability to experience that world.

The last of these qualitative changes is about interpreting and understanding reality in a different way. So again, if we go back to my example from geology, I had looked for years at a point of land jutting out into a lake; I had simply seen it as a point of land with some houses on it and some trees, but by arning the term, 'esker,' I could then start to see that, not just as a point of land in this lake today, but I could start to imagine the stream flowing under a glacier or through a glacier that created that landscape, that created what was looking at, so I saw it as a stream bed, an ancient stream bed rather than just a point of land, so I was able to interpret and understand reality in a different way. So these are some-, ive different ways of thinking about learning, some of those may match with what you've written down, and we can talk more about those later, and it may be that you have written down other things, which might be an extension of knowledge in this field.

▶ 1.3 Extract 3

Dr Kathleen Quinlan So that brings me to the end of the talk. We've talked about three main questions: what is university learning, how you can improve, how you can make the most of your education, and ultimately what benefits you might expect from it. So you've started down an important path, it's a powerful path, and I wish you all the best with that, may you enjoy the journey – it will be a challenging one – and benefit from the options that it opens up to you, whatever those might be around the bend. Thank you.

Unit 2
Listening

▶ 2.1 Extract 1

Dr David Howard Today's lecture's going to be entitled 'Sustainable living, changing aspects of urbanization and consumption'. What my research and teaching does is look at levels and styles of urban living, and **particularly I'm looking at aspects of** sustainable development and consumption in the way we live today in urban areas. The world's residents are in general young and poor, and living in cities, and are part of an unequal and unsustainable network of global production and consumption, **so over the next 40 minutes we'll be looking across** early ideas of urbanization, looking at aspects of sustainable development, and then looking at how ideas of consumption and production fit into this matrix, and how then we can go back to looking at ways of sustainable living in cities today.

So first of all, what does the 31st of October mean to you? It's an important birthday and-, be interesting if-, you think for a moment, if you could know why this date is significant. A slight clue here is the birthday announced of Adnan Nevic on the 12th of October 1999 in Sarajevo in Bosnia, and the particular date we're looking at is the 31st of October 2011. Now this date was announced-, the UN announced that it was the day of the 7th billionth living person to be born, and in 1999, 12 years ago, the UN announced the name of a single baby, born in Sarajevo, to commemorate this landmark occasion of him being the 6th billionth person being born. Whereas in October 2011, the UN didn't announce a single baby but said this is an important day, a day in general where you can note that the world population has passed 7 billion people. Now there are many cases where population growth is seen as problematic, it raises a lot of concern in the media; academics and scientists for many decades have considered the problems and the advantages of demographic growth, but

when we look at this figure today, of 7 billion people having lived in the world, we'll notice one thing. First of all, if we think in, in the years ahead, it's predicted that in 14 years' time, it will be the 8th billionth person and after that in another 18 years, it will be the 9th billionth person.

▶ 2.2 Extract 2

Dr David Howard Now that would seem a dramatic figure, a dramatic growth, but what we're really looking at here is not so much a demographic growth that's out of control, but actually, population increase is slowing down, and what is happening to the world's population by and large, yes, it's increasing; **but really what we're concerned (with) today**, if we're looking at development issues, if we're looking at issues of sustainability, **is** not so much the number of people living in the world but their distribution and the access of these world residents to resources, for social, economic, and physical resource consumption. So the news around the-, October 2011, brought a lot of attention to this notion of demographic increase and as you can see on the graph, towards the end of the graph it goes right up to 10 billion. But you'll see the curve of the graph is slowing off, **and that's what we're talking about, in some ways today,** the fact that it-, pop-, population is increasing but that increase is not intrinsically what we're concerned about, **what we're concerned about is** where people live and how they're living. The majority of the world's population are living in cities, **so that's why we're focusing on** sustainable cities, and looking at those aspects of urbanization and the consumption patterns of people globally, but particularly within those urban areas.

Now if you are-, are politically engaged, and if you are interested in-, in global leaders, you may have noticed that the birthday we've selected, the 4th of August 1961, is the birthday of Barack Obama, the President of the USA and you'll notice that when he was born 50 years ago, there are around just over 3 billion people in the world. So in President Obama's life span, the world has more than doubled, and the-, **these are the issues** of governance **that we're looking at today,** globally as well as at state level, but also at city, municipal level.

▶ 2.3 Extracts a–d

Extract a

Prof Richard Caplan Now another point to bear in mind is that the UN is not just the Security Council or the General Assembly or the Secretariat – these are three principal organizations, organs of the UN to be sure – but the UN is a family of bodies that also includes the International Court of Justice (also known as the World Court), ECOSOC (the Economic & Social Council), the International Labour Organization, UNESCO. and the World Health Organization among many others. **For purposes of this lecture, I'm going to be concentrating on** the Security Council, but you mustn't think that that's all there is to the UN.

Extract b

Dr Nazila Ghanea So in the UN, so, of the complex web of human rights mechanisms the world over – local, national, regional and international – I'm going to focus only at the international. **I'm not going look at** the UN **as a whole** and how all of its activities everywhere should have human rights as part

of their concern; **I'm going to focus narrowly on** what we call the UN human rights mechanisms and we said there are two types, treaty and charter, **I'm going to only focus on** the charter-based bodies.

Extract c

Dr Kerry Lock So today we are going to focus this lecture on community ecology, but first of all we must recap, what is ecology? So, it's the study of interactions between organisms and their environments, and I have this array of leaflets around the outside, just to show the sheer scope that ecology covers, especially in terms of the scale from molecular through to the landscape level.

Extract d

Dr David Howard Now that would seem a dramatic figure, a dramatic growth, but what we're really looking at here is not so much a demographic growth that's out of control, but actually, population increase is slowing down and what is happening to the world's population by and large, yes it's increasing **but really what we're concerned (with) today**, if we're looking at development issues, if we're looking at issues of sustainability, **is** not so much the number of people living in the world but their distribution and the access of these world residents to resources, for social, economic and physical resource consumption.

▶ 2.4 Extract 3

Dr David Howard So I'm just going to focus the next few minutes on one school of thought on sustainable cities and sustainable urban living, and that is New Urbanism. It evolved really in the last two decades, in North America and Europe, but again it sort of has some highlights, some of the aspects of sustainable living-, sustainable urban living that have been underpinning much of the literature and research over the last two decades. The Congress of New Urbanism in North America is set up principally to promote forms of sustainable, but also traditional, urban design, and again, we can see some of the principles they outline match very closely with some of the wider principles of sustainable city design. So again the New Urbanists would argue that **sense of** place, **community** building, really lies at the core of creating a socially sustainable neighbourhood. In terms of planning design, they look at interconnected street grid networks, but principally create cities and neighbourhoods in which the streets are **liveable**, they are arranged in compact, walkable blocks or areas to encourage that form of sustainable movement, and to encourage walkable spaces.

The New Urbanist movement will argue that housing choices should be varied to encourage a social mix of people within an area, to go away from what Engels looked at, the separate palaces of the rich and the slums of the poor; argue that a **social mix**, an economic mix is a-, is really one of the key aspects of creating a liveable neighbourhood. New Urbanists also say that modern **design** should be of **high quality**, it should last beyond 25 years, so, the notion of your building for the next century, not for the next 25-year profit cycle. And again, if you're a geographer, you'll be focusing on place and space, and again the New Urbanists argue that when you're designing a-, a town, it should be at a scale that really is-, allows the access-, easy access to educational, social, and commercial facilities that would-, can be walked-, that are **walkable**, or you can use public transport and you're not relying on the car. And finally there's a notion that urban areas should be designed with a human scale in mind; that increasing **public spaces**, the more shared spaces that people can mix (*in*) and-, and integrate, will create a more socially aware and socially sustainable society.

▶ 2.5 Extract 4

Dr David Howard Now the New Urbanists have been critiqued for being too **Utopian**, in many ways. We'll look at a couple of examples where their urban designs have created some very positive-, but also maybe some more … challenging aspects of a New Urbanist process; but as David Harvey has mentioned in *Spaces Of Hope*, he said that really Utopia is a key aspect for human development, that without Utopia, if we humans don't strive for a Utopia, they'll never really continue – the progress really relies on Utopia, and it's a failure obviously-, of gaining that Utopian landscape is what drives on the next generation. So you need Utopias, you need to dream in order to-, in order to progress in-, in social terms.

So we're going to look at two examples of the New Urbanist school. The first one is in Seaside. It's become a very well-known city, a well-known urban development, largely because it was a film setting for *The Truman Show*, which became a Hollywood film which in many ways created an **ideal** living urban environment; and the producers of the film visited Seaside and thought they were walking into a film set, the film set they'd been trying to design previously. Now Seaside was one of the first developments of the New Urbanist school, and it was designed along the principles outlined in terms of **small scale** neighbourhood development, it was first really discussed or mooted in the late 70s, and in the 1980s it was fully developed, the process had been developed in creating certain forms of liveability, **walkability** in Florida. The idea was to create a small-town neighbourhood with a projected population around 2000 people, this was deemed to be similar to the-, the **townships** in the USA, in Nor- in (*the*) United States in the 1920s and 30s. It was again to have a mixed form of land use, to create that mixed social, economic neighbourhood that arguably would make a city more pleasant to live in. And as you can see, they are Utopian in vision; they are referring to maybe a-, a notion of North American living, very **clean** streets, white picket fences, and we'll discuss some of the aspects of that form of the New Urbanism that have been critiqued in the following slide.

Celebration in Florida, for those of you who know Disneyland, was developed in the early 90s as part of a genera- an urban generation project inspired again by New Urbanism, as again it follows the same principles of walkability, high quality urban design, **mixed neighbourhoods**; and you can see it presents an image, particularly of-, an image of North American townscape that many would find attractive. But as you'll notice there, although there are different urban design-, different building designs, there are also a variety of … well, a variety of residents arguably in its planning; but you'll notice there's quite a strong level of uniformity. And in some ways the New Urbanism (*Urbanists*) have been critiqued because they are looking at urban design, they're looking at traditional ideas, almost (some have argued) **quaint** ideas of urban design; but there's a certain **conformity**

there, so you'll notice all the picket fences are white, and you'll notice there's a level of conformity within difference. And one of the aspects of living in this area is, you also sign up to, if you will, a **social code**, a form of conduct; so if you wanted to paint your, your fence a different colour, or your door a different colour, then that again probably would not be seen to be in fitting, and you-, you have to conform to (the) certain laws of the neighbourhood.

So although many aspects of New Urbanist design do fit into the wider aspects of creating a social sustainable city, a sustainable, sustainable city, in many cases that comes as forms of control, and so again, that has been seen as **problematic**. Also, the notion of having a city in which a variety of social groups may live becomes problematic when you-, you're working within a **market economy** and many of these desirable residences are indeed desired, and many of the houses now are really only **affordable** as vacation homes for the relatively wealthy. So in some ways the principle and design has worked very well, but in terms of reality, the market economy has created a-, some would argue, a **gentrified** community that really doesn't reflect some of the **social mixing** that New Urbanist or sustainable forms of development would encourage. And this has been reflected in some of the critiques of New Urbanist development, particularly Scully has argued, 'One cannot help but hope that the lessons of Seaside, and of other new towns now taking shape, can be applied to the problem of housing for the poor. That is where **community** is most needed and where it has been most destroyed.' So again we're going back to the issues of the social matrix of a city, that sustainable development isn't purely looking at urban design. It's not focusing on the economic or environmental aspects alone; it's the social aspect which many would argue is the most important form of creating a living, a liveable city and a sustainable city.

Speaking

🔊 2.6

A OK, so we're looking at the question, what makes a city liveable? And we're thinking about what are the main factors affecting the quality of people's lives. So, if I can start things off, I think for me, one of the main factors is transport, because it affects so many areas of people's lives. I mean, on a day-to-day level, people need to get around, get to work, or to school. And if you have to spend hours, you know, stuck in traffic, that has a big effect on your life. I mean, I, I grew up in London and sometimes it could take me, like, an hour to get to college because the traffic was so bad. You know, and that's a lot of time out of your day. And for businesses, if it's hard to get around, you know, if they're spending a lot of time travelling, then that has an economic impact too.

B How do you mean?

A OK, well, a basic example, if, if a company is transporting its products from a warehouse to stores in the city … if the truck gets stuck in traffic for hours every day, that adds to the delivery time and the fuel they use, and it just generally increases their transport costs.

B OK, I see what you mean.

A Well, then there's the pollution caused by traffic congestion; that's bad for people's

health and it's bad for the environment. I mean, not just in the local area, but globally too. All the greenhouse gases that come from emissions from cars are contributing to climate change. Take the London Congestion Charge; that's cars and trucks that have to pay to drive into the centre of London. And, you know, that's cut the amount of traffic in the city. It's reduced pollution and lots more people are using public transport.

B Sorry, can I just interrupt you there?

A Yeah, yeah, sure, go ahead.

B Well, I completely agree about transport, but I think there's a bigger picture we need to look at. Text 2 here, Bluestone, talks about distribution of income, so basic economic factors, and I think that really has to come before anything else. I mean, if you look at the cities at the top of this list in Text 1, they're all in wealthy, developed countries. So, we've got cities in Australia and Canada, they're both wealthy countries and, like the article says, they've got quite small populations. Then there are a couple of wealthy European countries represented, so Vienna in Austria, and Helsinki in Norway … is that in Norway?

A It's in Finland. It's the capital of Finland.

B OK, OK. Well, yeah. So, another rich Scandinavian country. It seems to me that if people are well off, they can afford to have a comfortable lifestyle. And governments in richer countries can spend money on things like transport and urban planning, because they're not having to deal with so much poverty and crime, things like that, yeah? Like we saw with examples in Dr Howard's lecture on New Urbanism, and those model towns in the States. It's easy to create a perfect city if you've got the money and you fill it with rich people.

A But there aren't any American cities in the top ten here, are there?

B No, but perhaps that's because there are lots of social problems in the States too, like crime and poverty in certain parts of society. Like the article says, it's not just about wealth, it's about the distribution of incomes as well. And I mean, look, look at the cities at the bottom of the list. Harare is right at the bottom. That's a classic example.

C Can I ask something? Where is Harare?

B It's in Zimbabwe, you know in Africa. It's been … well, there's a lot of political unrest there.

A Yeah, so that's about politics as well as economics, isn't it?

B Exactly, I think that's a really important point. But political instability leads to poverty, doesn't it? I mean, they've had hyperinflation and really high unemployment, and that was because of the political situation. So of course, there's going to be a lot of poverty, a lot of misery.

A Yeah, I think, I think you're right. I guess the economic factors have to come first before you can really deal with any of the other problems.

B Yes, and like you said, sometimes politics comes into the equation too; to have a healthy economy, you need political stability.

C I just wanted to say something about crime. I put down crime as a factor. I mean, you have to feel safe where you live, don't you?

B So you're saying a low crime rate is important?

C Yeah.

B Yes, of course we need to consider crime rates, but surely that comes back to economics again and distribution of wealth.

Unit 3

Listening

▶ **3.1 Extract 1**

Dr Jennifer Tilley OK, hello, my name's Jenny Tilley and I'm a biomaterials scientist at the University of Oxford, and today I'm going to talk to you about three materials that I think will play an important, if somewhat **controversial** role at London 2012 next year. Now Olympic fever is building, as people around the world anticipate the thrill of watching world class athletes push their bodies to the limits in order to be faster, higher, stronger, but as a materials scientist, I have to wonder whether athletes would break so many **records** without the help of us materials scientists.

So what is materials science? Well, materials science is the study of what gives materials their very specific **properties**, how can we play with the structure and **composition** of a material, in order to control its properties. It's a subject that sits at the interface of science and engineering. We need scientists who understand all about atoms and atomic **structure**, and we need engineers who understand all about <u>massive structures</u> like bridges, cars, nuclear reactors. It also covers a very diverse range of topics. We have chemists, physicists, and mathematicians, but we also have biologists, <u>biochemists</u>, computer scientists, and design technologists. And we all cover real life issues, we're all concerned with those things that affect the world around us every day.

So what do material scientists really do? Well, we can be split into two categories: those of science and those of engineering, and the scientists are concerned with controlling the <u>atomic structure</u>, so arranging atoms in a material and adding new atoms of maybe a different material in order to control the properties, and the main properties that they're concerned with, are those of mechanical **strength**. So I have a picture on here of some carbon **fibre**, and you can see some fibres aligned in one direction and fibres aligned in another direction, and so carbon fibre is able to be strong in two directions.

We're also concerned with the electrical properties; so I also have a picture on here of some carbon <u>nano-wires</u>. Now these are made of atoms all arranged into very tiny little wires, and that means that they conduct electricity in one direction, which is exactly what we want from wires. And then we-, I also have a picture up here about optical properties, and what I've got is so-, a-, a glass beaker made by the Romans that in normal light looks green, but when I put a candle inside it, shines red; and the reason for that is that the Romans added some tiny, tiny little particles, nano-particles, of gold, and this changes the optical properties of the glass beaker.

▶ **3.2 Extract 2**

Dr Jennifer Tilley Now what about materials in sport? Well, the sporting world has changed significantly in the past century, and one of the key examples of that is the Paralympics. **Paralympics** were introduced after World War II to give war veterans a sporting event that they could participate in. No one actually managed to run the 100-metre sprint in the Paralympics until about 1952, and in 1976, the-, a- bi-, sorry, in 1976, a double amputee ran the 100-metre sprint in 42.3 seconds, absolutely amazing, I can't imagine how he must have felt. So I wonder how he'd feel now,

knowing that Oscar, Oscar Pistorius, a <u>double amputee</u>, runs the 100-metre sprint in 10.91 seconds, just over a second slower than Usain Bolt, an Olympian.

And it's not just in the Paralympics that things are changing. As you can see from the graph, over the past century, we've slowly been knocking 0.1 of a second off the time it takes to run the 100-metre sprint at the Olympics. In 2008, Usain Bolt ran the 100-metre sprint in 9.81 seconds, last year he ran it in 9.64 seconds, in 2012 he's hoping to run it in 9.5 seconds, and so the question has got to be, how is he doing it? And it's not just sprinters who are getting faster. Weight lifters are lifting more weight, canoeists are canoeing faster, jumpers are jumping further and higher, and so there really has to be this question, how are they doing it?

Well, you could argue that it's the athletes' ability and dedication that's changed. Since 1981, fully professional athletes have been allowed to compete in the Olympic Games, so now those who get the decent sponsorship deals are able to dedicate every waking and sleeping moment of their lives to pushing their bodies to the limits. But as a scientist, I have to argue that it's actually the scientific advances in the past century that have played a more important role. Now these can be broadly split into those of biomechanical engineering and materials science. <u>Biomechanical engineering</u> is that study of how we move our bodies, and how we could move our bodies more efficiently in order to be faster; maybe you don't lift your arm out of the water as far when you're swimming front crawl, maybe you need to move your feet in a slightly different way when you're running the 100-metre sprint. It's quite complex, but it manages to shave 0.1 of a second off times. But as, as materials scientists, I actually have to argue that materials science advances in the past century have played an even more significant role. Gone are the days when men ran around dirt tracks wearing plimsolls and baggy sports clothing. The Olympics are a material world, and so I present to you my three medal-winning materials.

▶ **3.3 Extract 3**

Dr Jennifer Tilley Now it turns out the use of polyurethane can be quite controversial. Whether you swim or whether you don't, you've probably heard of a man called Michael Phelps, a medal-winning American swimmer. Now in this picture, you can see Michael Phelps in the middle, flanked by two fellow competitors at the 2009 World Championships, and you can see that they're all wearing funny swimsuits, it looks a bit like they're wearing wetsuits. What they're actually wearing is a polyurethane swimsuit. Polyurethane swimsuits were introduced because they reduce drag through the water, and they also, because it's a very light material, increase buoyancy, so your hips are further up in the water than the rest of your body, so it feels like you're swimming downhill. And the other thing they do is, they compress your body, because they're very tight swimsuits, and so they reduce your drag through the water even more, because they compress your hips, the bits that stick out and slow you down in the water.

Now when these suits were first introduced, people put them on, and automatically started knocking seconds off their personal best. At the 2009 World Championships, over 32 days, over 32 events, over 43 world records were broken, in other words, these suits are so effective that not only were they breaking

records in the finals, they were breaking records in the heats in the run up to the finals, these suits are just amazing. However in 2010, the governing body of swimming determined that these polyurethane suits were the equivalent of steroids; they were introducing too significant an increase in speed, and they banned them from use in any subsequent competition. Now in 2008, all the world records were set wearing these swimsuits, and so at the 2012 Olympics, how likely is it that we're going to see records smashed?

Unit 4

Listening

▶ **4.1 Extract 1**

Carolina Hello, and thank you for your interest in our poster. I'm Carolina Burquart, and this is Ben Foster…

Ben Hello.

Carolina … And we'd like to just talk you through the main ideas of our poster which we've been working on. So, over to Ben to start.

Ben Thanks, Carolina. Well, what we're going to be looking at is Knowledge Transfer, which is also known as 'KT', and the changing nature of KT and some of the challenges associated with it.
So, first of all, KT is basically the exchange and dissemination of knowledge, particularly the change in information. KT is increasingly being recognized as being a valuable activity, particularly for researchers and developers in universities.

Carolina That's right, and actually KT is at the heart of most activities at universities, if you think about it. Lecturers and professors are disseminating knowledge and information, not only to their students through lectures and seminars, but also to a wider audience, through their publications, especially online.

Ben And increasingly, publications are reaching a truly global audience.

Carolina Exactly, yes. In the past, publications tended to be more restricted in their reach, whereas nowadays they're essentially global – in terms of their access, and also in terms of their authors, the researchers who write for them.

Ben And this brings us on to our next point, which is the emergence of open access journals. Open access journals basically means free at the point of use. So students or the general public can access these journals in electronic form, directly, without having to pay for them. Obviously this is in contrast to the more traditional model, which was on a payment basis. Journals were published in print form only, which can be expensive obviously, because you have to pay for them. So it was usually the university libraries that subscribed to them, for the benefit of their students … rather than individuals.

Carolina OK, so as Ben says, things have changed. There are a lot of issues here. Although access is free, it's very important to maintain quality, so the content – the papers, the articles – these are still peer-reviewed. In other words, other researchers, from the same subject area, review the content … checking it for accuracy, reliability, quality, those sorts of things.

Ben That's right. And one other area we wanted to look at was plagiarism. One advantage of the fact that, basically, all articles are now available electronically, one advantage is that it's much easier to detect when something has been plagiarised, using anti-plagiarism software. And one other area, another area is innovation. Universities need to look at what they do in terms of innovation …

Carolina Well, just before we look at innovation I think we should just talk about our central idea here. Basically, if I could just explain this cycle here … This starts with direct investment in educational research. Now this investment could come from a government agency, like a Higher Education Council, something like that. Or alternatively it may come from industry. Because increasingly, companies are choosing to invest in aspects of university research that have economic potential. So this means increased levels of research at universities, because there's more funding available, and the emergence of more high-tech companies developing the ideas that come out of that research. So … the next stage in our diagram is an increase in economic competitiveness – the local economy surrounding the university benefits, resulting in economic growth. And finally, all this economic growth, all this activity, should lead to more funding, more money becoming available for research at universities, in other words. Ben, do want to talk about that at all?

Ben Well, looking at the time, I think we probably should move on …

▶ 4.2 Extract 2

1 KT is increasingly being recognized as being a valuable activity, particularly for researchers and developers in universities.
2 And increasingly, publications are reaching a truly global audience.
3 Exactly, yes. In the past, publications tended to be more restricted in their reach, whereas nowadays they're essentially global – in terms of their access, and also in terms of their authors, the researchers who write for them.
4 Obviously this is in contrast to the more traditional model, which was on a payment basis. Journals were published in print form only, which can be expensive obviously, because you have to pay for them.

▶ 4.3 Extract 3

Questioner 1 Could I ask a question?
Ben Yes, of course.
Questioner 1 Thank you. It says in part 5 that 'Britain must invest more strongly than in the past in its knowledge base, and translate this knowledge more effectively into business and public service innovation'.
Carolina Yes.
Questioner 1 What does that mean, exactly? Are you suggesting that universities are all about turning knowledge and education into business and profit? I mean …
Carolina Well, no, er, I mean actually this quotation is from the Science and Innovation Investment Framework.
Questioner 1 Yes, I can see that, but …
Carolina So I think what it's saying is that universities are, well, universities are expensive but they are an essential part of a country's knowledge base. And they're also really important in terms of innovation – they're where innovation begins. As the quote says, innovation is essential to Britain's growth and economic development.

Questioner 1 OK, but is that what universities are for primarily? I mean, what about knowledge for its own sake?
Ben Well, I don't think they're saying we shouldn't have knowledge for their own sake. But I think they're saying that we need to invest more in the university sector.
Questioner 1 OK. Could I ask something else?
Ben Absolutely.
Questioner 1 I was wondering if you could explain why you've included this other quotation? It says, 'dangers in positioning university research too close to market and thereby crowding out company innovation and undermining its value'. How does that fit in with what you just said?
Ben Well, OK, good question. What this means, as far as I understand it, universities have a more central part to play in research, and creating value and so on, but they should remember that they are primarily universities, not companies. They're about learning. They need to focus more on the more traditional areas like research, ideas, knowledge and leave companies to more market-based products.
Questioner 1 OK. Thanks.

▶ 4.4 Extract 4

Carolina Yes, another question.
Questioner 2 Yes, how do you see the future of knowledge transfer, and in particular, publishing in, say, five years? Compared with today?
Ben Me?
Questioner 2 Either of you.
Ben Well, … Carolina do you want to answer that?
Carolina Thanks! OK, I would say that there'll be bigger investment in digital publishing, obviously. And to some extent, open access publishing. But I think the biggest, most powerful publishing houses will probably stay focused on value. They're not going to give content away for nothing. So there could well be a divergence, on the one hand there'll be free open access publishing, on the other, more restricted, expensive, publishing more valuable higher-quality content for those who can pay for it.
Questioner 2 OK. That's interesting. Thanks.

Unit 5

Listening

▶ 5.1 Extract 1

Prof Jonathan Michie So the second thing I want to talk about is the fact that you have long swings in the global economy, something I've hinted at in that I've just been describing the whole era of the 1980s, 1990s and beyond, starting with Margaret Thatcher in, in Britain and Ronald Reagan in America, deregulating the financial sector, that was a long swing, 30-year era which came to an end, but we've seen those long eras before. In the **1920s, following the First World War**, there was an **era of, of laissez-faire**, economic orthodoxy, similarly allowing speculation to, to take place which led to the **1929 Wall Street Crash and** subsequent **Great Depression** … and it was only emerging out of the Second World War, that there was a feeling that that couldn't be allowed to happen again, we had to have regulation on a global scale but also nationally and that's what was put in place in **1945** globally with the **World Bank, the International Monetary Fund**, fixed

exchange rates but also domestically in most countries, with public ownership, public regulation and so forth. And that led to what has been described as the **Golden Age of Capitalism, 1945 to 1973**, almost 30 years, which saw more **sustained economic growth** and development than had ever been seen before or has been seen since. Following the, the turbulence of the **1970s** where there was high inflation, it seemed like the previous economic policies weren't working, we've had this **30 years** of **deregulation, 'capitalism unleashed'** from **1979** through to the, the **2009 global recession**.

▶ 5.2 Extract 2

Prof Jonathan Michie So what, what do we do about it? Well, in 2008, when it was clear that this was a, a really huge systemic crisis across the globe, national governments, in Britain, across Europe, in America did act, did act quite forcefully, nationalizing banks and also putting huge amount of government demand into the economy as Keynes had urged in the 1930s. Keynes, probably one of the greatest, er, and best-known economists ever, did most of his work between the wars in, in Britain, became famous at first after the First World War when Britain and France were imposing large reparations on Germany, saying that Germany would have to pay back Britain and, and France for the damage the First World War had caused. Keynes warned that that was economically wrong and therefore probably would lead to, to political suicide as, as well because the German economy would not be able to pay back these reparations so it would be self-defeating, it would, the demand to pay back the rep-reparations would, would actually prevent the German economy recovering, you'd have wide, widescale unemployment locked in, and that was bound to lead to political and social problems, on which of course, unfortunately he was proved correct.

▶ 5.3 Extract 3

Prof Jonathan Michie In Britain, in the 1920s, Britain tried to, well did rejoin the Gold Standard, which again Keynes warned against saying that was just old economic orthodoxy and it would, it would not work. The Chancellor of the Exchequer actually, who took Britain back onto the Gold Standard then, was called Winston Churchill, who then went onto become Prime Minister and, and er, led Britain during the Second World War, and so after the First World War, when Keynes wrote his first famous pamphlet called *The Economic Consequences of the Peace*, where he warned that the peace agreement after the First World War would cause political dangers later on because it was unsustainable to try and force a weak economy, as Germany then was after the First World War, to repay huge reparations, when Winston Churchill then took Britain back onto the Gold Standard, Keynes wrote another pamphlet saying the economic consequences of Mr Churchill, warning that again would … lead to British goods being, becoming uncompetitive, because, he said, the real world just doesn't work like the text books say. The text books say 'doesn't matter if goods become uncompetitive 'cause you can just reduce prices by cutting wages' and Keynes warned that the world just doesn't work like that; it's very difficult to just cut wages, drop prices and so on, and so it proved again in, in Britain, that led to the general strike of 1926.

And then, most famously, in 1936, Keynes published his major work, *The General Theory of Employment, Interest & Money*, where he basically said that economies don't naturally return to equilibrium and, and full employment; it's quite possible for them to get stuck in recession, depression, with large-scale unemployment, that was the first thing he said which, which quite radical at the time, might seem obvious, might seem now that it would have been obvious in 1936 when there was large-scale unemployment as a result of the, the Great Depression, but nevertheless economic orthodoxy then was still saying, 'no, no, just cut the budget deficit and everything else will follow'. Keynes warned that actually cutting the budget deficit in that situation makes matters worse, not better, because the only thing which is going to lead to recovery is people spending money. In a depression, consumers aren't spending money; it's hard to export if it's a global recession, companies won't be investing because they don't think that the markets are there, so the only other possible source of demand is government-, government spending and that was one of the, the key lessons from the general theory; and Keynes said it, it must be government spending, not just quantitative easing as it's called today or having low interest rates, it can't just be monetary policy which was the orthodoxy, well if you have lots of money then people will borrow and then, then spend that, Keynes said that you can't force people to borrow and if people aren't optimistic about the future, then companies won't borrow to invest 'cause they won't believe they'll be able to sell the goods and services they produce. So he likened, Keynes likened having a low interest rate in that situation or money, monetary policy in general in that situation as like pushing on a string, you might be doing but will have no effect elsewhere because people won't be taking up the offer of loans in order to, order to invest. So Keynes said you must use fiscal policy, which was what the leading governments around the world did in 2008, and did prevent that recession from being greater than it, it was.

▶ **5.4 Extract 4**

Dr David Howard From early times, many historians have looked at the, the living and working conditions of the urban poor and Friedrich Engels, in the turn of the, the middle of the 19th century, wrote about the condition of the working class in England. Now this was at a time of, a peak really of the industrial revolution, in many ways a, a moment of great industrial wealth and productivity for the British economy at the time, but Marx and, and Engels his co-worker, noted the great levels of poverty amongst many of the working class people. So in his book, written in 1845, called *The Condition of the Working Class in England in 1844*, Friedrich Engels looked very closely at city structures and he noted that 'every great city has one or more slums where the working class is crowded together. True, poverty often dwells in hidden alleys, close to the palaces of the rich; but in general, a separate territory has been assigned to it where, removed from the site of the happier classes, it may struggle along as it can'.

Speaking

◀)) **5.5 Extract 1**

A OK, so we need to research a person who's been influential in our subject area. And we're going to present a short profile of that person. So I guess the first thing is to decide who.

B Well, we're all studying science or engineering, aren't we? [1]**So probably a famous scientist would be the best choice.** Any ideas?

C [2]**We could do Schrödinger** ... Schrödinger? The Austrian physicist?

B Sorry, I haven't heard of him. Who is he?

C He did a lot of really important work in the early days of quantum mechanics. He won the Nobel Prize for physics. Come on ... [3]**You must have heard of Schrödinger's cat**.

A Yeah, but I don't really know what it's about. I thought he was a philosopher. [4]**Don't you think that a subject like quantum mechanics might be a bit difficult to explain?** [5]**Remember we need to present this in a really clear way because our audience won't necessarily be scientists**.

B What about Marconi? The guy who invented radio?

A Yes ... I think a lot of people will know the name, but [6]**they might not know much about him**. But it's a more accessible topic. It might be easier to explain than quantum mechanics.

C OK, that's a good point.

A I'll put him down as a possibility. Marconi. OK, any other suggestions?

C What about Professor Stephen Hawking? He's really well known.

B Yes, he'd be really interesting, but isn't he still alive? [7]**Aren't we meant to be** choosing a historical figure?

C No, I don't think so. It just has to be someone who's been influential in their academic field.

A OK. I'll put him down too. Anyone else?

B [8]**Perhaps we should stick with** what we've got rather than spending ages thinking of lots of different people.

A All right. So, are we agreed that Schrödinger might be a bit too difficult? So that leaves Marconi and Hawking. We could either make a choice now, or we could research both of them and see what we find, then decide later.

C [9]**I think it would be better to** focus on one person from the beginning. Otherwise we'll just waste time doing research that we don't use.

A OK. So which one do we want to choose? I think they're both good suggestions.

B Well, I know I suggested Marconi, but actually I'd go for Stephen Hawking. The brief says that we have to mention their key works and I know that Hawking has published some really important books. Marconi, well, he did lots of different things. It could get a bit messy, difficult to narrow down.

A Right, [10]**let's go with Hawking then**.

◀)) **5.6 Extract 2**

C Great. So what do we need to research?

B Well, we need some biographical data. I guess the basics would be date of birth and where he was born, and some personal details too.

A I don't know about that. This is an academic profile, isn't it?

B Yes, but Hawking's a bit different. The fact that he has motor neurone disease is ... well, it's a really important part of his life and who he is. I think that's relevant in this case.

C And then we need to research his work.

A Yes, but we don't need to go into too much detail. We just need to outline his most important work. I think it's important we don't get bogged down in technical details.

B So are we going to each research different topics? One person do a biography, someone else look at his work?

A I don't know. It's not a very wide topic, is it? Perhaps we could all just choose a different source and then compare what we find.

B OK. I'll start with Wikipedia, then.

C Erm, I don't think that's a very reliable source. We're always being told to avoid it.

B Yes, but we're only looking for some really basic facts, and we can check it against other sources. I think it might be a useful starting point.

C OK, I guess so. He's a professor at Oxford University, isn't he? Or is it Cambridge? Anyway I could check the University website, they might have a profile of him.

A That's a good idea. And I'll start looking in the archives for ...

Unit 6

Listening

▶ **6.1 Extract 1**

Dr Nazila Ghanea My lecture is going to be about the UN human rights machinery but **I'm going to focus on one of the newer bodies of the UN human rights machinery, which is the Human Rights Council and also a very new procedure which is called the Universal Periodic Review.** I think I'm going to point out some of the changes that have occurred organizationally to the UN human rights mechanisms and point out the innovation that is captured within this new mechanism called Universal Periodic Review.

So we, we see something of the Human Rights Council here, we should recall that the, the body I'm going to focus this lecture on is one where there are hundreds of people in one room, they are meeting for at least ten weeks a year, we have the presence of high-level delegations from governments, we have very senior diplomats that would be in this council discussing, focusing their sole attention on human rights at the international level and there will be a media presence, there are non-governmental organizations there and you know, amongst them also are victim groups, those whose human rights have been violated or their representatives.

Now the human rights machinery at the UN level is quite complicated and we shouldn't be too narrow in how we capture and understand this. The reason I say this is that almost every UN agency or whether at the local level, regional level, national level or international level, every UN body should be concerned with human rights amongst its other activities, so whether it's a monetary agency, whether it's a development agency, whether it's working with let's say maternal health or child nutrition or working in conflict, all UN activities should have human rights as part of their agenda, whether overtly so or whether you know, as a part of a range of concerns including health and you know, eradicating polio or whatever it is.

Nevertheless when we look, when we talk about the UN human rights mechanisms, we mean some particular mechanisms, we're not talking about when the Security Council acts taking note of human rights violations in a country, we're not really talking about the World Health Organization, so in the narrower sense, **the UN human rights mechanisms are of two types, one are charter based bodies and the other are treaty based bodies** and the distinction here is really quite simple, treaty based bodies draw their origin, their reason for being, their creation, to particular treaties that governments have been involved in drafting, they have voluntarily become bound by that treaty, just like, you know, any other treaty works and because of accepting and ratifying that treaty, then they are obliged to respect it and report what progress they have made in realizing its objectives, so it's a treaty, it happens to have a human rights focus.

And **in the UN human rights mechanisms, we have nine core human rights treaties. The treaties are not what I'm going to talk about today, it's the other,** the second prong of or type of human rights mechanism and these are the charter based bodies. So these bodies are the ones that were created by virtue of the UN Charter in 1945, saying that one of the objectives of the United Nations was to ensure not only peace and stability but also human rights and just from that one commitment in 1945, over the past six to seven decades, we have seen the evolution of a range of bodies to try to realize that UN Charter objective.

So in the UN, **so of the complex web of human rights mechanisms the world over, local, national, regional and international, I'm going to focus only at the international,** I'm not going to look at the UN as a whole and how all of its activities everywhere should have human rights as part of their concern, I'm going to focus narrowly on what we call the UN human rights mechanisms and we said they're **of two types, treaty and charter, I'm going to only focus on the charter based bodies.**

▶ **6.2 Extract 2**

Dr Nazila Ghanea So when we moved from the Commission to the Council, we also developed, adopted a decision to have a new procedure called the Universal Periodic Review, the resolution that brought this decision into being, into force said that Universal Periodic Review, I'm going to call it UPR from now on, *[1 What is the UPR?]* **UPR is the fulfilment by each state of its human rights obligations and commitments, a cooperative mechanism based on an interactive dialogue,** it sounds pretty good, the fulfilment of every state, of all its human rights obligations and commitments, you know, who would be against that, that seems a great idea.

[2 What are the objectives of the UPR?] **So the objectives of Universal Periodic Review, UPR, is first of all to assess positive developments but also challenges, so it wants to be balanced. It will assess the fulfilment of each member state of the United Nations, of its obligations and commitments in the field of human rights,** it can share good practice because all the states will be reviewed and therefore they can learn from each other and share experiences about, let's say, you know, the challenge of racism, especially you know, we see around us how austerity seems to have given rise to a, a push to the Right and with that unfortunately we see in many states, more racist organizations gathering support and becoming more vocal, so this is a shared challenge at the global level, it rears its ugly head all too often and you know, states can really share with each other, you know, that whilst respecting privacy, whilst respecting freedom of opinion or expression, how do you deal with the scourge of racism?

When the state lacks capacity, money and expertise to improve its human rights situation and you know, we're not talking about only civilian and political rights but also economic, social and cultural rights, so social benefits, training for employment, child literacy, maternal health, etc. etc., all these require expertise, require money and in many states where this experience and financial ability or infrastructure is lack- lacking, I mean in all human rights, if you want to track developments, you need detailed statistics and gathering detailed statistics and disaggregating them according to age, you know, so distinguishing, so let's look at literacy, we need to know the male and female, we need to know the minority populations, we need to know the border regions, we need to know the deprived areas, we need to know how illiteracy breaks down according to boys and girls, according to different age groups, that requires some expertise. *[3 How does the UPR system work?]*

UPR, along with welcoming positive developments and raising issues of concern, is also able to offer technical assistance to the state, if that indeed is the reason why there hasn't been an improvement in the human rights situation on the ground, so it's quite a well-rounded package within that mechanism.

Now this is the first time we have mobilized a procedure that looks at the human rights situation of all 193 members of the UN on an equal basis, it gives them exactly the same allocation of you know, funding, time and you know the examination is on exactly the same basis, exactly the same pattern is used for a country of 1.3 billion population or a country of let's say 300,000 population. Seems bizarre but on the other hand if we're living in a world of sovereign states, all states are equal, therefore they have equal obligation and should be equally responsive to their obligations of commitments in the field of human rights, so if we look at it in terms of sovereign equality, then it's quite right that they should be treated equally, even though if you were looking at it in terms of population it seems bizarre to give exactly the same attention to 1.3 billion as a few hundred thousand.

But **the system as we have it is every 190, each of the 193 member states will be reviewed every four years, that means around 48 states per year.** The aim for it is not to surprise the state and just launch into criticism, it's a cooperative mechanism, it should be based on reliable information so it's, the information has been sifted, it's been summarized into a standard format, it's an inter-governmental process so primarily you know, one state is under review and other states are making recommendations to it and the state which is under review, is fully involved.

So if you're concerned with the universal enjoyment of human rights, if you are concerned with the advocacy for human rights, you know, you might have your favourite human right, freedom of expression, freedom of religion or belief, the right to education, etc. etc., if you are concerned with the domestic impact of international commitments or have concerns about particular violations, then *[4 When are UN member states reviewed?]* **UPR is one procedure that gives us a very broad assessment about human rights situations in all 193 states, every four years.**

Now I said that the pattern being used for assessment is identical, so is the basis. I mean, on what basis are you going to review Brazil and Monaco? Lichtenstein and the People's Republic of China? Well on exactly the same basis. *[5 What does the UPR review?]* So it's on the basis of the UN Charter, the Universal Declaration of Human Rights, **all the human rights treaties that the state has ratified because if it's not ratified them, it's not bound by them,** that's, you know, the legality comes from the ratification. **Any additional voluntary commitments and pledges and taking note of applicable international humanitarian law,** so if there are situations of conflict, then that body of law is also applied.

▶ **6.3 Extract 3**

Dr Nazila Ghanea Just to end, the UN Secretary General, Ban Ki-moon, said that the Universal Periodic Review 'has great potential to promote and protect human rights in the darkest corners of the world' and I think this statement is quite profound on many levels, first of all some small states have never received the attention of the UN human rights mechanisms, they either weren't bad enough or they were too remote or there, you know, not, no- Non Governmental Organizations had produced a report on that country, I mean you know so some states and some regions of the world received a lot less attention than others, so first of all we get a picture, we get a global picture through UPR. Secondly, by the state being able to both accept and reject the recommendations, we see where the state explicitly doesn't have commitment regarding human rights, and thirdly and most importantly, I think we see every four years, how the state has lived up to those commitments. Thank you.

▶ **6.4 Extract 4**

Prof Richard Caplan OK, good afternoon, my name is Richard Caplan, I'm Professor of International Relations at the University of Oxford, I'll be lecturing today on the United Nations and international security.

For purposes of this lecture, I'm gonna be referring to the UN Charter, charters and constitutions are the very foundations of organizations, whether it's the European Union, ASEAN, the Association of South East Asian States, the African Union or FIFA, the international football association for that matter. Charters and constitutions tell us a lot about the basic principles of an organization and how that organization works or should work and the UN Charter is no exception in this regard. Of course practice doesn't always conform to theory and here too the UN's no exception, but nevertheless the UN is a useful starting point for gaining an appreciation of the role of the organization in the arena of international security and I would encourage you to take a look at it, I'll be showing you excerpts from the charter in my lecture today but before we turn to this charter, let me start with a few basic facts about the UN.

First of all the UN is an organization made up of member states, 193 member states to be precise, nearly every state in the world is a member of the United Nations, the near universality of the UN arguably gives it greater legitimacy than its predecessor organization, the League of Nations had. The United Nations – the United States was not a member of the League, nor was the Soviet Union initially and their absence from the League it could be argued, hampered its effectiveness and although virtually all states in the world are members of the UN, the UN is not a world government, the UN is what we call an inter-governmental organization, which is to say that sovereign authority remains for the most part with the member states. That means the UN can only do what its members allow it to lo and this is important because when the UN fails to take effective action as it failed to do with respect to the humanitarian atrocities being committed in Bosnia and Herzegovina or Rwanda in the 1990s, it's not the UN itself that bears responsibility but rather the UN's member states. Now that doesn't mean that the UN as an organization has no autonomous powers, the Secretary General has some as we'll see later but the autonomy of the UN tends to be exaggerated.

Now another point to bear in mind is that the UN is not just the Security Council or the General Assembly or the Secretariat, these are three principal organizations, organs of the UN to be sure, but the UN is a family of bodies that also includes the International Court of Justice also known as the World Court, ECOSOC, the Economic & Social Council, the International Labour Organization, UNESCO and the World Health Organization among many others.

For purposes of this lecture, I'm going be concentrating on the Security Council but you mustn't think that that's all there is to the UN. Now what's the purpose of the UN? Here it's useful to turn to the Charter. Article 1.1 tells us that one of the purposes of the UN and I would argue the primary purpose, is to maintain international peace and security. It also says that towards that end, 'member states will take effective, collective measures for the prevention and removal of threats to the peace and for the suppression of acts of aggression or other breaches of the peace.' Now it's the bit about collective measures that I want to focus on for a moment. The UN is a collective security organization. What exactly does that mean? The idea behind collective security is that all members of the organization agree to join forces to protect any one of its members from the unlawful use of force by any or any one or several states. Now I'll come back to the distinction between lawful and unlawful use of force a little bit later.

📺 6.5

Prof Richard Caplan The UN is not a world government, the UN is what we call an inter-governmental organization which is to say that sovereign authority remains for the most part, with the member states. That means the UN can only do what its members allow it to do and this is important because when the UN fails to take effective action as it failed to do with respect to the humanitarian atrocities being committed in Bosnia and Herzegovina or Rwanda in the 1990s, **it's not the UN itself that bears responsibility, but rather, the UN's member states.** Now that doesn't mean that the UN as an organization has no autonomous powers, the Secretary General has some as we'll see later but the autonomy of the UN tends to be exaggerated.

📺 6.6 **Extract 5**

Prof Richard Caplan So we've been through the major provisions of the UN Charter that deal with international security but what about peacekeeping? You know, the blue helmets? Probably the most visible contribution of the UN to international security, where does peacekeeping figure in the UN Charter? Well it doesn't. Peacekeeping represents an innovation, the first peacekeeping operation was established in 1956 in the Middle East, following the withdrawal of British, French, Israeli and Egyptian forces from the Suez, it was thought that some military presence was needed

to present- to prevent the resumption of hostilities, to keep the peace in other words and so it was decided to send lightly armed soldiers to serve as a buffer between Israel and Egypt. Some people date peacekeeping from 1948 when the first UN observer mission was established, to supervise the implementation of the truce after the 1948 war of independence but in that case unarmed observers were deployed, whereas in 1956 lightly armed soldiers were used.

Now I want to say a few words about peacekeeping because it is, as I said, one of the most important contributions of the UN to international security. Because peacekeeping falls between pacific measures, Chapter 6 of the Charter and enforcement measures, Chapter 7, it's sometimes referred to as Chapter 6½. We can define peacekeeping operations as UN operations in which international personnel, military and civilian, are deployed with the consent of the parties and under UN command, to help control and resolve an actual or potential international or internal conflict. The idea behind peacekeeping's a simple one: suspend the conflict and thus lower the temperature and gain time to allow the parties to the conflict, to negotiate a settlement that will resolve the conflict. In other words, peacekeeping is meant to create space for diplomacy to work, peacekeeping is not peace enforcement, otherwise known as war fighting, peacekeeping succeeds not because the UN deploys overwhelming force, UN peacekeepers as I said are only ever lightly armed and that's for self-defence, but – peacekeeping succeeds because the parties to the conflict want the peacekeepers there, because as UN forces, they're trusted to be impartial.

Now what I've been describing is what's known as traditional peacekeeping, lightly armed soldiers deployed with the consent of the belligerents for the purpose of maintaining a ceasefire and from 1956 or 1948 until about 1987, that's the only kind of peacekeeping there was but then two things happened with the end of the Cold War. First, there was an explosion in the number of peacekeeping operations. From 1948 to 1987, there were a total of 13 UN peacekeeping operations. Since 1987 there have been 53 new operations, in other words four times as many in the past 25 years as there were in the previous 40 years, this year alone there have been 15 active UN peacekeeping operations, the total cost to the UN of running those operations incidentally is US$7bn. Now the UN is sometimes criticized for being bloated and inefficient but just to put those costs into perspective, the US was estimated to be spending more than $6bn a month on just its operations in Iraq in 2007.

All right, so that's the first change that occurred with the end of the Cold War, a surge in the number of peacekeeping operations. The second important change that's taken place is with regard to the nature of peacekeeping. The UN mandate has expanded considerably in this regard, these forces are no longer just keeping the peace, they're also responsible for ensuring the delivery of humanitarian aid, for organizing and observing elections, for disarming and demobilizing armed forces, for training police, for verifying compliance with human rights agreements, among numerous other functions. Indeed in a few cases, Kosovo and East Timor for example, the UN's been responsible for governing the entire territory. These operations are sometimes referred to

as complex peace operations to distinguish them from traditional peacekeeping. OK but peacekeeping is just one instrument that the UN uses to promote peace, there are three other broad areas of UN activity in relation to international security and I'll mention them briefly.

Speaking

🔊 6.7

1 No one's mentioned the role of religious groups. I think religious leaders can play a really important part in many of these situations too: for example, in conflict resolution.

2 The problem with NGOs is that they're not accountable to anyone, not in the same way as, say, a UN agency. They're completely unregulated. So although they may have good intentions, they're going to have their own agendas. And sometimes their activities might clash with what governments or other agencies are trying to do.

3 On the whole, it seems like national governments should be primarily responsible for dealing with issues in their own countries. The trouble is that outside agencies, like the UN, don't always understand the situation on the ground. Look at the examples that Professor Caplan talked about in his lecture, like the situation in Rwanda back in the 1990s; international UN peacekeepers didn't help there.

4 Global problems like climate change aren't limited to national borders. Look at what's happening in the Arctic with the melting of the ice cap. It's going to have an impact on countries right across the world. So we need to have international regulations that all countries sign up to. So we try and tackle the problem together.

Unit 7

Listening

📺 7.1 **Extract 1**

Today I'm going to talk about the concept of work-life balance and how it applies to workers in the modern labour market. Traditionally, concerns in this area revolved around the amount of time individuals spent at work – 'in the office' – balanced against the time spent at home, in leisure activities, or socializing with family and friends. So I'm going to start by looking at average working hours and how they've been affected by general trends in the labour market.

However, we're also seeing an increasingly flexible labour market, with increased outsourcing and growing numbers of portfolio workers and freelancers. There's more pressure on workers to remain engaged with work *outside* of normal office hours. And with new technologies like smart phones and widespread internet access, the line between work and home life is becoming increasingly blurred. This is called 'extensification' or 'overflow'. So, in the second part of my presentation, I'll be looking at these phenomena, and how they've affected people's ability to maintain a reasonable work-life balance.

7.2 Extract 2

OK, so, let's start off by looking at how many hours workers in the UK spend at work on average.

So here we have some statistics from the Office of National Statistics in the UK, on working hours over the past few years. This first slide shows how the hours of everyone in employment have changed over the period from 1992 to 2011. And we can see that, overall, there's been a fall in the average working week from 38.1 hours in 1992 to 36.3 hours in 2011. If we look at some major sectors of the British economy, we can also see some differences in the average working hours. People working in construction have tended to work the longest hours, followed by those in manufacturing, with people in the service sector working the shortest hours. Although it should be noted that in the construction sector, there's been a fall of around three hours in the average working week over the past decade, the past ten years.

What's important to understand when considering the fall in the average number of hours is the influence of a changing economy in the UK. To illustrate this, let's look at the share of employment across the different sectors in 1992. What we can see is that 68% of people were employed in the service sector, 21% in manufacturing, 7% in construction and 4% in other areas, such as agriculture. Now, looking at 2011, what we see is that the service sector has a much larger share of employment and at the same time as this has gone up, the percentage of people employed in manufacturing has gone down.

So why is this important? Well, if we go back to our first slide for a moment, we can see that people in manufacturing tend to work longer hours, on average, than those in the service sector. So if we have more people employed in services and fewer in manufacturing, this will act to reduce the average number of hours worked by the UK workforce as a whole.

OK. Another important factor to consider is the effect on these figures of part-time working. Looking at this graph, we can see that the share of employment that is part-time working has been steadily increasing ... so from around 24% in 1992, to 27% in the second quarter of 2011. The effect of this, of course, is to bring down the overall average number of hours for all those in work.

Another interesting thing to look at is the percentage of people who are working part-time and who would like to work full-time. We can see that following the end of the 1990s recession, this was around 14%, but then this figure fell as the economy recovered. It started to rise again from around 2004, and this increase accelerated at the start of the recession in 2008. In 2011, it stood at 16%, or around one in every six people working part-time.

7.3 Extract 3

As I said in my introduction, statistics on working hours only tells part of the story. Achieving a good work-life balance doesn't just involve the number of 'official' or paid hours employees spend at their desks, especially within the growing service sector. In a competitive job market, workers are expected to be flexible both in terms of time and space.

I want to refer to a study done by two researchers from the London School of Economics, Andy Pratt and Helen Jarvis. This was a study of new media workers in San Francisco. Pratt and Jarvis came across a number of families who were living in small, cramped city-centre apartments, rather than moving out to live in more affordable, more spacious areas outside the city. This was because both parents were working, and felt that they needed to be at the centre of things for the sake of their careers. So a city-centre location was part of this. We also see this phenomenon in the UK with its huge focus on London as the location with really good career prospects, but also very high housing and living costs. This pressure on workers to move to where the work is not only impacts on their standard of living, but it also affects the rest of their family.

Pratt and Jarvis also identify a phenomenon which they call 'overflow', where work tasks gradually creep into people's home lives. This may be in quite obvious ways, like someone bringing their laptop home to look at some work after the kids have gone to bed. Or it may be more insidious. Does checking your work email on your smartphone in the evening count as work, for example? One study by a UK employment law firm found that staff who are issued with BlackBerries or other mobile technology work on average an extra fifteen hours a week outside of the office.

In the last few decades we've seen a period of 'intensification' of work practices, where new technologies have been brought in to make workers more efficient, and then this has had the effect of making work more intensive, and increasing productivity. It's been argued that following this, the trend in recent years has been towards 'extensification', where employers seek to 'extend' the role of their staff – providing them with smartphones, BlackBerries, whatever – so that they are always 'on call'. Of course, from the employer's perspective this is seen as a positive development, a way of increasing productivity, of getting the most out of your workforce. From the employee's point of view, though, it means their work inevitably overflows into their personal lives, their home lives. As I said earlier, the line between work and home life starts to become blurred. And this can be seen as a negative thing, something that makes achieving a healthy work-life balance much more difficult.

So, this view of the modern labour market moves us away from a 'balance model', where workers are able to balance their work and home lives, towards a 'depletion model', where the demands of work, both inside the office and outside, take away from the time available for family and social activities.

Unit 8

Listening

8.1 Extract 1

Dr George Pope Good afternoon, my name is George Pope, I'm a consultant physician working in the John Radcliffe Hospital in Oxford and an honour- honorary senior clinical lecturer in the University of Oxford and I have the privilege today of talking to you about stroke, an extremely exciting field of medicine evolving over the last 100 years and very, very quickly evolving over the last ten years.

So if I'd like to just go, go through the outline of my talk which really looks at introducing stroke and how important a stroke is in our population for patients and for society, how, what is a stroke, and try and go through some outline of giving you an understanding of what it means to have a stroke, the making of the diagnosis from the physicians' point of view, the classification which is relevant to the prognosis and the impact on, of, of stroke on people. I'd then like to go on to talk about the primary prevention, or the treatment strategy which is three-fold, primary prevention, secondary prevention, and the very exciting acute treatment which has now emerged over the past ten years as I've said, with thrombolysis and hemicraniectomy; thrombolysis is the use of clot-busting agents and hemicraniectomy is the use of surgical procedures to relieve pressure in the brain, both exclusive treatments that are restricted to a very select population of stroke patients.

8.2 Extract 2

Dr George Pope So if I can go through some of the facts to begin, every two seconds, somebody in the world has a stroke, and every six seconds, somebody in the world dies from a stroke. That leaves 5.8 million lives per year lost to stroke, and this is information coming from the World Health Report in 2007, the Geneva Report. Furthermore, it's the third commonest cause of death, with a third of strokes being fatal; one in six people in the world will have a stroke in their lifetime, it's unlikely to get through life without knowing somebody, a first degree relative or very close friend, who will not have a stroke. It is commoner than the combination of AIDS, TB, and malaria; one in six as I've said will have a recurrence. This is even more relevant in our current environment where our population is ageing; the risk of having a stroke is increased significantly by the-, as one ages, and we are living in an ageing population and this is some data published by Professor Rothwell in the *Lancet* in 2005, which shows the increased prevalence of vascular disease, especially stroke, with age. In the EU population, the over-65 group will increase by 2050, it is estimated by Social Trends Office for National Statistics, to be 29% of the population that'll be over 65 years of age.

8.3 Extract 3

Dr George Pope What is a stroke? Well stroke, the word 'stroke' comes from the Greek 'apoplexy' meaning 'to be struck down', and most people experience stroke in this way, that it is like a bolt of lightning out of the blue. What it is not, is a CVA, which is the old term for a stroke, known as a cerebral vascular accident and the, the terminology for, for stroke has changed somewhat over the last couple of years, the reasoning being mostly that this is not an accident, and we should consider it in an emergency, and something that is to be treated, and something that we look for risk factors for, to try and reverse, prevent future problems, and treat the current problem. Again **the World Health Organization definition for stroke, which is slightly wordy and I will go through it, the definition from the World Health is a rapid developing clinical signs of focal or global disturbance of cerebral function with symptoms lasting more than 24 hours or longer, leading to death, with no apparent cause other than vascular origin.** What does this mean? It means that this is a vascular event, blood vessels are involved, not necessarily a neurological event where brain tissue may be involved and it lasts for longer than 24 hours, the differentiation being events that are neurological events, that are vascular lasting less than 24 hours, are often called TIAs or transient ischaemic attacks, which are a forewarner of strokes and certainly increase your risk of subsequently having a stroke, but they are not an actual stroke.

How do we make the diagnosis? Well the diagnosis is made principally by history, so this is a detailed conversation with the patient, outlining how this event occurred in the first instance. Examination is obviously important in terms of the deficit following the stroke and indeed the risk factors that cause the stroke, or potentially cause the stroke, for example, problems with the carotid artery with narrowing or stenosis, subsequently can result in increased stroke risk, problems with the heart, with irregular heart rhythms equally can relate in, for in strokes from embolic or clots forming in the heart and moving to the brain. Blood pressure is of course vital, glucose is vital for diabetes and other tests are important such as brain scans, but ultimately the diagnosis is one made by discussing in detail with the patient, what the problem was.

Things that strokes can mimic are, we call them stroke mimics, are syncope which are collapses, usually secondary to blood pressure problems, a number of other causes also, space-occupying lesions, for example tumours, metabolic disturbances such as blood problems with liver problems, kidney problems, high or low glucose, seizures and the post-seizure state or a post-ictal state, migraine can rarely present with stroke-like symptoms, acute confusional state. How else can we classify it? There is no one classification system unfortunately that encompasses stroke completely and that is important, the reason we classify is to, is to gain an understanding of the underlying cause and the underlying prognosis, radiologically, i.e. through CAT scans or MRI scans, we can classify strokes into either ischaemic or haemorrhagic. **Ischaemic strokes are where a clot forms somewhere along a blood vessel and the blood supplied to the tissue that that blood vessel is supplying, is blocked and stopped.** That causes damage to the brain tissue and it's called an ischaemic stroke, this is the commonest cause of a stroke with 80% of strokes presenting as ischaemic strokes. **Haemorrhagic strokes are where there is a bleed from a blood vessel**, this is 20% of the stroke population and is broken down to primary bleeds in the brain tissue or intra-cerebral haemorrhages or bleeds outside of the brain in the subarachnoid space, the space under the meninges, the lining of the brain.

▶ **8.4 Extract 4**

Dr George Pope How do we approach the treatment of stroke? So, primary **prevention** in the population group, **reducing smoking, treating blood pressure, improving diet, promoting exercise** is obviously the principal strategy to prevent strokes. In those who have risk factors and they are **diabetes**, high to-**high blood pressure**, previous warnings or TIAs as we've discussed earlier, these groups of patients benefit from treatment strategies that are rather more accelerated than the normal population, for example, starting aspirin for treating blood pressure very well, and these have all been shown to reduce the, the **risk of subsequent strokes**. We all know about **aspirin** and it's been in treatment vogue for many, many years and that was the acute management for stroke up to ten, maybe fifteen years ago. What's very exciting now is the acute treatment of stroke with interventions and with **rehabilitation**, and one mightn't think that rehabilitation is that exciting but in fact it is, and it is probably *the* best proven treatment for any stroke patient.

(Secondary prevention I'll come onto in a minute.) So looking at rehabilitation, stroke unit patients versus non-stroke unit patients. The Cochrane Report in 2001 looked at the number of people who returned home and the number of patients that you need to treat in order to get an extra person home between a stroke population treated in a stroke unit, versus that treated on a normal non-organized, acute medical ward, I don't use the term non-organized with any disparagement, but it is organized care, organized stroke specialist care versus ordinary hospital care. Five more return home, four fewer died and three less are institutionalized from 100 patients and this is significant and this is a real benefit to treatment, this is, this is real patient impact.

Unit 9

Listening

▶ **9.1 Extract 1**

Dr Kathleen Quinlan So I said that this lecture was going to focus on three main questions, we've spent a lot of time on that first question of what is university learning? We've explored it from several different perspectives so that you could have a sense of what the fundamental cultural assumptions are, that underpin the educational process in English-speaking universities. How you – and er, so what I'd like to do now is to focus on the second major question of the talk which is how you can make the most of your university education in an English-speaking country. So how can you engage in deep learning, if we use Säljö's term or higher order thinking, if we use Bloom's term, or to use Newman's terms, the collision of mind with mind. So let's take a moment to do our third reflection and here I want you to think of a situation in which you learned something deeply, deeply in the terms we've just described and what did you do and what helped you the most? Good. We'll look at that more closely in the tutorials later because I know, I don't want to keep you over time today.

So what I want to focus on is the process of university learning in English-speaking countries. Now I'm hoping that some of the notes that you've written down to yourself include some of these key bullet points, that through, that the way in which you can learn involves reading, yes, it involves listening and listening – and particularly listening actively – so I've built in these reflection prompts throughout this lecture today in order to help you to listen actively, to help you to think about the key points in the lecture as well as just listen because I know that if all you did was listen to my voice for an hour, I would be waking you up to leave the room at the end, so I want to keep you awake with having you think about things along the way and it's important that you take that mindset into any lecture that you have, even if the lecture doesn't do what I've done today which is pause throughout the lecture, you should still be thinking to yourself, generating questions or paying attention to the questions that the lecturer might be posing, so that you are actively engaging with the content, even if the lecture is going through quite continuously.

Another key process of learning in universities is by writing and often we, mistakenly I think, think of writing as something you do after you've learned something, you read about it and all you

have to do is write it up but actually I want to challenge you to think that writing is in fact a part of that learning process, that we write in order to understand, we write in order to clarify our thinking, in much the same way that Socrates engaged his students in a dialogue where they said something and then explored it further and further.

▶ **9.2 Extract 2**

Prof Angus Hawkins Good morning everyone, my name's Professor Angus Hawkins and I'm here to talk to you this morning about a man called, or I have called the Forgotten Prime Minister.

Perhaps I should start by telling you about a parlour game perhaps I've been playing with acquaintances over the last few years, who when I've met them, have asked me, "Angus, what are you working on now?" and I say, "I'm writing a biography", they then say "Oh, interesting, who is your biography of?" and it's at this point. I ask them some questions. I say "Well, I'm writing a biography of the first British statesman to become prime minister three times", there's a pause and they try and er, guess who it is that I'm talking about and they will suggest Gladstone or Disraeli or Salisbury, to all of which I say "No, no, no, no" and then I say "OK, I'll make it easier for you, he is the longest serving party leader in modern British politics, led the Conservative Party for 22 years" and again, various suggestions but almost invariably, not the correct answer.

And then I say "OK, I'll make it very, very easy for you, he, I'm writing a biography of the man who abolished slavery in the British Empire" and at that point people usually begin to look slightly embarrassed and are still unsuccessful. Over a period of about three or four years, when I was having these conversations, the number of people who could give me the correct answer, who could tell me who I was writing about, you could number on the fingers of one hand.

As a result, the biography that I wrote, I entitled, *The Forgotten Prime Minister* because the 14th Earl of Derby, who indeed was the first British statesman to become prime minister three times, led the Conservative Party for 22 years from 1846 to 1868 and in 1833 as Colonial Secretary, abolished slavery in the British Empire, has been largely forgotten, has been as it were, airbrushed out of our history of modern British politics and British Conservatism.

So this was very interesting to me as a historical problem, the historical question, "Why has Lord Derby been written out of our history of modern British politics and our history of British Conservatism? Why has he been airbrushed away? Why has he been forgotten?"

▶ **9.3 Extract 3**

MT = Prof Marianne Talbot **S** = student(s)
MT Right, OK, I'm going to be talking about the mind-body problem and it's going to be a really brief introduction, it really is going to be brief. What I'm going to do is I'm going to introduce you to the mind body problem and I'm going to set out for you why the relationship between the mind and the body is considered prob-problematic and also why it continues to be problematic, this problem isn't going to go away. So going right back to the beginning, there was René Descartes, there he is, he wrote a wonderful book called *The Meditation on First Philosophy*, I'm sure you've all heard of that, if you

haven't read it, do try it, it's very easy, very easy to read, the ideas in it are very difficult but it is easy to read so try it. On the basis of conceptual analysis and we'll talk about that in a second, Descartes drew a very sharp distinction between the mind and the body and just before we go onto the distinction that he drew, let's have a look at what conceptual analysis is. Tell me what's characteristic of a triangle?

S Three sides.

MT It has three sides. OK, must it have three sides? Are there any triangles that don't have three sides?

S No.

MT No, there aren't, are there? What you were doing there, notice there isn't a triangle that I can see in this room, what you were doing was reflecting on your concept of a triangle, analysing it to see what was necessary for something to be a triangle and what you could see is quite clearly, if it hasn't got three sides, it isn't a triangle, is that right?

S Yes.

MT OK, you were using the tool of conceptual analysis and that's what Descartes used with respect to the mind and the body and what he did, when he thought of the mind and thought, "OK, what is it that's characteristic of mind? What is it without which the mind wouldn't exist?" and then he looked at the body and he thought, "What is it without which the body wouldn't exist?" and he came up with two things, he identified the essential property of the mind as thinking, so if you didn't think, would you exist? Your body might but would you exist if you didn't think?

S How about feeling?

MT OK, we could add feeling to that and in fact I'm happy to do so at the moment, if you didn't think and feel, could you exist? If you had no thoughts, no feelings, no sensations, no consciousness at all, would you exist? No, well that, that's the conclusion that Descartes came to, he, he thought without consciousness, it wouldn't be me, even if my body was around but there was no consciousness, it wouldn't be me because what's, what's important to me, what's essential to me is that I think, that's where he got his famous, "I'm thinking, therefore I am" *Cogito ergo sum*. He then looked at the essential property of a body so if we take a physical object, I wish I had a solid one here but I don't but this pen will do, what is it that's essential to, to a physical object like this? Is it its shape? You could have a physical object with a different shape, couldn't you? What is it and what he thought was its space fillingness, its extension which means solidity or space fillingness, so there couldn't be a physical object, thinks Descartes, that isn't extended in space. We're going to do a Cartesian thought experiment for ourselves so let's, let's do that, I'm going to use the flip chart ...

Speaking

▶ 9.4 **Extract 1**

Dr Kathleen Quinlan Another pros- part of the learning process are laboratories or practical experiences where you may get demonstrations of key ideas or you get to experience the process of the scientific disciplines in particular. Discussion, debate, critique and questioning are also all a

significant part of the learning process in English-speaking universities and I realize that for many students coming from other cultures, this can feel very uncomfortable, that you may be accustomed to listening to the teacher as the authority, as the one who knows the answers and that in order to be respectful to them, you ought not to ask too many questions, you should simply take that as given.

But the way we operate in English-speaking universities is quite different than that and you'll generally find that there are discussion sections, tutorials, small class settings where you are expected to bring questions, not only questions about the content that you've been reading but also to question other students in the class who may be putting an idea out there that you think isn't quite right or maybe it's a pretty good idea but if you can help them to clarify it, it will be an even better idea. And you can expect that your teachers will do that to you and it's quite all right to do that with your teachers, so that's a di- a really different way of operating than the situations that some of you may have come from and it's important that you understand that so that you can take the best advantage of your university education and we've talked already a lot in the first segment of this lecture, about the cultural roots of that critical thinking approach.

And finally, I want to encourage you to think about developing and supporting your own arguments, to think about the process of education as an opportunity to find your own voice, to develop your own thoughts about the subject at hand and also to think about what your place is then in what I'm calling a remade world because as you learn in this deep way, your perspectives will be challenged, your assumptions will be challenged , you'll see things you didn't see before and you'll start to see the world and yourself in it differently and that's part of the process, it's not always comfortable but it's part of the process when you're doing it really well, so bear with it and embrace it as much as possible and get the support that you need, so that you can experience it that fully.

◀ 9.5

A I'm interested in this idea that's come up several times about there being more interaction between students and teachers here. *[= example from source]* For example, from my own experience as a high school teacher in China, I'm used to students raising their hands to answer questions from the teacher. *[= example from own experience]* I think that's partly cultural, because of our ideas about respect and because there's always a kind of distance between the teacher and student. But it's also a practical thing too. So, in China, for example, class sizes are very large, maybe 50 or 60 students in one class. *[= general example]* Say that every student called out when they wanted to answer a question. It would just be chaos. *[= hypothetical example]*

B The example in the text we read about Americans not using formal titles ... I can really relate to that situation. There was this researcher in the United States that I was collaborating with last year. *[= example from own experience]* And he started his very first email to me with, 'Hi, Claus'. And to tell you the truth, I was a little bit offended. I mean, I know it's cultural, but I'd never met the guy and he was being just too friendly, too familiar. I would always use professional or academic titles, like 'doctor' or 'professor',

in that context. Certainly the first time I wrote to someone. I guess it's just a case of cultural difference. He didn't mean to be rude, it was just normal for him.

Unit 10
Listening

▶ 10.1

Good morning ... and thank you for choosing to attend my presentation today. So, as you can see, I'm going to be looking at the challenges facing the global pharmaceutical market today, and how those challenges can be addressed. I'd like to start with some background information on the pharmaceutical market as a whole.

As I'm sure you know, in the majority of cases the price of goods and services in a particular market normally find their equilibrium through the meeting of supply and demand. In other words, the price of goods or services reflects both the availability and the demand. So if demand rises, and a lot of people want something, then if the supply remains at the same level, the price will go up. And if that supply increases, we'd expect the price to come back down. And vice versa – if demand falls, the price goes down until the supply is reduced ... and so on. But as we'll see, the pharmaceutical market is different. The pharmaceutical market is not a perfect market where supply perfectly matches demand. And this leads us to the situation we have today.

So, I'd just like to outline the situation with regard to expenditure on medical products globally. We'll start with the figures from 1990 and 2000, and then we'll look at the most recently available figures, published in 2011, which come from the World Health Organization, the WHO. And I should say that I'm basing all of my figures on publications by the WHO. The WHO is the world's most visible global health organization, with a 193-country membership, which means it operates at both a global and a local level. This global reach means that they are able to collect data from more countries than any other organization.

OK ... As we can see, this table shows the private and government per capita expenditure on pharmaceuticals in 1990 and 2000. All the figures are in US dollars. There are several things going on here. First, private expenditure on pharmaceuticals outweighs government expenditure in all income categories – so, high, middle, and low incomes. Second, the total expenditure increased very substantially in this decade. If we compare the totals of the years 1990 and 2000, we can see that the increase is around 50% overall, with higher increases in middle-income countries. And third, there is a significant variation between countries with different incomes. If we look at the year 2000, the governments of low-income countries spent just over one dollar per capita on pharmaceuticals. Contrast this with the expenditure of high-income countries – 167 dollars. This is a huge difference, obviously.

There are some more recent figures, and these seem to show a similar trend, that per capita pharmaceutical expenditure has been increasing steadily for a number of years. In 2005 to 2006 this ranged from 7.61 US dollars in low-income countries up to 431.6 dollars in high-income countries. Compare this with 1995, when the highest rate of increase was in low- and middle-income countries.

The WHO figures also allow us to make some interesting observations regarding inequalities in expenditure. For example, 16 per cent of the world's population currently live in high-income countries, and they account for over 78 per cent of global expenditure on medicines and medical products. Now, total pharmaceutical expenditure – or TPE, as it's often referred to – TPE is much higher in high-income countries, as you might expect. However, compared with low-income countries, a much smaller proportion of this money is spent on actual medicines or drugs. Since 1995 the *private* share of TPE has been increasing in low- and middle-income countries, but not in high-income countries and I'll come back to this public–private distinction a little later.

So, having looked at the global market in pharmaceuticals, I want to now look at some of the associated problems. As I said at the beginning, the pharmaceutical market is not a perfect market where supply balances with demand, and I'd like to explore some of the reasons why. In this section of my talk I'll be basing my material on the work of Walley and Wright. And by the way, I'll give you all the references at the end.

OK, the pharmaceutical market is a bit of a special case for a number of reasons. First of all, in general consumers are not particularly well-informed about the medical products they're using. Consumers tend to be better informed about products like, well, the clothes they buy, food products, white goods, and the gadgets they use, and so on. Typically, most people don't know much about the quality and safety of their medicines. They tend to take these just on trust. And they're not especially well informed either about the effectiveness of their medication, or how appropriate a particular medication is for their condition.

Secondly, there actually isn't much competition in this market. There are a large number of consumers, or potential consumers, in the world – in effect, the entire population of the world is a potential consumer. If you compare that for a moment with manufacturers of other kinds of products, let's say for example satnavs, you're immediately limited to consumers who own a car. Nobody is going to buy a satnav if they don't have a car to put it in. But potentially, everyone is a consumer of pharmaceutical products. And while there's an enormous number of consumers, there are relatively few suppliers. Basically, there are health care providers, purchasers, and manufacturers.

Thirdly, there is the issue of monopolies. Manufacturers are known to create monopolies through the use of patents, which protect their medicines from being copied by other manufacturers for a fixed number of years. Manufacturers can also patent their manufacturing processes, which makes it even harder for competitors. Related to this, there's also brand loyalty, just as there is in many other sectors, which is achieved, partly at least, through intensive marketing. A great deal of money is spent on marketing pharmaceutical products in high-income countries like the United States. There have also been cases of price-fixing by producer cartels in order to keep market prices artificially high.

Finally, I just want to mention external factors, externalities, which exist in the sector. This means that treatment for some conditions, especially communicable diseases like tuberculosis and some sexually-transmitted infections, benefits not only

the patient receiving the treatment but also the wider public – because their risk of contracting the disease or infection is also reduced.

So, I hope this analysis shows that the pharmaceutical market is quite unlike most other markets. I would go as far as to say it is a market which has failed … it is a failed market.

A key point to emerge from this is that the financing of medicines, and the balance between government and private financing, plays a critical role in the market. So, I'd like to propose six ways of keeping costs down and improving the profile of the pharmaceutical market.

Most parties agree that medicine costs need to be kept down, so national governments have a key role to play in drawing up principled lists of cost-effective medicines. Alongside this, the generic market can be promoted, so that pharmacists can replace more expensive branded consumer drugs with the equivalent generic ones, which tend to be much cheaper. Therapeutic substitution is also possible … in other words, adapting a particular patient's therapy and moving to a lower-cost drug programme. Governments can use their buying power to negotiate with the manufacturer on prices. They can do this effectively by comparing the medicines with others on the market.

Another option for promoting competition and putting downward pressure on prices is parallel imports. Now this is where patented medicines are brought from another country where they cost less, this is often because the price has been negotiated down by that country's government. One further option is compulsory licensing. Compulsory licensing is where a local manufacturer is licensed to produce a patented drug under licence and usually at a lower price. In fact, the World Trade Organization allows compulsory licensing under certain conditions, normally related to the public interest.

So these measures illustrate the choices available to stimulate local pharmaceutical markets … and indeed the global market as well. Any health financing system has to be sustainable in the longer term. It needs to promote equality, efficiency, and the rational use of medicines.

I'd like to now consider some of the issues raised in managing medicines. I'd like to look at public financing, health insurance, and user fees. I've put these on a handout here for you to take away at the end. As far as public financing is concerned, this finance is mainly raised through taxation. This has a number of advantages. One is that it becomes easier to select supplies of various medicines and target them at the people who need them the most. Another advantage is that the government can control the quality of medicine. They can achieve economies of scale by buying in large quantities. And also, the cost of payment is effectively shifted to a wide base of the population – not just the sick, but everyone in work who is paying taxes. And since tax is normally collected as a percentage of income, it means that those earning higher salaries pay more.

In many countries, health insurance has an important role to play in the management of medical supplies. Health insurance is a mechanism for sharing risk among a section of the population. Health insurance schemes may be public or private, compulsory or voluntary. Basically, all developed countries, with the exception of the United States, have some kind of public health insurance system which covers part or all of the cost of

medicines for most or all of the population. However, in developing countries, this kind of scheme is much rarer. Health insurance schemes should be an attractive option for these countries too, since medicines account for a large share of total household expenditure in many developing countries. But there are risks too, and these include over-prescription, abuse, and fraud. If they're going to work effectively, health insurance schemes need to include measures to prevent costs from spiralling out of control.

OK, finally, user fees. In developing countries, user fees make up over two-thirds of the expenditure on medicines, mainly from the private sector, because people typically buy medicines from private sellers. An alternative is cost recovery schemes – these are where people have to pay back some or all of the cost of medicines after they've been prescribed. These recovered fees are then put back into the general medical expenditure budget. Now supporters of user fees tend to argue that they improve the general availability of medicines and efficiency in terms of the supply. Also, they help to reduce over-consumption and they allow public funds to be spent on the people who are most in need. But in reality the needs of the poorest are often not met, so there has to be some kind of system of checks and balances, such as exemptions for the poorest people in society, those who are least able to pay.

Unit 11

Listening

▶ **11.1 Extract 1**

Dr Kerry Lock So today we are going to focus this lecture on community ecology, but first of all we must recap what is ecology? So, it's the study of interactions between organisms and their environments, and I have this array of leaflets around the outside, just to show the sheer scope that ecology covers, especially in terms of the scale from molecular through to the landscape level.

Now in terms of organisms, we're obviously talking about individual forms of life and in terms of the environments, we have the **abiotic**, the non-living part of the environment, and the biotic, so that's the living part of the environment, and we're going to go into more detail about that a bit later on. So first of all, the abiotic factors, these non-living components, they include aspects such as water, wind, and solar radiation, and on the southern slope you can see on the foreground, which is currently in sun, it's likely that that slope receives more solar radiation than the slope opposite, the northern facing, but in reverse, actually the northern slope is likely to be wetter than the southern slope because it will have water fed down through the entire catchment onto that point. And in the centre of the photograph, you can see this rocky area, and that area is likely to be exposed to more salt water and potentially winds than these two grassland areas; and the key point is, that the environmental conditions that are present in these three areas will suit some populations of some species but not others. So what is a **population**? It- it's individuals of a single species living together in one geographical location at the same time. Now when we talk about species, that is organisms which are able to interbreed to produce fertile offspring, and when we talk about the geographical area, the physical area in which these species live, that's called their **habitat**.

So habitats such as forest or ponds or meadows are shared by many co-existing populations and an assemblage of two or more of these populations is known as a **community** and you've probably observed already, from this diagrammatic representation of a grassland, that some species are more associated with particular areas than others. So in the bottom of the diagram, you can see a click beetle species and a weevil species and they're particularly associated with the root systems, in contrast to the carder bee which is specifically associated with the flowers and pollen. And then in the centre there is the orb web spider which is actually using the architecture of the grassland itself. And these areas are sometimes called an **ecological niche**, they don't just have to be a physical area, they are specifically the conditions and the resources that those species need to survive and they can include a range of temperatures, and they can conc-include a temporal range as well, so whether the species is coming out at day or at night. And this means that ecologically similar species can actually co-exist in the same community, especially if their niches are able to differ by one or two significant ways, and this is what we call resource partitioning.

This diagrammatic representation of a grassland shows clearly a range of sward structures, you've got some tussocked, thick areas of grass compared to some open bare patches, and this is really important, because it enables quite a large array of **niches** to be available for a range of species. Now some species may need to reside in this open bare patch where maybe the temperature will be different, the moisture will be different than inside this tussocked grassland area. Some species may actually need both of those areas as part of their niche, so for example, a wading bird species such as a lapwing will need the tussocked area to shelter from predators and also to nest, but they will need this open bare patch to be able to probe for food, to be able to probe for invertebrates. Now this **niche separation** issue is really well represented in the spider community, and even within one metre square of this particular grassland area, you will see ground-dwelling spiders which will be hunting at that lower level, and at the same time, you'll see orb web spiders, and they will be up in the grassland, in their webs, so within a small area you will have very similar ecological species but are able to co-exist in a small area due to this niche separation.

▶ 11.2 Extract 2

Dr Kerry Lock So how are communities actually structured? First of all we look at species richness, so within a community there can be different types of species, and then there are relative abundance of those species, some will be more common than others. Then we have the physical characteristics of the organisms, so, for example, in very arid areas, some plants will have very thick succulent leaves and this is to reduce evapotranspiration, so that is to stop water evaporating from the leaf and that's an adaptation to that environment. And then lastly the trophic relationships among interacting populations within a community, this refers to the way in which energy is transferred through the system, so you remember from biology school days,

you'll have been taught that green plants had a compound called chlorophyll and that was able to capture energy from the sun and in, by using carbon dioxide and water through a process called photosynthesis, they were able to generate a carbohydrate, an energy source.

So how is this energy transferred through the community? Well, basically, it's transferred through a series of what we call food chains, and these are intricately linked to create a food web, which you can see here. Now at the very base of the food web we have the phytoplankton and phytoplankton are, are really the foundation of oceanic food webs, and they contain chlorophyll, so they are generating this carbohydrate source. Now in turn they are fed upon by the krill, which are herbivores, so they're primary consumers, and in turn, they are fed upon by the leopard seal, which we call a predator but we also call a carnivore, and a third title is a secondary consumer. And so energy is fed up through these chains, and actually only 10% of the original energy is passed on at each stage, so that puts a limitation on the, the number of steps you can have in any one food chain, and it's usually at about three or four, which is what you can see in this oceanic one here, so you've got the phytoplankton in Step 1 and the krill Step 2, leopard seal Step 3, and the smaller toothed whale, Step 4; and the reason that you can only have that many levels, is because these higher trophic level species require to consume an enormous amount of these lower trophic level species, to be able to survive. So there is only a certain level of primary producers and so only a certain number of the higher trophic species can be supported.

So we've talked a little bit about interactions between populations in the community and we've touched on **herbivory** already, so there's another example here. This is an epilobian species, that's a primary producer, the plant, and to the right is a hawk moth caterpillar, so that's our herbivore, that's this, the primary consumer. And we've also touched upon **predation**, so these are secondary consumers, so on the lower right hand side we have the water vole, that's a herbivore, and on the left is an American mink, which is our secondary consumer, so these are some very, very basic sort of connections in the, in the food web.

But there are three other interactions within the populations that I want to talk about, first of all is **parasitism,** so this is a symbiotic interaction in which the parasite actually derives part or all of its nourishment from a host, which is either harmed or in some cases is actually killed in the process. Now the first example I want to give you is a hemiparasitic plant and by hemiparasitic we mean that it only derives part of its resources from its host. So this example is *Rhinanthus minor*, the yellow rattle, which is depicted here in the photograph and it latches onto competitive grasses such as *Holcus lanatus* and by doing that, it impedes their growth so this is a fantastic plant to aid restoration of grasslands for example, because by sowing out the *Rhinanthus minor* seeds, you can actually impact on some competitive grasses which opens out the sward to enable less competitive herbaceous plants to come through. The second example I want to show you are parasitic hymenoptera, so these are the parasitic wasps and here this depicts a Chilean Rosé which is actually a tarantula which is about this size, just to give you an idea of scale, I mean it's so large, you can see

it walking across the road when you're driving along, so this photograph is actually taken in Argentina and it's been paralysed by the parasitic wasp which is now dragging it off to the nest and it will be brought down into the nest and the eggs will either be laid on top or within that host and when the eggs emerge and the larvae emerge, they will feed on that host, so ultimately this parasitism case will actually involve the death of the host.

So the second example I want to talk about is **mutualism**. Now mutualism basically means that there's an interaction between two different species and the interaction results in a mutual benefit for both species, so there's nothing more classic than the example of the large blue butterfly and the red ant interaction, so basically the large blue butterfly caterpillar feeds on wild thyme and marjoram and when it reaches its third instar level, it starts secreting a honeydew substance which attracts the red ant species. The red ants then carry that caterpillar down into their nest, still feeding on this honeydew secretion and the caterpillar there can actually feed on the red ant eggs, so there's this mutual benefit from both sides and the large blue butterfly will end up hibernating over winter there, so they'll turn into a chrysalis and in fact incredibly, the large blue butterfly can actually mimic the pheromones of the red ant and noises that the red ant makes, just to ensure its survival in the nest. Now when the next season comes around, the blue butterfly emerges and is actually taken up to the surface by the red ants, which then surround it and actually protect it as it pumps up its wings, ready for its first flight, it's, it's an incredible relationship, a very classic example.

▶ 11.3 Extract 3

Dr Kerry Lock So in terms of ecosystems, they are extremely vital to our survival as I've said, and back in 2001, 2005, a global millennium ecosystem assessment took place and the key objective was to assess the consequences of ecosystem change for our well-being, and this encompassed 95 countries, phenomenal number of experts, so it was the first and the largest assessment of the health of ecosystems in the UK. And effectively, these ecosystem processes were split up into four key categories that are called eco system services, now ecosystem services are basically the benefits that we gain as human beings from these processes, so they split it into supporting services, so that includes the nutrient cycling, the primary production, how the energy gets into our system in the first place; provisioning, obviously we gain food and fuel from these systems; regulating, so food, flood regulation and water purification; and then the cultural aspect, the aesthetics. But fundamentally, these systems are very vulnerable and because of the level in which we rely upon them, it is our responsibility to maintain them and to ensure their continuity. ... So the focus for the future is very much on reconnecting our fragmented landscape and this is going to be vital in terms of continuing these ecological processes and more fundamentally, maintaining the ecosystem services that we very much require for our own survival.

Unit 12

Listening

Dr Adrian Stokes Now, before we, given that it's all difficult, just to describe something in society, just to get some measures of anything is extremely difficult, costly, time consuming, we really ought to find out what's already known, we need to know whether it's worth doing, this research. I think just about everybody listening to this lecture will be familiar with the idea of a literature review, you can go and see what's been published on a particular research topic. But undertaking a **literature review** can be a complicated and time consuming business in itself, there are different forms of review, a narrative review would try to tell the story of how research has developed in a broad area, over perhaps a number of years, different traditions, try to make sense of it all and it would give a good flavour for what's gone on in a particular area but increasingly, people are suggesting that actually we should approach our reviewing systematically. This doesn't mean that people who've done narrative reviews were utterly unsystematic, you know, they just kind of went into the library, picked anything up off the shelf, just kind of had a quick look and, they were totally not unsystematic, but systematic reviews are systematic in a very, very specific sense. They have a specific search strategy to address a particular research question, that research strategy, sorry that search strategy needs to be set out in detail, so for example you would say which library databases you'd searched, on which day even, you'd identify the terms that you put into that search, the number of hits that you got back, why you chose to read the ones you chose, how you extracted the data from those that you chose to pursue and in fact, you'd almost certainly involve another researcher, it wouldn't be a lone effort sitting in a library, there may be a team of a dozen people working across the world, carving up this literature into manageable parcels, extracting the data from it and evaluating it and then comparing notes with one another, cross referring certain samples to check they've come up with the same conclusions. Systematic reviews are there to try and make sure that we don't repeat research that doesn't need doing and that we know which research does need doing.

Obviously that then begs the question of how we would combine this research and syntheses are probably one of the most important things going on. If there's been all this investment of time and money in research, we really ought to be in a position to combine it so that we get the full picture. There are no research studies that have given the definitive answer on any interesting question, it takes **multiple studies**, coming at it from different perspectives, repeating things to check against error, to really let us know that we know an answer or have a good idea of what the answer is on a particular question. Often that's done statistically with what's called meta-analysis where you can take the statistics reported in a range of studies, combine the data and do other forms of analysis that let you work out what the effects are over much larger populations and different circumstances. OK, well, let's assume we were doing something in the area around happiness, finding happiness, well there's the question of finding happiness in our own lives but leave that to one side, the question of finding research on happiness you'll see, it's actually not going to be very easy because happiness isn't a term that's very easy to define, it's not one that everybody would approach in the same way. So if you're trying to find literature on happiness, what **search terms** are you going to put in? Well you might use 'happiness' itself but just sitting there, you would be able to come up with lots of other terms, you might come up with broad kind of synonyms like 'contentment', maybe 'satisfaction', 'life satisfaction', maybe you're familiar with some of the literature so you come up with terms like 'well-being', 'quality of life' and you may of course come up with other things which are, relate to happiness but are quite different concepts so lack of anxiety, lack of distress might be qualities associated with happiness, you're not going to be very happy if you are very anxious and distressed. So mapping out those search terms is quite a complicated thing to do, unless you're working in a field that's very, very closely defined, very technical and where there's a long established kind of tradition of ways to approach it. So you may need a theory to help guide you in selecting those terms and knowing what you're going to mean by them. …

OK, well so we've sorted all that out, we know what humanity is, we know what we want to do and we know how we're going to investigate it. We also ought to think about whether we're going to do any harm because our orientation to this is that we're going to do good, none of us have come here into doing social research in order to foster some kind of deliberately malicious ends but it's very easy to do harm without intending it and the research literature is littered with examples of that. Research governance is what institutions like this university and others do to try and keep an eye on how research is being undertaken, to try to make sure that it is properly conducted. Key aspects of that are **research ethics** and research integrity.

In relation to the research ethics, you've probably heard the term 'informed consent' and probably familiar with the idea that research subjects, either people being researched should have anonymity. Those have not been assumptions that have been made throughout the history of the development of social research and there are many debates about how these things can be conducted. In the context of happiness, it's rather obvious that if you're going to start asking people about happiness, you may well draw them into consideration of unhappiness, if you're going to explore things like anxiety and distress and people's circumstances in their lives, it's very, very likely that you're going to, going into territory that may be really quite uncomfortable for them and of course for the researcher, so if you are part of the research programme and you're employing a lot of researchers, you've got to look out for their well-being as well as your research subjects, so there's the ethics of the research process, also research integrity and the P word, plagiarism, falsification. It's rather shocking and rather disappointing but there are many examples where researchers have cut corners, under pressure to publish, under pressure to produce results and I'm afraid, plagiarism and falsification of results, plagiarism being where you rip off somebody else's work and present it as your own and falsification, where you literally just stick in the numbers that suit you.

In terms of **research outcomes**, there are also problems for researchers because somebody will have funded the research, you hope people will use it but they may not use it in the ways that you intend. Use of research in the politics of blame is a big issue, for example in educational research where identifying things which appear to show weaknesses in one set of schools or whatever, can result in consequences that certainly weren't intended by the researchers. In the context of research into happiness, because people tend to be very resilient and actually report much higher levels of happiness than you might expect, that can result in, you know, there's no problem, let's ignore the other difficulties that people are under because they're saying on this scale, 7.7 happiness, that's fine. So these outcomes can be ones that aren't intended but which the researchers really need to think about in the way they manage what they're doing.

OK, so let's go onto some of the nitty gritty about the kind of data we might need to gather. Obviously we're doing it to **answer specific research questions** and that's something that has a whole field in itself and how you craft good research questions, but let's just point out for the sake of this lecture, that you need to have some, and you need to know what they mean but you're then going to have to deal with how you're going to **gather your data** and how it's going to be analysed. The two terms that you'll have already encountered here are quantitative and qualitative approaches, so these are broad orientations to the way in which the research is going to be conducted and they're also a hint to certain assumptions about epistemology for example, about what you take to be the forms of knowledge that are achievable in your research. So let's, rather than just do qualitative/quantitative as the main headlines, let's just consider aspects of those two in relation to the questions about how we gather relevant data and then how we analyse it.

Quantitative approaches turn things into numbers and the main ways they're conducted are through, for example, surveys; they may be questionnaires, those questionnaires may be conducted in a variety of ways, there may be interviews, you may do it online, on the web, you may have somebody phone you up and go through a set of questions with you. Obviously, there's also experimental designs, an experiment is where you'd have a particular action or intervention taken and you'd allocate people to receive that or to receive some kind of control, could be nothing, could be a placebo as they're called so you're, and you're making comparisons between a control group and an intervention group to see whether the intervention has had any kinds of effects, were they good ones, were they bad ones and what might they mean?

Some of the key concepts: obviously if you're surveying, there'll be a population but in relation to happiness index, for example, for the UK, that population is millions and millions of people and you may well not be able to, feasible to reach all those people, too expensive, too impractical, so you're going to work with a sample of those people. In **selecting your sample**, you've got to think about how you're actually going to get the information about those people, how you're going to reach them, so you'll have a sampling frame as it's called, so for instance, an example of a sampling frame would be the electoral roll, which is a specific database.

Now the electoral roll will not actually have in it all the people who are eligible in principle to vote, it has the people who are on the electoral roll, so there'll be omissions, but you'll have to make that kind of decision about how you're going to sample and what frame you would use to conduct the research.

You're probably going to be considering **randomization** because arguably the best way to avoid bias is not to select people, it is to randomly identify them, using some computer-generated number or some other method that just applies a step, a random step to a selection of people. You might randomize people, then you won't get bias in your results, you won't accidentally draw unduly from a particular part of your population because if you're dealing with a very large sample, from a very large population, randomization could easily result in ... unequal representation between men and women for example, so there you might do what's called stratification, you would make a decision, informed by a certain theory that gender differences are important and you might decide to randomize within those two chunks, so you're stratifying those two chunks and then you're randomizing within males and females.

Speaking

🔊 **12.2 Extract 1**

A I'm studying Law and I'm particularly interested in commercial law. Some of you may be familiar with the legal processes involved in transporting goods from one country to another, known as the carriage of goods. This is what I decided to focus on. A number of issues and problems have come up in the last few years and recent research shows that international trade is becoming a lot more complex. Very large quantities of goods are being shipped around the world all the time, and the legislation hasn't always kept up with the increase. Anyway, it's a topic that's quite interesting to me, but for other students, especially students who aren't studying Law, it could be quite dry, quite boring. So I decided to use an example that everyone could relate to. I set up an imaginary scenario with somebody ordering a book online in one country ... from Amazon or a company like Amazon ... and that book being shipped to the customer in another country. So, something that anyone might do, but without knowing about all the legal processes that might have to go on behind the scenes. I worked through the whole process, I used pictures of the book in its packaging at each stage, then I used some 'what if' scenarios to illustrate the possible problems.

B OK, I'm studying Management & Finance and my project was about the different business models that retail businesses adopt when they get in involved in e-commerce. So basically existing retailers who set up online shopping. I focused particularly on the food sector and I wanted to start with an example which shows how these business models worked in practice. I looked at two case studies, both involving supermarket chains which had used very different approaches. My presentation was to other business students, so I summarized the background and the theory quite briefly at the beginning, because we all know about that, and then the main part of my presentation was about the case studies. This was the most interesting part, really. I brought in examples from my work as an intern. I did think about demonstrating the two stores' websites live, as part of my presentation, but although I had an internet connection in the room where I was presenting, when I checked it out, it was too slow. So I just used screenshots instead and I think it worked quite well.

🔊 **12.3 Extract 2**

A In my home country, China, exports are big business. Despite growth in the domestic market, the majority of goods made in China are still for export all around the world. Goods labelled 'made in China' are being shipped across the globe every day, and the legal processes and the regulations involved in the transportation of these goods are of real importance to all Chinese businesses. In my research project, I looked at the legal procedures involved in the carriage of goods, and more specifically, I looked at some of the problems that are now being seen in the increasingly complex world of international trade.

B Today I'm going to be talking about e-commerce, so the sale of goods online. You may have heard in the news recently that online purchases now make up around 15% of all retail sales in the UK. This percentage is similar right across Europe and it's increasing steadily year on year. Established retailers in all sectors are realizing that an online presence is now essential in order to be truly competitive. However, how individual retailers go about setting up their online offering, and which business model they choose, can be vitally important in the success, or otherwise, of their e-commerce operation. In my presentation today, I'm going to look at two case studies, two different UK supermarket chains, who approached the task of selling their products online in very different ways, using very different business models.

Oxford source material used in this course

The reading modules of *Oxford EAP* include extracts from the following source material published by Oxford University Press. For more information about any of these titles, please visit: **www.oup.com**.

page 009
Oxford Dictionary of Economics
3rd edition

pages 009, 012
Health and Human Behaviour
2nd edition

pages 025–026
Winds of Change: The Environmental Movement and the Global Development of the Wind Energy Industry

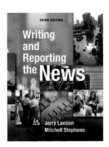

pages 057, 064
Writing and Reporting the News
3rd edition

pages 059–060, 062
Media and Journalism
2nd edition

pages 078, 185
Research Methods for the Biosciences
2nd edition

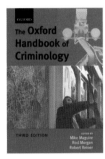

page 105, 106
The Oxford Handbook of Criminology
5th edition

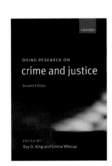

page 108
Doing Research on Crime and Justice
2nd edition

page 123
Child Public Health
2nd edition

page 137
Anthropology: What Does It Mean to Be Human?
2nd edition

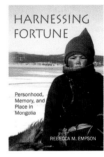

page 138
Harnessing Fortune: Personhood, Memory and Place in Mongolia

page 138
Social and Cultural Anthropology: A Very Short Introduction

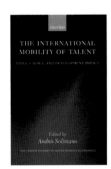

page 152
The International Mobility of Talent: Types, Causes, and Development Impact

page 153
Globalization for Development: Meeting New Challenges

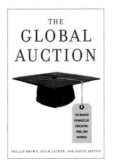

page 155, 156
The Global Auction: The Broken Promises of Education, Jobs, and Incomes

page 168, 169–170, 171, 187
Business Research Methods
3rd edition

pages 172–173
Marketing Research
2nd edition

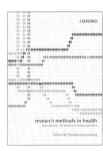

page 186
Research Methods in Health: Foundations for Evidence-based Practice

OXFORD
UNIVERSITY PRESS

Great Clarendon Street, Oxford, OX2 6DP,
United Kingdom

Oxford University Press is a department of the
University of Oxford. It furthers the University's
objective of excellence in research, scholarship,
and education by publishing worldwide. Oxford
is a registered trade mark of Oxford University Press in
the UK and in certain other countries

© Oxford University Press 2013

The moral rights of the author have been asserted

First published in 2013

2022 2021 2020 2019 2018

10 9 8 7 6 5

No unauthorized photocopying

All rights reserved. No part of this publication may
be reproduced, stored in a retrieval system, or
transmitted, in any form or by any means, without the
prior permission in writing of Oxford University Press,
or as expressly permitted by law, by licence or under
terms agreed with the appropriate reprographics
rights organization. Enquiries concerning
reproduction outside the scope of the above should be
sent to the ELT Rights Department, Oxford University
Press, at the address above

You must not circulate this work in any other
form and you must impose this same condition
on any acquirer

Links to third party websites are provided by Oxford in
good faith and for information only. Oxford disclaims
any responsibility for the materials contained in any
third party website referenced in this work

ISBN: 978 0 19 400177 9   Book
ISBN: 978 0 19 400179 3   Pack

Printed in China

This book is printed on paper from certified
and well-managed sources.

ACKNOWLEDGEMENTS

*The authors and publisher are grateful to those who have given
permission to reproduce the following extracts and adaptations of
copyright material:*

Reproduced by permission of Oxford University Press:

p.9 Definitions from *Oxford Dictionary of Economics (3rd ed.)* by
Black, J., Hashimzade, N., and Myles, G.D. © Oxford University
Press 2009. p.9 Extract from Herlihy, J., Gleeson, K., & Turner, S.
What Assumptions about Human Behaviour Underlie Asylum
Judgments? *International Journal of Refugee Law (2010)* 22(3): 351-
366. p.9 Extract from Hothersall, S.J. Review of Human
Behaviour and the Social Environment-Micro Level: Individuals
and Families, Katherine van Wormer, Oxford University Press,
USA. *British Journal of Social Work (2008)*, 38(7): 1447-1449.
p.29 Extract from Timilsina, G. & Dulal, H. Urban Road
Transportation Externalities: Costs and Choice of Policy
Instruments. *World Bank Research Observer (2011)*, 26(1): 162-191.
p.39 Extract from Wiebe, G. An Exploration into the Nature of
Creativity. *Public Opinion Quarterly (1962)*, 26(3). p.42 Extract from
Holmes, J. Making Humour Work: Creativity on the Job. *Applied
Linguistics (2007)*. 28(4): 518-537. p.42 Extract from Crescenzi, R.,
Rodriguez-Pose, A. & Storper, M. The territorial dynamics of
innovation in China and India. *Journal of Economic Geography
(2012).*, 12(5): 1055-1085. pp.51 and 216 Extracts from *Run,
Swim, Throw, Cheat: The science behind drugs in sport* by Cooper, C.
© Oxford University Press 2012. p.54 Definition from *Oxford
Advanced Learner's Dictionary (8th ed.)* © Oxford University Press
2010. Reprinted by permission. p.70 Definitions from *Oxford
Learner's Thesaurus.* © Oxford University Press 2008. Reprinted by
permission. p.73 Extract from Whelan, C. & Maître, B.
Comparing Poverty Indicators in an Enlarged European Union.
European Sociological Review (2010), 26(6): 713-730. p.74 Extract
from Howe, D.H., Hargreaves, J.R., Ploubidis, G.B., De Stavola,
B.L. & Huttley, R.A.H. Subjective measures of socio-economic
position and the wealth index: a comparative analysis. *Health
Policy and Planning (2011)*, 26(3): 223-232. p.74 Extract from
Bloom, D.E., Canning, D. & Fink, G. Implications of population
ageing for economic growth. *Oxford Review of Economic Policy
(2010)*, 26(4): 583-612. p.75 Extract from Anxo, D., Fagan, C.,
Cebrian, I. & Moreno, G. Patterns of labour market integration
in Europe—a life course perspective on time policies.
Socioeconomic Review (2007), 5(2): 233-260. pp.78 and 80 Extracts
from Schultheiss, P. and Cheng, K. Finding food: outbound
searching behavior in the Australian desert ant Melophorus
bagoti. *Behavioral Ecology (2013)*, 24(1): 128-135. p.80 Extract
from Thorup, K., Holland, A., Tøttrup, A., & Wikelski.
Understanding the Migratory Orientation Program of Birds:
Extending Laboratory Studies to Study Free-Flying Migrants in a
Natural Setting. *Integrative & Comparative Biology (2010)*, 50(3):
315-322. p.80 Extract from Starks, P., Johnson, R., Siegel, A., &
Decelle, M. Heat shielding: a task for youngsters. *Behavioral
Ecology (Jan./Feb. 2005)*, 16(1): 128-132. p.89 Extract from
Cruickshank, S. and Kendall, M. Low-emission vehicle adoption
in a UK local authority fleet: economic barriers and air quality
benefits. *International Journal of Low-Carbon Technologies (2012)*,
7(1): 16-22. pp.90 and 91 Extracts from Hundt, K. & Reddy, B.V.

Algal biodiesel production from power plant exhaust and its
potential to replace petrodiesel and reduce greenhouse gas
emissions. *International Journal of Low-Carbon Technologies (2011)*,
6(4): 294-298. p.92 Extract from Sqn Ldr (Retd.) Banu, S.
Aviation and climate change: a global sectored approach is the
need of the hour. *International Journal of Low-Carbon Technologies
(2012)*, 7(2): 137-142. p.93 Extract from Waung Hu, W., Batte,
M., Woods, T., & Ernst, S. Consumer preferences for local
production and other value-added label claims for a processed
food product. *European Review of Agricultural Economics (2012)*,
39(3): 489-510. p.94 Extract from Thilmany, D., Bond, C.A., &
Bond, J.K. Going Local: Exploring Consumer Behavior and
Motivations for Direct Food Purchases. *American Journal of
Agricultural Economics (2008)*, 90(5): 1303-1309. p.96 Extract from
Brown, C. & Miller, S. The Impacts of Local Markets: A Review of
Research on Farmers Markets and Community Supported
Agriculture (CSA). *American Journal of Agricultural Economics (2008)*,
90(5): 1298-1302. pp.100, 102 and 217 Extracts from *The
Globalization of World Politics (4th ed.)* by Baylis, J., Smith, S., and
Owens, P. © Oxford University Press 2008. pp.105 and 106
Extract from Criminal Statistics and the Construction of Crime
by Maguire, M. in *The Oxford Handbook of Criminology (5th ed.)*
edited by Maguire, M., Morgan, R., & Reiner, R. © Oxford
University Press 2012. p.108 Extract from *Doing Research on
Crime and Justice* edited by King, R. & Wincup, E. (2007). © Oxford
University Press 2007. p.109 Graph and text extract from
Lemieux, A. and Clarke, R. The International Ban on Ivory Sales
and its Effects on Elephant Poaching in Africa. *British Journal of
Criminology (2009)*, 49(4): 451-471. pp.111 and 112 Extracts from
Bradshaw, C. Little left to lose: deforestation and forest
degradation in Australia since European colonization. *Journal of
Plant Ecology (2012)*, 5(1): 109-120. pp.120 and 121 Extract from
Hatton, T.J., & Martin, R.M. The effects on stature of poverty,
family size, and birth order: British children in the 1930s.
Oxford Economic Papers (2010), 62(1): 157-184. p.123 Extract from
Child Public Health (2nd ed.) by Blair, M., Stewart-Brown, S.,
Waterson, T., and Crowther, R. © Oxford University Press 2010.
p.138 Extract from Rebecca M. Empson, *Harnessing Fortune:
Personhood, Memory, and Place in Mongolia*, Oxford: Oxford
University Press, 2011, © The British Academy 2011.
p.138 Extract from *Social and Cultural Anthropology: A Very Short
Introduction* by Monaghan, J. & Just, P. © Oxford University Press
2000. p.142 Extract from Eertmans, A., Baeyans, F., & Van Den
Bergh, O. Food likes and their relative importance in human
eating behavior: review and preliminary suggestions for health
promotion. *Health Education Research (2001)*, 16(4): 443-456.
p.152 Extract from *The International Mobility of Talent* by
Solimano, A. (ed.) © Oxford University Press 2008. p.153 Extract
from *Globalization for Development: Meeting New Challenges* by
Goldin, I. & Reinert, K. © Oxford University Press 2012.
p.166 Extract from Szmuness, W., Pick, R. & Prince, A.M. The
serum hepatitis virus specific antigen (SH): a preliminary report
of epidemiologic studies in an institution for the mentally
retarded. *American Journal of Epidemiology (1970)*, 92(1): 51-61.
p.166 Extract from Rabiee, P., Moran, N., & Glendinning, C.
Individual Budgets: Lessons from Early Users' Experiences.
British Journal of Social Work (2009), 39(5): 918-935. p.172-173
Extract from *Marketing Research (2nd ed.)* by Bradley, N. © Oxford
University Press 2010. p.175 Reproduced by permission of
Oxford University Press Australia & New Zealand, from *Political
Economy: The Contest of Economic Ideas (3rd ed.)* by Stilwell, F., 2012,
Oxford University Press. p.186 Reproduced by permission of
Oxford University Press Australia & New Zealand, from 'Focus
groups in health research' in Liamputtong, P. (ed.), *Research
methods in health: foundations for evidence-based practice*, 2010,
Oxford University Press. p.191 Extract from Masden, E. A.,
Haydon, D.T., Fox, A. D., Furness, R.W., Bullman, R., & Desholm,
M. Barriers to movement: impacts of wind farms on migrating
birds. *ICES Journal of Marine Science (2009)*, 66(4): 746-753. p.191
Extract from Bloom, D., Canning, D., & Fink, G. Implications of
population ageing for economic growth. *Oxford Review of
Economic Policy (2010)*, 26(4): 583-612. p.191 Extract from Heal,
G. Reflections—Defining and Measuring Sustainability. *Review of
Environmental Economics and Policy (Winter 2012)*, 6(1): 147-163.
p.215 Extract from Patterson, M. A Corporate Alternative to
United Nations ad hoc Military Deployments. *Journal of Conflict
Security Law (2008)*, 13(2): 215-232. p.220 Extract from *Stroke: The
Facts* by Lindley, R.I. © Oxford University Press 2008. p.221
Extract from Siemens, L. & Burr, E. A trip around the world:
Accommodating geographical, linguistic and cultural diversity
in academic research teams. *Literary & Linguistic Computing*, first
published online June 25, 2012. p.222 Extract from Gallagher,
H.C. Willingness to Communicate and Cross-cultural
Adaptation: L2 Communication and Acculturative Stress as
Transaction. *Applied Linguistics (2013)*, 34(1): 53-73. p.223 Extract
from *Public Health: an action guide to improving health* by Walley, J.
and Wright, J. © Oxford University Press 2010.

Reproduced by permission of Oxford University Press, USA:

pp.25-6 Extract from *Winds of Change: The Environmental
Movement and the Global Development of the Wind Energy Industry*
by Vasi, I. © Oxford University Press 2011. p.30 Extract from
Two Billion Cars: Driving Toward Sustainability by Sperling, D. and
Gordon, D. © Oxford University Press 2011. p.57 Extract from
Writing and Reporting the News (3rd ed.) by Lanson, J. and Stephens,
M. © Oxford University Press 2008. p.78 Extract from *Research
Methods for the Biosciences (2nd ed.)* by Holmes, D., Moody. P., &
Dine, D. © Oxford University Press 2011. p.137 Extract from
Anthropology: what does it mean to be human? by Lavenda, R. &
Schulz, E. © Oxford University Press 2012. p.155 and 156
Extracts from *The Global Auction: the broken promises of education,
jobs and incomes* by Brown, P., Lauder, H., and Ashton, D.
© Oxford University Press 2010. pp.168-171 and 187 Extracts
from *Business Research Methods (3rd ed.)* by Alan Bryman and Emma
Bell © Alan Bryman and Emma Bell 2011. p.180 Extract from
Naked city: the death and life of authentic urban places by Zukin, S.
© Oxford University Press 2009. p.185 Extract from *Research
Methods for the Biosciences (2nd ed.)* by Holmes, D., Moody. P., &
Dine, D. © Oxford University Press 2011. p.217 Extract from *The
Urban Experience – Economics, Society, and Public Policy* by Bluestone,
B., Stevenson, M., and Williams, R. © Oxford University Press 2008.

Other: p.59-60 Reproduced by permission of Oxford University
Press Australia & New Zealand, from *Media and Journalism (2nd*

ed.) by Bainbridge, J., Goc, N., & Tynan, L., Oxford Uni
Press 2011. p.112 Extract from Braithwaite, L.W. Co
of arboreal herbivores: The Australian Scene. *Austral
of Ecology (2006)*, 21: 21-30. Copyright © 2006, John W
Sons. p.112 Extract from Lepers, E., Lambin, E.F., Jan
A.C., DeFries, R., Achard, F., Ramankutty, N., & Schol
A Synthesis of Information on Rapid Land-cover Cha
the Period 1981–2000. *BioScience (2005)*, 55(2). Reprodu
by permission of University of California Press Journa
p.132 Reprinted from *The Lancet*, 380, Lee, I.M., Shiron
E.J., Lobelo, F., Puska, P., Blair, S.N., Katzmarzyk, P.T.,
of physical inactivity on major non-communicable di
worldwide: an analysis of burden of disease and life e
pp.219–229, 2013, with permission from Elsevier. p.1
Reprinted by permission from MacMillan Publishers
Reports. Wardle, J., & Cooke, L. One man's meat is ano
man's poison. *EMBO Reports (2013)*, 11:816–821. p.166
from Quine, L. & Pahl, J. Examining the Causes of Stre
Families with Severely Mentally Handicapped Childre
Journal of Social Work (1985), 15(5): 501–517.

Sources: p.67 www.mrc.ac.uk p.67 The Science and Inr
Investment Framework 2004–2014 p.67 The Council
Industry and Higher Education p.67 Universities UK 2
p.139 National Geographic Magazine p.139 ASA Globa
Association of Social Anthropologists p.154 www.
oxfordscholarship.com

*The publisher is grateful to the following for their permission t
reproduce photographs and illustrative material:* Alamy Ima
pp.7 (Students in library/Caro), 18 (Shape of skull in kn
wood of tree/imagebroker), 35 (Celebration, Florida/Ile
MacDonald), 35 (Vacation homes/Nik Wheeler), 49 (Bra
sprinter Alan Fonteles Cardoso Oliveira/Bob Daemmric
55 (Satellite dishes/McCanner), 67 (Students in lecture
Claudia Wiens), 104 (Policemen on motorbikes/Antipas
119 (Teacher with student/Tetra Images), 138 (Farmer w
cows/SuperStock), 142 (Child eating school dinner/And
Aitchison), 172 (Car factory production line/Mark Fagel
173 (Woman doing survey/Jeff Greenberg), 185 (West M
Safari Park/Robin Weaver), 187 (Radio assembly line/Ev
Collection Historical); Corbis pp.23 (Solar panels/Danie
Schoenen/Imagebroker), 39 (Speed skating/Max Rossi/R
53 (Lance Armstrong celebrates/Tim de Waele), 85 (Phys
Guglielmo Marconi/Hulton-Deutsch Collection), 85 (Pro
Stephen Hawking/Eleanor Bentall), 144 (Boy with sandv
mother image), 153 (Indonesian students wear face mas
CRACK PALINGGI/Reuters), 157 (Students taking test),
180 (Modern skyscraper and historic building/Image So
191 (Spix's Macaws/Patrick Pleul/dpa); FLPA pp.71 (Zebra
drinking at waterhole/Frans Lanting), 80 (Knotted wood
a tree/Horst Mahr/Imagebroker), 110 (African elephants/
Frans Lanting), 113 (Forest clearance/Chris Mattison); Ge
Images pp.18 (Forest path/Dietrich Bojko), 18 (Cairn, Hig
Stephen Spraggon), 18 (Pine tree/Takashi Sato), 18 (Tree
Elliot Elliot, Johner), 36 (Victoria, Melbourne/Ed Pritcha
40 (Student working on laptop/Don Bayley), 42 (Happy
businessman/Blend Images/Jon Feingersh), 64 (Chris Wa
interviews U.S. Supreme Court Justice Antonin Scalia on
News Sunday'/Paul Morigi), 67 (Scientist/Cultura Science
Sigrid Gombert), 85 (Erwin Schrödinger/SSPL), 95 (Woma
farmer's market/Ariel Skelley), 103 (Scientist in control r
Martin Barraud/OJO Images), 121 (Neighbours outside 'ba
to back' houses, 1950s/Haywood Magee), 135 (Butterflies/
Darrell Gulin), 151 (Flags/Hanquan Chen), 156 (Man with
computer/Trevor Williams), 167 (Girl looking at skyline/E
Carroll), 183 (Studying at computer/Silvia Jansen); Nature
Picture Library p.191 (Yangtze river dolphin/Mark Carwa
Reuters Pictures p.87 (U.N. water distribution in Haiti/Edu
Munoz); Rex Features pp.57 (Tourists reading headline, N
Resigning/Courtesy Everett Collection), 57 (Carl Bernstein
and Bob Woodward, Pulitzer Prize 1970s/Everett Collecti
Shutterstock pp.29 (New York traffic jam/Michel Stevelma
30 (Power plant, Russia/Kekyalyaynen), 32 (Students boar
school bus/Morgan Lane Photography).

Lecturer and presenter portraits by: Mark Bassett pp.19, 34, 50
83, 98, 99, 114, 130, 146, 148, 162, 178, 195.

Illustrations by: Peter Bull p.179 (food chain); Richard Ponsf
remaining illustrations and diagrams.

Cover photograph by: Gareth Boden.

Design by: Richard Ponsford.

*The authors and publisher would like to thank the following individe
for their valuable advice and assistance in developing the material
this course:* Kenneth Anderson (University of Edinburgh), Di
Charles Boyle (University of Oxford), Debra Farbey (INTO U
London), Jeanne Godfrey (University of Hertfordshire), Rob
Ledbury (INTO UEA London), Dr Jeffrey Verhey (Humboldt-
Universität zu Berlin).

*The authors and publisher would particularly like to thank the
following academic staff of Oxford University who generously gave
their time and participated so readily in the filming of their lectures
for this course:* Dr Sandie Byrne, Professor Richard Caplan,
Dr Elizabeth Gemmill, Dr Nazila Ghanea, Professor Angus
Hawkins, Dr David Howard, Dr Kerry Lock, Professor Jonath
Michie, Dr Cathy Oakes, Dr George Pope, Dr Kathleen Quin
Dr Adrian Stokes, Professor Marianne Talbot, Dr Jennifer Ti

Edward de Chazal would particularly like to thank all his fa
and his co-author Julie Moore, for their support and inspira

Julie Moore would particularly like to thank her co-author
Edward de Chazal for his support and guidance through the
whole process, and also Tristan Steinmann for his patience
understanding.

Special thanks to: Kate Chomacki

*Although every effort has been made to trace and contact copyright
holders before publication, this has not been possible in some cases. V
apologise for any apparent infringement of copyright and, if notified
publisher will be pleased to rectify any errors or omissions at the earl
possible opportunity.*